PEREGRINE BOOKS

NAPOLEON: FOR AND AGAINST

Pieter Geyl, D.Litt., was born in 1887 and held the chair of Modern History
in the University of Utrecht from 1935 until his death in 1966. One of the
great historians of his time, he was the author of several important books,
including *The Revolt of the Netherlands 1555–1609*, *The Netherlands in the
17th Century* and *Encounters in History*.

NAPOLEON

FOR AND AGAINST

Pieter Geyl

Translated from the Dutch by Olive Renier

SPIRIT SINISTER: '. . . My argument is that
War makes rattling good history; but Peace is
poor reading. So I back Bonaparte for the
reason that he will give pleasure to posterity.'

THOMAS HARDY, *The Dynasts*
Part First, Act ii, Scene v

Penguin Books
in association with Jonathan Cape

Penguin Books Ltd, Harmondsworth, Middlesex, England
Viking Penguin Inc., 40 West 23rd Street, New York, New York 10010, U.S.A.
Penguin Books Australia Ltd, Ringwood, Victoria, Australia
Penguin Books Canada Limited, 2801 John Street, Markham, Ontario, Canada L3R 1B4
Penguin Books (N.Z.) Ltd, 182–190 Wairau Road, Auckland 10, New Zealand

First published by Jonathan Cape 1949
Published in Peregrine Books 1965
Reprinted 1976, 1982, 1986

Printed and bound in Great Britain by
Cox & Wyman Ltd, Reading
Set in Monotype Bembo

Contents

Preface

I cannot claim to be an expert on Napoleon. To do so rightfully one must have devoted a lifetime of study to the man and to the period.

This book is a by-product of our recent experiences. In the early months of 1940, finding it difficult to pursue the work on which I was engaged, I plunged into reading about Napoleon, and wrote an essay which was to have appeared in the June number of one of our monthly reviews. After the capitulation, in May, the manuscript was returned to me, still marked with an instruction to the printer to be quick, and without a word of explanation. No explanation was needed for me to understand that, although I had not written a single word in it about Hitler or National Socialism, the parallel with our own times had seemed to the editor a little too pointed in the new circumstances. In September 1940 I used the article for some lectures in the Rotterdam School of Economics, where occasional bursts of laughter showed the audience to be equally alive to the parallel. Again, when I repeated those lectures, not much more than a month later, in very different surroundings and for a very different public, namely in Buchenwald concentration camp for my fellow hostages, it was the parallel that roused the keenest interest and amusement.

After Buchenwald, in the various places in Holland where I spent the remainder of my forty months of internment, I did a good deal of further reading on Napoleon, but it was only after my release, on medical grounds, in February 1944 that I conceived and executed the plan of the present book.

Let me state, in fairness to my own work, that I found a good deal more than the parallel to attract me. Napoleon had his own fascination, and French historiography a charm of its own. Even the article of 1940 had been in the first instance suggested to me not by the problem of the resemblance or contrast between Napoleon and Hitler, but by the historiographical problem, the problem of the endless variety of interpretations of Napoleon, his career, his aims, and his achievements. Yet – how could it be otherwise? – I had been struck by the parallel, no less than had my readers or hearers, and in this book too it has undeniably remained an element, even though I have alluded to it only very occasionally and have nowhere worked it out.

'I always hate to compare Hitler with Napoleon.' So, listening to the B.B.C.

the other day, I heard that Winston Churchill had been telling the House of Commons, only to continue with a 'but' and to enter upon the comparison all the same. So it is with all of us, and so it is with me. It is simply impossible not to do so. The resemblances are too striking. No doubt – and I want to state this with unmistakable emphasis – the differences, the contrasts, are no less obvious. History does not repeat itself. Between noticing a parallel and establishing an identity there is a wide gap. Between the two world assailants in question the differences, the contrasts, are such that, even when as in my case one had hated the dictator in Napoleon long before the evil presence of Hitler began darkening our lives, one almost feels as if one should ask the pardon of his shade for mentioning his name in one breath with that of the other. The Revolution which he represented – in so far as he did represent it – was a different one. The national civilization by which his conquests were accompanied was . . . but no! I do not want to say that French civilization was made of so much finer stuff than German: the difference is that under Napoleon, French civilization (albeit stifled and narrowed by him) still accompanied the conquest, while the character of the conquest that it has been the lot of our generation to undergo is not compatible with any civilization at all. Lastly, the personality of Napoleon – indeed, when I think of elaborating the comparison on that score, I suddenly feel a surge of revolt against the 'detractors', with whom generally (as will be seen) I am on quite friendly terms.

'But . . .' But the fact remains that we are here faced with phenomena that show an unmistakable relationship. In both cases there was a revolution – two revolutions, I am not forgetting it for a moment, animated by principles that are not only radically different but in some respects even diametrically opposed. But, for all that, in both cases a revolution moved by the conviction, by which all revolutions are moved and which causes them to be so incalculably dangerous, that it is bringing a new world, a new order; that therefore all the standards, all the laws of the past have become antiquated; and that it has on its side not power only, but right, so that everything must give way, and all opposition, if not contemptible, will be criminal.

Napoleon certainly did not embody, or did not embody in their purity, the principles of 1789; but he derived from the Revolution the conviction I have just described, and it made him the dictator and conqueror he was. He was a dictator who attempted to break with new legislation what resistance was left in the old society; who intensified his power in the State by means of a centralized administration; who suppressed not only all organized influence or control and expression of opinion, but free thought itself; who hated the intellect, and who entered upon a struggle with the Church which he had first attempted to enslave; and who thought that with censorship, police, and propaganda he would be able to fashion the mind to his wish. He was a conqueror with whom it was impossible to live; who could not help turning an ally into a vassal, or at least interpreting the relationship to his own exclusive advantage; who decorated his lust of conquest with the fine-sounding phrases of progress and civilization; and who at last, in the name of the whole of Europe, which was to look to him for order and peace, presumed to brand England as the universal disturber and enemy.

Methods of compulsion, and atrocities? The worst that our generation has had to witness, the persecution of the Jews, had no parallel in Napoleon's system. Indeed, that system remained true, from first to last, to conceptions of civil equality and human rights with which the oppression or extermination of a group, not on account of acts or even of opinions, but of birth and blood, would have been utterly incompatible. And yet methods of compulsion and atrocities are inseparable from the character of the dictator and conqueror, and we shall see that Napoleon incurred bitter reproaches, at home and abroad, for some of his acts. Nevertheless this is one of the points where the comparison is bound to do good to his reputation. What is the proscription of 'the general staff of the Jacobins' beside the annihilation of all opposition parties in jails or concentration camps such as has taken place in the Third Reich? What is the murder of the Duke of Enghien beside those of Dolfuss, of General Schleicher and his wife, and of so many others on 30 June 1934? What are the executions of Palm, of Hofer, what are even the severities with which so many villages and towns in Germany and Spain were visited, beside what in our time all occupied territories have had to suffer from Hitler's armies! The French police were hated and feared in the occupied and annexed territories, but when one reads about their conduct with a mind full of our present experiences, one cannot help feeling astonished at the restraints and resistances they still met with in the stubborn notions of law and in the mild manners of a humane age.

I do not grudge them, nor do I grudge the entire Napoleonic régime, the credit which here again accrues to them from the comparison. But if we are to be true to our own standards, if we want to live up to our determination that no retrogression in civilization shall be dated from our time, we must not in contemplating the past react less sensitively than did the men then living. The case of the persecution of the Jews remains singular: for the rest we must be alive to the fact, when we compare then and now, that although there is a difference in degree, there is none in principle.

There is another point to which it is difficult not to fear that the parallel may extend – it is only a later generation that will know for certain. I am alluding to the legend. When one sees the French licking the hand that had chastised them; when one notices how the errors and crimes of the Hero, the trials of the people,

9

the disasters and losses of the State, were forgotten in the glamour of military achievement, of power, unsound and transitory though it was; when one notices the explanations and constructions, ingenious, imaginative, grandiose, that were put up as much as a century later by historians – and such excellent historians! – then one seems already to discern among later generations of Germans the apologists and admirers of the man who was our oppressor and who led them to their ruin.

But, as I have said, I should not be fair to the present book if I gave the impression that it was written for the parallel and owed to the parallel, in my opinion, its principal interest. Certainly it has been a constant surprise to me, while reading and writing, to find the parallel presenting itself to my mind again and again at ever fresh points. The idea that the course of Revolution and of Dictators is predestined, or subject to some law, repeatedly forced itself upon my mind. But in the end the book has come to be what I wanted it to be and what the title indicates, a book on Napoleon as seen by French historians.

In two ways I have myself been constantly fascinated while I was engaged upon it. First, by the inexhaustible interest of the figure of Napoleon. I shall not attempt in this preface to give what I have not wanted to undertake in the book, a synthesized valuation of that figure. I am not suffering from the illusion that I have been able to relate the various interpretations without subjecting them to a judgement of my own. I have striven to give the more important of them their full due, but still the reader will easily discover that I have my preferences and my aversions, connected with personal convictions and principles, and – to use the somewhat over-simplified division of my sub-title – that my sympathies are with the *against* rather than with the *for* category. But I shall not on that account imagine that the entire Napoleon is to be found in Lanfrey or in Taine. I feel grateful to Masson and Bainville too, for having taught me to see other aspects of that many-sided personality, and to Sorel and Vandal for having expressed the historical phenomenon in terms which, problematical as they may be, make one hesitate before any all too single-minded rejection of Napoleon as the Dictator and Man of Violence.

And in the second place I have, I may almost say continuously, enjoyed the spectacle presented by French historiography. What life and energy, what creative power, what ingenuity, imagination, and daring, what sharply contrasted minds and personalities![1] And all the time the historical presentation turns out to be closely connected with French political and cultural life as a whole.

1. I do not claim to give a complete survey, but I do believe I may say that the omissions do not affect the general outlines of the picture.

I can only hope that I shall be able to communicate to the reader something of my interest in the protean figure of Napoleon and in the manifold problems of his régime, as well as in the picture given by his historians and its connexion with the modern history of France.

P.G.

Utrecht. 14 *October* 1944

All I want to add to the above preface, which was written nearly seven months before Holland was liberated, is a cordial word of thanks to the translator, Mrs Renier, for her devotion and patience, and to my friend Professor Renier, for his belief in the book as well as for his assistance.

P.G.

Utrecht. 23 *November* 1947

Part 1

The Antithesis at the Beginning

Argument Without End

My aim in this book is to set forth and compare a number of representations of Napoleon as given by leading French historians. Striking differences will emerge, but this is hardly surprising. History can reach no unchallengeable conclusions on so many-sided a character, on a life so dominated, so profoundly agitated, by the circumstances of the time. For that I bear history no grudge. To expect from history those final conclusions which may perhaps be obtained in other disciplines is in my opinion to misunderstand its nature.

I say this with some emphasis, for Professor Romein, in his inaugural lecture at Amsterdam, did take precisely this point of view. He was dealing with a subject similar to mine. He was tracing the various accounts that have been given at different times of the Dutch revolt against Spain, and the resulting chart of conflicting opinions seemed to alarm him considerably. He called his lecture 'An Image Shattered', and the scientific method as applied to history seemed to him to have failed, since its consequence is not unity but diversity.

Without entering into philosophical or methodological discussions, I must nevertheless make it clear that this lack of finality strikes me as both unavoidable and natural, and that the scientific method is certainly not to blame. The scientific method serves above all to establish facts; there is a great deal about which we can reach agreement by its use. But as soon as there is a question of explanation, of interpretation, of appreciation, though the special method of the historian remains valuable, the personal element can no longer be ruled out, that point of view which is determined by the circumstances of his time and by his own preconceptions. Every historical narrative is dependent upon explanation, interpretation, appreciation. In other words, we cannot see the past in a single communicable picture except from a point of view, which implies a choice, a personal perspective. It is impossible that two historians, especially two historians living in different periods, should see any historical personality in the same light. The greater the political importance of a historical character, the more impossible this is.

Is there anyone whose decisions have been more affected by the ever-widening network of international relations than Napoleon? Is there anyone whose decisions have had greater consequences for the whole of Europe? It goes without saying that the various writers who have tried to express their opinions of him

Central Europe in 1796

Kiel
Lübeck
HANOVER
Han
Amsterdam
Antwerp
Brussels
Cologne
Kassel
Lille
BELGIUM
Luik
Marburg
Erfur
RHINELAND
G
Rouen
Laon
Trier
Frankfort
Mainz
Bayre
Alençon
Paris
Rheims
Mannheim
Nurember
Metz
Karlsruhe
Stuttgart
Versailles
Orléans
Strasbourg
2
Tours
Troyes
Epinal
Ulm
Nantes
Dijon
Besançon
3
Poitiers
Nevers
Basle
E
Châlon
Neuchâtel
Zurich
Innsb
Geneva
Constance
Clermont
Lyons
SAVOY
Aosta
VENE
Grenoble
Milan
Turin
Parma
Savona
Modena
Bayonne
Avignon
Arles
Marseilles
Genoa
Flo
Toulouse
Nice
R. OF GENOA
LIGURIAN REP.
1797
Le
T
KINGDOM
A
SARDINIA
FR.
Barcelona

1 S. Netherlands
2 Wurtemberg
3 Breisgau
4 Avignon
5 Nice

0   Miles   300

and his career have reached different conclusions. No human intelligence could hope to bring together the overwhelming multiplicity of data and of factors, of forces and of movements, and from them establish the true, one might almost say the divine balance. That is literally a superhuman task. A man's judgement – for however solemnly some people may talk about the lessons of History, the historian is after all only a man sitting at his desk – a historian's judgement, then, may seem to him the only possible conclusion to draw from the facts, he may feel himself sustained and comforted by his sense of kinship with the past, and yet that judgement will have no finality. Its truth will be relative, it will be partial.

Truth, though for God it may be One, assumes many shapes to men. Thus it is that the analysis of so many conflicting opinions concerning one historical phenomenon is not just a means of whiling away the time, nor need it lead to discouraging conclusions concerning the untrustworthiness of historical study. The study even of contradictory conceptions can be fruitful. Any one thesis or presentation may in itself be unacceptable, and yet, when it has been jettisoned, there remains something of value. Its very critics are that much richer. History is indeed an argument without end.

1 Chateaubriand

NAPOLEON had his detractors and his glorifiers, even during his lifetime. To see him as he appeared to his detractors, it is not necessary to go to that part of Europe which opposed and finally brought him down. In his own France there were Chateaubriand and Mme de Staël, of whom the former painted a most repulsive picture of him at the critical moment after his first abdication, when the Bourbons were making their initial somewhat hesitating reappearance on the scene.[1]

Chateaubriand is a figure of great importance in French literature, one of the very few which the period produced. Mme de Staël, however greatly her work may differ from his, is the only writer whom one would immediately and unhesitatingly place on the same level. Romanticism is vested in him, not only in his original, lively style, but in his attitude towards himself and towards life. He is the nobleman, homesick for the *ancien régime*, with a real feeling for those values of beauty and tradition imperilled by the Revolution. Yet he had too deep an understanding, too developed a historical instinct, to be a pure reactionary. At an early stage Chateaubriand had made his peace with the régime, he was a *rallié*, as it was called, and had established his reputation by the publication of *Le Génie du Christianisme*, a wholly emotional and traditionalist apology for Catholicism, on aesthetic and sociological lines, which made a tremendous hit at that moment of reaction against the anti-clerical tendencies of the Revolution, and served the reading public as a suitable companion-piece to Bonaparte's Concordat. Young Chateaubriand was in good odour at the new Court, through the influence of Fontanes, the Consul-Emperor's Court poet and orator, himself a man of the *ancien régime*, but he was made of tougher stuff than the pliable self-seeking Fontanes. Two courageous actions, at a time when Napoleon's power appeared unassailable, had earned him the right to attack the Emperor in 1814. In 1804, after the murder of the Duc d'Enghien, he resigned from the diplomatic service during the stricken silence which followed the crime. In 1807 he wrote an article in his paper, the *Mercure*, which made an even greater sensation. In scarcely veiled terms he attacked imperial tyranny, summoning it before the judgement seat of history. The paper was immediately suppressed. But Napoleon still hoped to be able to do something with him, and the Academy

1. *De Buonaparte, des Bourbons*, 1814.

19

took the risk, therefore, of making him a member. His inaugural address, however, was of such a character that his meddlesome overlord refused him permission to deliver it without alterations, which he refused to make. If it was his pride, his vanity, as much as a fundamental dislike of despotism, which made him stand up to the Emperor, the fact remains that he did stand up to him, and Napoleon, though he took no measures against the *vicomte* (certainly to his secret disappointment), was worried by the opposition, however ineffective, of the great writer. Indeed this one testimony by a Catholic nobleman of royalist connexions encouraged all those who still in their hearts resisted, even when their emotional and intellectual background was very different.

The work that appeared in 1814 was simply a pamphlet, and its importance is largely due to the moment at which it appeared. In that atmosphere of uncertainty it sounded a positive note, hatred of the fallen Emperor. What was Napoleon? The destroyer, the despiser of men, the foreigner, the Corsican, especially scornful of Frenchmen, careless of French blood, devourer of generations of young men, suppressor of all free opinion, demanding of writers a toll of flattering unction as the price of permission to publish – in a word, the tyrant.

2 Madame de Staël

THERE was open war between Mme de Staël and Napoleon. In 1803 she was exiled from France, and her books, at first merely branded as indecent by the obedient Press, were banned. The angle from which she judged the régime, her personality and her methods, explain why Napoleon was less tolerant to her than he was to Chateaubriand.

Mme de Staël was the daughter of the Swiss banker Necker, who at the eleventh hour of the *ancien régime* was to have been the minister responsible for its reconstruction, and from whom, in the first stage of the Revolution, the National Assembly had expected so much. She admired her father, and remained faithful throughout her life to the original liberal aims of the Revolution. Perhaps this can be explained by her Protestant origins and upbringing. Perhaps it was also the fact that she was not French by birth, however deep her love for France, which made her immune to the lures of glory and power which undermined the resistance of so many others. Her personal fortune and the title of her husband, a Swedish diplomat, enabled her to play an important part in the social life of Paris, and this, thanks to her vivacious and energetic personality, she was able to maintain through many a change of government. Her *salon* was the centre of her life. Conversation, as she herself says, was her greatest pleasure, but perhaps it gave her even more satisfaction to exert influence, to play a part, through her friends and her activities, in the development of the great events going on around her.

As a woman with a devouring need for action, whose aim it was to know and if possible to influence everyone worth knowing in political circles, she had naturally tried to get hold of General Bonaparte after his triumphs in Italy. In this she had not much success, for Bonaparte did not care for intellectual women. Nevertheless Mme de Staël was still among his admirers after the Egyptian campaign, and rushed eagerly back to Paris after the 18th Brumaire to enjoy the spectacle of what she considered a reforming and conciliatory administration. But before long disillusionment set in. The young dictator's determination to do everything himself, his refusal to admit discussion, revolted her. She had a sharp eye for the dangerous implications of his cavalier attitude to the law. As a result, she egged on her friend Benjamin Constant to outspoken warnings and criticism in the Tribunate. Nothing more was needed to make Bonaparte see her as an enemy. The concentrated spite with which he persecuted her, and the energy with which she carried on the fight verbally and through her writings, combined to convert her from a celebrated into a great European personality.

There was something European about her. She was enthusiastically French, but she knew Europe better than most Frenchmen. Her Swiss Protestant youth gave her the key to a world which it was difficult for them to penetrate, particularly after the Revolution. Before her time, her great compatriot Rousseau had done everything he could to carry French culture beyond the limits of a narrow classicism which to most people seemed to be solely national. Though politically his spirit might have found triumphant expression in the Revolution, culturally this upheaval had given rise to a reaction against that interest in the intellectual life of Britain and Germany which had begun to show its broadening and fertilizing effect.[1] The Revolution followed the reactionary classical tradition of Voltaire, not only in those literary outpourings which later generations have found unreadable, but in that general idea of Man as a universal abstraction, in that indifference or even impatience displayed towards the individual distinguishing features of peoples and of national cultures. Naturally the features of this abstract Man were predominantly French, but the demands of universality made it necessary to exclude those special characteristics which are at the same time the deepest and the truest, with the most deleterious effects on the originality and vitality of French civilization.[2] These tendencies were only emphasized under Napoleon. His own outlook was classicist, universalist, in the typical eighteenth-century way, even though, as we shall see, there was a strong romantic streak in his personality. At the same time he consciously excited the pride and self-satisfaction of *la grande nation*. The wars automatically brought about a disparaging attitude towards cultures other than the French, and in particular hatred of Britain, and the isolation and sterile rigidity of French culture

1. cf. JOSEPH TEXTE, *J.-J. Rousseau et les origines du cosmopolitisme littéraire* (1895), p. 406 ff.

2. Voltaire cited the fact that Corneille and Racine were played everywhere, but Shakespeare, so far, only in Britain, as a sufficient proof of the inferior literary value of the latter. His reasoning has since lost its basis, but apart from that it is typical of the French classical spirit. The following point of view, which could be called traditionally British, would have been completely unintelligible to Voltaire:

'A man does not attain to the universal by abandoning the particular, nor to the everlasting by an endeavour to overleap the limitations of time and place. The abiding reality exists not somewhere apart in the air, but under certain temporary and local forms of thought, feeling, and endeavour. We come most deeply into communion with the permanent facts and forces of human nature and human life, by accepting first of all this fact – that a definite point of observation and sympathy, not a vague nowhere, has been assigned to each of us.' E. DOWDEN, *Shakspere . . . His Mind and Art* (3rd edition, 1883), p. 8 ff.

were never so marked as when the French were pouring over the whole continent of Europe.

The importance of Mme de Staël in the cultural history of France lies in the fact that in spite of unfavourable circumstances she kept up her opposition against this cramping of the spirit. This was the declared aim of her famous book on Germany, which especially called down on her head the thunderbolts of Napoleon and his policy. But politically she reserved her greatest admiration for Britain, the land in which popular forces had free play, the land of liberalism *par excellence* – a view which was not likely to make Napoleon regard her with more favour. At the end, in 1813, she visited princes and ministers who were getting ready for the last lap of the struggle and spurred them on, but only to the war against Napoleon, for the distinction between the tyrant and the France she loved was a fundamental in her view of the situation. She felt herself too much a part of the Revolution to glorify the Bourbons, as Chateaubriand had done. Her charge against Napoleon was that he had assassinated Republican liberty. Her ideal remained liberty, enlightened, moderate, the liberty of philosophers and writers.

It was from this point of view that she wrote her *Considérations sur la Révolution française*, which was published in 1818 after her untimely death. The idea of Napoleon which she develops in the second part, illustrating it by an account of his whole career, is remarkably well thought out. There are personal memories and observations, and yet the whole work has nothing in it of the *mémoire* or of the pamphlet. This woman of genius has succeeded in portraying her subject in historical perspective, which is not of course the same as saying that she has succeeded in giving the objective truth about Napoleon. But it is in her writings that for the first time it is possible to find unfavourable criticism allied to the actual events, in such a way as to set one thinking. Moreover, the problems with which the liberal spirit, the spirit of belief in the rule of intellectual and moral values, must always wrestle when it comes in contact with the phenomenon of power, its rise and decline, are stated by her in such a way that it sometimes seems as though later writers, though capable of finer shades and possessing a far richer store of data, can only elaborate her themes.

Here are the brief outlines of her portrait of Napoleon, his career and his personality.

He comes to the fore as a soldier. The principles of political warfare do not interest him. He destroys republican idealism, first in the army, then (with the help of the army) in the State. He is the complete egoist, for whom human sympathy does not exist, for whom men are despised tools, pieces on a chess board. He is a foreigner among the French. Having no faith and no fatherland, he pursues no other purpose than his own greatness. He is the sly machiavellian, who promises peace and makes play with the bogy of Jacobinism, but who when once power is in his hands can do nothing but make war. He is the man for whom religion and literature mean nothing, except in so far as they minister to his greatness or his power, and under whom both must wither. In short, as in Chateaubriand's pamphlet, he is the tyrant.

3   The Napoleonic Legend

THE first to provide a portrait in which there was nought but unblemished beauty, endearing humanity, greatness, and virtue was Napoleon himself. On St Helena he set about the task of shaping his reputation for posterity. The *Mémorial*, in which the Marquis Las Cases noted his conversations,[1] a book which had an immeasurable influence in France, and which was the first and foremost source of what is called the Napoleonic legend, was peculiarly suited to become a popular classic. Anecdotes and reminiscences chosen at random from the whole miraculous life are interwoven with speculations, the whole within the framework of the Longwood tragedy and the bitter struggle with Sir Hudson Lowe, which Las Cases describes from day to day. This plan gives the book its human note. It catches the emotions as well as the interest of innumerable readers. It presents Napoleon not just as the aloof mighty Emperor, but as somebody who for all his incomparable cleverness, greatness, and luck is nevertheless accessible, one of ourselves.

From this living variegated backcloth emerges the political Napoleon. He is before everything else the son of the Revolution, the man who consolidated the possession of equality, and made good his country's escape from feudalism, by restoring order, by ridding France of those factions which had practically dissipated the fruits of the Revolution, and by wresting peace from the monarchs who hated France and the Revolution. That peace (Lunéville 1801, Amiens 1802, when Bonaparte had only just become First Consul) was a breathing space, which brought sudden overwhelming popularity to the victorious young hero. There was nothing Napoleon liked better to recall after his downfall, and the fact could hardly be denied; but how brief was that respite! How endless, bitter, and bloody were the campaigns which followed, up to the disasters and the final collapse! It was all the fault, so the Napoleon of the *Mémorial* would have us believe, of those self-same monarchs, and of envious Britain. His conquests had adorned the name of France with undying fame – *gloire*, that word dear to the Frenchmen of the period – but they had been forced upon him. He had been obliged to conquer Europe in self-defence. And even this conquest was fraught

1. *Le Mémorial de Sainte Hélène;* some editions carry the title *Mémoires de Napoléon,* which properly belongs to the *Mémoires* dictated by Napoleon and dealing mainly with his campaigns.

with benefits. After the French it was the turn of the Dutch, the Swiss, the Germans, the Italians, the Spanish, to receive the blessings of the codes of laws and other revolutionary reforms. Had he been allowed to go his own way, or had he remained victorious, Europe would have become a federation of free peoples, grouped round enlightened and fortunate France in an eternal peace. It was the hatred of the monarchs and the envy of Britain, the mischief-maker, the pirate swayed only by low materialistic motives, which had destoyed this noble future for France and for Europe.

Such is Napoleon's apology. But I would give an incomplete outline of the *Mémorial*, and would fail to account for the impression it made, were I to omit to add that not only is this apology embedded among anecdotes, reminiscences, and daily particulars of the mournful exile, but that no sense of inconsistency prevents the fallen Emperor from enlarging with inexhaustible complacency on his military achievements. The whole work glows with the glory which surrounds Napoleon even in his fall, and which the people of France share with him. The glory of France is the thought to which he constantly returns; and what he did, he did for France.

POETS AND NOVELISTS

The Napoleonic legend was enriched from many sources, and it may well be said that the most important was Napoleon's own downfall. Was it not easier to glorify him when he was no longer there to oppress men, and when his insatiable demands had no longer to be satisfied? Chateaubriand says something of the sort in his *Mémoires d'Outre-Tombe*. Here, though he repeats all his indictments, he allows free rein to the admiration which obsessed him and which forced him to compare his own career, from his birth in the same year, with that of the All-Powerful, to compare, to contrast, to extol, in particular in connexion with his own opposition.

It is the fashion of the day [he writes] to magnify Bonaparte's victories. Gone are the sufferers, and the victims' curses, their cries of pain, their howls of anguish, are heard no more; exhausted France no longer offers the spectacle of women ploughing her soil; no more are parents imprisoned as hostages for their sons, nor a whole village punished for the desertion of a conscript. No longer are the conscription lists stuck up at street corners, no longer do the passers-by crowd round long lists of death sentences to con them anxiously for the names of their children, their brothers, their friends, their neighbours. It is forgotten that everyone used to lament those victories, forgotten that the people, the Court, the generals, the intimates of Napoleon were all weary of his oppression and of his conquests, that they had had enough of a game which, when won, had to be played all over again, enough of that existence which, because there was nowhere to stop, was put to the hazard each morning.[1]

Indeed it was all forgotten. People were forgetting their dislike of despotism, now that they were faced with the Bourbons, their Court of *émigrés*, and their priests, and now that France could harvest no new glory. They were forgetting it, as they saw the famous soldiers neglected by a despicable government. The opposition, the men of 1789, listened with emotion when General Foy voiced their complaints in the Chamber of Deputies, and praised them, and in them their dead leader.[2] Take the case of Beyle – Stendhal – who had been grumbling about trampled liberty while Napoleon lived, and who only now came truly under his spell.[3] The young people in his novels idolize Napoleon. Fabrice in *La Chartreuse de Parme* is an Italian, and in Stendhal's own view the French conquest of Italy meant an altogether desirable liberation from government by priests and obscurantism, while after Napoleon's fall stupidity, senility, and cruelty set the tone once more.[4] In *Le Rouge et le Noir*,[5] the action of which takes place in France, Stendhal proclaims his old dislikes through the mouth of an embittered republican, to whom Napoleon is merely the man who has restored all that monarchical nonsense and put the Church back on its pedestal again. But for Julien, the young Frenchman, Napoleon is a god, and the *Mémorial* 'the only book in the world, the guide of his life, and object of ecstatic admiration'. And yet he wants to be a priest! But the lesson he gets from the book is that one must be accommodating, that with will-power you can achieve anything in life. The world no longer belongs to the man with the sword, courageous and gay, but to the soft-voiced, ruthless dissembler, in his cassock.[6]

That was a lesson indeed. Not everyone dared to learn it, and so perplexity, a sense of powerlessness, of being crippled, overcame a generation 'begotten between two battles'. It was de Musset,[7] speaking with the melancholy voice of the romantics, who voiced their woes. He did not see in Napoleon that *professeur d'énergie* proclaimed, as we shall see, to the French youth of a later age, nor

1. III, 341. The *Mémoires d'Outre-Tombe* appeared in 1860, a few years after the death of Chateaubriand.

2. VAULABELLE, *Histoire des deux restaurations*, v, p. 295 ff.

3. A. CHUQUET, *Stendhal-Beyle* (1902), chapter 'Napoléon'.

4. The *tredici mesi* (1799–1800), when French rule was interrupted by an Austrian victory, appeared to Milan, according to Stendhal, as a return to gloom and darkness; only the monks and a few nobles like the Marquis del Dongo (the father of the hero), who 'professed a lively dislike of enlightenment', were disappointed when Bonaparte won the battle of Marengo and the French returned. In 1810 the more amiable characters look back upon 'ten years of progress and of happiness'. See *La Chartreuse de Parme*, 13, 17.

5. The subsidiary title is *Chronique de 1830*.

6. See note on Stendhal, p. 32 .

7. *Confession d'un Enfant du Siècle.*

did he know what to make of the advice 'faites-vous prêtre' which, according to him too, was addressed to his youthful contemporaries from all sides. But among the dreary ruins of his day, what an impression the figure of the Emperor made on his imagination, how overwhelmingly mighty, inspiring a sense of oppression and of admiration alike!

No criticism, no cynical inferences, no despair, nothing but open-mouthed astonishment at that supernatural good fortune, pity for that end, and a generous, satisfied acceptance of his glory as exalting all Frenchmen, and in particular the masses who had given him his soldiers – this is the reaction, as Balzac describes it, of peasants listening to an old soldier telling them about Napoleon's career. It is a tale of miracles that is unfolded to them.

The hero's mother dedicated him to God, that he might raise religion from where it lay prostrate. And so he was invulnerable. Though his comrades fell around him, the hail of bullets left him unharmed. His soldiers became accustomed to victories. Sometimes he would encircle and capture ten thousand of the enemy with but fifteen hundred Frenchmen. He began by conquering Italy, and the Kings grovelled before him. Was that a man like you or me? But in Paris they began to be afraid he might swallow up France too, and so they sent him to Egypt. 'There you see his likeness to the Son of God.' He promises land as booty to his soldiers. More miracles, and it was India's turn, but then there came the plague. So he returns, to save France (that is, from the Directorate).

'What have you done with my children, my soldiers?' he asked the lawyers. He shuts them up in their chatter-barracks, and makes them dumb like fish, and flabby like tobacco pouches. The Pope and the Cardinals come in state to his imperial coronation. 'Children,' says he, 'is it right that your Emperor's relations should have to beg? Let's go and conquer a kingdom for each of them.' 'Agreed,' answers the army. Those were good days! Colonels became generals, generals became marshals, marshals became kings. More victories. 'Vive l'Empereur!' you cry as you die. Was that natural? Would you have done that for just an ordinary human being?

Then comes his call to us to go and conquer Moscow, after all the other capitals, because Moscow had allied itself with England. Kings flock to lick his boots – difficult to say who is not there. The Poles, whom he wants to raise from their degradation, are our brothers. But the mysterious Man in Red, who has crossed his path more than once, warns him that men will abandon him, that his friends will betray him. Moscow: the fire: the fearful retreat. They say he wept at night for his poor family of soldiers.[1]

Betrayal as it was foretold, everywhere, even in Paris, so that he has to go away,

1. *Le Médecin de Campagne*, 1832.

and without him the marshals commit one folly after another. Napoleon had fattened them up till they would no longer trot. Even now he makes splendid soldiers out of conscripts and civilians, but they melt away like butter on a grill, and at his back – the British! They rouse the people to revolt, whispering nonsense in their ears.

His abdication at Fontainebleau; he says good-bye to us and we cry like children. 'Children, it is treason that has defeated us.' He comes back with two hundred men, and this is the greatest miracle of all. With them he conquers the whole of France. Waterloo! But Napoleon cannot find Death. France is crushed, the soldiers despised, in their places noblemen who never bore arms. By treachery the English seize the Emperor and nail him to a rock in the ocean. In France they say now that he is dead, but that only shows they don't know him! '*Vive* Napoleon, the people's and the soldiers' father!'

This is indeed legend, and in its most naïve form. As usual, the cry of betrayal goes up to mitigate the bewilderment and shame of defeat. But indeed in this story, so typical of Balzac, in whose pages we must not look for Stendhal's critical spirit but who can bring reality to life with so fine an imaginative skill, are to be found all the elements needed to dazzle the common man unused to reasoning. He appeals to the craving for the miraculous, to the national self-conceit, to religious feeling, to rapacity, to republican and anti-aristocratic tendencies, and to the simple need to give hero-worship and trust. The fact that these elements conflict does not make the mixture any the less heady. Napoleon is the man of the hero-worshipping boy, the man of the dreamy poet, but he is also the man of the people. 'The only king remembered by the people,' thinks Stendhal's Julien, hearing two workmen talking regretfully of the days of the Emperor.

But indeed Béranger, affecting in his bourgeois way a popular tone, at once frivolous and sentimental, lover of liberty and hater of priests and aristocrats, idealizing Napoleon in reaction to the Restoration, preferred to approach him through some old sergeant – memories of glory, of enthusiasm for liberty: the nations were made kings by our conquests, and crowned our soldiers with flowers, but our leaders, ennobled by him, have betrayed the good cause and flatter the tyrants. Let the People arise! – or through an old woman who has seen the Emperor in his glory, and in his adversity received him in her hovel, and set before him dry bread and her sour local wine:

> Il me dit: 'Bonne espérance!
> Je cours de tous ses malheurs
> Sous Paris venger la France.'
> Il part; et, comme un trésor,
> J'ai depuis gardé son verre.

But he fell into the abyss. There was bitter sorrow.

> On parlera de sa gloire
> Sous le chaume bien longtemps.

> Bien, dit-on, qu'il nous ait nui,
> Le peuple encore le révère.

'One asks oneself,' says Chateaubriand,[1] 'by what sleight of hand Bonaparte, who was so much the aristocrat, who hated the people so cordially, has been able to obtain the popularity which he enjoys. For there is no gainsaying the fact that this subjugator has remained popular with a nation which once made it a point of honour to raise altars to independence and equality. Here is the solution.

'It is a matter of daily observation that the Frenchman's instinct is to strive after power; he cares not for liberty; equality is his idol. Now there is a hidden connexion between equality and despotism. In both these respects, Napoleon had a pull over the hearts of the French, who have a military liking for power and are democratically fond of seeing everything levelled. When he mounted the throne, he took the people with him. A proletarian king, he humiliated kings and noblemen in his ante-rooms. He levelled the ranks, not down but up. To have dragged them down to plebeian depths would have flattered the envy of the lowest; the higher level was more pleasing to their pride. French vanity, too, enjoyed the superiority which Bonaparte gave us over the rest of Europe. Another cause of Napoleon's popularity is the affliction of his latter days. After his death, as his sufferings on St Helena became better known, people's hearts began to soften; his tyranny was forgotten; it was remembered how, having vanquished our enemies and subsequently having brought them into France, he defended our soil against them; we fancy that if he were alive today he would save us from the ignominy in which we are living. His misfortunes have revived his name among us, his glory has fed on his wretchedness.

'The miracles wrought by his arms have bewitched our youth, and have taught us to worship brute force. The most insolent ambition is spurred on by his unique career to aspire to the heights which he attained.'

But Chateaubriand's sombre warning was the voice of the past – or of the future. His contemporaries took refuge in illusion. So did Victor Hugo, who, in a manner quite different from that of Stendhal or Balzac or Béranger, found in the figure of the Emperor an outlet for his romantic longing for greatness, which was mysteriously combined with a love of freedom. In his 'Ode to the Column' – the triumphal column in the Place Vendôme, from the top of which

---

1. *Mémoires d'Outre-Tombe*, IV, 60.

on 31 March 1814, the day of the Allies' entry into Paris, a group of royalist noblemen with their plebeian hirelings had removed the statue of the Emperor – the poet, writing in 1830, dedicated to Napoleon 'his youthful muse, singing nascent freedom', and promised the departed hero that this generation, which, though it had not known him as master, honoured him as a god, would come and fetch him from his island grave. And what transports there are when ten years later his mortal remains actually return to Paris. 'The blessed poets shall kneel before you; the clouds which obscured your glory have passed, and nothing will ever dim its true lustre again.'

> Sainte-Hélène, leçon! chute! exemple! agonie!
> L'Angleterre, à la haine épuisant son génie,
> Se mit à dévorer ce grand homme en plein jour.
>
> Jadis, quand vous vouliez conquérir une ville,
> Ratisbonne, ou Madrid, Varsovie ou Séville,
> Vienne l'austère, ou Naples au soleil radieux,
> Vous fronciez le sourcil, ô figure idéale!
> Alors tout était dit. La garde impériale
> Faisait trois pas comme les dieux.
>
> Tu voulais, versant notre sève
> Aux peuples trop lents à mûrir,
> Faire conquérir par le glaive
> Ce que l'esprit doit conquérir.
> Tu prétendais, vaste espérance!
> Remplacer Rome par la France
> Régnant du Tage à la Néva;
> Mais de tels projets Dieu se venge.
> Duel effrayant! guerre étrange!
> Jacob ne luttait qu'avec l'ange,
> Tu luttais avec Jéhovah!

Here are elements which we shall meet with in the writings of historians right down to our own time. Here you have pity for the hero's personal fate, dislike for cold-blooded Britain, unregenerate pleasure in military power, and at the same time an attempt to give spiritual life to the great struggle by linking it to the spread of French thought all over Europe, to liberty, to world peace, so that the spectacle of the catastrophe may be lifted on to a higher plane.

Victor Hugo voiced the spirit of the time in his poem, while Chateaubriand's was an isolated independent view. This is true. Yet amid the chorus of adulation there were other discordant notes. One poem has remained famous; in it the Napoleonic legend is challenged and assailed with vivid force at the very moment of its clamorous emergence. It is all the more remarkable for the fact that the writer was a young man and spoke, not in the name of religion or of monarchy, but of liberty and republicanism. The young man was Auguste Barbier, and the poem *L'Idole* (1831).

Everyone knows the lines:

> O Corse à cheveux plats! que la France était belle
> Au grand soleil de messidor!
> C'était une cavale indomptable et rebelle,
> Sans frein d'acier ni rênes d'or.

The Corsican succeeded in controlling that marvellous animal, and rode it without pity, spurring it till the blood ran, pulling at the bit till its teeth broke, till it sank down dying – and crushed its rider. Certainly, cries Barbier (and here he is obviously aiming at Hugo), I too suffer from the memory of that humiliating day when they pulled down the statue under the eyes of the foreigner, the day when French women bared their breasts to the Cossacks, but I heap my curses on one man only: 'Be thou cursed, O Napoleon.' But the unholy image is set up again.

> Grâce aux flatteurs mélodieux,
> Aux poètes menteurs, aux sonneurs de louanges,
> César est mis au rang des dieux.

Ah, ends the poet, good princes, wise men who lighten the peoples' chains:

> Le peuple perdra votre nom;
> Car il ne se souvient que de l'homme qui tue
> Avec le sabre et le canon.

The masses honour those who force them to carry stones to build their pyramids; the masses are like a street girl who gives her love only to the man who beats her. . . .

STENDHAL

Stendhal consistently professed the most fervent admiration for Napoleon. In 1837 he published a little book on the great man ('the greatest man the world has ever seen since Caesar'; 'the more becomes known of the truth, the greater Napoleon will be'). When one tries to analyse his conception, however, one is struck by the most flagrant contradictions.

The book, although entitled *Vie de Napoléon*, describes in detail only the Italian campaigns, and indeed the writer says in so many words that 'the truly poetic and perfectly noble part of Bonaparte's life comes to an end with the occupation of Venice' (1797). He is careful not to say: the handing over of the Venetian Republic to Austria: with that betrayal he debits the Directorate and its baseness. Nevertheless: 'Here end the heroic times of Napoleon.' But in the preface, what he underlines as making out the greatness of Napoleon ('the love for Napoleon is the only passion that is left to me') is the fact that he 'has civilized the people *en le faisant propriétaire*'. Also, that he has made it possible for everybody to win the cross of the *Légion d'honneur*. He places Napoleon in the direct line of the Revolution: 'The true founders of present-day France are Danton, Sieyès, Mirabeau, and Napoleon.' Here, of course, he is thinking of the First Consul and Emperor. And while in other passages Napoleon is just the indomitable and unsurpassable warrior, the embodiment of an energy about the purpose of which one is not supposed to bother one's head, here he is annexed for the newly-propertied middle classes that had come into their own in 1830. This in spite of the fact that he was by no means blind to Napoleon's fear of the Jacobins and expressly deplores his weakness (when Emperor) for ex-royalists and aristocrats.

Both in this veneration for the *professeur d'énergie* and in this extolling Napoleon as the liquidator of the old order, it is possible to construct a line connecting Stendhal with contemporary as well as with much later historians (we shall see striking instances in Madelin for the first and in Thiers for the second attitude of mind). His being in so conventionally French traditions, as well as the ineradicable confusion reigning in his mind on this topic, will seem surprising only to those who accept the somewhat spurious reputation for 'intelligence' and 'independence' that it has been fashionable to cultivate for Stendhal among succeeding generations of intellectuals after his death in 1842.

Part 2

The First Chroniclers

1 François Mignet

ONE of the remarkable phenomena of the first generation after the fall of Napoleon is the association of Napoleonic legend with radicalism. Indeed we found from Barbier's hymn of hate that opposition under the banner of liberty and 1789 was never interrupted. With regard to historical writing in the earliest period I shall draw attention only to Mignet's short history of the French Revolution, which appeared in 1824, before the legend had really taken shape, but which was continually reprinted. This too was the work of a young man. Some hundred pages are devoted to the Consul-Emperor's administration. With a few deft incisive strokes Mignet gives us the portrait of a despot who subordinated both the Revolution and the country to himself.

The nation [says Mignet, speaking of the period of the Peace of Amiens] lay in the hands of the great man, or of the despot; his was the choice, either to preserve it in freedom or to enslave it. He preferred his ambitious schemes; he set himself above the rest of mankind, alone. Brought up in camps, a late arrival in the Revolution, he understood only its material side, the language of its interests. He believed neither in the moral cravings which had stirred up the Revolution nor in the convictions which had swayed it and which sooner or later were bound to emerge again and bring about his downfall. He saw a revolt approaching its end, a weary people delivering themselves up to him, and a crown which was his for the taking.

For Mignet the Concordat was nothing more than Bonaparte's plan to acquire domination over the Church, and, through the Church, over the people. He concludes his short account of it with the scornful reply of the general whom the First Consul asked how he liked the *Te Deum* sung after the ratification (all the unbelieving generals of the Revolution had had to attend, whether they liked or not): 'Pretty monkish mummery! Only those million men were absent who died to overthrow what you are setting up again.' In the institutions Mignet sees nothing but their lack of freedom. The Press, the representative bodies are crippled and muzzled, the authorities and the courts exercise arbitrary power. In the wars of Napoleon he sees nothing but an attempt to use Europe for his crazy dream of power.

Yet was there not something more in these wars after all?

As regards France, he was a counter-revolutionary because of his despotism, but as a conqueror of Europe he became a renovator. Several nations, which slumbered before he came, will live with the life he brought them. But in that Napoleon merely followed the dictates of his nature. Born as he was from war, war remained his inclination and his joy.

There is something doctrinaire and arid about this sketch; it lacks life. And life would result only from admiration inspiring an array of serious works; these in their turn brought about reconsideration – in which many of the young Mignet's ideas would be seen to emerge.

2 Baron Bignon

THE first historian who undertook a broad treatment of the subject, and whose work is still of value, is Bignon, whose *Histoire de France depuis le 18 Brumaire* began to appear in 1829. He died in the beginning of 1841, having brought his voluminous work as far as 1812.[1] His son-in-law, Ernouf, took it up to the Battle of Leipzig, on the basis of his notes.

In Napoleon's will, signed at Longwood, on 15 April 1821, the thirty-second legacy reads as follows: '*Item* to Baron Bignon, one hundred thousand francs. I commission him to write the history of French diplomacy from 1792 to 1815.'

Bignon entered the diplomatic service in 1797, and had filled important posts under the First Consul and the Emperor in various German capitals and in Warsaw, in the capacity of Minister, sometimes also as Governor. In the foreword to the first part of his book he gave an account of himself intended to allay the suspicions of a supposed inquisitive reader – the general attitude to Napoleon was still rather unfavourable.

It is true [he says, in effect] that I served Napoleon zealously, and that I flattered him. Who did not? It is also true that I was commissioned to write the book by the Emperor himself. Indeed I have the greatest admiration for him.

Does that necessarily imply that he supports despotism? Certainly not. Since 1817 he has sat in the Chamber of Deputies, on the left wing benches. 'Having served glory for a long time, I have devoted the rest of my life to liberty.' Then you will let us have some slashing attacks on imperial tyranny? suggests the reader. But the writer, having affirmed his dislike of despotism, whatever its label, and having confessed that in his youth, in common with many others, he had succumbed to republican illusions, explains that the imperial despotism was a dictatorship, not – as Turgot desired – to establish liberty, but to build the supremacy of France in Europe. The Empire inspires thoughts of strength, greatness, and glory. Bignon declares himself satisfied with constitutional monarchy, which through the Charter preserves the inheritance of the Revolution, and he would gladly see that strong, great, and glorious too.

1. Eleven volumes; in 1842 there appeared a double-column edition in two quarto volumes, published in Brussels, from which I quote.

For anyone familiar with French history, this career and this creed evoke an easily recognizable type. The officials who worked with Bonaparte from the beginning, and who remained faithful to him through every administrative metamorphosis, sprang from revolutionary origins. After them came the royalist *ralliés*, whose principles were less outraged by the monarchical evolution of dictatorship, but who on the other hand found it all the more easy to conform when the Restoration came in 1814. The old republicans had accepted Bonaparte's leadership because they considered that both the Revolution and the international position of France demanded a strong government. Unless their readiness to accept each successive stage in a conservative or frankly counter-revolutionary direction be ascribed entirely to concern for their own careers, it may be supposed that they were influenced by the glory and the power this matchless war hero was earning for their country. This particularly applied to a man like Bignon, whose official life was passed abroad. And it is perfectly natural that on the disappearance of this exceptional ruler he gave free rein once more to his old libertarian tendencies. The new government was far from strong. It could boast of no glittering triumphs won for a France forced back behind its old frontiers by the peace treaties and feeling cramped and sore, particularly over the loss of the Rhineland and Belgium, both conquered during the Revolution. Moreover the new government favoured priests and Jesuits. The point is important, for no old revolutionary Bonapartist could imagine Liberty as other than anti-clerical.

THE BOOK

What approach did Bignon make to the history of Napoleon? He was certainly no mere eulogist; indeed, he may be called remarkably independent. But before I illustrate this and attempt to define his limitations, I wish to deal briefly with his treatment of his material and to show what sources he had at his disposal.

He did not confine himself to diplomatic history, as Napoleon had directed. In plan his work became a history of France during the period. He tends to adhere to the method of the chronicler, so that within certain limits of time chapters on foreign affairs succeed chapters on domestic matters. His documentation is fairly extensive. Not only was he able to use his own papers and those of many other contemporaries, but in 1829, when a relatively liberal government was in office to which the name of Napoleon was not merely a bogy, he extracted permission to delve into the actual archives, so that he was able, especially in the later portions of his work, to quote from official papers and above all from Napoleon's own correspondence. He handled this material most intelligently. On a number of points the outline of events is firmly drawn by a man of experience and insight, skilled in portraying the official point of view, and capable also from time to time of showing its disadvantages. His work bears throughout the hallmark of the Foreign Office official who is thoroughly at home in matters of state and is accustomed to a clear-cut and lucid presentation.

When in the foreword to his seventh volume, however, he claims that the future historian worthy of Napoleon (he makes no pretence to be that man) will have need of no further discoveries, since his (Bignon's) work presents him with so faithful an account of the real facts concerning political events, the modern reader can hardly help smiling. That ideal historian, according to Bignon, will merely have to produce a work of art, in which the facts are more agreeably presented, the whole is better arranged, the details beautified and the story made more fascinating by improvements in the composition and by the use of a more elevated and more brilliant style.

He had no conception of the insatiable craving of later research workers to know more and know it more accurately, nor of the multiplicity of standpoints or of possible problems. The refinements of psychology and the bold flights of imagination were not for him. In short, he did not guess how never-ending would be the argument in which he was one of the first participants.

The mistake is typical of the work. I have mentioned Bignon's independence, but intimated that it had its limits. As a matter of fact it is severely circumscribed. Bignon the historian remains Bignon the diplomat, the official, Bonapartist to his finger tips. What makes his book so attractive is that its reader is offered access to the Napoleonic world. Even when he is critical, the writer takes for granted many things for the understanding of which we must grope backwards in time.

THE RELATIONS WITH THE POPE

Let us take as an example his account of the increasingly strained relations between Napoleon and Pius VII, the Pope with whom the First Consul had concluded the Concordat, who had later come to Paris to crown the Emperor, and whose secular power was finally destroyed by decree in 1809, his State, including Rome, being incorporated with France and he himself taken away as prisoner. We shall see this problem of the Church treated from various sides later on, but I know no other account which makes Napoleon's handling of the situation appear so completely reasonable and inevitable, if one accepts the Napoleonic point of view that the supremacy of the State and of the Emperor is irrefutable, and that all resistance to it is evidence of unendurable clerical ambition and medieval backwardness.[1] The matter is handled calmly; the opposition is neither

1. II, 201.

abused nor belittled. There is even a sympathetic sketch of the Pope, who re-remarked that having lived like a lamb he should know how to die like a lion.

FOREIGN POLICY

In dealing with foreign policy, Bignon undoubtedly shows his independence. Though the power and glory of France come first for him, though he served Napoleon so faithfully for these very ends, and still admires him on their account, he is not blind to the excesses, to the untenable position into which the régime had strayed. He dates this development somewhat late.

From the 18th Brumaire [he writes at the beginning of his seventh[1] volume] up to the Peace of Tilsit [that is, the peace of 1807, which was to establish amity instead of war with Alexander I of Russia, and by which Prussia lost half its territory and the subjection of Germany was confirmed] the greatness of France had steadily increased in the most marvellous fashion, but it could still be justified by the defensive nature of the wars from which it sprang, and it was still capable of consolidation.

Much might be said of the defensive nature of those wars, against England in 1803, against Russia and Austria in 1805, against Prussia in 1806, and I shall say something of this later.[2] The possibility, again, of consolidating French rule not only in the Low Countries and the Rhineland, but also in the whole of Germany and Italy seems dubious.

But from that moment [Bignon continues] the Empire, although still outwardly expanding, was to lose in real strength what it gained in territory. Napoleon understood as well as anyone how little durability there could be in an indefinite expansion. He could perfectly distinguish between that which was permanently necessary to the power of France, and that which appertained only to his own reign. 'After me,' he said, with reason, 'after me the Rhine, the Alps, and the Pyrenees.' And indeed, these were the conquests of France, the rest were his own.

It was certainly nothing unusual, even in the circles closest to Napoleon, to make this distinction between his earlier policy and that of his later years, between France's and his own private policy. The principal exponent of this view, even during the régime, was, as we shall see later, Talleyrand. It has remained current also among historians. But Napoleon himself rejected it wholeheartedly, in spite of Bignon's quotation. Many of his pronouncements at St Helena were solely intended to give the lie to this very distinction, and

1. Second, in the Brussels edition.
2. See, for example, p. 242 ff.; p. 270 ff.; p. 281 ff. Bignon affirms the justice of Napoleon's wars as of his peace conditions in 1805: Book I, 424, 482.

as we shall also see, many later writers were more influenced in this respect by the legend than was the practical, able, and sober Bignon.

Thus Bignon does not in the least hesitate to condemn Napoleon for certain excesses to which his power policy led him. The notorious Convention of Bayonne (1808), where the Spanish Bourbons were tricked and bullied into abdication, he described frankly as 'an ambush', and compared it with the crimes of Tiberius – a piece of erudition calculated to appeal to the prevailing fashion for things Roman. It is noteworthy that Bignon is here following the very writer – the bitter Tacitus – whom Napoleon could not forgive for his vilification of the Caesars.

Nevertheless the way in which even this writer deals with events in general gives us some clue to the reasons why French public opinion was for so long impressed by Napoleon's successes and by his methods. The joy in the military triumphs of France, the scornful relish of her enemies' discomfiture, the taunts – to take one example at random – when Russia and England deserted their ally the Kingdom of Naples after Austerlitz, in spite of their previous eloquent protestations, removing the troops they had there just at the moment when they were needed – such reactions show just how much the French identified themselves with their Emperor.

Throughout Bignon is particularly hostile to the British. Not that he allows himself to be carried away into declamatory tirades. Indeed he never departs from his flat diplomatic style, and remains throughout matter of fact and business-like. The argument, for instance, in which he maintains that Napoleon's attitude to the Continental System was completely reasonable is well worth reading.[1] He points out that the Emperor did not introduce it as being in itself lawful, but as a measure which was forced on him by the illegal nominal blockade proclaimed by the British, in which the neutral states were obliged, however unjustly, to acquiesce. Similarly, in a different class of matters entirely – though his judgement here is even more one-sided and lacks that insight into the opposite point of view which the historian should have – one might quote his defence of the severe sentence passed in Nuremberg on the bookseller Palm, who was shot in 1806 by the French army of occupation for distributing inflammatory litera-ture.[2] Bignon admits that in the peaceful and kindly Germany of that time nothing did more harm to the good name of France. Yet he unhesitatingly accepts the ruling of the laws of war as conclusive, and his dispassionate logical argument provides a revealing picture of the way in which the official mind works in such cases. But it is always the supporter of the régime speaking.

1. II, 28 ff.   2. I, 560.

'DESPOTISM'

For all that, Bignon does show his independence in the way he discusses 'despotism'. In 1800, after an attempt on the First Consul's life, penal measures were rushed through, without a trial, and the wrong men suffered. In dealing with this case, on which I shall have more to say later, Bignon expresses sharp disapproval,[1] and although he tries to find excuses for the killing of the Duc d'Enghien – this, too, I reserve for fuller treatment – he does not defend it. The creation of a new nobility, so characteristic of the reactionary tendencies of Napoleon's administration, he roundly declares to be in contravention of the principles of the Revolution dear to the majority of the French people. It is possible to detect a personal note in his complaint that abroad, 'where hitherto every French citizen enjoyed a prestige like that of the *civis Romanus* in the palmy days of the Republic, and where the whole French nation was regarded as the cream of humanity',[2] the distinction now made had the effect of degrading those who had no share in the new honours.

Such comments are, however, no more than incidental. Bignon refers with due respect to Mme de Staël and her friends (which can by no means be said of all later writers), but he is not so shocked by her banishment at the resumption of the war with England as the famous literary lady and Benjamin Constant would have liked the whole world to be. His exposition is shrewd, his estimate of the element of self-esteem just, and he is certainly right in thinking that it was not only Mme de Staël's brilliant conversation, but also the fact that her *salon* was a centre of the opposition, which earned her Napoleon's disfavour. Yet, having pointed out how small the minority was which gathered round her, and that the First Consul, as he then was, had offered her terms, he regards the subject as closed. The dictatorship itself, sensitive to the slightest opposition, he accepts.[3]

ADMIRATION

What delighted Bignon most, apart from military conquests, were the material benefits which accrued to France from that ever-watchful vigilance and care, that readiness of the ruler to use his power to get things done. And to those inclined to make fun of the adulations of his Minister for Internal Affairs (up to 1807 it was Champagny) in the annual reports in which these wonders were vaunted, Bignon would point out that the Emperor, 'nearly always animated

1. p. 93b ff., p. 94 ff.   2. II, 42b.   3. I, 307.

by generous feelings, passionately desirous of the good, and intelligent in his desire', at least worked hard for his glory.[1] He prefers to base his chronicle, and is deservedly proud of the fact, upon the actual orders and plans to be found in the Emperor's own correspondence; and even so, what a magnificent picture![2] Bignon allows himself a smile when he finds the Emperor meditating measures to improve literary criticism; he knows Napoleon's 'habit of mixing the State up in everything' sometimes leads him 'to take the wrong turning'.[3] Nevertheless the Emperor's aims and most of the time even his actions in the sphere of spiritual matters fill him with the purest admiration.

When he deals, for instance, with the Emperor's complete control over education, he does permit the voice of criticism to be heard for a moment, but among the reasons for the inevitability of the system he mentions not only Napoleon's dictatorial character, but the needs of a new régime, and the example offered both by the republics of antiquity and the Emperor's immediate revolutionary predecessors. 'Whether one agrees or not with his ideas on this delicate matter' – the political struggle during the Restoration had at least taught him that the matter was a delicate one – 'one must acknowledge that he was ever striving after what is good, that he was ever desirous of ennobling humanity through the education of the mind, and of preparing the way for generations which would contribute to the glory and well-being of the State.'[4] When it comes to the institution of the University, that formidable corporation whose task it was to wield the State monopoly in education, the point that seems of most interest to Bignon is that of the party affiliation of the Grand Master.[5] Fontanes, Chateaubriand's protector, was one of those supporters of the old régime who came to enjoy Napoleon's especial favour. Bignon calls him a man of the clerical party, in opposition to that of the 'philosophers',[6] and he is specially concerned to show that Napoleon was not really an enemy to progress, as though there were no more in it than that. On the significance of the University we shall be hearing comments of a very different character.

1. I, 500b.   2. II, 155a.
3. I, 667.   4. I, 491b.
5. II, 156a. Grand Master was the title of the Rector of the University.
6. The usual word for the rationalists of the Encyclopedia. Freethinkers would be another word for them.

3 Armand Lefebvre

IN 1845 two great works began to appear. They were Armand Lefebvre's *Histoire des cabinets de l'Europe pendant le Consulat et l'Empire* and Thiers's *Histoire du Consulat et de l'Empire*, a continuation of his youthful *Histoire de la Révolution française*, completed nearly twenty years earlier. Thiers's book became the great popular history of Napoleon. Volume succeeded volume in an inexhaustible stream, until by 1862 all twenty had appeared. In spite of the magnitude of the work, its success was overwhelming. For a generation Thiers's was the last word on the subject, and his book overshadowed that of Lefebvre. Lefebvre, who was a few years younger than Thiers, being born in 1800, a diplomat, and the son of a diplomat who had served Napoleon, suffered from this.[1] It is true that his book, the unattractive title of which conceals a history of Bonaparte's foreign policy, cannot stand comparison with that of Thiers for pace, fullness, and colour. Nevertheless it has its own special qualities. Even though the writer sets his diplomatic history in its wider background – the development of the Revolutionary idea and of the Consular and Imperial régime in France – the limits imposed by the subject give his work more unity. This becomes apparent when one compares him with Bignon. The contrast makes the latter take on even more the appearance of a chronicler, while in Lefebvre one can appreciate the attempt at truly historical presentation.

Lefebvre had his own interpretation of Bonaparte and his statesmanship, which he develops with a sure touch. The actual narrative is not the most important part of his book. His documentation is not up to present-day standards. Though he did draw from archive material he failed to consult non-French sources, in itself an irreparable omission in a book dealing with a subject of this nature. For all his positive tone, he is often wide of the mark, particularly in dealing with aims and motives. His style lacks personality. What makes his book worth examination is his view of the subject as a whole, his generalizations, his interpretation of the central figure in relation to the course of events. We shall see directly that he has much in common with Bignon, not only in descent

1. According to Sainte-Beuve in one of his *Causeries du Lundi*, reprinted before the first volume of the edition which was edited and completed by the writer's son in 1866. I quote from this edition.

and circumstances, but also in spirit. He too accepts the bourgeois ideals of the Revolution, supports anti-clericalism, equality, and even liberty, but his chief enthusiasm is reserved for the greatness and power of France.

DEFENCE OF THE 18TH BRUMAIRE

Lefebvre is more consistently realistic, in a sense, than Bignon, as appears from the introduction in which he discusses the rise of Bonaparte and the *coup d'état* of the 18th–19th Brumaire. The vigour of the reconstruction is certainly striking. The situation of France before the *coup d'état* is described as critical, what with administrative confusion, bitter popular unrest – the backwash of ten revolutionary years – leaders irresolute and incompetent, and all Europe watching for an opportunity to suppress that power which, after bursting forth with irresistible force during the first passionate confident years, was still sufficiently disquieting. The *coup d'état* was thus not only beneficial but absolutely essential. Given this view, there is no further need of argument concerning justice or injustice or the propriety of Bonaparte's ambition.

Once in the saddle, he had three courses open to him, according to Lefebvre. He could have accepted the support of the royalists, and brought about a restoration, but that would not appeal to a man who wished to be himself the master, and who was in any case aware that a restoration of the *ancien régime*, however strong the reactionary element, would arouse uncompromising resistance and bring to a head the latent civil war. He could have cooperated with the Jacobins, who wished for nothing better, but that would have meant a resumption of the war in its most revolutionary form, and a European convulsion which would not have accorded with Bonaparte's ideas; moreover he would in that case have had to share control of France with Jacobin clubs and radical demagogues, hardly a prospect to please a general 'who only loved popular energy when clad in military uniform'.[1] There remained the broad central mass of public opinion, tolerably satisfied with the social reforms of the Revolution and anxious to retain these, but longing for stability. Order, that was the slogan which Bonaparte understood, unity, an end to all that interminable bickering, a sweeping away of the parties, a chance to enjoy the fruits of the Revolution, work, reconstruction – and peace. But it must be a peace which would consolidate the powerful position that had been won.

Once in the saddle – but the horse was not yet quite broken in. After the *coup d'état* came a constitution (that of Year VIII) which still imposed certain parliamentary limitations on the dictator's power. From the beginning, Bonaparte secretly meditated shaking himself free from these limitations, to gain undisputed

I. I, 13.

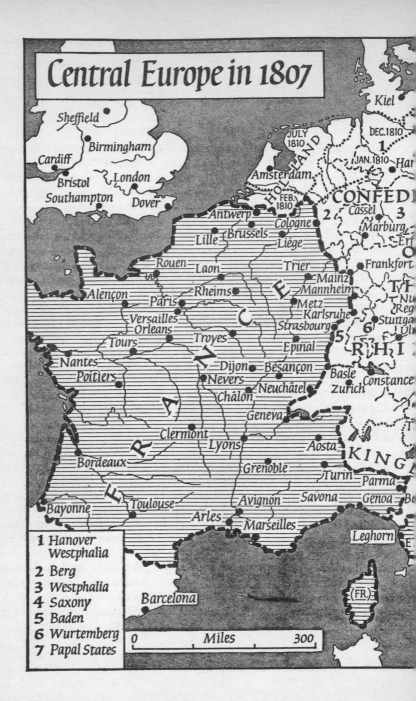

Central Europe in 1807

Kiel

Sheffield

Birmingham

Cardiff

Bristol
London

Southampton

Dover

JULY 1810

HOLLAND

DEC. 1810

1

JAN. 1810

Har

Amsterdam

FEB. 1810

CONFED

Antwerp

Cologne

Cassel

2

Marburg

3

Brussels

Lille

Liège

Erf

Rouen

Laon

Trier

Frankfort

Alençon

Rheims

Mainz

Mannheim

T F

Paris

Metz

Nu

Versailles

Karlsruhe

Reg

Orleans

Strasbourg

Stuttga

Tours

Troyes

Epinal

6

Ul

5

R H I

Nantes

Poitiers

Dijon

Besançon

Basle

Zurich

Constance

Nevers

Neuchâtel

Châlon

Geneva

Clermont

Lyons

Aosta

KING

Bordeaux

Grenoble

Turin

Parma

Bayonne

Toulouse

Avignon

Savona

Genoa

Arles

Marseilles

Leghorn

(FR.)

Barcelona

1 Hanover
   Westphalia
2 Berg
3 Westphalia
4 Saxony
5 Baden
6 Wurtemberg
7 Papal States

0   Miles   300

control of France. 'The constitution was not granted in good faith.' This calm statement, and still more the remark which follows, show Lefebvre's realism:[1]

And it could not be. There were lies everywhere, in words as in things. The nation, monarchical in its traditions, republican in its ideas, was all unconsciously a prey to the strangest contradictions . . . It was only through dissimulation and concealment and tricks that he was able to carry out successfully the most formidable undertaking ever shouldered by mortal man.

What was this undertaking? To reconcile the French people, to break resistance in the Vendée and elsewhere, to bridge antitheses, to bring into line the Church, which in the words of Lefebvre had been made, through the Concordat, 'one of the most useful instruments of his government';[2] in short to establish that unity under strong authority which was necessary to safeguard both France and the fruits of the Revolution against an envious and covetous Europe.

But could it stop there? After Marengo and Amiens, Bonaparte feels strong enough to throw out the opposition in the Tribunate; the more obedient Senate, too, is muzzled in 1802 by an appeal over the heads of the representative bodies to the people, who, blinded by his victories, make Bonaparte Consul for life by three and a half million votes to 8000. Having described all this, Lefebvre exclaims:

If God does not teach moderation to this man to whom he has given so much might, he will sooner or later abuse his good fortune and commit errors likely to jeopardize the future of a whole people.[3]

But is not this a somewhat belated reflection? Was not this possibility already implicit in the *coup d'état*, and was the 18th Brumaire in fact so fortunate a date in the history of France? Lefebvre does not draw this conclusion, and yet he says, and repeats at various points, that Bonaparte's first mistake, a fatal one, the source of all the disasters which later overtook France, had been committed before 1802.

THE FATAL ERROR OF LUNÉVILLE

This was the peace of Lunéville concluded with Austria in 1801, after her conclusive defeats, by Bonaparte himself in Italy at Marengo, and by Moreau in Germany at Hohenlinden. This peace, argues Lefebvre, could and should have been a peace of reconciliation.[4] 'We had two great enemies in the world, one

1. I, 26.   2. I, 194.   3. I, 209.   4. I, 94.

continental, that is Austria, and one naval, that is Britain.' Together they were already sufficiently formidable, and there was the possibility that if they both continued hostile, the two remaining powers, Russia and Prussia, with whom France's relations were in a state of flux, might join them. Such a four-power coalition would endanger the Revolution and even the nation. 'The First Consul should have taken thought, should have called up all the percipience of his powerful intellect, and should have spared his country this terrible and precarious hazard.' To this end he should have broken the alliance between Britain and Austria for ever, by concluding a real peace with one or the other. In practice this meant with Austria, for Lefebvre is firmly convinced that Britain was irreconcilable.

He paints a highly coloured picture of Britain, as a country whose social condition made war necessary for the ruling class (the 'British oligarchy', the expression which Napoleon also favoured). War was the only means by which to distract the people's attention from that oligarchy's policy of disinheriting the yeomen and sequestrating the land. The money-grubbing middle class, caught by a fever of speculation, could be induced to see in war the means of conquering world markets. A genuine peace with such an England would have been possible only at the price of renunciation of all naval, colonial, and industrial power. The surrender of Antwerp and Egypt, of San Domingo and Louisiana, of the merchant navy, of the French principles of maritime law (the principle that the flag protects the cargo, 'that sacred and inalienable principle', as the writer calls it elsewhere),[1] would hardly have sufficed, according to Lefebvre, to conciliate Britain. Thus he does not blame the First Consul if the peace of Amiens was merely a truce. It could be nothing more, owing to Britain's insatiable lust for power. (As we shall see, this point, which I shall not discuss further at the moment, was to give rise later to not a little difference of opinion.)

In passing, however, it must be noted that this view of Britain, as unfavourable as Bignon's, dominates the whole of Lefebvre's work. In fact, with his emphatic humourless style, he surpasses his predecessor in vituperation. According to him the British are always concocting new deceits and committing cowardly crimes. Coldly egoistical, unflinchingly heartless, they trample on the weak, desert the victims of their fair promises, and smugly count their gains.[2]

But Austria was another matter. Only, she should have been allowed a free hand in Italy, and Germany east of the Rhine should have been left alone. The archiepiscopal electors of Cologne, Mayence, and Trèves should have been compensated on the other side of the Rhine. Thus Austria would have been satisfied,

1. I, 114.
2. See for example I, 60, 66; 113, 134; II, 5: 'Un peuple froid, calculateur, qui n'estime la gloire qu' autant qu'elle s'escompte en argent.' And so on.

the spectre of coalition would have been laid, and 'master of our movements, we might have risen to our full height against our great naval enemy, confronting him face to face, and landing on his coast in order to strike at the heart of his power, all without the fear of a diversion on the Rhine'.[1]

Instead of this, Bonaparte at Lunéville took pitiless advantage of the power given to him by his victories. By the peace of Campo Formio the Directorate had deprived Austria of all her Italian possessions (in exchange, it is true, for Venice). Although Lefebvre does not say so, this had in fact been Bonaparte's own arbitrary policy, imposed on the Directorate after his first Italian triumphs in 1796. Subsequently, indeed, the Directorate had proceeded with it *con amore*. That had been the first step in the wrong direction. But now, instead of turning back, the First Consul went further. Venice, too, was taken from Austria, and in Germany all the powers through which Austria was accustomed to work – not only the ecclesiastical electors and all the clerical nobility and corporations, but the knights 'immediate to the Empire' – were dispossessed, for the sake of strengthening the States of the centre (particularly Bavaria, always jealous of Austria) and setting them all against her.

Is there any point in wishing to discount what has happened and make one's own programme of action, for the benefit of an earlier generation? Lefebvre recognizes that its realization would have met with almost insuperable difficulties. Fired with enthusiasm for the magnificent role which seemed prepared for her on the continent, France would not have understood voluntary renunciation of the fruits of her sacrifices. To give up Italy would indeed have damaged trade interests and the control of the Mediterranean vital for the maintenance or the reconquest of Egypt. But above all Bonaparte regarded Italy as his special domain. He desired to rouse the Italians from their age-long sleep, to awake their national feelings. And he was the last man to recoil from future dangers.

He was passionately keen on war, because he excelled in warfare. He favoured it above all as a means of rousing the nation and of impressing it, of strengthening his authority, and of establishing his dynasty. He thought himself able to reduce both Austria and England, and clever enough to make Prussia and Russia his allies.

In writing thus, Lefebvre is not so much laying down the law for the past, as trying to explain and to establish responsibility, which he tends to divide between the French people, in their intoxication, and the dictator, thirsting for power and action, whom they had wished on themselves.

From the womb of that fatal peace treaty [he concludes] have issued our glory as well as our disasters. It was no doubt a magnificent and an epic undertaking to bring about the rebirth of Italy; but at the end there yawned a chasm. For fifteen years

1. I, 99.

we did nothing but win victories and conquer countries, and what was the result of all that greatness? The treaties of 1815 and the martyrdom of St Helena.

We have seen that Bignon makes 1807 a landmark, and only begins to shake his head at Napoleon's foreign policy after that date. Lefebvre sets the beginning of the disaster much earlier, and from the point of view of historical perspective there is something attractive about his more organic, more concrete interpretation of events. We shall see the problem viewed from entirely different angles by later authors, but at times, and making allowances for appreciable differences, we shall recognize Lefebvre's approach.

APOLOGETIC TENDENCY

It should be noted, however, that Lefebvre does not always bear in mind the thesis which he has propounded so firmly. He is carried away by his admiration for Napoleon and his dislike of France's enemies. He describes, for example, how the Emperor, having subdued Austria in 1806, overthrows Prussia also, and is then faced with a situation which inspires him to ever more ambitious schemes, to the subjugation of half Europe and the foundation of *le Grand Empire* based on his brothers' vassal kingdoms. He is under no illusion as to this being 'a terrible situation'. 'Our own errors, our enemies' acts of violence, our disasters at sea' (Trafalgar) have brought it about. That is his first comment, but he goes on to conclude that

it was inexorable Fate, and not, as has been alleged, a contemptible dynastic pride, which compelled Napoleon to undertake this gigantic scheme. For seven years we shall see him, with incomparable mental vigour and consistency carrying it out.

If inexorable Fate, then what of 'our errors'? In this passage Lefebvre sounds a note of admiration which makes one wonder whether he was in fact able to discern his hero's faults. The answer is that the whole of his work is full of contradictions in this respect. That this is nothing unusual, we have already seen in the case of Bignon; and we shall find further examples.

No, Lefebvre is certainly not blind to Napoleon's faults. He sees the coarseness of his behaviour towards the Pope when the latter resists incorporation in Napoleon's power system.[1] He does not gloss over the stupidity and treachery of Bayonne.[2] He says somewhere, and with truth, that diplomacy was Napoleon's 'weak spot'.[3]

Here he was in every way at a disadvantage, and not the least in respect of his own character. Reared in the army camp, more aware of fact than of law, like all military men, too great a commander not to enjoy the gruesome game of war more than was good for his country's interests, he lacked in habit of mind and in method

1. III, 257.   2. III, 460, 501, 512.   3. III, 126.

the moderation, patience, and delicate dexterity which the art of negotiation in its highest form demands.

Elsewhere Lefebvre remarks that he was only too much inclined to use for this purpose military men like himself, General Beurnonville, for example, 'tough and imperious with a mouth full of threats, his favourite argument being war and the sword'.[1]

The writer seems to shrink from drawing general conclusions from these and similar observations, however. He generally palliates them, and cools his irritation and disapproval on the enemies of France, on Britain of course in particular. We see again and again, and not only when he is attacking the British, how much his mind is under the spell of the system. Sometimes the sort of fatalism which he professes seems designed especially to serve as an apology for Napoleon and for France. Nevertheless, and without for a moment wishing to subscribe to this fatalistic interpretation, it cannot be denied that the author thereby contributed a fertile idea to Napoleonic literature.

1. I, 193.

4 Adolphe Thiers

I HAVE already said that Thiers's *Histoire du Consulat et de l'Empire* was a work in twenty volumes[1] (of at least five hundred pages each), that it appeared between 1845 and 1862, and that it was a tremendous success. Apparently Thiers wrote more quickly than the printer could print, since his afterthoughts on the completed work date from as far back as 1855. Merely as a physical feat the *Histoire du Consulat et de l'Empire* is quite out of the ordinary.

Thiers was from Provence, like Mignet, his contemporary, and the two were close friends. Already in Thiers's earliest work on the Revolution, however, it is clear that they were poles apart in their ideas. Since that time Thiers had become immersed in politics. He was made for the daily hurly-burly and the struggle for power. He was one of the journalists who gave impetus to the revolution of 1830, and under Louis Philippe he was soon in the government. In 1840, as Prime Minister, he almost involved France in war with Britain. He was now in opposition to his successor, the conservative, cautious, peace-loving Guizot (also a first-rate historian), who negotiated an *entente cordiale* with England. To glorify Napoleon as the implacable enemy of British imperialism was for Thiers a form of opposition to Guizot. Thiers also paid homage to Napoleon as the representative of the Revolution, the Revolution as it was understood by the bourgeoisie, and as the creator of unparalleled *gloire*. During his premiership Thiers had given a powerful impetus to the cult of Napoleon, which had been flourishing for a long time, by arranging for his remains to be brought back in state to France. Even before 1830, the parliamentary opposition used the name of Napoleon as the symbol of enlightenment and progress against the reactionary tendencies of the monarchy. After 1830, too, the memory of the hero, the leader who had given greatness to France, spelled danger to that unimaginative dreary middle-class monarchy, under which, as Lamartine testified immediately before the revolution of 1848, the French people became so bored. Radicals and republicans appropriated the memory, and while he was busy with his great work Thiers suddenly woke up to find himself in a Republic, and was thereafter surprised in an even less pleasant fashion by the rise of Bonapartism and of Napoleon III.

1. I quote from the two-column edition published in Brussels in six volumes, and more readily available in Holland.

It would be most unjust to give the impression that Thiers's history was nothing more than a piece of propagandist writing. It was a respectable attempt to make a readable and orderly story out of the material on Napoleon which, though not nearly as extensive then as now, was already overwhelming. Thiers, too, made use of Napoleon's correspondence, then preserved at the Louvre, and also of course of whatever was available in the way of memoirs and documents of every description. Thus he was able to gain an impression of the infinitely varied industry of the ruler and the general. In this he was not breaking new ground, for Bignon had been before him. Indeed, he was in a sense the ideal historian for whom his modest predecessor had hoped. Lefebvre will have had his own thoughts on the subject, but the public was delighted.

Nor was the public wrong. Thiers is a master of historical narrative. One's first impression is of the unfailing lucidity of his presentation, throughout the work. In spite of its broad flow, its circumstantial manner, it holds the attention by its perfect clarity, logical arrangement, and orderly divisions. Knowledge of human nature and practical experience of political life inform it. In short, it is a triumph of 'intelligence', the attribute which, according to his own view,[1] the historian must possess before all others. Shall we admit that the 'true superiority' of the historian must be rooted therein? It must be said that his account has not thereby acquired profundity. Thiers asks no ultimate questions, he is quite content with answers that are little short of conventional, and his unfailing and plausible eloquence enables him to steer round any number of unsolved problems and contradictions.[2] But we need not judge him by his own standard. He possesses other qualities. He may not be witty, nor will he surprise; but when his story asks for dramatic effects or contrasts (and how could a history of Napoleon fail to do so?) he can rise to the occasion. In the last volumes, for example, his emotion at the disasters which his hero brings on himself and his country is genuine, and inspires some really forceful writing.

Thiers shows the influence of the Napoleonic legend more clearly than either of the two previous writers. This does not mean that he admires Napoleon more, or is less inclined to criticize. It means that he accepted a certain reading of the figure, and of the aims, which had been suggested by Napoleon's own propaganda.

He is critical of Napoleon, and more so as he proceeds. One might say that while before 1848 circumstances favoured the tendency to admire Napoleon, they made for an attitude of greater reserve when the later volumes were written. Thiers was not enamoured of the irresponsible and anti-parliamentarian activities

1. *Avis au lecteur*, before volume XII, 1855; Brussels edition after volume III.
2. Typical of the *grande histoire*. De Sacy feared that the increasing amount of historical criticism would put a check on this: FRUIN, *Verspreide Geschriften*, IX, 355 ff.

of the great man's nephew. But the more critical spirit of the later volumes was entirely in keeping with their subject. The further Napoleon advances in his career, the more difficult it is for the eulogist to find justification, in respect not of the general but of the statesman. Even at that stage, though he makes much of the dangers of despotism, with an eye to the new Emperor, Thiers excuses the faults of his hero wherever it is possible, and where it is impossible discusses them more in sorrow than in anger. He is critical; but in all the volumes, and especially the last, the dominant motif is admiration, and more than admiration – affection, love.

THE GENERAL; THE SON OF THE REVOLUTION

Perhaps I should mention first the intense interest Thiers felt in the art of war. I shall have little to say of Napoleon the general in this book. His greatness in this capacity is obvious, from his first amazing successes in Italy to the last wonderful defence on French soil in his adversity. The comprehensive view of positions, the eye for the key point, the capacity to read the mind of his opponent, the ability to take quick decisions, a personality powerful enough to impose obedience, all these qualities Napoleon possessed in their highest form. If the fact has sometimes been denied, it has only been in a paradoxical fashion or from hatred of the man, and no historian of any importance has ever done so.[1] Tolstoy's view of him in *War and Peace* is fundamentally unhistorical, even antihistorical; and he reduces the statesman too to nothing.

My object is to discuss the various opinions concerning the statesman, and concerning the political significance of the personality and achievements of Napoleon. But one would give an imperfect impression of Thiers's *Histoire du Consulat et de l'Empire* if one failed to point out the important part played in it by Napoleon's battles. Thiers's description of them is not only detailed, it shows a real understanding. The military experts of his day were loath to recognize his competence, although in 1870, when the old man was sought out to lead the country after its defeat, they felt some uneasiness in the presence of the politician who had so earnestly warned them. Marshal Foch, the general of a later generation, declared that it was from Thiers's book that he had learnt to read.

As regards Napoleon the statesman, for Thiers the peak of his career came at the outset. He recognizes this already in describing that early triumph:

The man who ruled France from 1799 to 1815 knew, no doubt, days of intoxicating glory in the course of his career, but surely neither he himself nor the France over

---

1. Unless it be G. FERRERO, in his little book *Aventure* (1938).

which he cast his spell ever again lived through such days as these, days whose greatness was accompanied by so much wisdom, and by that wisdom which prompts the hope of durability.[1]

These words follow his account of the bringing of law and order, of victory, (Marengo), of peace (Lunéville and Amiens), of reconciliation (the Concordat and the amnesty), and his description of the public's amazement at the part played by the young soldier in the Council of State towards the completion of the new Civil Code.

It is not only the statesman's strength and wisdom which Thiers admires. He sees in him, with fewer reserves than Bignon and Lefebvre, and in accordance with Napoleon's own presentation of himself, the consolidator of the Revolution at home and its promoter abroad. Above all, unlike Chateaubriand and Mme de Staël, he sees in him the good Frenchman. As Napoleon proclaimed at every stage of his life, as the French people were assured in countless proclamations and speeches, as the voice from St Helena tirelessly repeated, so did Thiers believe: that the mainspring of his life was his fierce love of France, her honour and her might, his desire to further her true interests.

THE FATAL CHANGE OF COURSE AFTER AUSTERLITZ

Nevertheless Thiers considers that Napoleon's policy was to blame for the disasters which ended his career and which engulfed France, that personal ambition and lust for conquest had a share in luring the peace-giver of 1801 and 1802 on the adventurous road which was to lead to Waterloo. He explains this as the corruption of a beneficent character by superhuman success, and sometimes, again, as the ravaging of a great spirit, in spite of the highest intentions, by a passionate temperament. He places the first fatal change of course only after Austerlitz (2 December 1805). This amazing victory inspired in Napoleon the dangerous belief that his genius and the power of France were invincible and made him lose all sense of moderation.[2] The conquest of Prussia in 1806 and her humiliation in 1807 were tremendous events, but they drew France outside her natural sphere of action. The conquest of the whole of Germany, the dizzy edifice erected at Tilsit in 1807, exceeded the limits of caution and of self-knowledge. And yet Thiers even then ventures to speculate that 'had not more and more been heaped upon the groaning foundations' they need not have collapsed; France's fortunes had not yet been compromised irretrievably, and ... 'his glory was immense'.[3]

It will be seen that this view bears some resemblance to that of Bignon; the difference lies in the moment at which the fatal change is supposed to have taken

1. I, 317b.   2. II, 87b.   3. II, 323b.

place. Thiers puts it earlier than his predecessor, but not very emphatically. In the passage just quoted, he allows his imagination to play with the idea, which Bignon had quite seriously entertained, that the position won for France at Tilsit could have been maintained. For the moment I leave on one side the question whether it is better not to speak of a change of course but to follow Lefebvre and seek (if I may so interpret an idea which he never expressed in so many words) ineluctable fatality in the fact that this wonderful brain always lacked the balance and self-control which an enduring peace would have demanded. And when Thiers stressed unfavourable circumstances, it must be remembered that these, by the peace treaties of Leoben and of Campo Formio, were largely of Napoleon's own making. I am ready to believe, with Thiers, in the honesty of Bonaparte's intentions regarding the peace treaties of Lunéville and Amiens (though we shall later see how much that of Amiens can be called in question). But even so I still find it difficult to accept the theory that he was not to be blamed for the breaking of the peace with Britain a year later, in 1803. Was not *that* year the turning-point?

THE RUPTURE WITH BRITAIN IN 1803

Thiers gives the impression – and here at least he is at one with his two predecessors – that in the renewed conflict with England the First Consul indisputably had the right on his side. True, he censures the notorious outburst of rage, not the first of a long series which became part of Napoleonic tactics, in which the British ambassador was shouted at in front of the whole diplomatic corps, and the most terrible misfortunes predicted for Britain if she did not leave continental affairs to Napoleon's pleasure. This outburst was but the outward sign, according to Thiers,[1] of a revolution which had taken place in 'the impressionable and passionate soul' of Napoleon. 'A fertile and hard-working peace', that was the dream which he had cherished. 'Now all of a sudden he was mastered by a patriotic and at the same time personal wrath, and from now on to conquer, humiliate, trample down, and annihilate England became the passion of his life.' Nevertheless he was able to control himself, and once more bore himself with an unshakeable steadiness, to make it perfectly clear that it was Britain, not he, which desired war.[2] This is the point in Thiers's treatment of the episode: he himself is completely convinced of this. He seems not to have the faintest notion that in using his position of power on the continent (which had been ceded to him at Amiens only with the greatest reluctance) to interfere in Switzerland, to

1. I, 460b.   2. I, 462b.

annex Piedmont, to march into other parts of Italy, to keep troops in Holland, the First Consul was bound to excite aversion and resistance in Britain against an arrangement which many there already regarded as humiliating and dangerous. And even before the scene with Lord Whitworth, there had been threats as well as actions designed to intimidate the British, and of a kind to arouse doubt as to whether the First Consul was so sincere in his dream of a fruitful peace as Thiers appears to think. There was Sebastiani's notorious report, published in the *Moniteur*, concerning the reconquest of Egypt; there was the dispatch dictated by Bonaparte, in which Talleyrand, who was just the man to realize the complete unreasonableness of such language, was made to warn the British that if they drove France to war, they would force her to conquer the whole continent. 'The First Consul is only thirty-three years old, he has so far destroyed second-class states only. Who knows in how brief a time, if he is forced to it, he will change the face of Europe and raise the Western Empire up again.' Thiers reports all this, but it does not shake him in his conviction that it was Britain who, by holding on to Malta, broke the peace treaty just signed and so brought about the war. He complains that Whitworth, who just before the famous scene (but after all these challenges and displays of power) had a quiet conversation with Napoleon, did not understand 'the greatness and sincerity' of the First Consul's words; and when Bonaparte insists on the integral execution of the peace treaty, he is only, according to Thiers, speaking 'the language of justice and of insulted pride'.[1]

THE MURDER OF THE DUC D'ENGHIEN (1804)

Thiers's attitude is strikingly shown in his account of the murder of the Duc d'Enghien. It is impossible in this connexion to use any other word than murder, and Thiers himself does not defend the action.

The war with Britain, resumed, as we saw, in 1803, was dragging on. A camp had already been in existence in Boulogne for a year, and feverish plans and preparations were being made. But was the invasion ever likely to come off? Relations were strained with Austria and Russia, but for the moment there was peace on the continent. Meanwhile the British were working up unrest in France, and the Comte d'Artois,[2] who was living in Britain, recklessly lent a hand. Royalists came secretly from overseas and hatched plots with their sympathizers. Attempts to assassinate the First Consul were all the rage. In England he was regarded as an adventurer who had made himself master of France.

1. I, 458a.
2. The youngest brother of Louis XVI, later Charles X.

People were expecting at any moment to see his ephemeral administration collapse. Bonaparte was infuriated by these conspiracies, about which a good deal had come to light. He could not get at Britain, nor at the Comte d'Artois. But in Baden, close to the French frontier, was another Bourbon, the young Duc d'Enghien, son of Condé. Was he waiting for a sign to play his part in the plot? Was he in touch with the conspirators? Suspicions of this kind – prisoners had let out that a prince of the blood was expected – in no way justified the kidnapping on neutral territory which Bonaparte ordered. Nothing could be proved to the court martial, save that Enghien was in British pay, nor was there any other charge.

On this ground he was shot, the same night. It was a warning, and at the same time a challenge, to the Bourbons and the royalists. It was a gesture for which a human life, and justice itself, were ruthlessly sacrificed.

Thiers does not deny this. But he puts the blame on the royalists who had driven the good First Consul to such a measure by their conspiracies and their collusion with Britain. 'His heart, generous and kind, whatever may be said by those who never knew him';[1] he does not scruple to write thus in connexion with this very crime. Nor is this an unconsidered statement: there is an entire theory behind it. For Thiers, Bonaparte is the exponent of the principle of the Revolution in its benevolent aspects. To the man of 1830, this is especially obvious when a question of opposition to the Bourbons is involved. 'Just as twelve years ago', he writes, 'the *émigrés* and their treason had incited the Revolution, guiltless till then, to the shedding of blood' – for had not the Terror been the answer to the invasion and royalist risings in connivance with the foreigner? – 'so now these same people' – still the hated royalists – 'caused the man who till that day had been wisdom incarnate at the head of the State to turn from good to evil, from moderation to violence.' 'The ingratitude of the parties' – to the man who had brought about reconciliation – 'the insolent enmity of Europe' – and the deplorable incident is explained.[2]

UNSHAKEABLE ADMIRATION

Thiers then regarded Bonaparte's conduct up to this moment as that of 'wisdom incarnate'. I have already said that he found much to question in the later years. He knew that Napoleon was subject to outbursts of passion, and he knew the dangers to peace this involved.[3] I have told, too, how dubious he was concerning the peace of Tilsit. He knows that Napoleon was so flushed with his victories that he lost all sense of proportion, and that France had to pay the bill. He realizes how irresponsible – looking at it merely from the pragmatic point

1. I, 532b.   2. I, 535.   3. I, 631a.

of view – was the imprisonment of Pope Pius VII in 1809, and he quite rightly links it with the murder of Enghien and the forced abdication of the Spanish royal family (the 'ambush' of Bayonne in 1808, of which more later), as episodes in that 'embittered struggle with the old European order'[1] into which Napoleon had thrown himself. He knows too that Napoleon could not bear to be contradicted either in his own circle or in France, that his system became more and more despotic, and that this state of affairs gradually undermined the self-reliance of his colleagues and servants and paralysed all their initiative, to the great detriment of both France and himself. He knows how weary the French people were of those endless wars, how fraught with peril the eastern digression of 1807 appeared even to contemporaries, and that Napoleon, though with his unerring perspicacity he could perfectly discern such feelings, would not have these storm signals actually discussed.[2]

Nevertheless Thiers's Napoleon, besides being incomparably great, both as ruler and as commander, remains a good and indeed an attractive man. His shortcomings are chronicled with a certain wistfulness. This appears even after one of the severest passages, in a reflection on the campaigns of 1810 and 1811 in Spain. Thiers states that Napoleon was a tired man, that he had been wilfully blind to unpleasant facts, and had given orders, uncertain and doubtful orders sometimes, based on numbers to which he knew that the worn-out armies could no longer attain, and that finally he put the blame on his generals and treated Masséna in particular with cruel injustice. Even then, when he comments that jealousy, vengefulness, anger, bewilderment, and error had taken possession of Napoleon's soul, it is only to ask how, if 'his own great spirit' was capable of these weaknesses, he could close his eyes to the inevitability that his generals would also succumb to them.[3]

And what of his greatness and wisdom as a ruler? In Thiers's opinion, Napoleon's correspondence with the brothers he had created kings 'deserves to be studied as a succession of profound lessons in the art of government'.[4] Certainly the reader of this correspondence feels himself in contact with an extraordinary mind. The decisiveness, the precisely expressed recommendations, the aversion to empty phrases, the ability to pick out relevant facts from the general confusion – it is a constant pleasure to observe these qualities. There are passages which fully deserve the praise Thiers bestows. One of these, from a letter addressed to Jérôme, the youngest brother, much younger than Napoleon, and created by him King of Westphalia, I shall quote:

Do not listen to those who will tell you that your people, used as they are to subjection, will receive your benefits gratefully. There is more enlightenment in the Kingdom of Westphalia than you will be told, and only in the confidence and

1. III, 210a.   2. II, 593.   3. III, 416b.   4. II, 130a.

love of the population will your throne stand firmly. What is above all desired in Germany is that you will grant to those who do not belong to the nobility, but possess talents, an equal claim to offices, and that all vestiges of serfdom and of barriers between the sovereign and the lowest class of the people shall be completely done away with. The benefits of the *Code Napoléon*, legal procedure in open court, the jury, these are the points by which your monarchy should be distinguished... your people must enjoy a liberty, an equality, a prosperity, unknown in the rest of Germany.[1]

Such a letter must have especially appealed to Thiers, with its picture of Napoleon as the conscious propagator of the principles of the Revolution. One might only express some doubt as to whether it was an example of the ruler's wisdom to lay a task so far above his powers on the shoulders of so useless a youth as Jérôme; but I shall not go into this matter at present. Even if one confines oneself to the correspondence, Thiers's unqualified praise seems strange.

Take for example the correspondence with Louis, separately published in 1875.[2] There is perhaps both truth and wisdom in the comment that Louis was too set on being regarded as good-natured, and that a prince who in the first year of his reign is regarded as 'so good' is likely to be laughed at in the second year. Louis's extravagance and his empty display were also assessed at their true value by his brother. But how arid does his severity appear after a time, what a lack of understanding is revealed by the ceaselessly repeated admonitions, as if the entire art of government consisted of the giving of orders and the application of force. I leave on one side the brutal tone used to the younger brother after the crisis of 1810, the scorn, the rubbing in of his stupidity and his powerlessness. Napoleon had enough of Louis's kingship, and any means seemed to him justified to induce Louis to abdicate. Among the deserved rebukes are some which are grotesquely unjust; and when Louis's retorts are to the point, no notice is taken. Or a reminder of promises made, an appeal to honour, is countered by a savage sneer: 'You might have spared me this fine display of your principles.' But what can be said of the warning that if Louis ignored his exhortation to be *français de cœur*, his people – the Dutch, by the way – would chase him away with scorn and contumely. 'One has to admit,' says the French editor of 1875,[3] 'that it would be difficult to show more hardheartedness and pride, combined with so little shrewdness in the appreciation of events.'

A succession of wise lessons! Are we to suppose that to these belongs 'that famous repression theory which Napoleon so frequently expounded, to Murat for Spain, to Joseph for the Kingdom of Naples, to Junot for Tuscany, to Davout

1. See for example RAMBAUD, *L'Allemagne sous Napoléon Ier*, p. 219.
2. By FÉLIX ROCQUAIN, *Napoléon Ier et le roi Louis*.
3. p. cxx.

for Northern Germany'?[1] The theory, that is to say, that severe punitive measures in occupied or annexed territories were humane, since they prevented a renewal of disturbances. But was even this remarkable humanity more than a pretext? Was it anything more than an unquenchable lust for power? In 1808 Napoleon wrote to Joseph, then still King of Naples: 'I wish the Naples mob would attempt a rising. As long as you have not made an example, you will not be their master. Every conquered country must have its rising.'

Meanwhile Thiers does not conceal the faults of Napoleon, nor the great weariness and reluctance, long before the end, of French public opinion. He gives a really telling picture of the reaction to the Emperor's retreat behind the Rhine frontier with his beaten army after his second military disaster, the German one of 1813, which succeeded that in Russia of 1812.[2]

In Paris he found the public profoundly cast down, almost despairing, and in particular greatly incensed by his actions. His police, however zealously and arbitrarily they worked, could hardly prevent those widespread feelings from breaking forth . . . He was not forgiven for having neglected the happy chance of concluding peace offered by his victories of Luetzen and Bautzen. His explanation of the peace negotiations of Prague was simply not believed[3] [and indeed it was false]; people were convinced that the failure was due to him. His ambition was looked upon as excessive, cruel to mankind, and fatal to France . . . The fettered and paid scribblers who alone were allowed to write the news-sheets, and who were believed by nobody any more, had received instructions from the Duke of Rovigo [that is, Savary, the Minister of Police] as to how they were to represent the disasters of the campaign. The frost having done service as explanation of the misfortunes of 1812, the defection of the allies was to make intelligible those of 1813 . . . 'He wants to sacrifice all our children to his mad ambition'; that was the cry rising up from every family, in Paris as in the remotest provinces. The genius of Napoleon was not denied; worse, it was ignored. People only remembered his passion for war and conquest. The detestation once felt for the guillotine was now evoked by war . . . France, which after ten years of revolution had had its fill of freedom, now, after fifteen years of military government, had learned to loathe despotism and the shedding of French blood from one end of Europe to the other. . . .

1814 AND 1815

Yet, as Thiers pursues the story further, Napoleon's downfall touches his heart more deeply. This of course is connected with the sorrow he felt at the consequences of France's downfall. In other words, unlike Mme de Staël, he will not

1. A. RAMBAUD, L'Allemagne sous Napoléon Ier (1896), p. 193.
2. v, 247b.
3. Cf. below the discussion of the negotiations of Prague, p. 271 ff.

separate Napoleon from his country. However much developments at that critical moment seemed to point to such an attitude, he is determined to make no such distinction. The profound difference between his view of Napoleon and that of Mme de Staël, indeed, between their whole social and political outlooks, makes this intelligible.

When the allies have reached Paris, in 1814, Napoleon is at Fontainbleau with the remnants of his severely battered armies. He still wishes to risk an attack, and Thiers, who thinks he had a chance (it certainly needs a fervent admiration to share this belief), bitterly reproaches the marshals for refusing to follow him in his last despairing attempt, and for thus forcing the abdication upon him. I do not wish to take up the cudgels for those children of the fortunes of war. They had been made great by Napoleon, from him they had their fancy uniforms, their high-sounding titles, and their broad acres; yet now they had no thought but of saving as much as possible of their gains from the wreck, and of seeking a quiet life at last. It is not surprising that in the public mind of the day Marmont ('Duke of Ragusa'), who played an important role in that praetorian resistance, and who became a great man under the subsequent régime of the Bourbons, was never regarded in any other light than that of the traitor of 1814.[1] But Thiers has more general considerations in mind. He imagines that the Rhine frontier could have been held. What binds the French patriot to Napoleon at this moment is the possession of the German Rhineland and of Flanders, the countries which the Revolution had conquered in its first onrush and which were now being lost in the last stages of the Napoleonic adventure. Had Napoleon by his mistakes gambled all this away? At any rate, only Napoleon can win it back. This idea must put an end to all criticism of the internal administration; to make a separation between the dictator and his country is betrayal.

The same problem appears again in 1815, after the return from Elba. As soon as Napoleon is once more in the Tuileries, Thiers considers it the duty of every Frenchman to support him in his resistance to the advancing allies. Those *départements* which struggle to make their young men available for yet another trial by battle are praised for their 'laudable attempts'.[2] The men of the Vendée who (as a generation before against the Revolution, and again under a de la Rochejaquelein), rise in revolt, are reproved. By doing so 'they withdrew fifteen to twenty thousand Frenchmen from the formidable rendezvous at Waterloo, and thus made their contribution to the most tragic disaster of our history.[3] This

1. In July 1830 Charles X made him Commandant of Paris, thereby irritating the people still more. 'Raguser' was used in the sense of 'trahir': VAULABELLE, *Histoire des deux Restaurations*, VIII, 209.
2. VI, 295b.
3. VI, 319a. '*Le désastre le plus tragique de notre histoire.*' Unfortunate France has since had to face worse disasters.

attitude towards Waterloo, this unconditional rallying behind Napoleon at the critical moment, we shall observe again in the work of many later French historians. Thiers is all the more prone to it in that he, as we know, is able to believe in the real goodness of Napoleon, in the purity of his motives, and so also accepts the sincerity of his conversion to liberal and peace-loving intentions.

For in that amazing final curtain of the great drama, the Hundred Days, the most astonishing sight is that of Napoleon in the role of the despot and conqueror chastened and made wise by misfortune. Freedom of the Press, parliamentary government, peace – all these he was now prepared to guarantee to the French people. Yet Thiers is not so naïve (although it is impossible not to use that word occasionally in connexion with this typical worldling, who prided himself on his shrewdness) as to be blind to the fact that there were good grounds for the distrust of the French people. He understands the suspicions of the French liberals and democrats, as well as those of the foreign princes and peoples. 'God', he says, referring to the first, 'sees our repentance and is satisfied. Men have neither this insight nor this pity. They are aware only of the transgressions that are committed, and their rough law demands actual, complete, and visible chastisement.'[1] Concerning the second category, he can up to a certain point sympathize with their fury against the destroyer of their peace, and admits that Napoleon had brought it on himself by 'an unendurable abuse of victory over a period of fifteen years'.

At the same time, Thiers is convinced of Napoleon's repentance. He gives a moving description of the Emperor's visit to la Malmaison, just before he set out for the final fatal battle and in the midst of urgent and pressing preoccupations. It was in the country house bound up with the memory of Joséphine, who had lived there after her repudiation until her death in 1814, and where he, when still First Consul, had passed his happiest days with her. How different things were then, how the world had honoured him in those days!

But at that time he had not yet wearied, enslaved, and devastated it; the nations regarded him not as a tyrant but as a saviour. Brooding over those days, he did not deceive himself, nor fail to mete out to himself the inexorable justice of genius, but still he told himself that, since he had renounced the error of his ways, the world might give him some confidence in return, and enable him to put into practice the new wisdom brought from Elba.[2]

Though Thiers repeats that men cannot be expected to grant a second chance, and that only God can judge true repentance, it is clear that for him despotism and lust for conquest had been only subsidiary faults, and that now that disasters had purified him, the true Napoleon, the benefactor of the French people and of

1. VI, 291b.   2. VI, 334b.

mankind, was once more appearing – only to be destroyed at Waterloo. There is here, then, deep human tragedy, quite apart from the blow sustained by France, for whom the new peace terms were harder than those of 1814. It is also clear that for a man who held such views, the St Helena pronouncements of Napoleon must be testimony worthy of trust, indeed of reverence.

FINAL JUDGEMENT

If one tries to get a view of the work as a whole, it must be admitted that there is some truth in the criticism of Sainte-Beuve that the picture of Napoleon as politician is somewhat vague, nebulous, and lacking in precision.[1] The great narrator, with his intelligence and his enthusiasm for the innumerable problems which he encounters, has given an admirable exposition which can still be used as a basis for further work. But synthesis is not his strong point. His own personality was too opportunist, too pliable, too adaptable.

Unprincipled, too impressed by success, said his enemies. Indeed, scarcely was the great work completed but there was a reaction against the Napoleonic legend, which had triumphed in Thiers's book for all his care for accuracy and his occasional severe criticism. The reaction was often directed against Thiers in person, in itself a recognition of his importance for Napoleonic studies. The fact will give me further opportunity to add to my all too scanty review of his inexhaustibly rich work.

1. In his review of Lefebvre's book *Histoire des Cabinets de l'Empire*, etc., printed at the beginning of the later edition: I xxxiii.

Part 3

Reaction Against the Legend

The Circumstances

THE reaction against the Napoleonic legend was closely connected with the opposition to the Second Empire, which grew in strength in the sixties.

One of the pillars upon which Napoleon III and his government rested was veneration for the first Napoleon. How much he himself realized this, appears from his sponsorship, in 1857, of a majestic edition of Napoleon I's letters, and still more from the decree of 1864 in which he disbanded the committee engaged upon the work, which had already produced fifteen volumes, and set another in its place under the chairmanship of Prince Napoleon (his cousin, son of Jérôme Bonaparte). The first committee had on the whole set about its task in a scholarly fashion. The second committee began by announcing to the Emperor that it would be guided by the 'very simple idea' 'that we were charged with the task of publishing what the Emperor would have made available to the public if he had wished, *se survivant à lui-même et devançant la justice des âges*, to display himself and his system to posterity'. Thus a number of letters which threw an unfavourable light on Napoleon were quietly omitted from the seventeen volumes issued by this new committee. It is amusing to note that since this official patronage did not go unobserved, its effects were the reverse of what was intended, and it was followed by a flood of writing prejudicial to the hallowed memory.[1]

1. Thiers had access to the originals in the Louvre, but when the committee started work this was apparently no longer permitted. There were, however, quite a number of letters in private collections, and while the committee, working from the minutes, made their selection, independent historians sometimes published letters which had been excluded by them. An example is d'Haussonville, with whose work I shall be dealing in a later chapter. After 1870 the great archive collection was of course reopened. As early as 1875, for example, Rocquain, whose work has been already mentioned, made additions to the *Correspondance*. In 1897 Léon Lecestre produced two volumes from material which the official editors had set aside (including material already made public variously by other hands). The work was called *Lettres inédites de Napoléon Ier*. There were later volumes of additions to this by other editors. In his introduction Lecestre wrote: 'Il convient de faire remarquer que ces lettres ainsi réunies laissent une impression bien différente de celle qu'elles auraient produite, si elles avaient été insérées à leur place respective dans la *Correspondance*. Encadrées dans les pièces si nombreuses où éclate le génie de l'Empereur, elles auraient peut-être passé presque inaperçues, ou du moins l'admiration inspirée par les incomparables qualités du souverain et du général aurat fait oublier dans une certaine mesure les coups de butoir du despote.' According to this view, which has much

At first many, like Thiers, who had scant liking for Napoleon III and his semi-dictatorial régime, shared the veneration for Napoleon I, and a popular method of attack was to point out the contrasts. Victor Hugo contemptuously called the new Emperor *Napoléon le petit*. Yet the *coup d'état* of 1851 had revealed in a flash the danger inherent in the combination of democracy and Caesarism, or to put it another way, the unreality of a democracy based on 'strong government' and militarism. The new régime, unable to conceal even though it might mitigate its authoritarian character, saw itself forced to interpret the Napoleonic legend less liberally than the first Emperor himself had done during the Hundred Days and on St Helena. It became customary to present the Revolution, of which Napoleon must still pass for the heir and exponent, as undertaken on behalf of civil not political liberty, and the French as being content with equality, and with social reforms safeguarded by a government which was not responsible to them. The fighters for trampled liberty could not avoid seeing that this had indeed been the position of the first Napoleon, and the never wholly forgotten tradition of rejection established by Mme de Staël was resurrected.

truth, Napoleon III's policy of falsifying the sources achieved an effect the reverse of his intention. Sainte-Beuve was among the members of the new committee which started work in 1864 with that remarkable declaration of principle: see the introduction volume XVI of the *Correspondance*. See on p. 148 below, the defence put forward by Prince Napoleon many years later.

1   Jules Barni

EVEN before the appearance of the historically more important works which
I intend to discuss, the problem was clearly set forth by Jules Barni in a critical
examination of Thiers's history. The writer lived as a political exile in Switzerland. His book, *Napoléon et son historien M. Thiers,* a series of lectures given at
Geneva in 1863, was banned in France. A certain number of copies were of
course distributed clandestinely, but in 1869 the writer had it reprinted in France.
He and his publisher believed that the court would leave that edition alone, and
indeed as far as I know there was never any prosecution. Jules Barni had translated Kant, and written books such as *La morale dans la démocratie* and *Les martyres
de la libre pensée.*

   In his examination of Thiers he begins by asking himself what the writer's
standpoint is. He finds that Thiers's only measure is success, and that he has no
moral scale of values. Lamartine had already remarked: 'This author is the
accomplice of Fortune: he only recognizes evil-doing when it is punished by
adversity.' The conflict between reverence for the historical fact as such (Barni
does not put it in these words), and the consciousness of an obligation to test
the fact by eternal moral values, always has existed and always will exist both
in historical study and in its object, the strife between men called politics. In
those years of resistance to arbitrary power, born of violence in the *coup d'état* of
2 December, Frenchmen became very much aware of that conflict.

   Barni's little book is no serious contribution to Napoleonic historiography,
for it is too purely polemical. But from the mass of Thiers's utterances, dis-
cretions, and palliations Barni skilfully extracts the spirit of the great work;
and most of the theses inspiring the four later works, which I shall be discussing
shortly, are to be found in his book.

   Barni has no patience with the idea of Napoleon as propagator of the Revolution. Rather does he regard him as the man who obstructed the Revolution, and
where he could not destroy it, debased it. I will glance at one or two of the points
he makes. Thiers admires the centralization introduced by the First Consul,
in which the prefects were the principal instruments of central authority. Barni
recalls de Tocqueville's demonstration that this was completely contrary to
the wishes of the *Assemblée constituante,* that it was a return to the *ancien régime*
and the *intendants.* 'The elective principle introduced by the Revolution was

suppressed.'[1] He is irritated by the way in which the suppression of representative bodies is glossed over, and the nonchalance with which those who attempted to organize a defence are brushed aside with the comment that 'they were blind to the general development of opinion and to the needs of the time'.[2] Against Thiers's enthusiasm for the setting up of the Legion of Honour, *'ce beau système de récompense'*, he quotes Bonaparte's cynical comment: 'It is with rattles that men are led.'[3] The institution was established for no other purpose than to undermine equality, still regarded as the great benefit brought by the Revolution, for the undisturbed enjoyment of which Napoleon claimed gratitude. The establishment of a new nobility under the Empire was of course an even more flagrant encroachment on equality. In his *Histoire de la Révolution française* the youthful Thiers had written that Napoleon carried out the Revolution by creating an aristocracy from among the people.[4] It is indeed not very plausible, but his view of the imperial coronation is closely connected with it.[5]

'Among the triumphs of our Revolution this was not the least, to see the soldier sprung from her own bosom consecrated by the Pope, who had left the capital of Christendom for that very purpose.' Barni comments:

As for me, I admit that I find it impossible to discover a triumph of the Revolution in the overthrow of her most sacred principles, in the ruin of her dearest achievements, in the restoration of such institutions and forms as were most opposed to her spirit.

Thiers continued: 'If only control of ambition had shared that throne with genius, that France might have been guaranteed a sufficient measure of freedom, and that a reasonable limit might have been put to heroic enterprises . . .'

Here I interrupt the historian [Barni says] and I exclaim: 'What! You praise that man when he tramples underfoot the fundamental laws and appropriates the sovereignty; you praise the Consular and Imperial Constitutions, which deliver all power up to him; and you want that usurper to control his ambition, you want that despot, who rules the country according to his whim, to guarantee a sufficiency of freedom, you want that omnipotent commander to limit his enterprises, which you call heroic? What a strange piece of reasoning, and, in a historian, what a surprising forgetfulness of all the lessons of history ! . . .'

Arbitrary administration of the law, the Press controlled, the Concordat, intended not to save religion but to make it an instrument of government – a censure, be it noted, very different from that of Mignet (see p. 37), though Mme de Staël had already written in these terms, and we shall meet it later *in extenso*

1. pp. 57 and 59.   2. p. 64.   3. p. 69.   4. p. 145.
5. THIERS, I, 602b; in BARNI, p. 158.

– and then the wars! Did no blame at all attach to Bonaparte for the breaking of the Treaty of Amiens? Barni merely poses the question, but he does protest against the systematic Anglophobia which Thiers displayed, in common with many other French writers. Next there were the acts of violence, the executions, the terrorism. Barni notes that Thiers does not bother to speak of the Tyrolean national leader, Andreas Hofer, executed in Mantua in February 1810. Napoleon had written to Eugène, his stepson and Viceroy of Italy, in whose hands the prisoner was:

My son, I had commanded you to send Hofer to Paris, but since you have got him in Mantua, give instant orders that a military commission be set up to try him and execute him on the spot. See that this takes place within twenty-four hours.

Not a word on this matter, says Barni, in spite of the deep impression made on German-speaking countries by the death of Hofer. But what we do get is a detailed account of the 'festivities, preparations, and details of etiquette' to which Napoleon 'devoted himself with so much pleasure' at the same moment, in anticipation of the arrival of the Austrian Archduchess, out of loyalty to whose house Hofer had sacrificed his life and who was now to be the wife of the conqueror.

Finally Barni contests, point by point, the 'portrait' of Napoleon with which Thiers had concluded his twentieth volume. I shall only take one of these. Napoleon, according to Thiers, 'était par son génie fait pour la France, comme la France était faite pour lui'. Barni's criticism is here in line with that of Mme de Staël and Chateaubriand. Napoleon, he says, was no Frenchman. He supports this view with quotations from Fichte (from his Reden an die deutsche Nation, 1813), and from Quinet, one of whose books I shall be discussing next, and who had already put forward his theory of the Italian origin of Napoleon's Imperial dream. Barni concludes:

That contempt of humanity, that misprision of the opinion of others, that Caesarean pride, that insensitive heart, and that profound moral indifference, these characteristics which distinguished Napoleon were not those of a Frenchman.

We shall see how all these ideas recur in the works of the writers whom I am now going to discuss, and which it might be thought must bring to an end the veneration of the French for their Emperor.

2 Edgar Quinet

THE WRITER

I AM going to begin with Edgar Quinet's book *La Révolution*, published in 1865. It is not so much a history as an interpretation of the Revolution. One should not go to it for a thorough examination of the facts. But in spite of the lack of detail, his portrait of the man of the 18th Brumaire has historical significance. (Quinet, it should be noted, closes the period of the Revolution with the coronation of the Emperor, that is, half-way through Napoleon's career.)

Quinet, a friend of Michelet, had been like him a professor at the *Collège de France*. In 1844 and 1845 the two had caused a great sensation by their lectures on the Jesuits, which were tantamount to a declaration of war on Catholicism. Indeed Quinet, though in no way an atheist or a man without religious feeling, regarded Catholicism as the great impediment to the development of the French social heritage. From a strictly scholarly point of view, his many writings on religious history, on German and Italian culture (he was acquainted before Barni with the German philosophers and poets, a most unusual accomplishment among his generation of Frenchmen), on the struggle for freedom in his own day and in antiquity, have little value. Quinet was a prophet, one of wide and real culture, and he preached his own undogmatic religion, his own anti-dictatorial liberalism. In 1851 he was obliged to leave France, and thenceforth lived in Switzerland. He was over sixty in 1865.

THE FRENCH AND FREEDOM

Quinet's *Révolution* was received with some surprise. So fierce an attack on the *Comité de salut public* had not been expected from a combative anti-clerical, who would not have scrupled to use the university monopoly to propagate a deism better calculated, in his opinion, to develop the social heritage of France than Catholicism. Perhaps his view concerning State education accorded ill with his liberalism, which was nevertheless sincerely held.

In his view, the Revolution in its earliest phase was most certainly the dynamic expression of a generous impulse towards freedom, and of a desire for a nobler, a more humane, and a more enlightened society. If in later years it engulfed the republic which might have realized these ideals, if it was satisfied with equality,

76

the *code civil*, and material welfare, if it took refuge under the sceptre of an ambitious soldier, by so much did the Revolution fall short of its own high ideals. But backsliding did not begin with the 18th Brumaire. Long before that time the French people had shown themselves incapable of fulfilling their Revolution. The massacres of September 1792 – '*les événements de septembre*', as they were called, a training in the hypocritical glossing over of horrors – were preparatory to the Terror by which the noblest minds of the Revolution were annihilated.

Quinet laments in particular the downfall of the Girondins, whom he regards as the true friends of freedom, for they wished to break down that centralization which was the product and the instrument of the old despotism. The Jacobins of the *Comité de salut public* desired nothing more than to make themselves masters of that instrument of the late domination. Their restoration of arbitrary power did even more moral harm than their savage methods with the leading figures of the Revolution. It left such demoralization that the Directorate was powerless to act, however good its intentions and however strong its desire to build firm foundations for the Republic. Indeed the Directors themselves were only too easily tempted to resort to force, and when in Fructidor 1797 three of them, with the help of the army, pushed aside the other two and attacked the legislative assemblies as well, the total rout of freedom was only a question of time.

The man who had directed this *coup*, from Italy, was General Bonaparte. Two years later, in Brumaire, after his Egyptian adventure, he gave the death blow.

As long as there had been a civilian government, and a constitution, and a republic, there were at least the roots from which liberty might still spring, to blossom once more; now there came, with the sword, a régime on principle opposed to liberty.

But after all that men had been through, after the atrocities, the shocks and disappointments, after the betrayals of principle, exhaustion and apathy were universal, and the parliamentarians' appeal to the people was powerless against brute force and met with no response. Indeed men *were* content with civil rights and material acquisitions. But what blindness, and to what disasters, degeneracy, moral and spiritual death, did it lead!

What is the explanation of this failure of the French people? It was not the only occasion. Whenever a liberal government was tried, in 1791 when the *Constituante* organized the constitutional monarchy, in 1795–99 when the Directory tried to clear the way for the republic, in 1848–51 under the Second Republic, the public failed to support it.[1] A people cannot free itself from its historical tradition in the space of a few years. The French had every reason to hate their

1. *La Révolution*, I, 137 ff.

77

history, which had nothing to offer them, no parliament like that of the British, no free cantons like those of the Swiss, nothing, indeed, save absolutism. In 1789 they revolted against it, and in a moment of joyous enthusiasm imagined themselves free. But the old ways, '*les mœurs serviles*', soon reasserted themselves, all the more easily since the French Revolution (unlike the English and the Dutch) was not accompanied by a religious reformation. In Quinet's view, freedom cannot coexist with Catholicism. It is one of his grudges against Rousseau, whose spirit governed the Revolution, that he shrank from this reformation, and still more that he made men's minds impervious to it by the doctrine[1] of his '*vicaire savoyard*' – 'I regard all the various religions as so many salutary institutions. I look upon them all as good, where God is served in fitting manner.' And so men adapted themselves to the old slavery once more.

What a melancholy spectacle they presented, these heroes of 1792, when after Brumaire they had to serve under a master. When friends reminded them of ideals formerly shared, there was only an embarrassed mumble, unless they snapped angrily back: 'Let us forget all that.' They decked themselves in the titles and the livery of the Emperor. And so this Revolution, begun as resistance to absolutism, to a stifling administrative centralization, and in Quinet's view[2] to the outworn Church of Rome, petered out in a government under which men could no doubt enjoy the lands they had acquired from the Church or from *émigrés*, and which introduced the codes, but which was as authoritarian as the monarchy had ever been, even more highly centralized, and with the link between Church and State restored by the Concordat.

The French who since 1804 imagined that they had salvaged the Revolution because they possessed their five codes, argued like the Byzantines, who also thought that they had preserved Athens and Rome and the heroic soul of ancient civilization, because Justinian had given them the Digests and the Pandects.

The First Consul's description of his régime, which turned everything into its opposite, as 'definitely consolidating the effects of the Revolution', was nothing more than an audacious sophism. 'The most surprising part is that this sophism and the ambition of a great commander became the guide for the historian's judgement (a thrust at Thiers), and the bait by which a portion of posterity allows itself to be snared.'[3]

This civil freedom itself, so cunningly used as a pretext for the destruction of political life,[4] was but a fragile possession, in the absence of political guarantees.

Everything had been sacrificed to equality, the divinity which devoured all others; it came first in the tables of the law. And yet this equality was suspended, by the creation of a new nobility and of entailed estates, which brought the old privileges with them. The nobility of the old France is revived and resumes its proud position,

1. II, 481.   2. II, 537.   3. II, 535.   4. II, 596.

as the democrats who cannot penetrate into its ranks are seen to be forging new titles for themselves ... Equality perished twice, when the new men repudiated her, and when the old names were restored.

There was a spiritual servitude so great that literature withered away.

Neither Kant, Fichte, Schelling, nor Hegel could have put forward in France those daring theses which gave a new content to the moral world; they would have been imprisoned at the first word.[1]

Mme de Staël was not allowed to live in France.

You know what the Empire asked as the price of restoring to her her country, her fame, her honour, and even the two millions that were owing to her. Two lines of praise; and these she had refused.[2]

But to exile she owed the opportunity of gaining strength and fresh life from the new ideas springing up elsewhere. Because of this, and because she had not needed to subjugate her mind to the All-Powerful, as the others had been compelled to do, because of her solitary sojourn at Coppet and her wanderings through Europe, at a time when the world and the French liberals were getting used to the yoke and were losing their way, she was able to echo the voice of 1789 in her *Considérations*. That almost forgotten sound aroused wonder and trouble of spirit. As if by a miracle, the tradition of free minds was restored.

THE CONCORDAT

Was the Church at least free from persecution? We know that Quinet could no longer regard it as a force for freedom. As we shall see, people never tired of citing the famous Concordat of 1801 as the conclusive proof of the young First Consul's statesmanlike wisdom. If Quinet condemned it, it was largely on the grounds that this measure was no true liberation for the Church, that it was in fact servitude. With a stroke of the pen, he writes, the First Consul had abolished the healthy modern principle of the separation of Church and State, established in 1795 (in place of the *Constitution civile du clergé*, which had proved unworkable).

Religion is henceforth no more than a matter for authority and police; conscience is again in the clutches and under the seal of policy. Nobody shall pray to his God without the permission of the State, which authorizes only those ancient forms of creed which have been consecrated by time. Hence the impossibility of renewing anything in religious life. Death is made into a rule ... Every non-salaried faith, every non-official god is suppressed; and that change actually takes effect as soon as

1. II, 560.   2. II, 570.

the order is given. Not a soul offers resistance. The officially admitted religions rejoice that life has been made impossible for others; and what strikes one dumb is that this spiritual régime, of which police supervision is the most constant feature, could be called the régime of religious liberty, so completely and suddenly had every idea of real liberty been driven out.

The clergy, enslaved by the sovereign, itself sovereign over conscience; a despotic church in the power of a despot. Such was the Concordat! A mace in the hands of Hercules! Yet it can be turned against him.

In the speech of Portalis [the Minister of Cults] by which the Concordat of 1802 was as it were prefaced, lies the origin of that conventional Catholicism, seen by no mortal eyes, fabulous, liberal, tolerant, without monastic orders, without monasteries or convents, without ultramontanism, without theocracy, almost without Pope, a mere figment of the imagination of a great lawyer serving a great soldier. We talk of Utopias: the first Utopia is the Concordat.

Here is its true significance: as regards policy the Revolution was seeking a refuge with Caesar, as regards religion with the Pope.[1]

I hardly need remark that all these views were so many attacks on the régime of Napoleon III. Quinet too was living in Switzerland, able to draw strength from the world of ideas outside France because he had not been willing to bow to the tyrant. In his day, too, a materialism reigned supreme and was to reconcile men to the loss of their freedom. Were not the intellectuals and the lawyers well satisfied, did not the air resound with praise for the blessings of imperial rule, uttered by those who were sunning themselves in its favour and enjoying its decorations, and who, many of them, had formerly served Louis Philippe or dreamed of liberty under the second Republic?

Under Napoleon III, Church and State were linked together as closely as ever, Lamennais had fallen into disfavour at Rome shortly after 1830, and the Concordat of 1801 seemed sacrosanct to priests and officials alike. But that Quinet wrote under the influence of his own experiences does not lessen the importance to history of his ideas concerning Napoleon and his work.

THE PICTURE OF NAPOLEON

For Quinet, Napoleon is first and foremost the general, the military man. He does not question his merits as such, though he does hint that Bonaparte neglected no means to make them apparent. Masséna, for instance, whose campaign in Switzerland during Bonaparte's absence in Egypt had just as much title to become legendary, confined himself to the most meagre dispatches, which failed to fire public imagination. Bonaparte used his military reputation as political

1. II, 525 ff.

capital. Precisely at the moment when in Brumaire he had to throw everything into the balance, the successes of Masséna in Switzerland and of Brune in Holland caused the danger to the Fatherland, which he was going to save, to appear much less threatening. Had not public opinion been so thoroughly prepared and ready to follow his lead, this might well have upset his calculations. However this may be, Napoleon is the soldier, the enemy of civil administration, of discussion and of freedom, the man of power, of brute force, the man, too, who was afraid neither of advertisement nor of deceit.

One thing assured Napoleon's success. He perceived from afar the goal towards which he strove. Among the men of his generation he was the only one who had known for a long time what he wanted. While the others were running aimlessly backwards and forwards, he went straight ahead. Absolute power was his compass.[1]

The case of Venice showed how unscrupulously he brushed aside everything which stood in his way. It was in 1796, at the very beginning of his career, after his sensational success in Italy. He was only a general in the service of the Republic, but already he was giving orders and negotiating in a high-handed way, establishing States here and doing away with them there. Thus, after finding pretexts to gain control of the neutral republic of Venice, he delivered it up to Austria, high-handedness which aroused a certain uneasiness even in Paris. And what a piece of sophistry was his justification after the event.

It was intended to strengthen the patriotism of the Venetians, to prepare the way for their future independence, and to ensure that at some later time they should receive a national government, whatever its composition.

It was at St Helena that the fallen Emperor made this statement; there 'where passion was stilled, and only posterity was his witness', he invented, in cold blood, this worse than Machiavellian example of special pleading. By his writings we may know him.

What writer, what philosopher [says Quinet mockingly] has the good fortune, in all religious, political, and sociological difficulties, and at the moment when the road seems closed to all others, to possess a star which shines exclusively for him, so that he can reply to every question: 'My interest was that of the universe, my rule was liberty for the others, my victory was that of earth and of heaven, my defeat is that of Providence, the key to all mysteries is my sceptre. I was the alpha and the omega. After me nothing remains, neither kings nor peoples, the old world and the new are empty.'[2]

Quinet can see nothing of the Frenchman, nothing of modern man, in Napoleon.

1. II, 489.   2. II, 487.

The ideal of Napoleon was the Empire of Constantine, and of Theodosius. He inherited this tradition, as did all the Italian Ghibellines, from his ancestors ... Instead of assisting the liberation of the individual conscience, he always postulated a Pope, of whom he would be the Emperor and master. It is a conception which takes its origins from the idea of the Ghibellines and the medieval commentators. When he dreams of the future, it is always of the submissive world of a Justinian or a Theodosius, as imagined by the medieval imperialist thinkers. In the midst of such concepts, modern freedom seemed an anachronism; worse, to him it could appear only as the people's whim, as a snare for his power.

That is Napoleon – an Italian strayed into France, a victim of the superstitions of the *Monarchia del mondo* and testamentary executor of the wild imaginings of Dante – whom he had never read. None of the generals of French descent who had at first been sometimes regarded as his rivals, men like Moreau, Hoche, Joubert, Bernadotte, would have discovered the tradition of Roman universal monarchy in their ancestral archives. More grandiose than great, the vision of *le grand empire*, limitless, unbounded even by the sea, belongs to Napoleon and is Italian, says Quinet. And it is the true setting for his triumphant restoration of Catholicism, by which he hoped to give his authority the necessary foundation. What he had gained by surprise on the 18th Brumaire, he consecrated with the Concordat.

CONSTANTINE AND THEODOSIUS

Quinet has one more interesting observation to make concerning Napoleon's ecclesiastical policy.[1] In order to bring the earth once more under the yoke of Constantine or Theodosius, he had been compelled not only to restore the Papacy along with Catholicism, but thereafter to put himself in the place of the Papacy. Thus the Pope would merely have been a patriarch in the power of the Emperor. Like Constantine, Napoleon would have been able to preside over Councils of Nicaea. He would have had absolute authority over men's souls as well as over their bodies. Such was his aim. But in trying to realize it, he made one mistake. It concerned the so-called liberties of the Gallican Church. Here his discernment failed. He did not realize that those liberties, which he intended to convert into servitude, had already disappeared with all the others ... He believed that with the four articles of Bossuet he could tie the Church fast to his triumphal chariot. But the Church would have nothing to do with them any more. 'These articles, by which he imagined he could limit the Papacy, were an illusion ... That was the weakest side of the Empire.'

Napoleon, argues Quinet, could not remedy his mistake, because he did not

1. II, 534 ff.

dare touch doctrine. As a true Latin, he was suspicious of the Greeks, he was lacking completely in the audacity of the pioneer or the reformer. The Church remained for him an unsurmountable obstacle to the attainment of his Byzantine ideal.

How businesslike and sober, after these vast and timeless philosophizings, appears the account of Thiers. Or should I say that, compared with Thiers, Quinet seems fantastic and far-fetched? As regards the ecclesiastical policy, in any case, I shall later show, when dealing with one of the writers whose books were soon, in a sense, to provide the factual basis for Quinet's conceptions,[1] that it is necessary to assume neither Italian descent nor Byzantine model, since it was in line with French and general European tendencies. No doubt it has an excessive air, but then Napoleon carried everything to excess. For the rest I shall refrain from comment, as later chapters will afford opportunity for explanation and discussion.

1. cf. below, p. 102 ff., on D'HAUSSONVILLE, *L'église romaine et le premier Empire.* Much that may seem obscure here will be explained there.

3 Pierre Lanfrey

THE MAN AND HIS WORK

IN 1867 there appeared the first volumes of a new *Histoire de Napoléon*, the aim of which was to do away with the legend once and for all. It was indeed the first scholarly attack made on it. While Barni contributed only scattered observations, and Quinet confined himself to generalities, Lanfrey, the author of the new work, undertook to give a straightforward and matter-of-fact account, and to support his critical attitude in every particular. Thiers's work, as I observed, cannot be regarded as purely polemical. There can be no doubt, however, of the polemical character of Lanfrey's book, in spite of the customary introduction in which the writer affirms that now that both the vilifiers and the apologists have shot their bolts, he will provide that calm, just, perspicacious assessment which the passage of time makes possible.

As well-known journalist and publicist, he is trying to attack the government of his own day by undermining the foundations upon which it rests. He desires to show the falseness of the current view of the 'great' Napoleon, particularly as coined by Thiers. Of Constantine or Theodosius, of the ten-century-old tradition of the French monarchy, he has nothing to say. Yet, even so, his view is strongly reminiscent of that of Quinet. He recognizes no springs of action in Napoleon other than ambition and the lust for power. He sees not the man who consolidated the Revolution, but the man who suppressed liberty, the man of violence and trickery, from whom France had nothing save misery, who took away free speech, enslaved parliament and the Press, who expelled all men of independent mind, and who created a new aristocracy, supremely vulgar and flashy, from among his sword-rattlers and his bootlickers. There were, besides, those endless wars with all Europe, yielding sterile victories but a rich harvest of distrust and of hate and finally the disasters of 1812 to 1815.

Lanfrey's book is a piece of polemical writing because he is nearly always more concerned to prove these contentions, to spar, so to speak, with both Napoleon and his eulogists, than to give a true picture of the man. In so far as he attempts this, one has the feeling that his pen is guided by aversion and hostility. Wherever it is possible to choose between a favourable or a less favourable interpretation of Napoleon's actions and intentions, one can be sure that Lanfrey will always choose the less favourable, and put it in the most unpleasant way. His reading of Napoleon's character, too, is composed from the least attractive testimonies.

If there is one characteristic and striking trait [he writes] in the innumerable conversations noted down by those who could approach him most intimately, it is the absence of all unforced utterances. He is always seen concerned either to gauge the intentions of the other person or to make an impression on his mind so as to lead him towards a certain conclusion; it would be trouble wasted to look for a moment of abandon, of enthusiasm, of sincere outpouring, be it about himself or others. Even when he allows himself to be carried away in these coquetries of cat-like grace, the charm of which contemporaries have so repeatedly described, he does not lose sight of the effect that he is aiming at; even his rash words are calculated. He is impenetrable to those near to him as well as to strangers. It would even be impossible to point out, in the whole of his life, a single one of those sayings of philosophic self-mockery which delight us in Caesar or in Frederick, because they show us the man rising above his role, commenting on himself with a judgement unclouded by his own success . . . Napoleon is always on the stage, always concerned about the impression he is making . . . He is lacking in that final human greatness which consists in estimating one's self at its true value, and as a result of his incurable self-conceit he remains on the level of small minds.[1]

That is a striking passage, and no doubt it gives a recognizable picture of Napoleon. But does it give the whole Napoleon? We shall come across other representations of him, later on, based on the very opposite impression, and yet these too are not without a certain truth. But Lanfrey is blind to the greatness of the figure, if only as the creator of power, as conqueror, as ruler setting his stamp on France and on Europe. He is blind to the magnitude of his operations, even if regarded as nothing more than a breathtaking adventure.

Since Lanfrey had the substantial volumes of the *Correspondance* at his disposal, he was able to make a much fuller use of the letters than Thiers, faced with the overwhelming mass of archive material, and he used them with much perspicacity. But the importance of his book, in the final analysis, is its point of view. It is one closely related to that of Mme de Staël and Quinet, the point of view of a man who sees in history primarily the moral problems. What I said above concerning greatness and power he would probably have rejected as rhetoric, or even denounced as dangerously misleading. He instinctively sets his face against hollow phrases about national honour and glory, and judges, unshaken by success or popular approbation, by his standards of freedom, love of truth, humanity, and reverence for spiritual values.

The living Napoleon is not to be found in Lanfrey's book. For absolute
1. II, 336 ff.

historical truth one would also search in vain. It has no place among these sharp judgements, this setting of black against white. The available material was still too one-sided, and Lanfrey is sometimes completely positive about relationships which later research has shown to be far more complicated and intricate. To give only one example, there is the passage in which he presents Napoleon in 1812 as preparing 'with the utmost secrecy' the attack on Tsar Alexander, while the latter had only set in motion 'a few defensive operations', and had otherwise 'loyally accepted the consequences of his declaration of war on England'. Since the Russian archives have been opened and the story of Alexander's ambitions, plans, dissimulation, and tricks told in great detail,[1] nothing remains of this theory of the innocent Tsar and the wicked Napoleon.

Lanfrey must therefore be used with caution. His picture is not the one which history can mark as her own. Nevertheless, where he did possess the necessary data, he again and again provides irrefutable arguments which are of the greatest importance for the formation of the picture. Any number of illusions perish before 'the keen, searching north wind'[2] which blows through this book.

BONAPARTE BEFORE BRUMAIRE

In Thiers's opinion, as we have seen, Napoleon's authoritarian and military excesses were due to the fact that his better nature succumbed to the temptations of overwhelming success. Lanfrey – who thus continues in the direction pointed by Mme de Staël – shows us a very different Napoleon, consumed with ambition from the first, thirsting to succeed and to reach the top, and yet, with all this fiery passion, coldly calculating, completely unscrupulous in his methods, absolutely unprincipled himself but capable of making skilful use of the principles of others when he deigned to notice them at all. Long before the French, to their own undoing, made him First Consul, they could have realized, had they not been so blind and so frivolous, what sort of man he was.

There was his little book, *Le Souper de Beaucaire*, published in 1793 when he was not yet twenty-four years old, in which, at the very opening of the terror and the domination of the *Montagnards*, he exhorted the Girondist population of Marseilles to submission. And why? On no other ground than that of the accomplished fact. Young Bonaparte does not care for justice or reason, but with frightening maturity recognizes power as the all-important factor.[3]

He makes one further contribution to the cause of the revolutionary left,

---

1. By VANDAL, in his *Napoléon et Alexandre Ier* (1893–4); cf. SOREL, *Lectures historiques*, p. 192.
2. According to G. P. GOOCH, *History and Historians of the Nineteenth Century*, p. 257.
3. I, 30 ff.

this time with cannon shot. It is in October 1795; he is just twenty-six, and (since Toulon) a man of some importance. What caused him to join forces with Barras against the royalist revolt?

His personal sympathies were as little with the one as with the other [writes Lanfrey]. He was guided more by calculation than by principle.[1]

He gets his payment, the command of the army intended for Italy. In the famous proclamation delivered by the young general to his shabby troops, Lanfrey reads the signs of an ominous deviation from the spirit which had up to then inspired the republican armies. The call was no longer to their patriotism, but to their greed.

Soldiers, you are ill-fed and almost naked . . . I shall lead you into the most fertile plains of the world, where you will find big cities and rich lands. You will gather honour, glory, and riches.

Such language heralded a war no longer of liberation but of conquest.[2] Thus Lanfrey, who says later on:

Our national self-love has generally cast a veil over those motives of shameless rapacity which characterized our first occupation of Italy . . . People prefer to let themselves be beguiled by the fine-sounding phrases and rhetorical commonplaces intended to befog the crowd . . . But in that way the true meaning of events remains hidden, and there is surprise when so much alleged heroism and virtue result in so cynical a peace treaty as that of Campo Formio. People do not understand why our work in Italy was so quickly undone,[3] nor why in the end our own Republic was doomed to suffer extinction at the hands of its own republican soldiers.[4]

It will be seen that his point of departure is quite different from that of Thiers. The *coup d'état* of Brumaire, a few years after, was not regarded by Lanfrey as salvation from confusion and impotence, but as the downfall of the Republic set up by the Revolution. He admits that the Republic had fallen into bad hands, with the Directorate. But the worst deed which the Directorate had on its conscience was to have given a free hand to this young general. There he was, sending money and art treasures to Paris, turning a blind eye to the corrupt practices of his subordinates, making political arrangements on his own authority, like the shocking one whereby the old Republic of Venice was first dissolved and then, at Campo Formio, handed over to Austria. And meanwhile he was

1. I, 72. 2. I, 83.
3. The Italian republics set up by Bonaparte collapsed as early as 1798, under the fresh Austrian attack.
4. I, 102.

building such power for himself and the army that the French Republic itself would be safe no longer.

With what calculated cunning the young man already played men off one against another! How unctuously he describes the state of political inferiority in which the Venetian Senate was wont to keep the nobles on the mainland.[1] They are not likely to fare any better under Austria, those nobles – but that plan is not yet made public. The whole of that Venetian tragedy, the cunning design, the impudence with which weak opponents are put in the wrong, the demagogic exaggeration of occasional resistance to the French troops in order to have a grievance against the Venetian Senate[2] – Lanfrey uses it all to show that Bonaparte practised the unhallowed arts of dictatorial government as to the manner born. Most revealing of all is the instruction given by Bonaparte on 26 May 1797 to a general whom he sent to take possession of the Ionian Islands. For the time being the general was to show outward respect to the authority of Venice, but he must have the control all the same.

If the inhabitants should prove to be inclined towards independence [that is to say, inclined to free themselves from Venetian rule] you are to encourage that inclination, and in the proclamations which you will be issuing you must not omit to speak of Greece, Sparta, and Athens.[3]

Lanfrey considers that the last phrase 'is one of the most characteristic passages ever written by Bonaparte, shedding light into the darkest recesses of his soul'. We can certainly see from it that he had learnt the technique of propaganda appropriate to a conqueror even before he came to power in France, and that he did not scruple to use noble ideas for the purposes of deception.

The Ionian Islands meant for Bonaparte a springboard to the East, for an attack on Turkey. The impetuousness with which he threw himself into this dream, forgetting Italy, as it were 'betrayed', says Lanfrey, 'the unsoundness of that immoderate spirit, which at a later stage imagined itself to be building for eternity when it did but collect the material for a gigantic ruin'.[4] The Egyptian adventure falls into the same category.

But even before relinquishing his command in Italy, Bonaparte used the independent power he had acquired there for an intervention in France. The Directorate had let him go his own way, had allowed him to train himself, as it were, for the role which he designed for himself in France. The Directorate, however, was even then divided: two of its members, Carnot and Barthélemy, especially the latter, were in contact with an opposition group in the Councils. Anti-Jacobin and liberal, this opposition wished to curb violence and abuse of power. It desired peace, a lasting peace, and thus was prepared to moderate the

1. I, 261.　　2. I, 244 ff.　　3. I, 123 and 269 ff.　　4. I, 285.

war aims. This 'constitutional' opposition was inevitably urged on from behind by the royalists. But the member of the Five Hundred who put a question on the war with Venice, in which the country had become so unexpectedly involved, was certainly no royalist. It is characteristic that he spoke up for the right of the Five Hundred, and not without a reference to British parliamentary usage, to consider matters of war and peace. Bonaparte's fury at this timid attempt at criticism of his leadership is of the greatest significance. In his protests to the Directorate he complained that after the services he had rendered he was being persecuted and put under suspicion. He said that the speaker in the Five Hundred was 'inspired by an *émigré* and in the pay of England', and with his letter he sent a dagger. It was one taken from the conspirators on Venetian territory who had given the pretext for the occupation, but it must now serve as symbol for the daggers with which the opposition in the Five Hundred were, according to Bonaparte, threatening his life . . . Nor did he confine himself to protests. He used his eighty thousand men quite openly as a threat; he quotes the figure repeatedly as an argument which must stop all criticism. They were, he said, longing for the moment when they could save the constitution from royalist conspirators. In this Italian outburst his adversaries were referred to as 'cowardly lawyers and miserable chatterboxes'. When one knows what was to happen two years later at Brumaire, one recognizes the same brand of demagogy. It is nevertheless somewhat unexpected to find Bonaparte and the most fiery Jacobins in the same boat on this occasion, to find him appealing to the fiercest revolutionary instincts of his soldiers, instincts which were then still easy to arouse. He allowed the army to demonstrate and draw up addresses to its heart's content, and finally supplied the general, Augereau, needed by the majority of the Directorate and by Barras his patron in particular, in order to liquidate Barthélemy and Carnot and the opposition in the two Councils. And indeed it was by means of physical force, by the use of troops, that this was carried out on the 18th Fructidor (3 September 1797). The victims were not guillotined, as after previous crises: that time was past. Instead they were transported without trial to Guiana, where most of them died.

This then was the famous act of violence which so undermined the moral strength of the régime, the Directorate, and the Councils alike, that once the pear was ripe and he himself in a position to undertake his own *coup d'état*, Bonaparte had an easy task. Meanwhile Lanfrey, in giving his account of the story, has taken care that we shall note (though later historians, as we shall see, sometimes appear to forget it again) that Bonaparte, who was to profit from this moral decline in Brumaire, had had a leading part in the crime of Fructidor, simply because he would not suffer a word to be breathed against his arbitrary government in Italy.

There follows the Egyptian expedition. Lanfrey has nothing to say about the romantic side, the serious conversations with scholars whom Bonaparte had invited to Egypt, the admiration for ancient monuments. He is more interested in the famous proclamation to the population, in which the invader presented himself as nearly as possible as a Mohammedan. It is a striking example of Bonaparte's propaganda style, but it was too crude to make the desired impression. And then, when the situation – what with the failure of the Syrian campaign and the defeat of the French fleet – became dangerous, and a crisis was developing in France of the kind which he had always hoped to exploit, there was the return journey, alone, except for a small band of the best generals, leaving the army to the command of Kléber. Kléber, earnest and loyal republican, was deeply indignant at the impossible task with which he was burdened. He sent the Directorate a bitter accusation, fully substantiated. When it arrived, however, Kléber was dead, and so was the power of the Directorate. Bonaparte was First Consul, and could take on himself the adjudication of the charge made against him. He published it, with the most tendentious and dishonest annotations; and who was then going to call him to account?[1]

THE PROSCRIPTION OF THE JACOBINS (1800)

That Lanfrey must look upon Bonaparte's accession to power with emotions other than those of Thiers or Lefebvre is now intelligible. His attitude will be that of Mignet or Quinet. But his introduction was intended to provide the reader with something more than theoretical principles or general ideas. He was to be made to see and as it were to touch the truth that nothing good could be expected of this man, that France would not be safe in his hands. The *coup d'état* of Brumaire itself is laid bare with all the deceit and lies.[2] And the story does not end with Brumaire.

Thiers, as we saw, considers that until the unhappy affair of the Duc d'Enghien in 1804 Bonaparte behaved like a philosopher at the head of the State. Lanfrey, on the other hand, shows the extent to which in the years after the 18th Brumaire the First Consul resorted to stratagem and broken promises, in order to get rid of those limitations to his power which still existed, and how

1. I, 414 ff. I must here add the warning that all these matters could be presented very differently. For example, the opposition in the Five Hundred against Bonaparte's Italian policy was most certainly to a large extent royalist, or at any rate an instrument in the hands of those royalists who were aiming to overthrow the Republic; Kléber's accusation was greatly exaggerated, according to other authorities, and Bonaparte had done what he could for the army he left behind: see for example MADELIN, *Histoire du Consulat et de l'Empire.*

2. I shall deal with this subject more fully in connexion with Albert Vandal.

impatiently he reacted to any criticism or independence. It goes without saying that Lanfrey will not ignore the protests of doctrinaire republicans still sitting on representative bodies. That these no longer had public opinion behind them does not put an end to the argument, for him: one may, if one likes, call him a doctrinaire or abstract liberal on that account. Certainly it was the uncritical approbation of the people which made it possible for Bonaparte to draw the stings of parliamentarians and journalists. But the people were to be cheated in the end. Besides, Lanfrey argues, there are methods which nothing can excuse.

Leaving aside Lanfrey's treatment of Bonaparte's constructive work as First Consul, to which I shall have occasion to return later, I shall give one example of this point, in connexion with an incident concerning which I have already briefly quoted Bignon.[1]

These first years had also had their conspiracies. Just before Christmas 1800, an 'infernal machine' exploded in the street as the First Consul was driving to the Opéra. He was unhurt, but there were a number of dead and wounded. Bonaparte took this opportunity to purge the left opposition. In spite of considerable reluctance on the part of his nearest associates (he was as yet far from being the Emperor at whose voice all objections ceased), he forced through an extraordinary measure: one hundred and thirty well-known republicans – they were for the occasion called terrorists – were proscribed without any legal process. Among them were quite a number who had opposed him simply on grounds of principle, men, for example, who had resisted the *coup d'état* of Brumaire in the previous year and whom he hated for that reason. The hundred and thirty were either interned or deported, and most of them failed to survive the climate of Guiana.

But a few days after the decree, Fouché, Minister of Police, who had not for one moment believed that the republicans were guilty, found the real perpetrators of the crime. They were right-wing opponents, *chouans*, royalists. The new batch of prisoners were found guilty and guillotined, but the Jacobins who had been deported were not set free. Bonaparte was much too pleased to be rid of them, and he had had the foresight to see that the ground for proscription was given in the decree as concern for the safety of the State, not the attempt of 24 December. He laughingly pointed this out to a member of the Council of State who had the courage to come and plead for the innocent victims.[2]

Thiers too gives these facts.[3] The conduct of Fouché he condemns, but he says of Bonaparte, without a word of blame, that he troubled himself little about

1. See p. 44, and LANFREY II, 264 ff.
2. I must point out here that I take this from Lanfrey, who does not give his source – certainly *mémoires*.
3. I, 211b.

'unorthodox methods', provided he was rid of the 'general staff of the Jacobins'. It is only in reading Lanfrey's account that the real cruelty and hideousness of such arbitrary action emerges, and Thiers's later remark about Bonaparte's *'cœur généreux et bon'* acquires an odd flavour.

NAPOLEON AND THE DETHRONING OF THE SPANISH BOURBONS (1808)

There is one incident in Napoleon's career, undefended save by his most fervent supporters,[1] which did him an immeasurable amount of harm at the time, and which in its consequences contributed to his fall. This was the dethroning of the Spanish Bourbons in 1808. We have seen that neither Bignon nor Armand Lefebvre concealed their disapproval (pp. 44 and 53).

The old weak King of Spain, Charles IV, was a Bourbon, a direct descendant of Louis XIV, whose grandson had acquired the Spanish throne in 1700 after the Spanish Habsburg line had died out. Under the influence of his wife and her lover Godoy, who was Prime Minister and was known by the somewhat ridiculous title of Prince of the Peace, Charles IV had all the time held fast to the alliance with France, in spite of the fate of his relative Louis XVI. How little this could be relied upon, however, Napoleon had discovered in 1806, when Godoy, who thought that the war with Prussia would prove the grave of imperial greatness, revealed his secret hostility – just too soon, for immediately afterwards came the battle of Jena. Although Godoy beat a hasty retreat, even agreeing to the dispatch of a Spanish army corps to the Baltic to purchase his forgiveness, the Emperor had not forgotten. After the fall of the Bourbons in France and in Naples, where he had driven them out himself, he regarded the continued existence of the rival dynasty – for in that light he now saw the relationship between Bourbons and Bonapartes – as a dangerous anomaly. In addition, the weak misgovernment of Charles IV and Godoy offended Napoleon in what one might call his professional self-respect, and harmed his interests in so far as it destroyed the value of Spain as an ally.

Now at last the moment had come for Napoleon to give his attention to the affairs of Spain, and it was the most radical solution to which he felt himself driven. The Bourbons were to be forced to abdicate, and their place was to be taken by one of his brothers. It was true that Ferdinand, the heir, had approached him. Ferdinand's quarrel with his mother and his attempts to open the eyes of his father had given rise to a scandal, in which Spanish opinion was passionately

1. For example by Prince Napoleon (see below); others who condemn it emphasize strongly the objectionable nature of the Spanish Bourbons and Napoleon's conviction that he could do better than they (e.g. VANDAL, see below).

on his side; with him the nation was ready to await deliverance at the hands of the great Napoleon. But Ferdinand displayed a pitiable weakness and lack of loyalty in this family quarrel, and though the Spanish people were not disillusioned, it is not surprising that Napoleon was not very anxious to put his trust in him. What gives so unpleasant an air to the whole business is the manner in which he carried out his scheme.

He already had troops in Spain, on their way to Portugal, where the British had landed – the beginning of great events. More and more Frenchmen arrived, and fewer and fewer went on to Portugal. No explanation was given. Murat was in command of these troops in Spain, but not even he was told of Napoleon's intentions. Suddenly, in an atmosphere of fear and uncertainty, there was a revolt against the miserable trio of husband, wife, and lover, and at Aranjuez the King was forced to abdicate in favour of Ferdinand. Not for a moment did Napoleon think of allowing this event to shake his resolution, and he continued at first to recognize Charles IV. Under French protection, still accompanied by his wife and Godoy, Charles renounced his forced abdication. This was now to serve as a weapon in Napoleon's hand against Ferdinand. But as long as the Prince was surrounded by his Spaniards, Napoleon was careful not to disturb his hope that at the final account the French would be on his side. Murat was still left in the dark, but meanwhile Napoleon had sent Savary to Spain, Savary, the man he liked to use for delicate tasks, for the dirty work, one might say. Of him he said: 'If I ordered Savary to murder his wife and children, I know he would do it without a moment's hesitation . . .' Savary's task was to entice the ingenuous Ferdinand to France. There, at Bayonne, Napoleon was to compose the differences between him and his parents.

The King and Queen, with Godoy, were brought to this frontier town, and there too came Ferdinand, still the darling and the hope of his people, and never suspecting but that Napoleon would confirm him in his recent greatness. But he found himself in a trap. From the first he was virtually a prisoner and was told he must relinquish his crown. With a certain devilish glee, if Lanfrey is to be believed, Napoleon watched the unedifying and noisy scene between father and son. Old Charles threw himself into his arms as though he were his saviour. Ferdinand resisted for a long time, but coward as he was, he crumpled up when Napoleon openly threatened his life, and he recognized his father as King. The father then handed his crown to Napoleon, who gave it to Joseph, and a junta of francophil Spaniards summoned to Bayonne confirmed the choice. Ferdinand and his brothers remained in France under observation. It was an ironical touch, typical of Napoleon, that he chose Talleyrand for the 'honourable' task, as he described it, of offering them hospitality on his estate, for Talleyrand had for a long time been opposed to the whole tendency of his foreign policy and particularly disliked this Spanish adventure. Or did he perhaps play a double game? Was he, while really urging Napoleon to the action he took, trying to hide his own responsibility from the outside world? Concerning this and other matters to do with this complicated character there are conflicts of opinion; but even if the second interpretation be the correct one, the task must have been given to Talleyrand with the intention of compromising him.

Europe reacted with shocked abhorrence. There was the terror of the old dynasties at the upsetting of one of their number by that son of the Revolution, the role which Napoleon again saw himself acting. Worse still was the violent recoil in Spain itself, where the French had not been unpopular as long as they could be expected to support Ferdinand, but where now the betrayal of Bayonne was all the more keenly felt. Even before that tragi-comedy was played to a finish, there had been a rising in Madrid on 2 May 1808 against the French occupation. Murat suppressed it with much bloodshed, and Napoleon did not doubt but that 'this good lesson'[1] would ensure peace in the future. He was revolving great plans for Spain. If he brushed the Bourbons so unceremoniously aside, it was that he might set up under his own auspices – for Joseph would really be merely his lieutenant – an up-to-date régime in that backward priest-ridden country. He would regenerate them, he promised the Spaniards; their children would bless him. They themselves certainly did not. *Dos Mayos* became a battle cry for the Spaniards. Who does not remember the terrifying picture of hate and resistance which Goya's imagination created from the executions of that day? A popular revolt was organized throughout the country, led by the aristocracy and inspired by the priests, which made Joseph's rule a hopeless undertaking from the very first, and this was to prove a turning point in the history of Napoleon. Spain, with the British on the spot, remained a continuous drag on his system, and no less important than the military aspect was the moral impression made in Germany and elsewhere.

As I have said, practically all writers recognize Napoleon's error, though not always with the same intensity. Lanfrey treats the whole deceitful business with cold contempt; he lays it bare point by point, to bring out the whole treacherous intention. He puts far more emphasis than Thiers on the complete belief in brute force and power. This he shows was the basis of Napoleon's action, contempt for a people as such, a conviction that every nation will allow itself to be moulded into the desired shape by the use of a sufficiently strong force. In this connexion he has one very remarkable point.

There appeared in the *Mémorial de Sainte-Hélène*[2] a letter from Napoleon to Murat, purporting to have been written on 29 March, that is, between the rising

1. From his letter of 6 May, LANFREY IV, 297.
2. Under the date 12 June, 1816.

of Aranjuez and the meeting at Bayonne. Although they found no minute of it, and there was no trace of the original among Murat's papers, the editors of the great *Correspondance* inserted the letter as an authentic document: its having been communicated to Las Cases on St Helena by Napoleon seemed to them sufficient. Nevertheless, when the rest of the story is known, it makes curious reading. From Napoleon's day-to-day correspondence with Murat and with Savary – which was not of course known at the time when the *Mémorial* was published – it appears that the Emperor had the threads of the intrigue firmly in his hands and was controlling everything. In this one letter, however, we see him hesitating. He lectures Murat for having given him incorrect information concerning the state of public opinion in Spain. He warns him not to go too fast. He prophesies the whole obstinate resistance of the Spanish people, and foresees the furious energy they were to display. Something seems to be wrong here. What are we to make of it?

Thiers, who already knew the other letters of Napoleon, has recognized the existence of a problem here, and devotes an appendix to it.[1] He asks himself whether it is a forgery. But the letter bears the indubitable marks of Napoleon's style. Is it possible that Napoleon put it together himself on St Helena, to provide an excuse for the crudest error of his reign? This solution, too, Thiers rejects, firstly because one unimportant fact, which Napoleon could not possibly have remembered, is correctly mentioned in it, but also because the great Emperor was too proud to stoop to such a trick.[2] Finally he gets out of the difficulty by suggesting that Napoleon wrote the letter during a moment of doubt occasioned by some particular piece of information, but never sent it. He must have forgotten on St Helena that he had not sent it. . . .

Lanfrey is scornful[3] of the way in which idolatry and his critical spirit struggle for mastery of Thiers's mind. The only advantage presented by the desperately forced conclusion was that it allowed him to proclaim the 'almost superhuman' perspicacity which even in this case his hero displayed, without – it had to be admitted – any practical results . . . And yet it is so obvious that this is just another of Napoleon's customary tricks, by which he hoped to create just that unmerited impression and so put the blame for his mistake on someone else who might be supposed to have misled him with over-optimistic information, on Murat who was no longer in a position to answer when Napoleon indited that charming piece of fiction, because he was dead, shot by the Austrians. As for Napoleon being too proud, was he not quite at home in the art of forgery? Every day he packed the *Moniteur* with trumped-up diplomatic dispatches, fanciful news

1. In the later part of volume II; volume VIII of the Paris edition.
2. II, 663b.
3. IV, 265 ff.

from abroad, debates in the Chambers, edited to suit his purpose. And is not every line of the massive *mémoires* of St Helena a lie?

Thus Lanfrey. There is no question but that he was right in considering the letter as a forgery. Whether Napoleon was actually the author is another matter, on which I do not venture to pass judgement.[1]

NAPOLEON AND THE ABDUCTION OF PIUS VII (1809)

I shall now introduce another case, in some respects reminiscent of the previous one. It does not involve falsification this time, but it does show that for Napoleon to put the blame on others was nothing unusual. At the same time it once more illustrates Thiers's tendency to credulity.

In 1809, when Rome and the Papal State had been occupied for a full year by Napoleon's troops, and were in practice governed by him, relations with the Pope – that same gentle Pius VII with whom the Concordat had been arranged and who had visited Paris to crown Napoleon – had become so strained that the Emperor's not very large stock of patience was exhausted, and he decided to remove his refractory antagonist from Rome. I shall have more to say later concerning the view taken of Napoleon's actions with regard to the ecclesiastical problem. Here I am merely concerned with the question whether it was really he who decided upon the abduction of the Pope.

The Emperor was at Schoenbrunn (where he stayed for quite a time after Wagram) when he heard that the thing was done, and he appeared extremely upset.

I take it ill that the Pope has been arrested; it is a very foolish act. They ought to have arrested Cardinal Pacca, and have left the Pope quietly at Rome.

Thiers, who publishes this letter to Fouché, dated 18 July 1809, in a footnote writes that 'Napoleon greatly deplored the act of violence which had been resorted to'.[2] But immediately before, Thiers had given other letters from Schoenbrunn, dated a month earlier, in which Napoleon wrote to Murat, who was then King of Naples and who had to keep an eye on affairs in Rome:

1. PH. GONNARD, *Les origines de la légende napoléonienne* (Paris 'thesis', 1906), draws attention to the fact that the document, which he regards as a forgery, was published in the periodical *La bibliothèque historique*, with other forgeries, in 1819, that is, while Napoleon was still alive and before the *Mémorial* appeared. It is also produced in *Récits de la captivité*, by another member of the St Helena group, Montholon, published in 1847. It is there given as having been dictated to Montholon by Napoleon, a considerable time after the departure of Las Cases. Gonnard's theory (op. cit. p. 110 ff.) that Napoleon could not therefore have forged it himself does not convince me.

2. III, 212b.

I have already let you know that it is my intention that affairs in Rome be conducted with firmness, and that no form of resistance should be allowed to stand in the way ... If the Pope, against the spirit of his office and of the Gospels, preaches revolt and tries to misuse the immunity of his domicile to have circulars printed, he is to be arrested ... Philip the Fair[1] had Boniface arrested, Charles V kept Clement VII in prison for a long period, and those popes had done less to deserve it.

This was the letter which served as authority to the French officials in Rome. Thiers believes that Napoleon later regretted having given this instruction.

Lanfrey's interpretation is very different. He notes that Napoleon's order, in spite of its severity, remains general and leaves something to the initiative of his subordinates.[2] He has no doubt that this was intentional, and indeed, did not the Emperor wash his hands of the whole business afterwards? In the letter to Fouché of 18 July he does not, as Thiers asserts, regret the instruction he gave; he writes as though no such instruction had been given. In a letter to Cambacérès, quoted by Lanfrey, he goes even further:[3] 'The Pope was removed from Rome without my orders and against my wishes.' It is surprising, if that is the case, that he acquiesced in the accomplished fact. But indeed it is a flagrant untruth. It is all part of the system. In the Enghien affair, he sheltered behind the alleged over-hasty action of Savary. In the case of Spain, it was Murat. And now it was Miollis, the Governor of Rome, who had to bear the discredit of a deed which Napoleon had undoubtedly wished done.[4]

NAPOLEON AND LITERATURE

Before I leave Lanfrey, there is one more subject with wider implications to discuss.

One of the famous occasions in the life of Napoleon was his meeting with Goethe during the Congress of Erfurt in 1808. The intercourse with his friend of Tilsit, the Tsar, soon to be his enemy; the homage of the multitudes of German princes, to all intents and purposes his vassals, on some of whom he had bestowed their royal crowns; the quiet opposition of Talleyrand – all this has failed to

1. King of France 1285–1314.
2. Bignon, again the typical official, therefore refuses to regard it as an instruction. He says that a definite instruction from Napoleon would have named those who were to carry it out, the place of imprisonment, the route to be taken, etc.
3. LANFREY V, 16.
4. One could make a comparison here with Queen Elizabeth I, who was also very ready to saddle her servants with the blame in difficult situations. The best known but certainly not the only example is that of her rage against Davison on the pretext that he had given the order for the execution of Mary Queen of Scots without her authority.

dim the memory o´ the encounter between the Emperor and the poet. It is worth while noting the differences in the historical treatment of the episode.

From Thiers's account, one would hardly guess that perhaps not everything was quite as it should be.[1] He describes Napoleon at a *soirée* of the Duke of Saxe-Weimar, whose minister Goethe was, having a long conversation with Goethe and Wieland. He spoke of Tacitus, in whose dark picture of Imperial Rome he said he did not believe; he spoke of Werther, was extremely gracious, and 'let the two famous writers see that he deserted the cream of noble society for their sake'. Finally 'he left them flattered, as they well might be, by so distinguished an attention'. He afterwards presented them with the Order of the Legion of Honour, 'a distinction which they deserved on every ground, and which lost nothing of its brilliance by being given to men of their merit'.

One might conceive a report in the *Moniteur* drawn up in this style. Thiers is obviously overwhelmed by the honour done to Goethe. He does not even work himself up to lyrical raptures, such as have often been indulged in, concerning the Man of Action and the Man of Thought, face to face, each doing honour to himself in his appreciation of the merits of the other. Of course, as Thiers knew no German, or very little, Goethe was not much more than a name to him, while Napoleon was not only his hero, but in his estimation a very great mind as well. Some chapters before he had discussed the condition of French literature under Napoleon and had been obliged to admit that it was not much to boast of.[2] Chateaubriand, certainly, must be called a writer, though Thiers did not care much for all that nostalgia for the past. But, and here our practical-minded author lets himself go, 'that age did have one immortal writer, deathless as Caesar. It was the ruler himself, a great writer because he was a great mind, inspired orator in his proclamations, the singer of his own epic actions in his military dispatches, powerful exponent of policy in his innumerable letters, articles in the *Moniteur*', and so on. 'How wonderful was this man's destiny, to be the greatest writer of his age as well as its greatest commander, legislator, and administrator!' It is not to be wondered at that Thiers considered Goethe to be the one honoured when the two met.

That Lanfrey was not rendered dizzy by the spectacle of His Majesty the Emperor of the French doing honour to a great poet, will be readily believed. But on top of the many reservations we have seen this stern critic make when dealing with the greatness that seemed so blinding to Thiers, came his conviction, which in fact he shared with Mme de Staël, Chateaubriand, and Quinet, that Napoleon had a nefarious influence upon the literary life of France.

Thiers saw grounds for commiseration of Napoleon in the fact that the contemporary literary scene was not more brilliant. He took enough trouble about

1. II, 583b ff. 2. II, 363b.

it. There were prizes, annuities. He demanded a report from each section of the Institute on the progress of literature and the arts. In the Council of State when the chairman of the section of literature had read his report – 'simple, forceful, elevated' – he answered with a few short sentences of which Thiers says: 'If governments are to meddle with the works of the human mind, may they always do it in so noble a manner . . . Moreover Napoleon was able to give that most fruitful of encouragements, the approval of genius.'[1]

Lanfrey, on the other hand, made Napoleon's despotism answerable for the petrified condition of the literary landscape. As to prizes, who can read the list of names without laughing? And the two great figures, Chateaubriand (whom Thiers mentions here without recalling the awkward fact) and Mme de Staël (whom he does not mention in this connexion at all), were in disgrace because they were too independent, because they had the courage to put the mind above material power and did not abase themselves in the dust before success. Mme de Staël was obliged to seek in Germany for the French spirit, enslaved by its government.[2] Her book (*De l'Allemagne*, 1810) was banned, and Savary, now Minister of Police, 'the hero of so many unpleasant or sinister jobs', wrote an unmannerly letter to her in which, between gibes, he explained that her book was 'un-French'. The Press, which Napoleon described as 'a public service', was under control, the number of news-sheets soon reduced to one for each *département*, and all types of journal, including scholarly and ecclesiastical, subject to the arbitrary powers of the censor. There were annuities too, granted by the Emperor, but they were charged according to the whim of the moment on the budget of some periodical, which kept quiet and paid up. Nothing bloomed in France save official flattery and rhetoric.

Sire [thus the President of the Senate addressed Napoleon after Tilsit] these are miraculous achievements for which probability would have asked centuries, and for which a few months have sufficed to Your Majesty . . . It is impossible worthily to praise Your Majesty. Your glory is too great. One has to place oneself at the distance of posterity to become aware of your immeasurable elevation.

And the President of the Court of Appeal:

Napoleon stands above human history. He stands above admiration; our love alone can rise to his level.

And a prefect:

Truly, these miracles surpass our capacity. Only the astonished silence which admiration imposes upon us can express them.[3]

But the false pathos and hollow rhetoric are even more repulsive than these

1. II, 364a. 2. LANFREY V, 306. 3. IV, 178.

99

hyperboles. When Napoleon called once again on his Frenchmen to show him their love and give him the necessary support, this time for 'the restoration of order' in Spain, which 'was to assure the safety of their children', the same President of the Senate answered:

Anarchy, that blind and ferocious monster, of which the genius of Napoleon has freed France, has lighted its torches and reared its scaffolds in the heart of Spain. England has been quick to throw her phalanxes into that country and to plant her standards among the terrible banners of the satellites of the Terror. The Emperor's strong right arm shall liberate the Spaniards. Ah, what a comfort must this generous decision of Napoleon be to the royal shades of Louis XIV, Francis I, and of Henry the Great ... The French will respond to his sacred voice. He is asking for a new pledge of their love. With what glowing hearts will they run to meet him.[1]

That was the tone of the period. How differently Chateaubriand spoke – it was his immortal merit – when, albeit tucked away in a book review in his *Mercure*,[2] he dared to write a passage like the following:

When in the silence of humiliation there is no sound save the clanking of the slave's fetters and the voice of the informer, when everything trembles before the tyrant, and to earn his favour or incur his wrath implies equal danger, then the historian appears to avenge the peoples. It is in vain that Nero prospers; the Empire has already borne a Tacitus.

The paper passed from hand to hand, and the brave words were greedily read. Young Guizot comes to Coppet and knows them by heart. He has to recite them to Mme de Staël and her circle of friends, who listen breathlessly.[3] But the censor stifles the discordant sound immediately, and once more the air is full of the sickening chant of hypocrites and flatterers. 'In his ascent,' writes Lanfrey, 'Napoleon already understood how false rhetoric might be used for the benefit of his false greatness, and so had given it the encouragement of his example.'

It is hardly necessary for me to state that to regard Napoleon the writer and orator as an empty rhetorician betrays as much partiality as to proclaim him the greatest writer of his century. But it will now at least have become clear that the scene of Napoleon making himself pleasant to Goethe could affect Lanfrey with nothing but contemptuous boredom. As he saw it, moreover, Napoleon was oppressing and humiliating Goethe's fatherland. We shall see later that here, too, other views were possible. For German patriots at any rate it was natural

1. IV, 398 ff.
2. IV, 192. See above, p. 19, for a previous allusion to this famous article.
3. P. GAUTIER, *Mme de Staël et Napoléon* (1902).

to be pained by the scene enacted at Weimar, though a Frenchman needed to have steeped his mind in the liberalism of Mme de Staël to understand this. There were actually Germans, says Lanfrey, who glorified Goethe because he was able to rise above these low earthly conflicts. They ought to take example from the poet himself, who said apologetically to Eckermann that it is not everyone's task to fight. In his reminiscences of the talk with the Emperor, Goethe notes, not without satisfaction, that after looking at him silently for a few minutes, Napoleon cried: '*Vous êtes un homme, monsieur de Goethe.*' Lanfrey comments: 'Great praise indeed; and deserved, at that. But while we admit that Goethe was certainly a man in the highest sense of the word, we must add that on this occasion he was but a courtier.'[1]

Although Thiers so often speaks of the ever-growing tyranny of Napoleon and of its injurious effects on French society, yet when one reads writers such as Quinet and Lanfrey, the older man seems at times to be lacking in the true sense of spiritual freedom. We get the same impression from reading another book which appeared towards the end of Napoleon III's régime, and which dealt in particular with the relations between the First Consul and the Church.

1. IV, 410.

4 Comte d'Haussonville

WE have already touched upon aspects of Napoleon's ecclesiastical policy, and have noticed differences of opinion with regard to it. With the work of d'Haussonville we meet for the first time a systematic and thorough treatment, from a point of view which, though liberal, I would regard as primarily religious, and if we take Bignon, or perhaps rather Thiers, as typical of a worldly *étatisme*, we shall be able to make comparisons. For the convenience of the reader, however, I shall begin with a survey of the events such as would be acceptable to all writers whatever their tendency.

THE CONSUL-EMPEROR AND THE CHURCH (1801–1814)

The Revolution had begun by trying, in spite of the protests of Pius VI, to force upon the Church a ready-made settlement, the *Constitution civile du clergé*. This attempt had merely led to persecution, and within the Church to confusion and out-and-out schism. It was abandoned in 1795, and the State ceased entirely to meddle with the Church, in theory at any rate. In practice, the Church was no better off under the separation régime now prevailing. The clergy felt itself misunderstood and ill-treated, and its attitude to the Republic remained hostile. The reconciliation effected by the Concordat was valuable to Bonaparte, because it afforded him the gratitude of the priests, who were in any case subjected to his influence by the recognition of his right to appoint bishops. This gratitude was understandable. The Pope felt it too, in spite of his irritation over the Organic Articles which the First Consul unexpectedly tacked on to the Concordat. The unity of the Church had been restored, it had a recognized position in the State and was relieved of financial worries, and there was matter for satisfaction in the mere fact that the attempt to impose a revolutionary *Constitution civile*, with a view to withdrawing the French Church completely from the Pope's authority, had failed. More than that, in order to facilitate the reorganization of the Church, Bonaparte got the Pope to dismiss the whole episcopate. For the impatient dictator, this was the easiest way to break the resistance of royalist and of 'constitutional' bishops. To far-seeing Rome, it was an unhoped-for and unheard-of precedent for papal interference, a negation of apparently victorious Gallicanism.

How grateful the Pope remained, and how set on good relations with the powerful son of the Revolution, was apparent in 1804, when, not without much inner conflict, he allowed himself to be persuaded to come to Paris and consecrate as Emperor the second Charlemagne, indeed, the greater Charlemagne, for the earlier ruler was crowned only in Rome, in the papal city. But after this event relations soon became strained. The Pope was disappointed that his sensational step brought him no concessions in respect of ecclesiastical grievances or ambitions. Moreover, after the tremendous extension of Napoleon's power policy arising out of the defeat of Austria at Austerlitz, the overthrow of Italy and the subsequent inclusion of the Papal States in the French system gave the Pope as temporal prince every reason to tremble for his independence. Napoleon would brook no neutrality within his orbit. After the victory, all resistance to his wishes and schemes for the reorganization of Europe irritated him more than ever.

Already in February 1806 he had written a letter to the Pope full of complaints and reprimands. It included the famous dictum: 'Your Holiness is sovereign of Rome, but I am its Emperor; all my enemies must be those of Your Holiness.' The gentle Pius (who was so much more capable of resistance than the Emperor imagined) answered proudly 'There is no Emperor of Rome', and maintained his full sovereignty. Napoleon was no longer accustomed to hearing such language – and from this feeble creature, too! Continual difficulties over the application of the Continental System, which he was demanding from all his allies and vassals, aggravated a relationship which was already hopelessly disturbed.

In 1808 Napoleon ordered the occupation of the Papal States, including Rome. The defiant attitude subsequently maintained by the Pope in his capital annoyed Napoleon in the extreme. In 1809, after Wagram, a victory which seemed to have brought Europe to submission, he issued the decree from Schoenbrunn whereby as heir of Charlemagne, the original donor of the temporal power, and vested in his rights, he declared the sovereignty of Pius over the Papal States abolished. When Pius answered with excommunication, he was immediately taken away, and after being carried to Grenoble was finally interned at Savona on the Gulf of Genoa, which was then of course part of the French Empire.

The Pope now refused to carry out any papal functions, on the grounds that he was not at liberty and was out of reach of his councillors. The cardinals had been called to Paris when he was removed, and graced Napoleon's court festivities in their crimson robes while the Head of the Church was in bondage. The most zealous upholders of church law in the Sacred College, however, thirteen in number, fell into disfavour with the Emperor in February 1810, when they failed to attend the reception given after his marriage with Marie Louise. Indeed, important issues were raised by this abstention. The declaration of nullity of

Napoleon's marriage with Joséphine had taken place quite independently of the Pope, in the Officiality of Paris. Naturally this ecclesiastical court was unable to refuse any request of Napoleon's, but was it within its powers to give a verdict of this kind? The demonstration made by the thirteen seemed to cast doubt on the legality of the new marriage and of the hoped-for heir. The Emperor was furious. They had to doff their crimson robes – hence the nickname by which they were known, the 'black cardinals' – and were interned in various parts of France.

There was at least one function which only the Pope could perform, and which was essential to the satisfactory management of affairs in the French Church, according to the Concordat. This was the canonical 'institution' of bishops 'nominated' by the Emperor, who became bishops only by that papal act. Even before his imprisonment, the Pope's refusal to institute bishops had perpetuated vacancies in Germany, where he was already at loggerheads with many of the princes owing to the secularizations after the peace of Lunéville in 1801. And what concerned Napoleon even more, although he was increasingly involved in German affairs, was that the Pope was doing the same thing in Italy. In February 1810 the Emperor issued a *sénatus consulte* by which he hoped to cut the Gordian knot. This arranged the particulars of the annexation of Rome by the French Empire. Rome was to be the second city of the Empire. The heir to the throne, still to be born (but the All-Powerful expressed himself quite positively concerning his sex) would have the title of King of Rome. A prince of the blood was always to hold his court in Rome, and the popes, bound to the Empire by a handsome allowance and an oath of allegiance, would spend part of their time at the Emperor's side in Paris, whither the papal offices and boards would be transferred, henceforth to be maintained on the imperial budget. Was there any chance of getting the Pope to agree to these arrangements? Napoleon thought it possible. Faced with his supreme power, urged on by so many cardinals and by the majority of the higher ranks of French clergy, how could the Pope avoid bowing to the inevitable?

However, the opposition of the Pope to the Emperor's plans was unexpectedly discovered to be much stronger than the latter had imagined. Napoleon had decided to make his nominees for the vacant sees (of which there were now twenty-seven) fulfil their functions even without canonical institution, by prevailing upon the chapters of the various sees to give them vicarial powers. The canons, whatever their reasons and feelings, gave their cooperation, and finally the Emperor had commanded the nominees to go to their dioceses and to take up their duties. Scarcely had this taken place, when at the end of 1810 his police got wind of letters from Pius smuggled out of Savona to trusted canons in the chapters of Paris and of Florence, urging them in no way to recognize the archbishops nominated by Napoleon but not instituted by himself, and not to give them vicarial powers. This discovery was not such as to incline Napoleon to concessions. He was stung to violent outbursts of rage. One of these achieved notoriety. Its immediate object was his Privy Counsellor Portalis, son of his former Minister of Cults and cousin of the Paris canon, recipient of a papal letter. The canon had made a clean breast of it to Portalis. Thereupon the latter had uttered a general warning to the Minister of Police to the effect that something was afoot, without mentioning his cousin. 'In league with my enemy! Traitor!' Napoleon had shouted at him in full Council of State, and had finally ordered him out of the room, while the others remained silent and ill at ease. Napoleon also meted out severe punishments – imprisonment for an unspecified term – to the incautious canons, and more rigorous and oppressive treatment to his prisoner at Savona. The Pope was deprived of the few trusted followers who were still with him, and was guarded more closely than ever.

At the same time Napoleon called a National Council in Paris to obtain the ecclesiastical approval for his programme, which he intended to use for putting pressure on the Pope. The threat in the background was the formation of a national church, a schism; and Napoleon, who had always compared himself with Charlemagne, at this time frequently let fall the name of Henry VIII. Conscious of this, and apprehensive of fresh troubles if there should be resistance to his power, a few French bishops obtained the Emperor's permission to go to Savona before the opening of the Council, to persuade Pius to come to an agreement. They wrung from him a few reluctant promises, which they took down in writing, but which he partially retracted as soon as they had gone.

Nevertheless, assertions concerning the Pope's capitulation had to do service to influence the Council to a pronouncement in line with Napoleon's policy. What the Emperor wanted was an arrangement concerning the episcopal institution whereby if the Pope withheld it, the archbishop of the relevant see would be empowered to grant it. The main point to him certainly still was that the Pope should submit to the *sénatus consulte* of February 1810, should resign himself to the loss of his temporal power and accept the comfortable dependence offered him; but to this he thought the Pope would have to come in any case, if the means of defence offered by institution escaped him. To Napoleon's complete surprise, however, a hitch occurred over this apparently not so unreasonable preliminary demand. Anxious though the prelates were to carry out his wishes, and for all the terror inspired by the arrest of the canons of Paris and Florence, the clerical spirit, which individually could not but lie low, roused itself to action in the assembly. Sympathy with the prisoner in Savona created an atmosphere in which these old, venerable, frightened ecclesiastics were moved to an attitude at which they were themselves surprised. In spite of all the efforts of the henchmen of the Minister of Cults in the assembly, and of the chairman – no less a person than Cardinal Fesch, the Emperor's uncle – it proved impossible to persuade the Council to accept as a decree the draft agreement of Savona, which as we have seen had been disowned by the Pope in the meantime. More, the Council declared itself incompetent to deal with the institution question.

Never had Napoleon felt himself so thwarted, in his own empire, and by those whom he called 'my bishops'. Once again he had recourse to fury, penal measures, and a more rigid insistence on his policy. Three of the ringleaders (one of whom was the Bishop of Ghent with whom William I of Holland had trouble some years later) were arrested without warrant, like the canons, and thrown into prison. This frightened the remainder, so that the great majority agreed to the decree which they had just rejected. Care had been taken, it is true, to make sure that they should not seek courage from one another. On the advice of the new Archbishop of Paris (who was recognized as such in practice, solely from fear of the consequences), the Minister of Cults had interviewed each member of the Council separately in his office.

With the decree thus obtained, the bishops who had been at Savona before made another journey thither, and a couple of trustworthy – that is, of course, 'red' – cardinals were also permitted to see the Pope. These clerical ambassadors were now able to obtain concessions from Pius on both the main points, the institution and the residence of the Pope in France at the State's expense. Napoleon, who received the news during his tour of Holland, was still not satisfied with certain reserves and claims made by the Pope. He ordered the negotiators, who were congratulating themselves on the peace they had achieved, to make further demands. The Pope, however, refused to make any more concessions. At that moment Napoleon's mind became preoccupied with his plan for a campaign against Russia, and he considered that he would be able to impose all his desires when he returned, after a brief interval, crowned with fresh laurels and more powerful than ever. So the Pope was once more completely isolated in Savona, till in the summer of 1812 he was suddenly removed to Fontainebleau.

At the end of that year, however, Napoleon came back from Russia, defeated. He felt his position endangered through loss of prestige, and in these circumstances the ecclesiastical question, which he had once hoped to settle in his favour once and for all by the Concordat, seemed to him a danger. So to Fontainebleau this time went the same negotiators, but soon the Emperor arrived there himself. In the course of talks which lasted several days, he obtained his prisoner's signature to the preliminaries of a new concordat in which his leading ideas were embodied, though in a weaker form than before his Russian campaign. One stipulation, however, which the Pope had refused to forgo was that his cardinals should have unimpeded access to him. No sooner had the 'black cardinals' arrived in Fontainebleau than the Pope realized that the new Concordat was a mistake, indeed an offence against the Church, and he informed Napoleon that he withdrew his signature. Thus before the Emperor embarked on his German campaign, which was to be as disastrous as that of the previous year in Russia, he once more made war against the Church, ordered the arrest of a cardinal, threatened others, and conscripted seminarists from dioceses whose bishops had incurred his displeasure.

To the defeats of 1813 succeeded the invasion of 1814. Once more Napoleon began to negotiate, but when the Pope said he wished for nothing but to return to Rome, he was allowed to leave Fontainebleau. At one moment, when Napoleon hoped that he might defeat the invaders, he sent orders to have him detained once more; but he countermanded them after a fresh defeat. Only after the first abdication was the Pope able to return at last to his States. Of the rejected Concordat of Fontainebleau there was naturally no question any longer. Relations between the Holy See and France remained based on the Concordat of 1801, and since an attempt made under the Restoration at a new settlement never led to anything, so they remained till 1906.

THE WRITER AND HIS BOOK

Through his marriage to a daughter of the Duc de Broglie, Comte d'Haussonville already belonged to that liberal *élite* which honoured the memory of Mme de Staël. De Broglie, himself a leading figure in that group, had married a daughter of the great writer. In religious matters the liberalism of these men was far removed from the Voltaireanism so powerful in France, so self-assured and often so intolerant. Nor did it savour of that spirit of secular bureaucracy which frequently seemed related to the other tendency, and which out of suspicion of the Church favoured its control by the State. D'Haussonville, in fact, was a practising Catholic. His combination of liberalism and Catholicism suggests the influence of Lamennais, an influence which remained a stimulating one to faithful Catholics even after Lamennais's quarrel with Rome, while at the same time penetrating into Protestant circles. Montalambert's slogan, 'a free church in a free state', was found convenient by a worldly-minded statesman such as Cavour, but when d'Haussonville uses it, as he does in his introduction, it cannot be doubted that he is arguing from the point of view of the Church, and it was out of consideration for religion that he advocated the separation of the two powers. Nevertheless, in so doing he showed a certain independence of Rome, for Pius IX had shortly before condemned this solution in his *Syllabus errorum*.

He indicates his point of view quite frankly in his introduction. Like Quinet he reacts against the current glorification of the Concordat of 1801, but there is naturally no trace of Quinet's impatient disapproval of Catholicism or of Rome. Both the clergy and officialdom, surprisingly enough, are pleased with the Concordat. The Church officially honours its tradition. But according to d'Haussonville it is the temporal partner in the combination that has the best of it, and the spiritual partner is blinded to the true interests of the Church by satisfaction with material advantages. Without saying so in so many words, and entirely in the spirit of Lamennais, he argues against the Gallican spirit, the worldly tradition of the French Church, its readiness to be dependent on the régime of the day. That this for him was the régime of Napoleon III is really hardly relevant, since after every change, and the French had seen a good many, the Church never failed to accommodate itself with equal zest. It is true that under Napoleon III praise of the wisdom shown in 1801 and enthusiasm for the fine spectacle of 1804 and the joint display given by the Pope and the Emperor in Notre Dame were particularly fashionable, and d'Haussonville wishes to show that this view can only be supported from contemporary official phrase-making, that is to say from lies. He is desirous of seeking the truth behind the outward appearance, and finds it in the official correspondence; he wants to show, too, how the unedifying scenes of 1809 and after, about which official spokesmen of his day preferred to remain silent, were implied in the origins of the existing connexion between Church and State.

THE CONCORDAT

Napoleon the restorer of the altars, Napoleon the saviour of the Church – Pius VII himself never tired of testifying to that view. In the eyes of d'Haussonville, the pure, gentle, and thoroughly well-meaning Pius showed his weakness in this. The Pope was led to his position, as were most of the higher ranks of the clergy, by his conviction that the Church was now near to its total dissolution. The Revolution, and the devastation it had wrought in the field of religion, coming after a century of increasing scepticism, had profoundly shaken their confidence. It was not long since Pius VI had died on French soil, a prisoner of the Directorate after a revolt in Rome in which a French general had lost his life, and the Papal States had then become a republic. The Austrians had soon put an end to this situation, but the Pope had not found comfort from them for very long. In any case the French were there once more. What a blessing then that Bonaparte, the man sprung from the Revolution, talked of reconstruction. Pius VII and his circle were inclined to regard him as an instrument of heaven. His assurances that he would make religion respected once more were as balm for their souls. They trembled at his warnings that if they did not do what he wanted, he would oppress religion still more, he would even destroy it, or (as was his favourite expression) 'change' it.

D'Haussonville considers this attitude defeatist and pusillanimous. Religion did not thus hearken to the commands of the First Consul. Regeneration was taking place spontaneously in the hearts of the multitude, and this process had begun before his accession. Thousands of priests were labouring in spite of indifference or persecution. But the Church no longer dared trust to their power alone. When it allied itself with Bonaparte, the notion that he was indeed the restorer had to be officially accepted, and the hierarchy fell over itself to express its thankfulness and adulation. All this served to strengthen Bonaparte still more in his infatuation with absolute power, and made a conflict unavoidable.

In their faint-heartedness, the Pope and his councillors had shut their eyes to the fact that the First Consul was not himself a believer even though the Concordat asserted that the head of the French State was a practising Catholic. They had not allowed themselves to be deterred by his cynical remarks, which showed so clearly that he intended to use the Roman Catholic religion as he had used the Mohammedan in Egypt. Thus they passed over the Organic Articles, which still further increased the power of the State over the Church, already sufficiently established in the Concordat itself, and they ignored the lack of good faith displayed by Bonaparte when he surprised them with the Articles.

If we now turn back to Thiers's account of the birth of the Concordat, we find none of these doubts. That the promulgation of the Organic Articles ('that wise and profound law')[1] was an act of bad faith towards the Holy See, he contests with the argument that 'it was purely a matter of French internal administration, and did not concern the Holy See'. Nevertheless the Articles include regulations which forbid the publication of any bull, pastoral letter, or any other papal communication without permission of the government. There are others concerning the catechism, which is to be introduced for the whole country and for which the approval of the Government will be required; and concerning the four Gallican theses of 1682, which are to be taught to the clergy. The Holy See must obviously asseverate that these matters were indeed within its province, and if the French Government answered that they were all included within that Gallican tradition of 1682, '*ces beaux principes de soumission et d'indépendance*', as Thiers says,[2] the Holy See might retort that for that very reason Rome had condemned those theses. What Thiers does dislike on the other hand, and what *he* regards as little short of bad faith, is the attempt of the papal nuncio to obtain at the eleventh hour a recantation from the 'constitutional' bishops – those, that is, who had worked under the *Constitution civile* and had thus become schismatics, and who were now included in the episcopate along with the former

1. I, 350b.   2. I, 350a.

réfractaires. The two writers start from such different points of view that one cannot expect them to agree in their evaluations.

When Thiers describes the induction of the Concordat with a solemn *Te Deum* in Notre Dame as the triumph of a wise and courageous policy of conciliation, he is undoubtedly, within certain limits, justified in his contention. The measure had to be pushed through against the opposition of the republican old guard in the representative bodies. The generals of an army born of the Revolution only the day before almost rebelled against the order to attend the *Te Deum*. Only Bonaparte's formidable ascendancy forced them, grumbling and scornful, to give way. Mignet's story of a typical comment will be remembered (see p. 37). But however little the healing of the schism had touched the intellectuals of the Revolution, its soothing effect was noticeable in the country at large. There can be no doubt that the measure was popular with the masses, and on this basis Bonaparte now ventured to introduce an amnesty for *émigrés*. D'Haussonville would find it difficult to deny all this, but he is concerned with tendencies and perils which at the time were visible to very few. The remarkable fact about his position is that his dislike of the Concordat is based on considerations entirely different from those held by the contemporary opposition. If that opposition was almost satisfied by the promulgation of the Organic Articles, for him these make the whole transaction only more offensive.

D'Haussonville was the first to describe in detail the beginnings of the Concordat and its working under the Empire, but his point of view, though different with regard to Catholicism, is closely related to that of Quinet. This can be seen if both accounts are compared with that of Thiers. To my mind d'Haussonville's view means an advance. One might ask if it is fair for the historian to approach a past action by the light of values and conceptions which were then scarcely valid. It goes without saying that his later wisdom does not justify him in taking up a patronizing attitude towards his characters, and that his imagination must primarily help him to see them within the limits of their period. But with this proviso, the taking of a new perspective is an inalienable prerogative of the historian. More than that, it is only by doing so that historical presentation can be enriched and kept alive.

THE CORONATION IN NOTRE DAME

D'Haussonville considers, then, that the Church underestimated its own strength, and moreover was insufficiently aware when it accepted the Concordat of the dangers threatening it from Bonaparte's conception of the State and from his ambition. Pius and his councillors made the same mistake once more in 1804, when they reluctantly decided, in spite of many warnings, to go to Paris. Was this not a humiliation, a Canossa in reverse? Was it necessary to be a counter-revolutionary to take the view[1] that Pius took too little account of Enghien's freshly spilt blood, or that religion lost as much as it gained when its representative took his part in that ostentatious show, in that court of worldlings and atheists? The more so as bad faith had once more to be taken into account. For Pius, who certainly felt that his dignity and that of the Church was endangered, had stipulated among other matters that the coronation should take place according to precedents. In spite of this, at the last moment Napoleon took up the crown himself and placed it on his head. This was a symbolic gesture which delighted the whole anti-clerical section of the public, and which also corresponded to Napoleon's own deepest conception of his attitude to the Church. But the Pope would never have left Rome merely to perform a consecration.

I mentioned in an earlier chapter (p. 74) Thiers's satisfaction at the scene in Notre Dame, where in his view the Revolution itself was consecrated by the Pope. The ruthless self-calculation of Napoleon in his relations with the Church he never noticed. With regard to the Organic Articles, which we know he thought a model of wisdom, that is not surprising, however much of a blow their unexpected declaration was for the Pope and his Secretary of State, Consalvi. As regards Napoleon's action in crowning himself, Thiers simply does not mention the bargain previously made.[2]

CARDINAL CAPRARA AND THE IMPERIAL CATECHISM

The worst of it was that all this confirmed Napoleon in his overweening pride, which was to prove a disaster for the world, but especially for the Church. Immediately after the signing of the Concordat, Pius and Consalvi were put in a difficult position because the First Consul intimated his desire to have Cardinal Caprara and no other for papal nuncio. Thiers describes Caprara as a man 'too enlightened and too wise to appeal to the other cardinals',[3] and when one thinks of the demands which Pius thought himself entitled to make after the coronation, and which could not possibly be granted, the judgement is intelligible. These demands were drawn up by the most reactionary party at the papal court and Caprara had warned against them. But in general Caprara's 'enlightenment' appeared to consist in a blind zeal for the service of the First Consul, soon to be the Emperor. Even those cardinals who like Pius himself

1. cf. DR BARTSTRA in *Pelgrimstocht der mensheid*, p. 508.
2. ARMAND LEFEBVRE tries to prove Napoleon not guilty of deception, but on very weak grounds: *Histoire des Cabinets*, II.
3. I, 613b.

realized that a certain recognition of the new spirit was inevitable, regarded Caprara with the greatest suspicion. Weakness in respect of the powerful worldling, which overcame them all at times, was with Caprara raised to a system. 'His absolute power is everywhere recognized,' he was in the habit of saying, 'and, given his character, the only way to save Rome from total defeat is to submit systematically to his wishes.'[1] Later Consalvi wrote that under pressure from Napoleon Caprara repeatedly acted arbitrarily, sometimes even against the strict orders of the Pope. More than once there was question of recalling him, but the necessary courage was never found.

I shall deal with one instance only in which Caprara took his orders as it were from Paris rather than from Rome. Mme de Staël had already expressed her indignation concerning the section of the new catechism of 1806 which dealt with the duties of subjects to their Emperor. She did not know – and d'Haussonville was the first to give documentary proof – that this chapter was forced upon the Church, which offered only feeble resistance. (Thiers has nothing on the matter.)

Some years before, the Minister of Cults had set up a committee of clergy to draw up a catechism under his supervision. It was laid down in the Organic Articles that there should be one single liturgy and catechism for the whole Empire. It was not one of the provisions to which Rome objected, since the thought occurred to no one that Rome would not be consulted in this beneficent work of unification. And indeed as early as 1805 a project was handed to Caprara which he passed on to Rome. The Secretary of State, Consalvi, thereupon charged him most emphatically to prevent such a catechism being proclaimed. Not only did the draft document submitted contain errors, but it was fundamentally unacceptable that the temporal power should dictate a catechism to the bishops: 'The Holy Father trusts that His Majesty will not take unto himself a function which God has reserved for the Church and for the Vicar of Christ.'[2] In spite of this letter, dated September 1805, eight months later it was from the public Press, from the *Journal de l'Empire*, that Consalvi learned of an imperial decree of 4 April 1806 which after specifically mentioning the approval of the nuncio Caprara, announced a catechism for the use of the whole Empire. It was actually published in August. On 11 March 1806 Caprara had given his formal approval in an interview with the Minister in his office. From the beginning the Minister had indeed been convinced, as he wrote to the Emperor, of the Cardinal's 'good disposition', but he was nevertheless a little anxious lest he should raise 'theological quibbles'. Less than a fortnight after Caprara had removed these doubts, Napoleon wrote to Eugène de Beauharnais, his stepson and Viceroy of Italy, instructing him to buy for Caprara his palace in Bologna (where he was arch-

1. D'HAUSSONVILLE, I, 145.   2. D'HAUSSONVILLE, II, 279.

bishop), so as to relieve him of his monetary difficulties ... Here we have the explanation of Caprara's enlightenment, so praised by Thiers.

And what were the duties of the subject according to the new catechism? The seventh lesson, which dealt with this, was for Napoleon and his Minister of Cults the one that mattered. The catechism had been practically ready for signature as early as 1803, but the First Consul saw the change in his position coming, and had suspended the work till he knew where he was. And now Portalis, in a letter to the Emperor, put forward the suggestion that a general statement of the duty of obedience to the ruler was not enough. Bossuet's catechism merely laid it down that it was everyone's duty according to the fourth commandment 'to respect all superiors, pastors, kings, magistrates, and others'. 'History does not relate,' writes d'Haussonville, 'that Louis XIV regarded himself as slighted because he was put after the pastors and only preceded the magistrates.' But Portalis thought, and Napoleon heartily agreed with him, if indeed the idea was not originally his own, that it was necessary in present circumstances 'rightly to direct the submission of the subject', and to mention the ruler by name. After a thorough exchange of views between Emperor and Minister, the ecclesiastical committee received a text which they dutifully adopted. It had become quite a treatise.

SEVENTH LESSON

Christians owe to the princes who rule them, and we in particular owe to Napoleon I, our Emperor, love, respect, obedience, loyalty, military service, the dues laid down for the conservation and the defence of the empire and of his throne; we also owe him fervent prayers for his safety and for the temporal and spiritual prosperity of the State.

– Why do we owe all these duties towards our Emperor?

Firstly, because God ... plentifully bestowing gifts upon our Emperor, whether for peace or for war, has made him the minister of his power and his image upon earth. Secondly, because Our Lord Jesus Christ, both by his teaching and his example, has taught us himself what we owe to our Sovereign. ...

– Are there not particular reasons which should attach us more closely to Napoleon I, our Emperor?

Yes, because it is he whom God has sustained, in difficult circumstances, so that he might re-establish public worship and the holy faith of our fathers, and that he might be their protector. He has restored and maintained public order by his profound and active wisdom; he defends the State with his powerful arm; he has become the anointed of the Lord by the consecration he has received from the sovereign pontiff, head of the universal Church.

– What must one think of those who should fail in their duty to our Emperor?

According to the apostle Paul, they would resist the established order of God himself, and would render themselves worthy of eternal damnation.

Before the catechism was introduced, rumours of its contents had got about, and the bishops were somewhat troubled. One of them expressed his indignation – the letter, it should be noted, was private – that such a glorification of the Emperor should be smuggled into religion.

Is it within his province to take a hand in these matters? Who called upon him to do so? He is concerned with earthly affairs, we with heavenly. If we allow him to proceed, he will soon lay hands on the censer, and then perhaps will mount the altar.[1]

In practice, Napoleon's interference went much further even now, for it was at his wish that the doctrine of no salvation save within the Church, which appeared unmistakably in Bossuet's work, was dropped from the catechism. Episcopal dissatisfaction, not daring to attack the objectionable seventh lesson, vented itself in opposition to this point. Even here the need of a privileged spokesman was felt. Such a one was found in the Emperor's uncle, Cardinal Fesch, who did indeed succeed in obtaining redress in this matter. For the Emperor's enlightenment, which had revolted against this intolerance, was not quite so firmly attached to principle but that it could not wink upon occasion at a deviation, if by so doing he might obtain the damnation of those who denied his own omnipotence. The catechism appeared with the seventh lesson intact, and no one ventured a word of disapproval. Far from it – most of the bishops greeted the work with a great show of gratitude and joy. Rome kept silent.

SUBMISSIVENESS OF THE BISHOPS

It is this submissiveness which presents so alarming a spectacle. Before talking of the blessings of the Concordat of 1801 – this is one of d'Haussonville's theses – one should have a clear picture of the enslavement to which the French bishops were brought under that régime. From Thiers no such picture is to be got. He keeps extolling the peace-loving qualities of the bishops, and thinks it perfectly natural that they were inclined to be pliant in order to keep the Church's benefactor, that irascible potentate, in a good humour.

Meanwhile Naopleon knew perfectly well, as always, what he was about. Later he wrote in his *Mémoires* that he had intended to adapt religion to his policy without actually interfering in it, and entirely by exerting temporal influence. As d'Haussonville rightly remarks,[2] he was under an illusion in believing that this involved no interference with religion. Its close association with him was a real danger to the Church. He was after all not a Catholic, and made no bones about it. He had no desire to detract from the dignity of the Church: he gave

1. II, 289.   2. II, 213.

no encouragement to scoffers. On the contrary, at his court bishops had precedence over generals, and cardinals over marshals. But Napoleon negotiated with
the Church as he negotiated with other allies: the lion's share of the profit derived
from the association was to be for him. The form in which he demanded his share
from the priests was that they should exercise their influence on the faithful invariably in the direction of blind submission to him and to the demands of his
policy.

Napoleon, who never contented himself with general directives, and who
with an unbelievably concentrated personal attention concerned himself with
the smallest details of his administration, was not satisfied with the spontaneous
demonstrations which the bishops hastened to give him. They frequently received special hints, as well as general advice. When he was at war with Russia,
for example, he indicated in detail how, in sermon or pastoral letter, they should
arouse the zeal of the faithful by drawing their attention to the schismatic nature
of the Greek confession. Another time, they were to remind their hearers of the
Protestantism of the English. A bishop in the Vendée, where the *chouans* might
now be quiet but where there was always a possibility of a revival of royalist
agitation in conjunction with England, would do well, Napoleon wrote to
Portalis, to emphasize in his pastoral letter the persecutions suffered by the
Catholics in Ireland. The Minister was urged to write 'un bel article' in the
Moniteur which would serve as an example. A careful eye was kept on all ser-
mons, and a thoughtless word might result in a term of imprisonment without
trial for the priest. Napoleon hit on the idea, which he passed on to Portalis,
that the disposition of the higher ranks, including deacons, might be controlled
by demanding from them a degree in the Imperial University, that powerful
monopolistic organization. The University would have to refuse the degree in
the case of candidates known to cherish ultramontane or other notions dangerous to the Government. When he became aware, in 1806, of the existence
of various clerical papers, he ordered at once that they should be amalgamated
into one journal, entitled *Le Journal des Curés*. At the slightest sign of deviation
from Gallican ideas in the paper, Napoleon urged his Minister of Cults to take
action.

In addition there must be incense for himself. This was achieved, for instance,
by the cult of St Napoleon, of whom nobody had heard until the Emperor
achieved greatness. Now chapels and fraternities were set up, although it was
difficult to find out anything in Rome about the saint. De Broglie, the bishop
of Ghent, relates how Réal, the Minister of Police, once told him that he should
give more praise to the Emperor in his pastoral letters. De Broglie, who for his
sermon on the birth of the King of Rome had used as his model Bossuet's
sermon on the occasion of the birth of a grandson to Louis XIV, thought his

course must be safe under that flag. But what was good enough for the *Roi Soleil* would not do for the second Charlemagne, neither in the case of the lesson on the fourth commandment nor in this instance. 'Please give me the yardstick,' said de Broglie.[1]

THE POPE IMPRISONED: THE COUNCIL OF 1811

When Thiers comes to treat of the abduction of Pius in 1809 and of the high-handed way in which the Council was managed in 1811, he is hardly less disapproving, particularly of the latter case, than d'Haussonville. He even has an impressive passage[2] concerning the delusion which had attacked Napoleon that all problems, including spiritual and moral problems, were included in the one which preoccupied him in 1811, that of the war with Russia. If he could defeat Russia, the only country which, if it did not actually oppose him, was inclined to cross him in some of his wishes, he would also have overthrown all the various open or hidden oppositions still rampant in Europe. Of what account then was this poor priestly prisoner, who ventured to dispute Rome with him? Of none, or hardly any; and the Church would recognize the might of Caesar, as she had so often done.

And yet here too Thiers judges events and lays his emphasis very differently from d'Haussonville. He is shocked by the methods used, he disapproves of the plan to deprive the Pope of his last weapon, by putting a term to canonical institution, and to make him the obedient servant of his prince, albeit in the lap of luxury, on French soil. All this he regards as the overthrow of that 'beautiful edifice', that precious balance, which is his idea of Gallicanism. But when it comes to the point, his sympathies are almost automatically with the Emperor. Those ecclesiastics who let themselves be used as go-betweens and who tried to force the aged Pope to make concessions by threatening him with the wrath of the Emperor, were men after his heart. They are described as being among 'the most venerable, the most learned, the most conversant with the traditions of the French Church' and also 'those best shaped for the handling of business', since 'they joined to a profound knowledge of ecclesiastical affairs a first-rate intelligence, extreme tact, the art of dealing with men, in short, a remarkable political sense of the kind that was growing rarer every day among the leaders of the Church'.[3] The opposition party, which drags the Council into resistance, he calls 'imprudent, passionate, wild, unenlightened, fanatical'.[4] The bishop

1. II, 239. From a letter of de Broglie dated 11 September 1810; d'Haussonville does not state where the letter is to be found.
2. IV, 47b (Quoted by D'HAUSSONVILLE, V, 64).
3. IV, 31a.
4. Prince Napoleon used the last word (see p. 148) in the same way; it was an expression in the party jargon of the anti-clericals.

whose annoyance at the way in which the Emperor meddled with the catechism I referred to above was naturally one of these frenzied and backward priests. The rejection of the institution decree by the Council, the first warning to Napoleon that his writ did not run everywhere, gives Thiers an opportunity to write: 'Those crazy spirits, who were only longing for confusion, might congratulate themselves.'[1]

Thiers, however, told only half of the ecclesiastical section of his story. As d'Haussonville remarks in his introduction, with the necessary respect for the *doyen* of Napoleonic historiography: 'He knew practically everything, but it did not suit him [in the structure of his work] to tell everything.'

There are no blacker pages in the history of Napoleonic despotism than those devoted to his 'negotiations' with the Pope, in which the Council was forced to provide him with an additional weapon. Thiers's much-praised bishops made themselves accessories to the almost intolerable moral pressure brought to bear on their chief. They did so out of fear of the Emperor. In the interests of the Church, they put it themselves; but if so, they took a petty, mundane, and short-sighted view of these interests.

One must picture to oneself Pius, whose very over-conscientiousness often enough made him a painfully irresolute old gentleman, gentle, none too strong, cut off completely from the outside world since the interception of his letters to Paris and Florence. He had been deprived of books and papers and even, by express instructions from Napoleon, of the Fisherman signet ring. His servants, including his personal physician, were bribed. The prefect of Monte-notte, Chabrol, supervised everything and gave to the prisoner such information as the Emperor wished him to have.

When Napoleon instructed Chabrol to express to Pius his sorrow for the Church which had such a master, a man who did not know what was due to the temporal sovereign, and to add that the good work would go on without him, one is shocked at the impudence. Yet utterances of that kind were nothing new with Napoleon. He always knew much better than the Pope and was ready at all times to air his theology. Once, for example, when he was visiting Belgium, he had told a number of Brabant priests that he was prepared to protect the religion of St Louis, of St Bernard, of Bossuet, of the Gallican Church with all his might, but not that of Gregory VII, of Boniface VIII, of Julius II, who he was convinced were burning in hell because of all the dissension to which their extravagant claims had given rise. 'The Popes have committed too many follies to allow us to believe in their infallibility.'[2]

1. IV, 45a.
2. D'HAUSSONVILLE, III, 363. Many such utterances of Napoleon's exist; he was free with the names of popes and saints.

It became worse, however, when Chabrol was ordered to assure the Pope that 'all canons and theologians of France and Italy are indignant at his letters to the chapters, and that he is the cause of the arrest of' a large number of Florentine and Parisian priests, all mentioned by name, and of a cardinal, 'that he brings misfortune to everyone with whom he corresponds'.[1] The impudence might be called irresponsible, but the lie – for the statement about widespread ecclesiastical indignation was nothing else – had something devilish about it.

But that was the game in which the three bishops came to take their allotted part. When one reads in d'Haussonville the daily reports of Chabrol to the Minister of Cults about the way in which the Pope was being besieged; how tired he was; how he suffered from insomnia; how the forsaken old man was plied with sophisms and misleading suggestions, as though the whole Church was accusing him of offering obstruction merely for fear of losing his temporal power; how the doctor had his part to play – when one reads of Pius's collapse after the ambassadors had gone, of his despair at the thought that he had conceded too much – it becomes difficult to feel any admiration for the ecclesiastics who might have torn through the web of intrigue but who failed to do it.

After the Council, pressure was again brought to bear on the Pope, with the help of the decree extorted from it. This time, in addition to Napoleon's tame bishops, several of the 'red' cardinals were let loose on him. The old man had to make up his mind without knowing anything of the real state of affairs in the outside world. There was a complete conspiracy of silence concerning all that had happened in the Council. Before being sent to Savona, the cardinals, whom Pius regarded as his natural councillors, had actually been made to bind themselves in writing to the views officially favoured. They had promised to advocate these with the utmost vigour to the Pope.[2] It is no wonder that Pius gave way in the end.

When Napoleon was still not content with his agreement, and the Pope on his side set himself firmly against further concessions, the Emperor arranged that Chabrol should read him a letter[3] not directly addressed to him, though the Pope had just written one to the Emperor. The letter began with a declaration in Napoleon's most domineering style that direct correspondence between crowned heads was seemly only for the exchange of compliments. Thus the letter was addressed to his Minister of Cults, and was supposed to be intended for the negotiators, who had in fact just left Savona. In it he first refused the Pope's request to be allowed to communicate freely with the faithful. The Pope, he said, had forfeited this freedom by his act of excommunication. He seemed to

---

1. IV, 481. It should be noted that a letter like the one quoted was not included in the official *Correspondance de Napoléon Ier*. It is also printed in LECESTRE, *Lettres inédites*, II, 107.

2. D'HAUSSONVILLE, v, 8.   3. D'HAUSSONVILLE, pp. 127 ff.

want to forget that now, but Napoleon did not: 'Is it for the sake of cursing sovereigns that Jesus had himself nailed to the Cross? Is this the principle of the Supreme Redeemer?' Next, he had forfeited it by inciting the chapters.

Has he since tried, out of love for truth, for religion, for humanity, to persuade the thousands of kindly priests who allow themselves to be excited by the idea of their allegiance to him, to give their sovereign what is his due? ... He must have no hopes of any intercourse with the 'black' cardinals. In the meantime, there is no interruption in affairs. In the absence of bishops, the dioceses are administered by capitular vicars. He [the Pope] had counted on trouble. But he was mistaken. Public opinion today is too enlightened. For this criminal speculation, however, frustrated by men and condemned by his divine master, the Pope will one day have to account. His Majesty pities the Pope's ignorance. He is sorry to see a pontiff who might play so great and noble a part sinking to be the misfortune of the Church. All the advantages possessed by the papacy he might have retained, but, egged on by his prejudices, he preferred breaking with me, in spite of what the doctrine of the Church enjoins.

The negotiators – they were, as we know, actually on their way back – were then instructed to leave Savona if they did not obtain complete submission within three days. And the document proceeds:

Simplicity, sincere and faithful hope in His Majesty's generosity, is the only course remaining to the Pope. H.M. has a better knowledge of all these matters than His Holiness, much too good a knowledge ever to allow himself to be pushed off the course he has laid for himself ... Seeing the Pope in this false situation, H.M. looks forward with equanimity to his rejecting the decree and covering himself with the dishonour attached to ignorance. If he does not feel himself sufficiently justified, not sufficiently enlightened by the Holy Ghost and the hundred bishops [that is, by the hundred, out of the hundred and twenty, for whom the pressure applied in the office of the Minister of Religious Cults had been too much] then why does he not acknowledge that he is unable to distinguish what belongs to the dogma and the essence of religion from what is merely secular and subject to change, and why does he not abdicate? That distinction is simple enough for the greenest seminarist to understand. If the Pope cannot grasp it, why does he not vacate the papal see, for somebody with a stronger head and a firmer grasp of principle, who might at last repair the untold damage done by him in Germany and in all the countries of Christendom?

This churlish piece is nothing out of the way among Napoleon's writings, but as an example of unbridled exercise of power against the weak it is in the running for a place of honour. Pius endured the recital patiently, but weak though he might be he rejected decisively the suggestion that he might abdicate, and the dictator was left with his insoluble problem.

THE DRAFT CONCORDAT OF FONTAINEBLEAU (1813)

There is nothing of all this in Thiers's account. If only for this reason, the affair of the Concordat of Fontainebleau a year later is shown by him in quite another light. It is only when we know what pressure was put upon Pius at Savona that we appreciate the shamelessness of the embrace with which Napoleon greeted his victim on the occasion of their so-called unexpected encounter. Only then can we imagine what fresh moral pressure must have been brought to bear on that impressionable old man, still surrounded only with councillors picked by his jailer, by an Emperor whose heart, in his decline of fortune, was set on compromise. It was a pressure all the more painful for the fact that this time he did not scorn the weapons of amiability, and even of concessions on subordinate matters. It is therefore not surprising that the Emperor obtained the assent he so greatly desired, and without waiting for a definite treaty triumphantly authorized the bishops to order a *Te Deum*. But at the same time one can readily believe that the Pope did not put his signature without grave doubts, and that when, some days later, the 'black' cardinals were at last allowed to see him, his conscience was already troubled.[1]

Thiers believed – and this was of course what Napoleon tried to make the world accept – that the 'black' cardinals were the mischief-makers who changed Pius's mind for him; the argument they were supposed to have used was that of the approaching downfall of the autocrat, the possibility of which had not even occurred to Pius, in his innocence and isolation from the world. Such explanations are not strange coming from a writer who appears to regard the new Concordat as reasonableness itself, though that he should take that view is indeed odd, when at the beginning of his account of the negotiations concerning the right of institution he had expressly described this as indispensable to counterbalance the temporal right of nomination.[2]

It is only as one realizes the way in which the Concordat of 1801 was misused that it is possible to understand how a harsher edition of it was bound to give rise in the Pope's mind to reflections very different from those relating to temporal power in the States of the Church or to the fortunes of war. Indeed, every lover of liberty will be disturbed at the thought that this unscrupulous government would have removed the Pope's only remaining means of defence by a new

1. On both points d'Haussonville quotes the memoirs of only *one* of the 'black' cardinals, Pacca, indomitable among the indomitable. The evidence is perhaps not completely satisfactory, and Thiers has apparently rejected it, but now that the previous history is known from sources additional to his work, it has internal probability.

2. IV, 32. The treatment of the Concordat of Fontainebleau, IV, 412 ff., seems to me utterly irreconcilable with this earlier passage.

settlement, and would have established him in its own territory as a kind of high ecclesiastical official. Did Thiers not see this? In theory he recognized it, but as I have shown, he had not given the essential facts in the earlier volumes of his history.

HISTORICAL BACKGROUND OF THE THEORIES OF CHURCH AND STATE AS HELD BY NAPOLEON AND THIERS

We must, however, carry a little further our interpretation of his attitude of mind. To understand it, and to do justice both to him and to Napoleon, it is necessary – if we are to observe the conditions under which I said that the historian uses historical perspective – to keep before us the values and ideas which both saw still prevailing in their own time. Nothing can ever excuse the broken promises, the pride degenerated into pedantry, the use of moral violence, which is worse than physical coercion; but the spirit of Napoleon's clerical policy will then become more intelligible. And at the same time, harking back to Quinet, we shall come to the conclusion, which I indicated when I discussed his *Révolution,* that in this connexion Byzantium and Constantine provide no short cut to an explanation.

Thiers was a liberal with a strong eighteenth-century background, a man of the Enlightenment with outward respect but little real feeling for religion, penetrated with fear and at the same time scorn for 'rule of priests' and 'superstition'. 'A free Church in a free State' was a conception only beginning to attract attention. The old tradition, a very old tradition, but one which was in full flower during the second half of the eighteenth century, and of which Thiers like many thousands after him had not yet freed himself, pointed to the placing of the secular power above that of the Church as the only means of defence. In Protestant no less than in Catholic countries the leading intelligentsia of Europe had long familiarized themselves with the exaltation of the claims of the State as a means of defence against ecclesiastical ambitions, which it was feared might endanger public order by their influence over the masses. Grotius and Oldernbarnevelt, Hobbes and Spinoza have their place in this current of thought.

In France the tradition had acquired a strong national colour; it appeared as one of the pillars on which rested the unitary State. Bossuet, who had formulated the famous four Gallican theses within the Church itself – though the Assembly of the French clergy in 1682 did not actually possess much more freedom than the Council of 1811 – was not regarded as the instrument of Louis XIV's despotism but as the defender of national rights against sinister jesuitical Rome. Thiers swore by this Gallican tradition. We have seen that he sometimes tried to allow the claims of the Church a fair place in that compromise; but for the most part he used the slogan to further the triumph of the State, and even of the State as personified by Napoleon, though he sometimes disliked the latter's extremism. Already in the eighteenth century the French *philosophes* had taken possession of these ideas and sealed the ascendancy of them in the spirit of *étatisme*. The enlightened despots took them as directives for their policy with respect to the Church. Just as the Gallican tradition had gained a footing in the French Church itself, so did a considerable part of the German episcopate now follow the teaching of Febronius. The *Constitution civile du clergé* (1790) was extreme in a typically revolutionary manner, but its origins were in the current tradition.

Thus Napoleon also, though at first he reacted against revolutionary trends. In any case it should not be thought that his harsh driving of the French clergy, or even his brutal treatment of the Pope, caused much of a sensation in that part of Catholic Europe which had remained outside the Revolution. Austrian diplomacy was less upset by the annexation of the Papal States than by the excommunication which was Pius's answer. Indeed, 'upset' is too strong a word in either case. The Austrians shrugged their shoulders over the excommunication, and laughed. Yet memories of Pope Gregory VII caused a slight shiver, and even the suggestion of an attack on secular sovereignty was looked upon as a bad example. In his prison at Savona, the unfortunate Pius received the visit of the former Austrian ambassador to his court; Metternich had just arranged the marriage of his master's daughter with Napoleon, in itself a proof of how little the Catholic court of Vienna troubled about the Pope – particularly when one remembers that the Habsburg had not allowed himself to be deterred from the match by the irregularity involved in the annulment of the previous marriage without the Pope's consent. The smoothly official report which the Austrian diplomat gave of what was nevertheless rather a pathetic encounter shows how right Napoleon had been in thinking he could safely let him visit the prisoner.

On this point there was much agreement between the men of the world. Everywhere the Church was looked upon as something at once old-fashioned and dangerous. Modern institutions – those of Joseph II in Austria as well as those of the Revolution in France – had to be protected against it. States which had adopted civil marriage and the subjection of the whole of society to civil law inevitably wished also to break clerical control of education. To recall the ambition of medieval popes in times so different was foolish, but such reminiscences helped to justify the national centralized state, run by bureaucrats who allowed little scope to pastors or priests and kept a careful eye on the relations of the Catholic clergy with their chief outside the country. This tendency continued with unabated vigour into the nineteenth century. Metternich, mentioned above, was powerful in Austria till 1848. Dutch William I was a disciple. In France, Gallican principles survived the Restoration.

As I have said, it is worth while recalling all this, because one has to see Napoleon's actions against the Church within the framework of his day, in order to judge of them fairly. But it is just as necessary to explain Thiers's attitude. I believe it is not going too far to say that the most important factor was not Thiers's admiration for Napoleon so much as his sense of spiritual kinship. It seems at first sight strange that the Napoleonic legend was so successful among just those radical sections of the French people which drew their inspiration from the Revolution. Anti-clericalism – the restorer of altars had long before the end revealed himself as the tamer of priests – anti-clericalism is a connecting link of prime importance.[1]

D'HAUSSONVILLE'S IDEAS IN THE CATHOLIC WORLD

D'Haussonville's book is imbued with respect for spiritual freedom. He did not feel that the Restoration had completely restored this freedom. For most of the clergy, in spite of their former enthusiasm, in spite of the papal consecration and of the lessons in the catechism glorifying the Bourbons, continued to believe – and until the reaction started by Lamennais they believed it, one would almost say, as a matter of course, innocently – that a close association with the State was healthy for religion. D'Haussonville's work made a valuable contribution to the knowledge of Napoleonic despotism, which by no means all the writers who succeeded him have digested, however.

His treatment could find no favour in leading Catholic circles in France, or indeed in Rome, where under Pius IX a sharp turn was taken against liberalism, and where even before him Lamennais had found no mercy. There the attack on the Concordat met with no approval, as was demonstrated with the appearance of a history of the Concordat by Father Theiner (a German, though he wrote in French), archivist of the Vatican, which amounts to a glorification not only of the famous agreement but of Napoleon also. A generation later another history of the Concordat was written, this time by a Frenchman, Cardinal Mathieu, also pro-Concordat. At that moment, at the beginning of the twentieth century, attacks were being made on the Concordat by those who wished to 'laicize' the State. To defend it seemed a Catholic duty. After the separation of Church and State in 1906, however, the Church seemed to prosper well enough in the secularized state; there was even a Catholic revival.

1. That men in England and America rejoiced at the fall of Pius, and prophesied the ruin of the Roman Church as a result, is not without connexion with such ideas, but naturally has a specifically Protestant and anti-papist inspiration.

In these circumstances there is greater inclination in Catholic circles to entertain d'Haussonville's view.[1]

1. A deft characterization of Bonaparte's attitude at the negotiations of 1801 is to be found in J. CRÉTINEAU-JOLY, *Bonaparte, le Concordat de 1801 et le cardinal Consalvi* (1869), 56:

'Bonaparte a l'instinct des belles choses; mais, enfant gâté de la fortune et de la victoire, il veut, il décrète, il ordonne que ces belles choses s'improvisent à son heure et à son temps. Il n'y a pas de délais, pas d'atermoiements, pas de transactions, pas de réflexions possibles avec lui. Il a jugé opportun et nécessaire de rompre avec l'athéisme légal et de renouer la chaîne des temps. Il y procède comme à coups de canon; il tente d'enlever le Concordat à la baïonette.'

This agrees with the account of d'Haussonville. The writer, a fervent Catholic, proud of the approbation expressed at his work by Pius IX, also considers the Concordat a blessing for religion. This does not prevent him from polemicizing furiously with Father Theiner.

One point on which Crétineau-Joly disagrees with d'Haussonville is on the latter's contention that Bonaparte was personally not a Catholic. It seems to me that it is impossible to maintain the thesis that Bonaparte was a sincere Catholic. It can be said that his conviction of the social and political importance of religion – religion in general, and as far as France was concerned the Catholic religion – was not necessarily pure self-interest or 'cynicism' but was derived from a sincere religious feeling. That is a typical eighteenth-century sentiment, such as was expressed by Rousseau's *vicaire savoyard*, and not everyone, naturally, condemns it so severely as Quinet. See p. 365 below, for what Hanotaux wrote concerning Napoleon's strong religious awareness.

5 Jules Michelet

THE two last works, those of Lanfrey and of d'Haussonville, have this much in common, that their authors could not shake off the influence of Thiers. They correct, they amplify him, but he still dominates the territory in which they operate.

This is not so in the case of two writers who took issue with the Napoleon problem in the period that opened with the downfall of Napoleon III, but whose conception had been formed (as was that of every one of those I have so far discussed in this section) under the impact of the nephew's disenchanting caesarism: Michelet and Taine.

I shall deal very briefly with Michelet. Having interrupted his many-volume history of France in 1843 at the close of the Middle Ages in order to deal first with the Revolution, he had filled the gap (and disposed of the seventeenth-century and eighteenth-century kings with ferocious contumely) in the early sixties. Now, in his old age, in 1872 and 1873,[1] he wrote three more volumes, the first dealing with the Directorate and the rise of Bonaparte, the second and third with the period of the First Consul and Emperor, from Brumaire to Waterloo.

In the preface to the first volume he had said that he was going to disburden himself of the severe opinion he had all his life held about Napoleon, while others 'looked without seeing'. Now, certainly, Napoleon is to him the mere self-seeking adventurer, the betrayer of the Revolution and of the peoples. But twenty-five years ago he had in fact shared the view then so commonly held by the devotees of the Revolution tradition that Napoleon had been its champion in Europe. In his book on the Revolution (in 1851) he had rebuked the Belgians for jibbing at the demands made upon them by the French conqueror. 'When France undertook, for the Belgians and for the world, the war which cost her from 1792 to 1815 ten millions of her children, it did not, in the face of that terrible effusion of French blood, become them very well to grumble about a little Belgian money.' From 1792 to 1815! Napoleon's wars, too, were waged on behalf of Belgium and of the world!

Now, on the contrary, he sees the youthful Bonaparte already in his Italian campaigns 'waging war *against* the peoples'. '*Le glorieux traître de Campo Formio*'

1. *Histoire du XIX siècle;* vols. II and III were published posthumously in 1875.

debased himself to acting as 'the devoted minister of Austria'. The annexation of Genoa to France and the handing over of Venice to Austria were two 'crimes'. Bonaparte was a 'corrupted soul'.

Michelet is still the fervent believer in the Revolution as the bearer of a message of liberation for mankind; France to his mind is still the chosen country deserving eternal admiration and gratitude, and the Britain of Pitt, on the contrary, the home of base materialism and cunning. But after the Terror, the magnanimous French nation had gone through a spell of moral lassitude and indifference, and of this the unprincipled Bonapartes (he is thinking of Napoleon and Lucien) availed themselves 'to dig the abyss of Brumaire, which contained for Europe and for us fifteen years of atrocious warfare and the death of three millions of men'. He is still convinced that 'the wars of the Revolution were far from excluding the true human fraternity', but he now admits that their sequence under Napoleon led to a disastrous divorce between the conception of France and that of Europe (otherwise to him synonymous). When the catastrophe is there, and Alexander of Russia is approaching Paris with the victorious allies, Michelet can even bring himself to quote with approval the '*mot beau et vrai*' pronounced by the Tsar on that occasion: 'I come to reconcile France with Europe.'

Meanwhile the whole of Napoleon's career has been reviewed in an impassioned and exclamatory style, and the work is a sustained denunciation rather than a history. Nothing is left to Napoleon. The vulgarity of his character is illustrated by anecdotes which sometimes seem to the writer so revolting that he can hardly bring himself to relate them. His military successes he represents as due to luck as often as to ability. He insists on the cowardice displayed by the spurious great man on the 18th Brumaire, again in the face of hostile crowds on his journey to Elba after the first abdication, and finally at the battle of Waterloo and in the hectic days that followed upon the defeat. A cowardice accompanied by an insane egotism. Napoleon did not think of the safety of Paris or of France, only of securing the succession to his son and of his possessions. When in the heated discussions in Paris Lucien suggests that the baby King of Rome should be proclaimed, La Fayette, revolted, uttered 'a terrible word, a veritable sentence by which that disastrous family will for ever remain marked: "What have you made of France?"'

The British – even to them Michelet is now almost reconciled – committed one grievous mistake. By shutting him up at St Helena, they provided him with 'a towering stage, from where the scoundrel could surprise the pity of the public and by dint of lies prepare a sanguinary repetition of all the calamities of the Empire'.

6 Hippolyte Taine

THE WRITER

TAINE'S book on Napoleon is a very different proposition from Michelet's diatribe. Michelet was miles apart from Thiers, not because he did not accept the Revolution, but because in his view it belonged to 'the people', instead of as with Thiers to 'the bourgeoisie'. Taine on the contrary definitely breaks with the liberal school of the forties, because he rejects the very principle of the Revolution.

But, moreover, his method is so different that the reader forgets his immediate predecessors. And yet there is a relationship with all those who have come under review in this section. Like them (if we except Michelet, who is *sui generis*), he was a spiritual heir, if a bitterly disillusioned one, of Mme de Staël. Like them, he had his place in the reaction against the Napoleonic legend. Indeed, although he did not indulge in the abuse with which Michelet startled his readers, in him this reaction culminated.

The first volume of the two devoted to Napoleon in Taine's great work *Les Origines de la France contemporaine* appeared in 1890. It contained the brilliant 'portrait', as an introduction to a discussion of the institutions which Napoleon gave to France. I shall in the first instance confine my attentions to this portrait.

Taine is in a different category from writers such as Thiers, d'Haussonville, or Lanfrey. Nor can Quinet compare with him. The hundred and forty pages of the chapter on Napoleon belong to literature. No one has a greater capacity for making his readers see a character. Taine's Napoleon, a creature devoid of all humanity, an evil demon let loose on France and Europe, is alive, is alive with a gripping, an overwhelming intensity. This does not mean that Taine's Napoleon must be true to life. Imagination plays too important a role in the writing of history, and what is imagination but the projection of the author's personality? It is to a supreme degree the Napoleon of Taine, and Taine, a creative imagination without a peer, was by no means the calm objective observer he declared – and believed – himself to be.[1]

Deeply shocked as he was by the defeat of 1870, and no less by the Commune which followed, he wanted to show his compatriots how the conditions and state

1. See the Introduction to the *Origines*.

of mind arose from which had sprung those disasters and the other ills that visited France. It was for this reason that, though his fame hitherto rested on books of philosophy and literary history, he now undertook the purely historical work of *Les Origines*. The *ancien régime* could not have been painted in darker colours than it was in his first volume. But the Revolution aroused even greater abhorrence. He hated the triumph of frivolous theorizing, the blindness to historical growth and to indispensable order, the letting loose of the animal in man. He might have gone on to celebrate Bonaparte as the man who scorned the ideologists and restored order. But when his friends somewhat reproachfully commiserated with him on the compromising approval accorded to him by conservatives of every colour for his withering attacks on the Jacobins, Taine would answer with a smile: '*Je les attends à Napoléon*.'[1] And indeed it was with hate that he painted the portrait.

Taine's mind was so constructed that everything and everybody in history was seen by him subjected to a few precisely-defined guiding ideas. It is curious that this tendency has much in common with that passion for general ideas which he condemned in his eighteenth-century Frenchmen, and from which, as he was never tired of declaring, derived their blindness to realities. Not less curious is the way in which, in spite of this cramping and sometimes highly artificial structure into which he forces his subject, he contrives an astonishingly close contact with life. Yet his is in no sense a historical method. Taine has no understanding of development. He has no power to trace the origins and connexions of events and to extract from them their meaning. He tries to distil the quintessence of a whole period, a career which embraced so many lands, wars, revolutions, reformations. It is the weakness of his *Ancien Régime* that he neglected the differences between the period of Louis XV and that of Louis XVI, using his notes concerning the one or the other indiscriminately, without regard to the circumstances, to make a composite picture which for that very reason cannot have existed in reality. His *Révolution* is, in my judgement, a complete failure as a history, because he is only interested in describing feelings and states of mind, and never places the actions, incidents, and utterances from which he deduced these in their natural relation to the wider course of events. And it must be admitted that his *Napoléon* suffers from the same defect.

THE PORTRAIT OF NAPOLEON

Napoleon is not portrayed as the course of an amazing life, as contact with mighty events *made* him, but as he *was*. Taine knows only one Napoleon. He sees the Emperor implicit in the Corsican boy or in the poor lieutenant

1. SOREL, *Nouveaux essais d'histoire et de critique*, 1898, n. 138.

of the royal army. It is therefore not the Napoleon of any one stage, but the quintessence of Napoleon which he gives us. To what central ideas is this portrait related?

Napoleon, says Taine, is not a Frenchmen of his time. He is a foreigner, an Italian. Here we are reminded of Quinet, but Taine's Italian is of the Renaissance, as it were preserved in isolated Corsica. From this follows his mental attitude ('*l'intelligence*'), his independence of the eighteenth-century French tendency to generalization, his complete indifference to all current theories and principles, and his unfailing and tireless instinct for facts. I must remark here that this interpretation seems even more fantastic to me than Quinet's. Napoleon's brain was brim-full of conventional ideas, among them many that were typical of the French of his day. We have already noticed examples of these in his attitude towards religion, his respect *à la Rousseau* for the established religion of any country, and his general 'philosophical' and Gallican conception of the correct relationship of Church and State. Nevertheless no one has given so telling an account as Taine of the insatiable passion for facts of that extraordinary human mechanism called Napoleon.

Next, Taine describes his character. The Italian Renaissance is again called in to explain the violence of his passions. And this extraordinary mechanism, this emotional violence, are in Taine's view subject to one ruling trait, egoism. This egoism, the tendency to make oneself the centre of things, to recognize no other motive than that of one's own advantage of greatness, was, Taine says, nourished by social conditions in Corsica, where no notion of law or of common interest served to moderate the struggles of the chiefs and their clans. The confusion in France after the upheaval of the Revolution offered just such an arena on a larger scale.

The complete egoist is a solitary being, irrevocably shut off from his fellow men. He is self-insulated against all spontaneous feelings of sympathy, admiration, or pity. That is how Taine paints Napoleon. So intense is his egoism that he is unable to conceive of any other driving force in other men. This great realist is morally blind, and his scorn for men leads him into stupid blunders. High motives lead to independence, and without realizing the cause, he is always impatient of that effect. He surrounds himself with servants instead of collaborators. If someone inclined to independence compromises himself in his service – like Caulaincourt, however innocently, in the Enghien affair – he rejoices at the greater hold over the man this will give him. Napoleon demands the performance of turpitudes: Savary and men of that kidney are his ideal. He can see men only as instruments. He hounds on his ministers, his generals, his officials, even his puppet kings, his brothers, like a slave-driver. His harsh commanding voice easily takes on the accents of brutality, even of a refined cruelty. He wounds, he humiliates, he tries to break spirits.[1] The lot of those nearest to him was far from enviable. Strict etiquette and a tone of eternal constraint prevailed at the court. Everyone trembled before the master, who could not cease, even for one moment, to be a master.

Finally, in a score of pages of irresistible power, Taine links all this up with Napoleon's attitude to the world beyond France. An insatiable thirst for conquest; the fact that compliance and promises never meant anything more than tactics; that for him allies were but instruments of policy to be broken when they had done their service.

As long as his reign lasts there will be war . . . no barrier is sufficient to fence him in, no treaty can bind him. With him peace will never be anything but a truce, he will only make use of it to recover himself, and as soon as he thinks himself recovered, he will begin again; he is in essence anti-social.[2]

One cannot live with him. 'On that matter, Europe's mind is made up, definitive, unshakeable.'

France's interests are not what matter to him. Indeed he takes advantage of her trust to drive her to the abyss. In later days at St Helena, Napoleon sentimentalizes over 'that French people he had loved so much'.[3]

The truth is that he loves it as a horseman loves his horse; all the grooming and smartening up, all the stroking and encouragement, is not for the benefit of the horse, but to prepare it as a useful animal for his service, so that it may fulfil his purposes, even to exhaustion, so that he may force it on over ever wider ditches and ever higher obstacles – come up, now, one more ditch, another wall . . . But after what seemed the last obstacle, there are always new ones to overcome, and in any case the horse always and inevitably remains what it always was, that is, a mount, and an overburdened one . . .

For, says Taine, imagine for a moment that this Russian expedition, instead of turning into a frightful disaster, had been a triumphant success; what would the outlook for France have been then? At best a French European Empire undermined by European resistance: French residents and commanders at St Petersburg and Riga, as at Danzig, Hamburg, Amsterdam, Lisbon, Barcelona, and Trieste; all fit Frenchmen employed, from Cadiz to Moscow, in maintaining and administering the conquest, in hunting down refractory conscripts; no career left save that of policeman or bully, to keep down subjects and to gather in tribute, to seize and to burn merchandise.

1. An example can be found in the correspondence with Louis, previously referred to, p. 63 ff.
2. *Origines de la France contemporaine, Régime moderne*, I, 129.
3. Words from the Emperor's will. The comparison of the rider and the horse which follows is not entirely original; the reader will remember the poem of Barbier; see p. 32.

But these beautiful prospects came to nothing; in 1812 the *Grande Armée* lies prostrate in the snow. The horse has bungled its jump completely. Fortunately it is only a horse ridden to death. 'His Majesty's health has never been better.'[1] The horseman is unharmed, and all he thinks of is not the death struggle of the wretched beast but his own mishap, his damaged reputation as a horseman.

It is the catcalls, it is the comic effect of a *saut périlleux* announced with fanfares by so large an orchestra and ending in so pitiable a fall.

When he reaches Warsaw, he keeps on repeating the phrase: 'There is but one step from the sublime to the ridiculous . . .' And the upshot for France? Not only the collapse of Napoleon's empire, which all things considered was not a French Empire any more; but the loss as well of the conquests of the Republic, the Rhine frontier and Belgium, which had been entrusted to Napoleon in 1799, 'the natural frontiers [to which *we* shall hardly admit France to have so obvious a right, although this is a point on which practically all French writers are in agreement] those too, Napoleon, with his policy inspired by nothing but egoism, has lost for us', so Taine concludes.

THE INSTITUTIONS

The portrait of Napoleon is merely an introduction. The work as a whole is concerned with an analysis of the institutions for which France has to thank Napoleon, though Taine would certainly not have put it in that way; 'the institutions inflicted on France by Napoleon' would be more in accordance with his approach. The general tendency of '*le régime moderne*', as Taine sees it, he describes in his arresting and picturesque manner as follows:

A new France, not the communistic, egalitarian, spartan France fondly imagined by Robespierre and Saint-Just, but a practicable and durable France, the France of reality, yet levelled, made uniform, fitted together according to logic and after a general and simple principle, a centralized and bureaucratic France, which, apart from the petty and individualist activities of private life, was to be set in motion entirely from above; in short, the France which Richelieu and Louis XIV would have wished to bring about, which Mirabeau saw coming already in 1790; there you have the creation which the practice and theory of both the monarchy and the Revolution had prepared, and for the achievement of which the ultimate concourse of events, I mean the alliance of philosophy and of the sword, made ready the First Consul's sovereign hands.

Nor could he, with his character as we know it, with the quickness, the activity, the range, the comprehensiveness, and the style of his intelligence, have willed any

1. The famous closing sentence of the bulletin in which the disaster was at last announced.

other construction or have been satisfied with a lesser. His itch to administer and to manage was too great, his capacity for it was too great; his genius swallowed everything up. Moreover, for the external task that he took upon himself he needed internally not only the undisputed possession of all executive and legislative power, but more than that, the annihilation of all moral authority other than his own, that is to say, public opinion silenced and every individual isolated; and consequently the systematic destruction, in advance, of all initiative, be it religious, ecclesiastic, educational, charitable, or literary, departmental or municipal, which in the present or in the future might group men against or even by his side. As a good general, he covers his rear; in his struggle with Europe he sees to it that, in this France which he drags along with him, the recalcitrant souls or minds shall not be able to come together . . . The end of every thread which might draw together a number of men for the same objects is in his hands; he keeps a firm hold on all these threads together, guards them jealously, that he may pull them as taut as possible. Let no one be bold enough to try and slacken them, above all let no one attempt to seize them; they are his, his only, they constitute the public domain, *his* domain.

Even so the ruler admits the existence of a carefully defined territory within which, for all his power, he does not enter. Taine hastens to add that here too Napoleon is only acting from an enlightened sense of self-interest. He was realist enough to take the men of his day, the products of a civilized epoch with a long tradition of law, as they were. And it was in order to make them the more ready to work for his aims that he guaranteed them the free and untrammelled enjoyment of their own little plot, their property, for that is what is meant. I remark in passing that on this point considerations which did not occur to Taine are bound to present themselves to the modern reader. In the first place he did not foresee that rulers might arise who would violate this frontier too. In the second place this self-control, whatever its motives, is regarded by Taine as an undoubted boon, so great in his day was the domination still exercised by liberal economy over men's minds. At the present time many observers will inevitably consider this respect for private property a characteristic through which Napoleon ranges himself on the bourgeois, or even the reactionary, the anti-social, side of the Revolution.

However much one may wish to criticize Taine's view, the pages which I have quoted form the starting-point of bold and penetrating speculations concerning Napoleonic institutions. Their sombre tone may perhaps find more echo among our own contemporaries than among the author's, though doubts had already begun to make breaches in nineteenth-century optimism. In any case the shattering of individuality and of group, the uprooting of local government, the destruction of all initiative and all conviction in political matters – these constitute for Taine the distinguishing features. When he compares the work of Napoleon with that of

Diocletian and Constantine, without suggesting, as does Quinet, that their spirit was still working in the Italian blood of the Corsican, it is in order to note that in their day, too, human material was smashed to make that classically simple and symmetrical structure. I shall not follow him further in these considerations, and I shall merely note that he does not deny Napoleon's work all merit. Order was restored, the bureaucratic machine itself became a model of tidiness, regularity, and equipoise. The incidence of taxation was regulated most excellently and the principle of opportunity for all – *la carrière ouverte à tous* – had a stimulating effect. But the driving force that was continually brought into play was the purely personal one of competition, while all direction came from above.

After having discussed Napoleonic institutions in general, Taine planned to show how various departments of life fared under the régime. He was able to finish only two chapters, which together make one volume, on the Church and on the schools. Remembering d'Haussonville's book, it will be readily understood that Taine found the Church a rewarding subject. I shall confine myself to discussing something of what he has to say about the schools under Napoleon.

EDUCATION

What is the aim Napoleon sets himself in his educational policy? He indicates it himself: 'My chief aim is to have a means whereby a lead may be given to political and moral conceptions.'[1] Quite agreeable to his way of thinking, then, is this statement of advantages of uniformity as set forth by a minister to the *Corps Législatif*:

Education must impart the same knowledge and the same principles to all individuals living in the same society, so that they will make as it were one body, informed with one and the same understanding and working for the common good on the basis of uniformity of views and desires.

This then was the purpose to be served by the monopoly accorded to the Imperial University. This University is in no sense to be regarded as a college; it is the organized totality of public education in France. This powerful body acquires more and more privileges, so that private education may be crushed out of existence. Heavy pressure indeed is needed, for parents do not much care for the new imperial *lycées*. They are too militaristic for their taste, there is a barracks atmosphere about them. Parents prefer to send their children to the private schools which try to maintain themselves against the tide of State education. This is made more and more difficult. Not only does the State make life impossible for the private school, but it frequently seizes upon the children too. In 1808 the

1. In the Council of State, 1806; TAINE, *Origines*, VI, 157.

Emperor had a list drawn up of old and rich families throughout the country who must send their sons to St Cyr. In 1813 a similar measure was drawn up on a wider scale. This was the institution of the *garde d'honneur*, which aroused such perturbation in Holland, and the object of which in France also was to force the notables to offer up their sons to Moloch.

To get the type of education at which he aimed, Napoleon wanted to train a body of teachers who would be filled from youth onwards with the spirit of obedience and sacrifice to the Empire. He thought with a certain envy of the Jesuits. Naturally he could not use them, and distrusted them as servants of Rome, but his ideal would have been 'a corporation, not of Jesuits whose sovereign resided in Rome, but of Jesuits who had no other ambition than to be useful, no other interest than the public interest'.[1] The *École Normale* would have to supply the need. Napoleon had his ideas concerning the syllabus and the kind of literature which should be read. He frowned upon the use of books such as Montesquieu's *Dialogue de Sylla et d'Eucrate*, Thomas's *Éloge de Marc Aurèle*, or the *Annals* of Tacitus. Such reading smacked of republicanism and stimulated the readers to independent judgement and to criticism.

Let youth rather read Caesar's *Commentaries* . . . Corneille [the supreme example of classicism in the drama, and the eulogist of will-power and unhesitating fulfilment of duty], Bossuet [the preacher of unity and obedience, to whom Napoleon was especially drawn, as we have seen, because of his Gallican ideas, and his ecclesiastical support for Louis XIV's state ambitions]; these are the masters they need, for they navigate with the sails of obedience set in the established order of their period; they strengthen it, they adorn it.

Among the 'fundamentals of education' Napoleon included 'the precepts of the Catholic religion' (see p. 165.) Taine does not omit to point out that in doing so he was in no way governed by disinterested conviction. He wanted to obtain the sympathy of the clergy, but took good care at the same time that religion did not spoil his officials, his officers, or even his subjects. As he explained in 1806 in the Council of State: 'The end to aim at is that the young people should grow up neither too devout nor too sceptical; they should be made to fit the state of the nation and of society.'

Let me remark here that judgement on sayings such as this depends entirely on the general outlook of the historian. Thiers too quotes similar utterances of Napoleon. On one occasion, for example, during the establishment of schools for children of necessitous members of the Legion of Honour, the Emperor declared[2] that religious instruction was only of secondary importance for boys, though in the case of girls 'a solid piety' was the first consideration.

1. TAINE, VI, 170.   2. THIERS, II.

Make of them women who believe and do not argue. The weakness of the female intellect, the volatility of their ideas, their appointed lot in society, the necessity of promoting in them, together with a constant resignation, a tender and yielding charity, all this makes the yoke of religion indispensable for them.

Thiers is not in the least shocked by this view of the usefulness of religion in relation to social needs, and these very one-sidedly estimated at that. At least he makes no comment on it.[1]

Taine continues with his description of the schools, and expatiates upon the strict discipline and mechanical regulation of life in the *lycées*. These boarding-schools were 'ante-rooms to the barracks', and the militaristic tone which reigned there was far from popular. Nevertheless the education given stamped their pupils' minds for life. Systematized competition as an incentive was taken over from the Jesuits. Prize-givings, which were turned into grandiose and theatrical performances, went with this. Loyalty to the Emperor, admiration for his military prowess, ambition to share that glory – such were the virtues that were fostered above all others. The presence everywhere of imperial scholars, sons of officers and officials, who owed all to the imperial favour and whose future fortunes depended on it, did much to secure the dominance of this spirit in the schools. The blind submission and enthusiasm of these boys set the tone. But everything was arranged to maintain it at that pitch. Reports of victories were read aloud and commented upon. Essays dealing with the latest triumph received the prizes.

In this teaching [Taine concludes] literature and science are of secondary importance. What matters is the training, an early, methodical, continuous, irresistible training which through the concentration of all means – lesson, example, and practice – inculcates *the principles* and permeates the youthful souls for good and all with the *national doctrine*, a kind of social and political catechism, the first article of which enjoins fanatical subjection, passionate devotion, and complete surrender of self to the Emperor.

THE CRITICISM OF PRINCE NAPOLEON; MME DE RÉMUSAT

Lanfrey's book was already almost forgotten.[2] Taine's work, so much more powerful in its brevity – I am thinking now of the portrait of Napoleon, the publication of which in the *Revue des Deux Mondes* (February–March 1887)

1. Thiers, who was not shocked by a purely social valuation of religion, also admired the rigid organization of education under the *Université*. Of all Napoleon's creations, he thought it 'perhaps the most beautiful': II, 132b.
2. At any rate among the general public, though it has always found interested and grateful readers, and still does.

preceded the main work by a year or two, and which certainly has since found twenty readers for one who was willing to wrestle with the institutions, the schools, and the churches – this study, which was not merely destructive but which within the temple of Napoleon worship unveiled an idol of monstrous aspect, caused a tremendous sensation. It was not to be expected that it would tempt the faithful to apostasy. The French people had fed their pride too long on that wonderful epic, had been too ready to admire their own greatness and energy in the conquests and the expansion of revolutionary principles, to allow their Napoleon to be taken away from them. Thus the horse attaches itself to the most exciting rider.

But indeed it was only too easy to point out exaggerations and weaknesses in the portrait. The first who did this, and it must be admitted with much perspicacity, was Prince Napoleon, who had 'edited' his uncle's correspondence (see p. 71) with so disconcerting a mixture of frankness and clumsiness. I shall discuss his book, *Napoléon et ses détracteurs*, which appeared in 1887, at a later stage; here I want to deal only with his criticism of Taine.

His general characterization of the great writer as a man without style who could present us with a string of notes from his card index, like an entomologist with a purely microscopic vision who failed to see the broad lines and was blind to moral values, is so obviously a caricature born from indignation – though certain traits of the original are indeed recognizable – that we might seriously ask ourselves whether this passionate Bonaparte was equipped to give a judgement on moral conceptions. But his actual criticism is much to the point. Let us ignore a number of errors due to negligence, which he lists, and merely mention in passing that a passage in the *Revue des Deux Mondes*, in which Taine, carried away by his comparison of Napoleon with the Italians of the Renaissance, and in particular with the Borgias, boldly asserted that the Corsican had seduced all three of his sisters – a story often whispered – is not reprinted in the book. I shall confine my remarks to the main charge that Taine was in general too much inclined to rely on memoirs, and preferably those of hostile writers, and that he failed to subject these sources to a much needed criticism.

That criticism Prince Napoleon proceeds to give. One after another Metternich, Bourrienne, Mme de Rémusat, l'abbé de Pradt, Miot de Mélito, are considered. Metternich's was a special case. The others had this much in common, that they had served Napoleon when he was in power and uttered their destructive or hostile criticism only after his fall. The apologist who attempts to discredit witnesses for the prosecution on this ground alone – that of inconsistency, ingratitude, and treachery – will not readily receive support from the historian. He is more likely to have his way with the general public, which is liable to be moved by nationalistic or political passions. In France, any reminder of the humiliating circumstances to which the régime which succeeded Napoleon owed its existence – the defeat, and the patronage of foreign conquerors – never failed to touch a chord. So did any representation of Napoleon symbolizing in his downfall the fate of the fatherland. Prince Napoleon certainly does not disdain to use these themes in a demagogic manner, but he also has arguments which cannot but impress a cooler critical judgement. I shall deal here only with the case of Mme de Rémusat. It is undeniable that her memoirs, which were published only in 1880, had strongly coloured Taine's view of the personality of Napoleon.

Mme de Rémusat had come as a young married woman to the court of Joséphine, then still wife of the First Consul. Her husband accepted a post as *préfet du palais*. They were aristocrats, not of the highest rank but authentically of the *ancien régime*, people such as Bonaparte thought he should have about him in his rising fortunes. They had been among the first to 'rally' to his side, in the golden spring of the Consulate, and Mme de Rémusat had begun with genuine admiration and enthusiasm. The memoirs describe her disillusionment. The book is certainly among the most fascinating written about Napoleon by contemporaries. The writer gives the impression of being a serious-minded, highly-cultured woman. She had an eye for the colourful event, and could tell an amusing incident with the best, but what sets her apart from most writers of memoirs is her judgement, and the independence with which she seems to have maintained her own standards against Napoleon. Her attitude is not purely individualistic, and it is not simply a question of an over-sensitive ego, as in the case of Chateaubriand. She represents a definite tendency, she is spiritually akin to Mme de Staël. In this connexion it is significant that her son, and later also her grandson, under the Restoration and the Second Empire, became important figures in French liberalism, which was then intellectually rather than politically influential.

The picture she gives of Napoleon tallies to an extraordinary degree with that of Mme de Staël. That he was completely heartless, without any spontaneous human feeling, without any generosity, nothing but self-love, and accomplishing all his works in a whirl of egoism or of crafty calculation – all this one can read in Mme de Rémusat, and of course one is reminded of Taine's portrait also. So conscious was Napoleon of these qualities in himself that he measured all others by the same standard, thus committing the gravest psychological errors. He was quite unable to believe in disinterested charitable actions. If he was forced to admit their existence, he only despised the doer, doubly despised him, for he started with a low opinion of mankind in general, and in particular of the French, among whom he still felt himself a stranger, though he tried to conceal it. Mme de Rémusat believed that she had seen him descend to these depths by slow degrees, or rather the Enghien crime had accelerated the process, making him lose all respect for moral values and all sense of moderation. She and her husband, she tells us, belonged to the secret opposition which had Talleyrand for its centre and longed for the return of the Bourbons and freedom.

Prince Napoleon's most telling charge against the reliability of Mme de Rémusat is that her later memoirs contradict her letters of the time. What admiration and enthusiasm she was still expressing for Napoleon and his victories, Napoleon and his gracious ways – at a time when according to the memoirs she already saw him as the conqueror run mad, as the heartless robot.

When exactly were these memoirs written? In 1818, to take the place of a previous version, which had been burned by the writer for security's sake during the Hundred Days. According to her son's introduction, occasion was given by the appearance of Mme de Staël's *Considérations*, containing a study of Napoleon with which Mme de Rémusat felt herself in general accord but which she wished to check by her own reminiscences, particularly as she was conscious of having at one time had other opinions of him. I have already remarked on the kinship between Mme de Rémusat's account and that of Mme de Staël. It gives a slight but salutary shock to be reminded that the former was not written absolutely independently of the latter. Prince Napoleon suggests an even more unpleasant possibility. Had the writer, in presenting matters as she does, some special object or interest in view?

At the moment of the first abdication, in 1814, when Chateaubriand's pamphlet appeared, and her son – brought up in the customary adoration of the Emperor – expressed great indignation at it, Mme de Rémusat gave him a lesson in worldly wisdom which, though delicately expressed, makes one wonder whether when everyday problems arose she did not exchange her high moral standards for more practical ones.

Mr de Chateaubriand's book is not a pamphlet. I could put my hand to each of his pages . . . We shall explain to you how we, respecting your tender years, took care to shield your eyes from a thousand matters which it was better for you not to know. Destined as you were to enter his service, you had to be fed on illusions respecting him. For the last three months [compared with the memoirs, this period must indeed be accounted short] your father and I have anxiously been looking for a change such as is now impending . . . Do not forget at this juncture to draw upon yourself the good regard of the public.[1]

THE MOST IMPORTANT PART OF THE WORK UNTOUCHED

How far the testimony of the memoirs is weakened by these letters I do not intend to assess, nor shall I attempt to judge how far Taine's portrait would be

1. *Napoléon et ses détracteurs*, 108.

affected by being deprived of those touches which were contributed from the memoirs. It is clear that there is a problem here which Taine, with his customary assurance, did not recognize, and not only in the case of Mme de Rémusat's memoirs.

I should add, however, that the criticism levelled at Taine for excessive and uncritical use of memoirs does not hold good for the most important part (in content and range) of his work, the brilliant study of the institutions of the Consul and Emperor. Naturally he uses memoirs here too, but the names of Mme de Staël, Miot, Bourrienne, and Mme de Rémusat will hardly be found any more, and generally speaking the quotations given are of a kind less liable to objections. Moreover, much use is made of official documents, of the *Moniteur*, and of Napoleon's correspondence.

However this may be, Taine's description of Napoleon was very far from henceforth dominating French historical literature.

Part 4

Admirers

The Political and Intellectual Background

TAINE'S book, one might almost say, was the starting-point for the best in Napoleonic literature which accepted and eulogized Napoleon. I would not go so far as to assert *propter hoc*, but the *post hoc* is undeniable. It was only now that the real stream of studies, monographs, serious histories of this or that aspect made their appearance. They were much more thorough than previous works, and were based upon the archive material which was slowly being brought to light. And most of this new output was favourable to Napoleon.

There is indeed something symptomatic about this trend, and the question arises whether it can again be explained by the circumstances of the day. The answer must undoubtedly be in the affirmative, but not every admirer of Napoleon should be labelled Bonapartist. After Napoleon III's fall, Bonapartism possessed little weight as a party with pretensions to an imperial restoration. The humiliating memory of 1870 was an unsurmountable obstacle. In 1879 a further blow was dealt the cause by the miserable death of the young former Prince Imperial in South Africa. This was followed by paralysing divisions in the party. Bonapartism was still affected by the cleavage which had characterized the career of the great Napoleon. There was the radical tendency, to which the Napoleonic legend had from the first given prominence, harking back to the Revolution, anti-clerical and almost republican. But there was also a conservative tendency, to which Napoleon III had most closely adhered, though not without contradictions and hesitations. His *coup d'état* of 1851 had cast him for the role of 'saviour of society', like the First Consul in Year VIII. And just as the latter had seen in the Catholic Church a useful basis for his power, so did Napoleon III rely on the clergy, and this without relapsing into those conflicts to which his great forebear had owed the support of the anti-clericals.

Yet, divided though it was, and played out in the realm of practical politics, in one respect Bonapartism still showed its unity and reflected a trend existing among large sections of the French people. Whether radical or conservative, whether on the side of the workers or of the capitalists, whether anti-clerical or clerical, it was filled with suspicion, contempt, and hostility towards parliamentarianism and towards that liberalism and intellectualism with which this had its closest associations. These were the forces on which the Third Republic had to rely, but they did not show to the best advantage in its service, nor did the régime succeed in winning for them universal respect. Many who would certainly not have called themselves Bonapartists were sufficiently antagonized to become conscious of a sense of kinship with the Consul-Emperor.

This was aggravated by a feeling of discomfort in wider intellectual spheres. There was a sharp reaction against the high expectations held in the third quarter of the century with regard to science, and against the exclusive domination of the analytical spirit and of reason. Youth turned away from the spiritual leadership of Renan and Taine, and even Zola had already passed the zenith of his influence. But to explain the readiness of the public to accept the Napoleonic legend, we must point to political events before everything else.

People were smarting from 1870, and it seemed to many as if this peaceful bourgeois government was taking that disgrace lying down. How strong this impatience was appeared in 1888, with the senseless adventure of Boulanger, the general and Minister of War, who had little to commend him save his easy eloquence and his handsome charger, but who stirred up ideas of *revanche* and thus for a moment endangered the existence of the Republic. It appeared possible to arouse elemental feelings of scorn and contempt against the parliamentary régime. In the case of some, anti-German feelings were offset by Anglophobia. Colonial expansion, that dominating feature of French history after 1870, brought about much friction with the leading colonial power. In the nineties, the Fashoda incident nearly led to war. It is true that at the same time it was argued vehemently that overseas interests must never be allowed to wipe out the painful memory of the loss of the Rhine. And in any case, the anti-British tendency gave rise to a sense of kinship with the man who had hated *la perfide Albion* so bitterly. There was so close a connexion in the French mind between Britain and parliamentarianism, Britain and liberalism, that in moments of tension these great conceptions appeared almost un-French, and Napoleon the autocrat was instinctively seen as a patriot.

THE DREYFUS AFFAIR

Then there came the Panama scandal, which poured discredit in large doses on both Parliament and the Republic. Hard on its heels came the Dreyfus affair. At first it threatened to raise the army into an independent force, as the only true exponent of the State, on a wave of anti-semitic and chauvinist passion, supported by every conservative and reactionary interest, drowning parliament, free speech, justice, and reason. But the forces of the mind, armed with the best traditions of French civilization, put up a brave defence, and after a struggle which will always be among the finest episodes in French history, the Dreyfus affair ended in a severe defeat for fascist tendencies – if I may use this word *avant la lettre* – in French intellectual and political life.

All this had a direct effect on the view taken of Napoleon. It must of course not be imagined that all the defenders of the innocent but condemned Dreyfus were hostile to the historic figure of the Emperor, or vice versa, although at first glance this oversimplification seems not untenable. In any case the mental attitude which was suspicious of all analysis and inquiry – especially when the hero of Austerlitz, the martyr of St Helena, was the object – which accepted the legend as worthy of veneration, which preferred to deal in such categories as patriotism versus defeatism, the true Frenchman versus the servant of the enemy, of the hate-ridden envious outside world, the servile imitator of British politics and culture (a hit at all liberalism this – Mme de Staël, Quinet, Taine, were always citing the example of Britain): this mental attitude came into its own with the agitation against the Jewish 'traitor'. When Dreyfus was found to be innocent, there was a collapse. The masses reflected this, however; and through them political life. The Republic was now based on firm foundations. But as far as cultural life was concerned, the victory of justice and common sense was not so fruitful. In particular many of the intellectual leaders who had risen in support of the army's honour, as though it would have been damaged by the reversal of an unjust sentence, kept their minds obstinately shut to evidence, and the mental mood which had given rise to the tragic mistake was proudly carried into the new century. Maurice Barrès remained more of a leading figure in literary circles than Anatole France, who, sceptic though he was, had seen where justice lay in the Dreyfus affair.

MAURICE BARRÈS

In 1899 Maurice Barrès had written from Rennes some sensational articles on the re-trial, in one of which, after his own fashion, he had given a sketch of the noble figure of Colonel Picquart, the officer who had dared to break right through the officers' plot. Of this article he says in his memoirs that his mother took it and read it by the grave of his father. 'And therefore', a French literary historian says sarcastically, 'the *bordereau* was indeed by Dreyfus.' Barrès also wrote in his memoirs:

I have never felt the need of any other ideas than those in which I was soaked from birth onwards. Thanks to them I have always had a perfect knowledge of what was truth.

The same literary historian quoted above, having contrasted Anatole France's relative loneliness with Barrès's circle of kindred spirits, also states:

The basis of objective truth, on which the intellectuals of 1897 triumphed juridically, morally, and politically, has therefore proved, from the literary point of view, an ungrateful ground compared with the basis of organic, inherited, passionate truth.[1]

In 1897, when Barrès was thirty-six years old, his famous novel *Les déracinés* appeared, the first part of a trilogy, *Le Roman de l'Énergie nationale*, in which he proposed giving a sociological study of French youth, for whom at the same time he developed a social philosophy. The figure of Napoleon is given the central place in the first volume. Barrès's young people, burning with desire to do something, to place their lives in the service of a purpose, visit the tomb in *Les Invalides*, to receive inspiration from Napoleon. They do not seek out the Napoleons of history, nor do they attempt to choose between them, for

they have disentangled from among them *the Napoleon of the soul*. Without any social or moral preconceptions, without weighing the benefits of his wars or the worth of his governmental despotism, in all simplicity, they love Bonaparte.

And indeed, the author speculates, what was Napoleon's profoundest capacity? He has stated it himself: 'As for me, I had the gift of electrifying men.' His enduring significance, so Barrès concludes a rhetorical passage which I shall spare the reader, will for ever remain: 'NAPOLEON TEACHER OF ENERGY.' Even today, 'his touch still has the power to enlarge the soul'. Nor is the character made up merely of what Napoleon Bonaparte was in his lifetime: all that has since been said or sung by the admirers and the poets, the great man's voices, has made it expand in the world of imagination, and the lads who are now meeting round his tomb add their tribute of sound to that triumphant symphony of the still lengthening cortège of Caesar.

There is no need to quote further. It is obvious that Barrès is purely pragmatic in his view of the Napoleon figure. What does he care for this or that interpretation of the wars or of the centralized administration, or for moral or social 'preconceptions'? The great Napoleon is what he wants, his greatness still increased by tradition and legend, to provide inspiration for youth, to spur them on, to give them courage to perform great deeds and make great sacrifices. Barrès was a disciple of Taine, and in many respects continued to venerate him. In Taine's writings, too, can be found this idea of the value of tradition, of what is a nation's own, the respect for what has grown. But in resolutely putting those values above morality and truth, Barrès was joining the reaction against Taine, as is conclusively proved by his glorification of Napoleon. Resulting from a combination of political and spiritual factors, it is typical of the period. That is why I have included it in my introduction to the historical glorification of Napoleon.

I intend to illustrate this historical glorification from the works of four writers, but first I must pause to consider the curious figure of Prince Napoleon.

1. A. THIBAUDET, *Histoire de la littérature française de 1789 à nos jours* (1936), pp. 413, 420.

I Prince Napoleon

POLITICAL CONCEPTIONS

PRINCE NAPOLEON, son of Jérôme (the king for a day of the shadowy King-dom of Westphalia), was sixty-five years old when he took up his pen to refute Taine. He was an excitable and crotchety but by no means insignificant figure. Robust, dark, with aquiline nose and flashing eyes, he seemed when the Second Empire crumbled the epitome of vital will-power as compared with the ailing, disheartened, and vacillating Napoleon III.[1] He had played a political role under his cousin, if only that of an impotent grumbler. Against Eugénie's aggressive conservatism and clericalism, he had been the spokesman at court of a popular anti-clerical tendency, the opponent of the attempt to preserve the favour of French Catholics by bolstering up the temporal power of the Pope in his last bastion and thus raise a barrier against Italian unity. He was a representative of the Napoleonic legend in its most radical version.[2]

The historic figure of Napoleon, which he defended with such asperity against its traducers, had for him a profound significance, not only, as he was wholly convinced, for his own personal life but for that fatherland which had banished him after his family's second downfall. 'To defend Napoleon's memory is still to serve France', he declared. As to the principles which Napoleon bequeathed to posterity, he believes that only these can solve the problem of the coexistence of democracy with a strong authority.

Executive authority springing from a direct, particular, and separate mandate, legislative power confined within the sphere of deliberation and supervision. Our parliamentary régime, which is becoming impracticable, if only as a result of the multiple divisions of public opinion, is condemned by all far-seeing minds. We are faced with this alternative; either the country will be subjected to the dictator-ship of an assembly, or it will return to the true conception of democratic and representative government.

1. cf. P. DE LA GORCE, *Histoire du Second Empire*, VII, 164; G. HANOTAUX, *Histoire de la France contemporaine*, IV, 472; the same work, I, 488: 'Le prince était un homme de haute valeur intellectuelle, ambitieux, intempérant, plus embarrassant peut-être pour les siens que pour ses adversaires.'

2. 'N'oubliant pas [writes Hanotaux] les origines révolutionnaires, il avait recueilli, dans l'héritage des Bonaparte, la thèse républicaine, populaire, et plébiscitaire.'

PRINCE NAPOLEON AND HISTORY

Given this attitude, how does he view the history of his famous uncle? We have already seen how his work as editor of the correspondence had been influenced by it. He defends himself against the attacks which he had to endure on that score, though without adding any new arguments. His argument that the publication on such a scale of the whole political correspondence of so recent and hotly debated a figure was in itself an unusual and a courageous action, has some force. A Dutch historian, remembering what has happened to other royal and non-royal archives, cannot venture to reproach the Prince and his principal Napoleon III too sternly for having omitted a small part of the correspondence, from a number of considerations of tact and prudence.

On all points Prince Napoleon is ready to defend the great Consul-Emperor. Throughout he sees him as the man of the people, the man of the Revolution, and if he grew too authoritarian during the period of the Empire, it was only under the compulsion of the wars which the rulers inflicted upon him out of their hatred for young, dynamic, and promising France. In the end, during the Hundred Days, he was able for once to show himself in his true colours, though it was a pity, says the writer, permitting himself a faintly critical note, that with his new Chamber he followed the British system, instead of 'developing consular institutions to their full possibilities of representation'.[1] But on St Helena his radiant wisdom at last appears to the full.

There he prophesies the future, and he, the captive of kings, forces them to hearken to his lessons. Freedom dawns in his spirit, as the necessary shape of the new society. He foresees the republic as democracy's own form of government.

But although this final wisdom had only been revealed to Napoleon on St Helena, his nephew is not less ready to defend everything, literally everything, he had done before attaining this state of grace. Take the case of Bayonne. How could the Emperor, faced with that spectacle of baseness and folly, stand aside and leave Spain to the British? And if he came up against Spanish resistance he did arouse national consciousness, there as in Italy and in Germany. Even though it was aroused against him, it was he who had awakened it, and to him the nations owed their liberty. Or take the treatment of the Pope, and the scene against Portalis. Without hesitation Prince Napoleon approves of it all. In his eagerness, he leaves out that half of the story which might excuse Portalis; but the canon who had received the Pope's letter was a 'fanatical priest'. With regard to the failure to

1. An example of how the antithesis French-British was equated with the antithesis authoritarian-liberal; see p. 144 ff.

secure peace in the summer of 1813 at Prague, he here presents Metternich in the role of criminal. The plot to truncate France existed already, in spite of all the fine phrases. (We shall be hearing more of this.) So Napoleon was above all the hero whose strong arm defended France. Hero he remained to the very end.

Weariness invades the hearts of his generals. He alone, who carries within him the destiny of France, struggles to the last.

Prince Napoleon's popular and plebiscitary Caesarism, which sometimes approached out-and-out republicanism – were not the republicans among the most ardent disciples of the Napoleonic legend? – included a strain of intense and chauvinistic patriotism, vainglorious, sabre-rattling. Taine had said hardly anything about Napoleon's battles. And yet, writes Prince Napoleon –

Arcole, Rivoli, Marengo, Austerlitz, Jena, Friedland, Montmirail, these victories of which we can see the names inscribed on our banners, remain to us [he means after our defeat of 1870] as an inexhaustible treasure of glory and honour, as an intangible inheritance, which will enable us to recover all that we lost [Alsace and Lorraine] . . . These are the memories which constitute the soul of a people. M. Taine speaks with the true sceptic's contempt of 'those poor trusting and gullible Gauls' [the French who threw themselves into the arms of Napoleon]. Indeed, to them Napoleon gave the most precious of gifts: self-respect, confidence in their own work, the fame of a limitless courage and of an immeasurable energy. In the passing days of our misfortune [before long *la revanche* !] the value of those priceless boons is felt more deeply than ever. The glory of Napoleon is a national possession: whoever touches it defaces the nation itself.

It may be said, all this is no longer history. But among the historians I shall be discussing next, and not only among the first four, these same ideas and emotions may be detected, not so fervently expressed, and barely emerging from a more sober historical context, but even so the driving force of historical imagination and reconstruction.

2 Henry Houssaye

HENRY HOUSSAYE'S *1814* appeared in 1888. The book had an amazing success, and brought its author into the Academy. (I must remark in passing that from that day to this the writer who was or is pro-Napoleon has had a much better chance of becoming a member of that illustrious company than one who had or has indulged in criticism. Besides Houssaye there are Vandal, Sorel, Masson, Madelin, Bainville, among those with whom I am concerned.) Houssaye, who had previously devoted himself to Greek history, continued to exploit his new mine, and followed up the weighty volume on 1814 with three weighty volumes on 1815. The last of these appeared in 1905.

1814 gives a very detailed account of the events of that year, the campaign in France, the abdication at Fontainebleau. The writer does not enter into discussions as to intentions and responsibilities. With all the greater assurance does he distribute blows and favours. The previous events which had landed France and Napoleon in that tragic situation he brushes aside in his introduction, with a remark supposed to have been made by a peasant: 'It is no longer a question of Bonaparte. Our soil is invaded. Let us go and fight.' From this reasoning – or refusal to reason – follows naturally the thesis of complete solidarity between France and Napoleon. It leads the writer to take up a position of fierce hatred against all those who thought that in this crisis France could be saved at the cost of Napoleon. When finally, after miracles of leadership and energy, Napoleon's resistance against the allied armies is beginning to collapse, he appears at Fontainebleau (Paris is in the enemies' hands) as the true hero of tragedy, abandoned by cowards, and Marmont, the marshal whose defection forces him in the end to abdication, is the traitor. We already know this interpretation, from Thiers.[1] With what vehemence does Houssaye's clear-cut account, for all its constant matter-of-factness, drive it home!

The villains of 1814 are Talleyrand and Marmont (the Prince of Benevento and the Duke of Ragusa). Houssaye considers the sole motive of the marshal to be 'vanity'[2]: he succumbed to the appeals that were addressed to him to raise

1. cf. above, p. 65.

2. *1814*, p. 593: 'Marmont trahit – car livrer à l'ennemi une position et un corps d'armée s'appelle trahir – uniquement par vanité, par la vanité de jouer un grand rôle glorieux.' (See above, p. 65, n. 1.)

France out of the depths. He was flattered that it was to him that men turned. He already saw himself as a second General Monk (at Charles II's Restoration in 1660), receiving Louis XVIII and making a name for himself in history. Nor is Talleyrand any better. He is nothing but an intriguer and a self-seeker. Houssaye scornfully describes the log-rolling and wire-pulling, the whispering and scurrying, going on in those Parisian circles which had for so long (certainly since 1807, and more or less enthusiastically according to circumstances) indulged in Frondist activities. These were the circles of the aristocracy, recently and in many cases only apparently 'rallied', with ramifications among the Emperor's higher officialdom. Houssaye scoffs at the ca' canny liberals; the royalists were at least active. The most cunning, and the most careful, was Talleyrand. What was he after? Not a restoration of the Bourbons, on whom he could not rely for his own future and who could not in any case give him more than a premiership. His dream was a Regency Council for the King of Rome, of which he would be the President, and for fifteen years . . . But Napoleon had to be got out of the way first. If only he would get himself killed in action! If necessary there were other methods, and Talleyrand did not shrink from them. This model of 'perfidy', writes Houssaye, was no more fastidious than the allied rulers.

Talleyrand was certainly used to treading labyrinths. In his career as Minister of Foreign Affairs, he had not forgotten his own interests, and his fortune was mostly built up in the years after the peace of Lunéville, when the German princes scrambled after secularizations of Church property, and used to come to Paris to obtain – or to buy – the necessary authorization. But does he therefore deserve to be accused of basing his actions after 1814 solely on personal motives? No better treatment can be expected from a writer whose mind is hermetically sealed against the idea of a distinction being made between Napoleon and France. But is this idea so foolish? We have already encountered it a number of times, as entertained by men of some account. It was not surprising if in 1814, all of a sudden, it became a matter of practical politics. Houssaye does not discuss the matter. Yet in order to persuade the well-informed reader, he ought first to have disposed of the theory, which is on the face of it only too acceptable, that Napoleon's mad lust for power, his overweening pride, had led to this catastrophe. He ought to have refuted the thesis – denied, as we saw, by Prince Napoleon[1] – that Napoleon could still have obtained peace in the summer of 1813 at Prague on reasonable terms, but had thrown away that chance; that even in the spring of 1814, as long as he saw the ghost of a chance that the fortunes of war might yet turn, he went on putting difficulties in the way of the eleventh-hour negotiations undertaken by the unfortunate Caulaincourt, his Minister of Foreign Affairs, and that he had thus brought upon himself the suspicion of the allies. Must

1. We shall meet more discussion of this matter; cf. SOREL, p. 266.

France meekly suffer his moods, and pay the price in the end? If Talleyrand thought otherwise, and saw a chance to come to an agreement with the allies without Napoleon, if necessary against Napoleon, that was surely not a policy to be set aside as treacherous, cowardly, interested, or false. Talleyrand's policy has its own relative justification, and at least deserves serious consideration. When I go more deeply into the problem of Napoleon's foreign policy in the next section, the problem of Talleyrand will inevitably crop up again. He had his own well-thought-out system, to which he tenaciously adhered even though his actions were not always in conformity with it. But generally French historians are little inclined to praise Talleyrand, least of all Houssaye, who in this connexion too, fails to see beyond the year 1814.

Resistance to the uttermost is the only policy he recognizes in the tragic circumstances of the invasion. He continually emphasizes that the people would have supported such a policy. A defeatist mentality was to be found only among the aristocrats, the well-to-do middle classes, the inteliectuals; and against this the high officials hardly dared to take strong measures, if indeed, like the marshals themselves, they were not tarred with the same brush. Hence those scenes, which so disgusted Houssaye, when the allies entered Paris and while Napoleon was still at Fontainebleau with his army. Cheering crowds flaunting the white of the Bourbons greeted the foreign troops, the statue of Napoleon was pulled down from the triumphal column in the Place Vendôme, and the next day there was a gala performance at the Opéra, with Alexander of Russia and Frederick William of Prussia as the guests of honour, and a packed hall listened excitedly to the hymns specially made for the occasion:

> Long live Alexander
> Long live this King of Kings . . .
>
> Long live William
> And his valiant warriors . . .[1]

Far be it from me to say that I cannot sympathize with the shame and irritation felt by the Frenchman at memories like these. The exhibition was certainly not distinguished by taste. Shame at the scene can, however, be expressed in a variety of ways. Barbier expressed it, as we have seen (p. 32), by passionately cursing Napoleon. Houssaye gives vent to it in a bitter recollection of French peasants driven from their homes by the invader, of French women raped by them, of those who died on the battle-fields of Craonne, la Fère-Champenoise, and so on. We are growing familiar with such contrasts through what we have already seen of French reactions to the Napoleonic drama. But to us, who have seen a similar situation elsewhere develop so differently, other considerations are suggested.

1. p. 504.

How much more intelligible, in view of the Paris scenes, is the consistent distinction made at the peace by the allies between the French people and Napoleon. Talleyrand's policy is explained thereby and to a certain extent justified. But how did it come about that the Napoleonic régime had so loose a hold on the French that it could be thrown off, as it were, in one jerk?

I mentioned in passing the slackness of the high officials, even Savary, Minister of Police, in dealing with the conspiratorial activities of Talleyrand and his colleagues. Houssaye tried to explain this, and in so doing gives one proof that he did not after all confine his view entirely to the year he was describing. Indeed, it goes without saying that no historical presentation can take shape without awareness of the events which have preceded it. I want, at any rate, to draw attention to the fact that Houssaye here seeks an explanation in an error committed by his hero in the past, an error proceeding from a profound instinct in the man – Thiers, too, repeatedly referred to it. With his oppressive and unrelenting supervision, and his demand for complete blind obedience, Napoleon had undermined the initiative of his ministers and servants. Of Joseph – who, driven from Spain, in 1814 was entrusted with a sort of regency – Houssaye says that what will he once possessed had been broken by Napoleon.[1]

But there is another factor of more importance, of which he seems dimly aware; it is indeed implicit in his repeated observation concerning the difference in attitude between the people and the upper middle classes. What was the use to Napoleon of the people's readiness – always supposing it in fact existed, which is a debatable point – when the people had no place in his government and had fallen into a state of complete incapacity under his rule? One of two things would have been necessary, for resistance to the last ditch. Either the lower levels of the nation would have had to be associated with the public interest by a democratic system of government, or (and this was an idea which could hardly occur to the generations before our own) the dictatorial régime would have had to organize the nation as well as the State. At the critical moment for Napoleon's government, however, the defection of the men at the top was sufficient to overthrow the rigidly organized and centralized state structure, while the nation, abandoned to its own devices, looked passively on.

1815: THE SAME PROBLEM ONCE MORE

In 1815 the same problem had to be faced. Napoleon is back. Without meeting resistance anywhere, he has reached Paris, and is Emperor as before. Not quite as before, though; for he is now to be a liberal Emperor, and before departing for the wars he has permitted the election of a parliament. Houssaye admits, like

1. *1814*, p. 415.

Thiers (see p. 66), that in spite of his full realization of the need for peace, Napoleon had inevitably to bring war once more to France. He might promise what he liked, he might even believe his own promises, for war certainly did not suit him at that moment, yet, writes Houssaye,

who is going to believe that he did not cherish the hope that the moment would come when he could tear up the humiliating peace treaty of 1814 with one blow of his sword? He only wanted to win time and choose his hour. It was thus good policy and good strategy to attack him in the midst of his preparations, rather than to wait till he had established his authority and built up his army once more.[1]

Much, indeed, is implied in this admission. But Houssaye does not remain consistent to the view he appears for a moment to hold, and when a volume and a half later he comes to describe the situation after Waterloo, he puts it like this:

The broad masses, with their common sense, realized that the Emperor, even though he might be the occasion *or the pretext* [my italics] of the war, had by no means promoted its outbreak. That formidable and detested war had been willed and made inevitable by Europe ... French pride was revolted by the idea that the powers wanted to impose a government on the people of the Revolution. The more ardently peace was loved, the greater was the bitterness against those who disturbed it with that insolent intention. The peril of a new invasion ranged all hearts on Napoleon's side, for in him men still saw the sword of France.[2]

But though these were the feelings of the majority, they were not, says Houssaye, shared by everyone. There was the small group of royalists; there were the liberals, who were strong among the better classes and who dominated the recently elected Chamber. Among these the old doubts and difficulties stirred again. La Fayette, for example, the hero of 1789, was now a man of importance, and his thoughts were centred on liberty. Indeed, should Napoleon enter upon a desperate struggle for life or death with the invading allies, what would the future be? Probably another defeat and still worse confusion; and even in the event of a triumph, would not the newly acquired constitution founder in its wake? If they supported Napoleon in this gamble, might they not be saddling themselves with another despotism, and start an endless succession of fresh wars and conquests?

It seems to me that the situation made such considerations unavoidable. As for the passion of the crowd, its blindness, its readiness to forget, one might well describe these as weaknesses which the dictator-demagogue is ever wont to abuse. The history of France in the preceding fifteen years seems to prove nothing so strikingly as the fatal attraction exercised on the people by the call to adventure, by the dizzying choice between greatness and downfall, the usual lures offered by conquerors and gamblers; the fatal conjunction, one might say, over the heads of

1. *1815*, I, 446.   2. *1815*, III, 2.

the thinking minority, of Dictator and Demos. But Houssaye will have none of these hairsplittings: he admits nothing but dereliction of duty.

Betrayal, personified for him in the previous year by Talleyrand, is now embodied in Fouché. This ex-terrorist, created Duke of Otranto by Napoleon, and in his element in the Department of Police, was certainly a much less attractive figure. Houssaye ascribes it to his cunning, and particularly to the rumours he spread, against his own better knowledge, about Napoleon's plans to dismiss the Chamber, that this body, in terror, got in first with a demand for abdication. By thus increasing the importance of Fouché's intrigues, the figure of Napoleon is made to stand out still more radiantly.

The Chamber asks me to abdicate [so Napoleon burst out in his ministerial council]. Have the consequences of my doing so been calculated? If I abdicate, you have no longer an army ... Are declarations about rights [of the King of Rome, of the French nation to decide about its own régime], are speeches, likely to prevent a collapse? People are blind to the fact that I am no more than the pretext of the war, which is in reality aimed at France ... By delivering me up, France will be delivering herself up ... I am to be deposed, not for the sake of liberty, but from fear.

This was eloquence, striking and to the point. These were the arguments Napoleon was bound to put forward, and he did it with an incomparable clarity and energy. But the argument cries out for criticism. How much was passed over in silence or twisted! Yet Houssaye's comment is as follows:

These words, whose eloquence was like piercing steel, and burning like a flame, galvanized the ministers ... Fouché became most anxious. 'That devil of a man!' he said a few hours later to a royalist friend, 'he did frighten me, this morning. As I sat listening to him, I believed he was going to start all over again. Happily, one does not start all over again.'[1]

The second abdication, like the first, Houssaye regards as a pitiable spectacle in which true greatness is deserted or assailed by puny beings. He girds at the Chamber for its impudence in asking that the abdication should come speedily. For Napoleon was hesitating; a strange inability to make up his mind had come over him. Was there still a possible way out? Perhaps an alliance with the restless masses – But this would involve giving a free rein to their revolutionary instincts. He shrank from it in the end; out of sincere regard for the interests of his country, says Houssaye. Or was it because he feared that that kind of excitement would be a straw fire, useless for the purpose of carrying on the war? Anyhow, our author

1. *1815*, III, 22.

can only feel bitter scorn for the impatience of the Chamber in the face of the hero wrestling with his fate. [1]

FRANCE 'TORN TO PIECES'

Did the second peace of Paris justify Napoleon's warning that the Allies' animus was directed against France? Certainly many Frenchmen, then and later, believed it. This explains the bitterness with which a man like Houssaye regards the collapse of the united front against the invader. France had to relinquish a number of frontier towns. Landau, Saarlouis, Philippeville, and Marienbourg were the most important, and the total area involved was about 2000 square kilometres. She had to pay reparations of 700 million francs, and was to be occupied for a period of five years (which in fact was reduced to three). She was also made to restore the stolen art treasures which had been left to her in 1814. The Duc de Richelieu, the Prime Minister, signed the treaty with trembling hand, and returned deathly pale to his colleagues, so Houssaye related: 'He burst out "I am dishonoured!"' [2]

When one considers what France had brought upon the world for nearly a generation, and once again after her first defeat, it must be agreed that she was treated very gently and that the allies did indeed stick to their distinction between France and the disturber of the peace to whom she had entrusted herself.

HOUSSAYE'S WORK

These four volumes of Houssaye are nevertheless exceptionally fine books. His method is that of the mosaic maker. From left, from right, from every possible source, memoirs, correspondence, newspapers, often also from unpublished archive material, from police reports to diplomatic documents, he takes quotations, figures, authentic conversations, intimate details, significant incidents, and reports of the state of mind in the army or among the general public. He does not throw his light solely on Napoleon; events in the whole of the country are brought to life. And this, not by means of eloquent phrases or by the display of his own theories and views. Every statement is backed at once by apposite data, if he does not allow it to emerge automatically from the facts. Yet the general effect is not in the least jerky; the work has pace, and remains clear and comprehensible.

I trust, however, that my comments will have been sufficient to dispel the illusions of those who think that such methods would leave a writer little

1. *1815*, III, 55 ff.   2. *1815*, III, 561.

opportunity to infuse historical narrative with his own political beliefs and preferences.[1]

1. Even so sceptical a critic as Anatole France has allowed himself to be taken in. 'M. Henry Houssaye a écrit là, d'un style sobre, une histoire impartiale. Pas de phrases, point de paroles vaines et ornées; partout la vérité des faits et l'éloquence des choses.' *Vie littéraire*, I, 184. France compares the attitude of the French in 1814 with that of their descendants in 1870–71, very much to the disadvantage of the former. In the latter crisis there were no Frenchmen on the side of the enemy; patriotism is now purer, and more proud, a consequence of democracy . . . He has not discerned the ideological element in 1814.

3 Arthur-Lévy

POLEMIC AGAINST TAINE

In 1892 appeared a book which is still popular, Arthur-Lévy's *Napoléon intime*.[1] Unlike Houssaye's volumes, it extends over the whole career and is designedly polemical and defensive. The book exudes a certain charm, yet at the same time it continually provokes the reader. For Arthur-Lévy really goes too far. His Napoleon is amiability itself. If he had a fault, it was that of excessive kindness. So anxious is the writer to depict the humanity, that he overlays the greatness with homely touches – about his relationship with his mother and brothers, with Joséphine, and later even with the Habsburg archduchess. The whole is supported with a wealth of quotations. If the resulting somewhat mawkish picture is laid beside that of Taine, one is inclined to wonder if the two writers are dealing with the same man. The contrast is instructive as to the possibilities of partisan representation open to the historian through selection from superabundant material.

MME DE STAËL AND MME DE RÉMUSAT

The first aim of Arthur-Lévy (whose later work, *Napoléon et la Paix*, equally the antithesis of Taine, I shall discuss further on) was no doubt to refute the representation in the famous 'portrait' of an inhuman, or, if I may so call it, a non-human Napoleon. Like Prince Napoleon, he attacks the crown witnesses Mme de Staël and Mme de Rémusat. What he says about them had already been said or hinted innumerable times, and was to be endlessly repeated.

Mme de Staël's initial enthusiasm for the victor of Lodi and Arcole and for the man of Brumaire (followed, as I have previously told, by disappointment and hostility) he reduces by slight touches to the story of a tiresome ambitious woman pursuing a celebrity, who keeps her at arm's length, not without some asperity; this, he says, the malicious Mme de Staël, who had passed from enthusiasm to tender emotions, never forgave.

But is it so strange that she did not at first perceive the objectionable nature of the young hero, as she later described it in her *Considérations*, and took him not

1. The edition in the 'Nelson Library' is somewhat shortened; and what is more unfortunate, the sources have been omitted.

only for a republican but for a sincere friend of literature, scholarship, and culture generally? Putting aside all evidence (which did not at that moment meet the eye) of consuming ambition, of pitiless trampling on the weak, of unscrupulous power politics, there was something uncommonly attractive in the spectacle of that court at Mombello, for a court it was, where Italian poets were welcome, of that journey to Egypt, which might almost be thought to have been undertaken for the exploration of Egyptian antiquities. Scholars accompanied the general, and he won their hearts by the seriousness, the insight, and the imagination with which he discussed their subject, be it literature or the stars, in short by the impression he gave of a disinterested taste for the things of the mind. When he gushed over Ossian's excessively romantic archaic nature poetry, faked by Macpherson, everyone thought it charming. In Paris, in those weeks before the *coup d'état*, the general was nowhere so much at home.as at the *Institut*, the centre of the learned world and of the Revolution's intellectual strength. There is nothing surprising about the fact that Mme de Staël did not discover ambition behind this innocent façade, and nothing is more natural than to accept the explanation that the coolness she showed immediately after the 18th Brumaire was due to her disappointment at the authoritarian direction taken by the First Consul.[1]

As regards Mme de Rémusat, she frankly admitted, as we have seen, that her ideas about Bonaparte changed with the years. She had started by admiring him, at a period when Mme de Staël had long passed that phase. Even after the Enghien affair, she still felt affection for him and listened eagerly to those long stories about his life which the great man was so pleased to relate. She tells of one small incident in her *Mémoires*. When she visited the army camp at Boulogne, where her husband was ill, the Consul, as he still was, would sometimes have long talks with her alone in the evening; the intimacy even gave rise to scandal. This is enough for Arthur-Lévy.

Is it not pitiful [he writes] to see philosophy of history [an obvious dig at Taine]

---

1. cf. PAUL GAUTIER, *Madame de Staël et Napoléon* (Paris thesis, 1902), p. 32 ff. Ed. Driault accuses the writer in his review of the work (*Revue d'histoire moderne et contemporaine*, V, 57) of having attached too much importance to the testimonies of Bonaparte himself, such as are to be found in the *Mémorial* and in Bourrienne. 'M. Gautier a beaucoup exagéré les sentiments particuliers de Mme de Staël pour Bonaparte; la vérité est sans doute tout simplement que, comme tant d'autres, elle l'a cru d'abord républicain, qu'elle a été vite détrompée, et que reconnaissant en lui le "Tyran", elle l'a alors combattu.' To this I would add that Sorel too in his charming, but, as regards her ideas, far from sympathetic little book on Mme de Staël (see p. 233 below) accepts on very insufficient evidence the view that she had visualized herself in the role of Cleopatra to the new Caesar, and that the hypothesis of a Mme de Staël disappointed in her amorous dream remained current; see for example LACOUR-GAYET, *Talleyrand*, 1930, I, 270 ff.

pay attention to the chatter of two bluestockings both smarting from wounds to their feminine vanity and not inclined ever to forget it?[1]

Anyone who can say nothing better of Mme de Staël and Mme de Rémusat than that they were bluestockings who could not resist the common feminine weakness for retaliation upon a man who has scorned them, puts himself in a category of writers from whom no important judgement on the intellectual and moral character of Napoleon is likely to emerge.

Of Mme de Staël it is true that Arthur-Lévy has something more to say, namely that as she herself tells us[2] she was hoping for a setback at the time of the Marengo expedition, the Consul's first feat of arms. The only explanation he can give is that her love had turned to hate, and therefore she wished him ill 'even if the fatherland were to be ruined'. Mme de Staël, however, feared that the ruin of France was implied in a victory which would make the dictator all-powerful. It is open to anyone to question her judgement, but here an appeal to the reader's patriotic feelings serves to cover a completely false presentation of the case.

RUTHLESSNESS

Arthur-Lévy skates all too lightly over a number of other points. I shall only quote the passage[3] in which he attempts to deal with 'the main, if not the sole, reproaches upon which his detractors have based themselves to assert that Napoleon was by instinct cruel and a persecutor'. To exaggerate the indictment in order to win an easy triumph is a well-known advocate's trick. That Napoleon was cruel, and enjoyed persecution for its own sake, is certainly not a current assertion made by his 'detractors'. The real indictment is that he stopped at nothing to reach his ends, and that in so doing he did not shrink from extreme callousness and severe persecution. But according to Arthur-Lévy these 'main, if not the sole, reproaches' are 'the execution of the Duc d'Enghien at Vincennes, the banishment of Moreau, and the exile of Mme de Staël'. I shall leave his defence in these three cases for what it is worth, but the contention that he knows of no other of sufficient importance to rouse him to a similar effort is really going rather far.

I have already dealt with several such: the liquidation of the 'general staff of the Jacobins' in 1800-1; the capture and imprisonment of the Pope in 1809; the arrest of canons, cardinals, bishops in 1811; the execution, by order, of the bookseller Palm in 1806 and of Andreas Hofer in 1809. I have also mentioned (p. 64) Napoleon's 'theory' that ruthless action in occupied territories is 'humane',

1. *Napoléon intime*, p. 494.   2. *Dix années d'exile.*
3. *Napoléon intime*, p. 472.

because of its preventive effect. Indeed, his correspondence is strewn with incitements to pitiless repression. Here are a few further examples.

In April 1806 Napoleon wrote to Murat, whom he had just made Grand Duke of Berg:

I am astonished that the notables of Clèves have refused to swear allegiance to you. Let them take the oath within twenty-four hours or have them arrested, bring them to trial, and confiscate their possessions.[1]

When news came of an insignificant revolt in Hesse, which till it became part of the new kingdom of Westphalia was under military rule, Napoleon wrote to the commander-in-chief on 8 January 1807:

My intention is that the main village where the insurrection started shall be burnt and that thirty of the ringleaders shall be shot; an impressive example is needed to contain the hatred of the peasantry and of that soldiery. If you have not yet made an example, let there be one without delay . . . Let not the month pass without the principal village, borough, or small town which gave the signal for the insurrection being burned, and a large number of individuals being shot . . . Traces must be left in the cantons which have rebelled.

In succeeding letters on the Hesse question, Napoleon demanded that sixty (twice that of his first order), then 'at least two hundred' people, should be executed. The general had long suppressed the petty revolt, and considered one execution quite sufficient. He could not help doing a bit more now, and Napoleon's 'theory of repression' cost about ten more lives, while one house symbolized the burning of a town. Throwing priests into prison was also a usual method of government. In 1809 Eugène was ordered to arrest a hundred priests from Parma and Piacenza, fifty from among the 'disaffected' of each territory, and to send them to Corsica. The newcomers found several hundred fellow sufferers already there. Many of these cases, those of Palm and Hofer for example, are such as to throw doubt on the efficacy of the notorious 'theory'. The most striking example of how such punishment can lead to more bloodshed is certainly the *Dos Mayos*, about which we are already informed (see p. 93 ff.). This was not directly ordered by Napoleon, but was a result of his only too well known inclination.

What I have said above is enough to give some idea of the 'reproaches' which Arthur-Lévy should have considered if he wished to cleanse his hero of all stain.

1. See RAMBAUD, op. cit. pp. 132, 193.

NAPOLEON AS MAN AND CITIZEN

I do not want, however, to give the impression that this book has completely missed its purpose or that it is historically without value. The writer is not strong on general statements, and will stoop to the cheapest devices for the sake of debating points. Yet, reading his book, one has the impression of coming into contact with a man who was really intimate with the Emperor, though perhaps he did not understand him. His judgement concerning the major political decisions and the tendencies of that remarkable mind is not of much value. But he saw Napoleon as he appeared in daily life: of this there can be no doubt. It is impossible to read the many extracts from his own letters, letters to Joséphine and Marie Louise, to brothers and sisters, from the mass of official correspondence, and the many testimonies concerning him made by men of all sorts, officers and officials, ministers and courtiers, men and women, Frenchmen and foreigners, without beginning to question the picture drawn by Mme de Rémusat and Mme de Staël.

Not that this picture should be ignored – far from it. As copied and enlarged by Taine, it may be unacceptable, but Arthur-Lévy has not proved more than that. These two women have undeniably made their own approach to the truth. The cynicism, the scorn of mankind, the lack of belief in nobility of motive – these observations have all been made from other quarters[1] and are confirmed only too patently by public actions. A portrait like the one put forward by Arthur-Lévy, which preserves no trace of these traits, is unconvincing. Those gentle pastel tints of melting blue and delicate pink could never be Napoleon.

Yet the book gives us something nevertheless. It is after all a reply to Taine. It is strictly limited in scope, for the whole of Taine's work is not dealt with. Arthur-Lévy does not attempt to discuss the figure of the statesman, nor his work as reorganizer of France. With these limitations, the author has proved something in his debate with Taine.

Napoleon cannot have been so completely cut off from normal human spontaneity. He did love Joséphine, and she did make him suffer. He continued to feel affection for her; and though he cast her off, it hurt him. He moved his brothers about like pieces on a chess-board, he sacrificed their feelings to his policy, trampling on their self-respect and initiative in his reckless forward march – though Arthur-Lévy says nothing of all this, it is none the less true. But he also had a great deal of patience with them, he felt himself tied to them one might almost say stupidly, and if one thinks of the fortunes and the peoples

1. A striking example is the agreement in the memoirs of Chaptal.

he shared out among them, high-handedly, at least there was nothing calculated about it and it was all too human. He could sometimes treat his generals and ministers with atrocious unfairness, and if his interest demanded it he could break them without mercy. But with them, too, he was extraordinarily long-suffering, he overlooked much and showered favours and benefits upon them, certainly with the cynical indifference of a man who considers everyone has his price, but also frequently with a certain geniality and even graciousness.[1]

And is it true to say that he could break them without mercy? True it certainly is, if one thinks of Admiral Villeneuve or General Dupont. But what is one to think of his curious indulgence to Talleyrand? Though he dismissed him as Minister of Foreign Affairs, and though he did not spare him sarcasm and even some of his famous fits of rage, he allowed him to remain in a position in which that man, the most dangerous of his opponents, could work against him. And long before the notorious scene at Fontainebleau in 1814, it was no secret to Napoleon that his marshals had had enough of his everlasting ambition and his oppressive superiority, but it was as though he felt as much tied to them as to his brothers.

'Alas,' exclaims Arthur-Lévy, after having once more quoted Taine on the crushing burden his arbitrariness imposed even on the most devoted, and the way in which he stifled everyone in his vicinity,

Alas, how very much the contrary! It was the gravest shortcoming of Napoleon's character in his capacity as leader, it was if not the chief yet the decisive cause of his greatest setbacks, that he was not always capable of imposing on his inner circle an inflexible authority, that he lacked the courage brutally to break the underground or open resistance of those on whom he had heaped riches and honours, that he was not able to hurt, to trample underfoot, to crush down or to stifle [these last words having been used by Taine].

The conflict is not so absolute as Arthur-Lévy's simple psychology allows him to imagine, but in any case his interpretation causes one to reflect.

Naturally, Arthur-Lévy cannot begin to compete with his antagonist in creative power; but the pages he devotes to Napoleon as a worker are well worth reading alongside those of Taine.[2] Here again it is by means of a string of quotations, mostly from the letters themselves, that he gives an impression of the tireless concentrated attention which Napoleon was able to turn on the most diverse affairs, down to the pettiest details; of his expert knowledge of

1. Thiers is so impressed by it as to write, in a style that Arthur-Lévy could not have improved upon: 'Voir le sourire sur le visage de ses serviteurs, le sourire non de la reconnaissance, sur laquelle il comptait peu en général, mais du contentement, était l'une des plus vives jouissances de son noble cœur.' II, 126a.
2. *Napoléon intime*, pp. 588–618.

every branch where he wished to impose his will; of his devoted and indefatigable industry.

To return once more to the central point of what I called the debate, was Napoleon indeed the complete egoist, the man who stood apart from his fellowmen? The very opposite, says Arthur-Lévy. He never tires of repeating that Napoleon combines genius with the simplest humanity. He has all the normal instincts, the ordinary middle-class virtues. He is above all the social man. How otherwise, one is bound to ask, could he have become a lawgiver with such ease and such success? He was industrious, he had a sense of order and economy. His understanding of conjugal fidelity and of religion, though it went together with personal laxity and unbelief, was not merely intellectual, not just the calculation of a realist. All these mental habits belonged to Napoleon the man, were natural and spontaneous.

I said that Arthur-Lévy was hardly in a position to reach any important conclusions on the intellectual and moral character of his hero. If his book provokes one to disagreement, it is not so much because he exaggerates, as because one feels the lack of balance between these humdrum, virtuous interpretations and the greatness of the historical figure. But one might also suggest, though not without hurting the feelings of more romantically inclined admirers, that just because our author was equally conventional and equally bourgeois in his views on morality and religion, in his appreciation of success and of property, he was able to get on these easy and genuinely familiar terms with Napoleon – or with one side of Napoleon.

4 Frédéric Masson

HIS MENTAL APPROACH AND HIS VIEW OF HISTORY

AMONG writers about Napoleon there is no more singular figure than Frédéric Masson. None was more wholehearted in his admiration, none more passionate, more one-sided, more partisan, and also none more sincere, more honest; none was more convinced that he served truth, or more courageous in its service and more indifferent to what others would say of his revelations and his assertions. He had need of both courage and indifference. Not only did he arouse the irritation, the fury, the sarcasm of his opponents – what did he care about that, being magnificently contemptuous of the 'detractors'! But even his fellow-Bonapartists were disconcerted, hurt, incensed, when he began his great work on the Bonaparte family and in no way spared the 'Napoleonides', rather enjoying pulling them down, that the greatness of his hero might appear the more brilliant. This was hard on the descendants, who fancied themselves as the bearers of the glorious tradition, while it gave unholy joy to the detractors. But Masson did not allow himself to be put out, and went on fearlessly, year after year, volume after volume.

As regards his attitude to Napoleon himself, it had nothing apologetic. One has only to read the introduction to *Napoléon chez lui*, at the outset of the enormously lengthy series which he announced in 1894, with great self-assurance, at the age of forty-seven. Napoleon is for him the representative of military glory, and also of the State, of Authority. Nothing seems to him more natural than that professors, journalists, and lawyers yapped at his hero. In his own day Napoleon's inexorable laws 'muzzled these three mouths of the Revolution'.

He obliged the lawyers to defend their clients without insulting either the government or any private persons. He obliged the professors to teach their pupils the subjects for which they were paid, without preaching to them either atheism or contempt of the law. He obliged the literary men to respect their country's lawful government, not to reveal to the enemy the weak points in our defence, not to lead the people's imagination astray.

Hence the hatred of all three of these groups. (Here we have the true Bonapartist method of disposing of the detractors. Reason, proofs? That would be serving their turn! Lay about them, beat them up! *Vive l'Empereur!*)

But fortunately, the writer continues, the tide is turning. When Prince Napoleon (a real man, with whom he had been on friendly terms) entered the lists against Taine and his 'pamphlet', a shudder went through the whole land. In the army, thank God, young Frenchmen were taught to honour the great general. A fresh wave of interest and admiration swept over the minds of men. Masson dreams of a Hero – in Carlyle's sense, as he says later[1] – like Napoleon, who shall arise and chase out the rabble of tub-thumpers and hirelings who have made France their prey. May his work serve to prepare the way for this saviour!

This was written before the Dreyfus affair. After the *débâcle* for the adherents of the army and the enemies of the parliamentary Republic in which this ended, Masson expressed himself with the same vehemence and clung to the same hope. 'I am a Frenchman, a patriot, and a militarist', he snapped at the socialists, who had spoken tauntingly of his election to membership of the Academy as evidence of the decline of that honourable body. He insisted that he would be proud if his glorification of Napoleon, the man who made France great, should fire some youth of genius to nourish 'wholesome ambitions' and to take 'curative decisions'.

Oh, would that he would come at last, the Liberator! Oh, that he might disturb the parliamentary carousal over which Circe presides, and that these swine of the sorceress, rolling in the dregs of their laws and with their bloody fangs disputing the quivering fragments of France's divine flesh, might hear their death knell in his approaching step.

Oh, that 'those fatted pigs', mad with terror, might disperse in all directions, while the young hero, with a godlike and expiatory gesture, thrusts his sword into Circe's throat . . .

The *Affaire* had not allayed Masson's excitement. This, then, is the political faith which inspired him in the task he had chosen, and which he was to carry out with unbelievable industry and pertinacity, the task of interpreting Napoleon the man. There was to be no romanticism, no rhetoric, no imaginative touches or poetry, nothing but facts, hard facts, with no other consideration than that of bringing the truth to light. 'The Hero must appear entire, his every aspect illumined by an implacable light.'[2] Thus not only the vicious pamphlets but the ingenuous childish apologies will be refuted. With the latter category he alludes to Arthur-Lévy, who reduces everything to 'a bourgeois, banal, and staidly respectable formula'. He, Masson, will shrink from nothing. Indeed, if it can be said of Arthur-Lévy that he reduced Napoleon's humanity to his own level, Masson takes a plunge into it. He tells everything, including much which was grist to the detractors' mill.

1. In the introduction to volume v of *Napoléon et sa famille* (1902).
2. *Napoléon chez lui*, 1894. Introduction.

These thirteen volumes of *Napoléon et sa famille*, in particular, not only damaged the reputation of the brothers and sisters but did not do much good to Napoleon's. It was not only that the distribution of favours and of fortunes and afterwards of kingdoms among the whole following seemed to come strangely from the son of the Revolution, particularly when one thinks of the excessive greed, envy, and inefficiency, only matched by self-conceit, displayed by that peculiarly unpleasant set of people. No; what was really unbearable and inexcusable was the way in which, as demonstrated almost *ad nauseam* by the facts, Napoleon persisted obstinately and for years in trying to build up his *Grand Empire* from such impossible material, and how he allowed his own position and the position of France, French property, and French blood to be jeopardized through their caprices, self-seeking, and folly. Was it not after all Arthur-Lévy's view which Masson used to undermine Taine's theory and destroy what was left of it? Far from being inhuman, the Emperor was only too human. But what is left of the statesman or of the sense of responsibility for the French people?

That spectacle did not shock Masson, however. What upset him was the baseness of the family, and later, in adversity, its ingratitude. In its activities he saw one of the main causes of the downfall. But his faith remains unshaken. One wonders how it was possible for a man who was at that very moment engaged in describing the family relationships of Napoleon to call for a Dictator to fight corruption. If it is a question of 'fatted pigs', Napoleon's brothers and sisters had the advantage of the parliamentarians. But for Masson Napoleon remains great and wise. Mistakes, weaknesses, what do they matter? 'The most astonishing exemplar of humanity'; 'truly a human prodigy'; 'this man who, with all the humanity he bears, with all the execration heaped upon him, all the apotheoses that put a finish to his ascent, is the most admirable specimen of the human race'.[1]

Hence that devotion and that tenacious zeal to find out every scrap of information about Napoleon, hence that conviction that the tiniest fact is of historical importance. If it be retorted that what interests us is not Napoleon the man but Napoleon the statesman, the writer has yet another line on which to defend his life's work.

It is time [he writes] to cease at last from making this senseless distinction between the public man, whom history may claim, and the private person, in whom she has no right. There is only *the human being*; a person's character is indivisible, like his nature. As soon as a man has played a historic part, he belongs to history. History lays her hand upon him wherever she happens to come across him, for there is no fact in his existence, however petty, no insignificant utterance of his sentiments, no microscopic detail of his personal habits, which may not serve to make him better known. I am sorry for him if he has any vices, or abnormal

[1]. *Napoléon et sa famille*, Introductions to volumes v (1902) and xii (1918).

inclination, or ugly sides to his nature, for history will tell; and also if he squints or is crippled, she will tell. She will collect his words, even those murmured in love; . . . she will question his mistress as well as his physician, his valet, and his confessor. If she is lucky enough to get hold of his cashbook, she will peruse it carefully and relate how his services were paid, how he enriched and ruined himself, what fortune he left behind him. She will lift his winding sheet to see what illness he died of and what was his last emotion when confronted with eternity. From the day he attempted to play a part in history, he delivered himself up to her.

This is how history shall be, no longer either political or anecdotal, but human; no longer a chronological arrangement of dates and words, of names and facts, but something which will remind you of life itself, which gives off a smell of flesh and bone, the sounds of love and cries of pain, in which the passions play their part and from which may at last emerge the lineaments of men whom we can greet as brothers.

What, shall poetry be allowed to appropriate the right to express all the passions of humanity, drama to show them on the stage, fiction to reproduce them from the imagination; and shall history, condemned to wear for ever the harness of a false modesty and an assumed dignity, strangled in the swaddling clothes in which the traditions of a monarchical historiography have wrapped her up – obliged, if she will not be regarded as frivolous and incur the strictures of the sticklers for deportment and the *Philamintes*, to keep within polite generalities and to speak about human beings as she would about heavenly bodies – shall history, which records mankind, only be allowed by dint of dexterous circumlocutions and of kindly suppressions to suggest, in noble phrases, that this same mankind has known passion, love, and sin? Political actions which had none but political motives – they do occur; but how rarely![1]

I could make this already lengthy quotation still longer, but this will be enough to show that Masson has his theory of history. It is a very one-sided theory, as I hardly need point out. The individual is certainly important in history, and it is pleasant to come across so lively an expression of this truth at a time when mechanistic ideas were to the fore. Nevertheless, it is the historian's task to deal with the individual in relation to the community. Furthermore, his task is a very different one from that of the novelist. Though the historian cannot do without imagination, he remains tied to the event, to data, to testimonies, and he lacks the omniscience which enables the poet to plumb his characters to the most secret places of their hearts. Fortunately Masson is too much of a real historian to let his imagination run away with him, and his work is in no way a collection of *vies romancées*. Happily also, in spite of this profession of faith, he has an eye for the true connexions with what is historically important. But even so his exaggerated interest in the personal side, as we shall see, does constitute the weakness of what is in many respects an excellent study.

1. Introduction to volume v.

THE INTELLECTUAL DEVELOPMENT OF NAPOLEON

I shall confine myself for the most part to a discussion of Masson's main work on Napoleon and his relatives. I would gladly say something about his *Napoléon chez lui* (1894), in which the Emperor's court and his daily life are minutely described. Here you can learn how he shaved himself, what paper he used for his letters; no detail is too insignificant for Masson, but he also discusses in a most interesting way the importance attached by Napoleon to etiquette, the reasons which led him to take costumes and titles from the days of Charlemagne, and many other matters. I must, however, limit myself to the discussion of another early work, *Napoléon inconnu*, and leave on one side not only *Napoléon chez lui* but a whole shelf-ful of others, about Napoleon and women, the divorce, St Helena, and many others which cannot be listed here. Many of these books appeared while the thirteen volumes of the main work were being written.

The two fat volumes of *Napoléon inconnu* which appeared in 1895 contained hitherto unpublished papers dating back to Napoleon's youth and by him entrusted to his uncle Cardinal Fesch. The papers consist of manuscripts and drafts of treaties, many referring to the Corsican party strife in which the Bonapartes enthusiastically participated in the early nineties of the eighteenth century. Then there are notes on books he was reading, one copybook after another, mostly from the years when he was garrisoned at Valence and at Auxonne. One unfinished extract from a geographical treatise has become famous: it breaks off with the words: 'Sainte-Hélène, petite île . . .' The historical importance of the whole collection is that it gives some idea of Napoleon's intellectual development. Masson's comment is interesting.

The young Napoleon, he says,[1] was heart and soul a Corsican, the more ardently because he was living in France. In the military academy he felt himself foreign, different, at a disadvantage with the French-born youths. He formed for himself a visionary picture of Corsica as a community where the ideals of simplicity and civic virtue, of equality in poverty and nobility of soul, were carried into effect. How beautifully this all fitted in with the theories of Rousseau! His mind filled with Rousseau's eloquent words, he imagined that he was called to save Corsica from the oppressive and corrupt French domination. But when as a young lieutenant he returned to the island during the Revolution and learned to know reality, when he failed to make himself heard in the midst of the furious strife between groups and family connexions, and finally suffered defeat, a complete change took place in his mind. 'Just as France had made him a Corsican, so Corsica made him a Frenchman.' Other factors, too, were at work. The

1. *Napoléon inconnu*, II, 500.

Revolution opened new possibilities for him in France – much greater possibilities than he could have found in Corsica, which in any case was now closed to him. Military honour and a dislike of British interference in French affairs also had their influence. At the same time there was another change. He turned away from Rousseau. Even his style shows the effect. The sweeping sentence of Rousseau the theorist, the ideologist, ill became a realist, a man of action. That sweeping sentence, which can be observed in the youthful political writings of Bonaparte 'is now broken, splintered, narrowed, dried, hardened, like steel'. He continues to command Rousseau's flourish, and is able to use it to express emotion. But for daily use he has found the style which will serve him throughout his life – *Le Souper de Beaucaire* at the end of his youth shows it.

As to the contents, the books read so thoroughly by the young lieutenant make an extraordinary collection. Masson finds in them the whole of Napoleon.

No literature; no classical reminiscences whatever; not a word of Latin . . . no striving after rhythm. No poetry . . . no novels . . . But on the other hand history and again history. History is his teacher, who supplies him with his arguments, who moulds his outlook and his philosophy, who from the beginning stamps him as a statesman.

The origins of his military genius will not be found here, but for the rest, once more, 'as far as outlook on life and politics are concerned, the whole of Napoleon is in those youthful notes'.[1]

He read and made extracts from the memoirs of Baron de Tott on the Turks and Tatars (1784), and from the history of the Venetian Government by Amelot de Houssaie (1740). He made extracts from the chapters on Persia, Greece, Egypt, and Carthage in the *Histoire Ancienne* of Rollin, and from the *Histoire des Arabes* by l'abbé de Marigny (1750), also from the *Histoire philosophique et politique des établissements et du commerce des Européens dans les deux Indes*. From this famous book of l'abbé de Raynal he extracts not only the 'philosophical' and political views, but all kinds of facts about the country and the peoples of Egypt and India. From the Swiss travel book of William Coxe he took pages and pages of notes, mostly on history and political institutions.

Everyone will be struck by the choice of subjects – Egypt, Turkey, the East. Now one understands, too, how it was that the young general knew the weak spots in the Venetian state machine, and that the First Consul could intervene with such assurance in the constitutional quarrels of Switzerland. In Year VIII he immediately showed himself well primed for constitution making, and here from this old chest comes a complete 'Constitution de la Calotte', consisting of extremely detailed and carefully worked out statutes for the subalterns' associa-

1. Masson's conclusion is quite untenable: see pp. 172, 352 ff., 378 below.

tion of his regiment, drafted by Lieutenant Bonaparte in 1788 when he was not yet twenty.

There is also an extremely long extract devoted to the history of Britain, at least eighty printed pages. The author used is a certain John Barrow. A history of Frederick the Great is not lacking.

On one subject which was going to be of incalculable importance in the career of the ruler of France, the young man is seen to have already formed his ideas; that is, on the question of the relationship between Church and State. Among the notes are extracts from the *Histoire de la Sorbonne* by l'abbé Duvernet (1790), from Voltaire's *Essai sur les mœurs*, and from *L'esprit de Gerson*, a work dating from 1691, in which, under the name of the fifteenth-century ecclesiastic of the University of Paris who had suggested royal intervention and a General Council as means to put a stop to the scandal of the papal schism, all the arguments were assembled in support of the Gallican conception, that is to say in support of the independence of the French Church from Rome and of the obligation of the French ruler to protect this independence. In 1791 Bonaparte noted down a number of conclusions from that book; that the Council is above the Pope, that temporal princes may call Councils, and that these do not need papal confirmation before they are valid; also that the Pope cannot touch the temporal power of princes, and that Gregory VII and Boniface VIII were guilty of flagrant abuse of their powers. The history of the Sorbonne is remarkable for its abuse of monks. From Voltaire, Bonaparte extracted details concerning Constantine, Charlemagne, and the decretals of Isidore. All this is most striking. It seems indeed possible to detect here the directives which were to govern the development of this man's mind to the last.

Masson, who shows all this very pointedly, is at the same time delighted. The later Napoleon, he says,

is anti-clerical, which does not imply that he is anti-religious. This Gallican doctrine, which was that of France as long as France was great, apart from which there was no salvation for sovereigns or nations, which alone could render religion acceptable because it resisted the abuse of power by the regulars, because it rejected ultramontane superstition, and preserved the humanity of God – had he not come to understand the greatness of this doctrine through his reading at Auxonne? In his early youth he was more radical, and wished to ban the Christian religion. Later he believed that the priests could be restrained and to a certain extent be made the gendarmes of the conscience ... At least he never tolerated that the head of the Church should arrogate to himself any power in France, and hardly bore with his spiritual influence. These good principles he owed to the reading of his youth.

Masson, younger friend of Prince Napoleon, did not try to conceal the revolutionary tendencies of his Bonapartism. He had no sympathy with Christianity.

He thought the Church 'unmanly', and somewhat ridiculous when it trespassed outside its own ground. But how differently can what he brought to light concerning the intellectual beginnings of Napoleon be appreciated!

I cannot refrain from quoting here another French writer, though he cannot really be included among the 'admirers' dealt with in this section. Geoffroy de Grandmaison, whose principal work was a study of Napoleon and Spain, as a fervent Catholic struck an obstinately dissonant note in the chorus of praise prevalent in his day. In an essay entitled *La formation intellectuelle de Napoléon* he discussed Masson's publication appreciatively and gratefully. But he is not nearly so enthusiastic as Masson over what is revealed to us of Napoleon's youthful studies. The young man worked hard and methodically, but look at the authors he used!

A collection of writers well below the average, full of paradoxes in the eighteenth-century manner. His historical education was warped for ever.[1]

Philosophy represented by Rousseau, religion by Raynal, and history by Mably ... And this Barrow, from whom he gets his knowledge of Britain, what anti-papist twaddle the man talks. Note that Bonaparte seems very impressed by the slanderous page on St Thomas à Becket. Mably, whom he read on French history, is even worse. 'An empty rhetorician, and almost publicly a deserter from the Church.' And then there is Duvernet, the historian of the Sorbonne, a mercenary scribbler, a hanger-on of Voltaire, who presumed, to the indignation of the whole circle, to write the master's life, a man who tried to turn a penny by making cheap fun of religion.

'Napoleon', says Masson at the end of his book, 'is twenty-four years old, and his intellectual education may be regarded as ended.' To de Grandmaison this is a horrifying thought.

The gravest problem which he later had to solve was that of the restoration of the Catholic Church in France. He solved it, alas, with good intentions I am ready to believe, with sincerity I hope, but with what profound ignorance of the Church's dogmas, history, and discipline. What! without knowing or having retained a word of the catechism, his mind stuffed with the stupidities of a literary hack like Duvernet, of a phrase-maker like Mably, of a protestant compiler like the unknown Barrow, and (here at last we can mention a man of some parts) with the views of Gerson, who on the very point where Bonaparte sought his guidance had been condemned by the Church his Mother – such is the way in which the future restorer of worship in France prepared his mind.

A non-Catholic will not entirely agree with de Grandmaison's judgements, but it was nevertheless worth while to point out not only the direction but also the contents of part of Napoleon's youthful reading – part only, since the notes

1. *Napoléon et ses récents historiens* (1896), p. 23.

published by Masson do not actually give the complete picture. Napoleon also read, both as a young man and later, Montesquieu, Adam Smith, Corneille, Plutarch . . .

THE FAMILY

Let us come now to the thirteen volumes of *Napoléon et sa famille*.

Napoleon had a mother,[1] an uncle,[2] four brothers,[3] and three sisters.[4] In addition Joséphine had two children[5] from her first marriage. There were nephews and nieces, brothers-in-law and sisters-in-law with their families. It was a motley crowd. The Corsican origins were humble. But from the first Napoleon Bonaparte carried the whole retinue along with him in his dizzying ascent. Even while his life was still a struggle, he spared himself no trouble to help his brothers. When he became commander-in-chief in Italy, the others shared his greatness as a matter of course. Without 'Napoleone', Joseph would never have become ambassador in Rome, nor would Lucien have achieved a seat in the Five Hundred. From the point of view of later years, the sisters' marriages did not seem very brilliant, but they were at any rate above the Corsican level, and it was already prosperity, riches, for everyone, in that time of shifting relationships of the later phases of the Revolution. In 1798, while Napoleon was still in Egypt, Joseph purchased that splendid estate of Mortefontaine in the vicinity of Paris where he was to keep open house as *grand seigneur* throughout the period, the equal even then of the leading politicians of the Republic, the protector of writers and intellectuals.

After the 18th Brumaire, to the success of which Lucien, young as he was, had greatly contributed in his capacity as President of the Five Hundred (this was practically the only instance in which a member of the family furthered Napoleon's career), Joseph became a senator and diplomat; Lucien, with whom, however, there was soon a split, became a minister; Louis, without having served at all, became a brigadier-general. Jérôme, at this time still too young, was to have an equally meteoric career in the navy. A most surprising advancement began for uncle Fesch – he was only a few years older than his nephew Napoleon. As a young priest, Fesch had taken the oath to the *Constitution civile* but had soon so to speak forgotten the Church. He had made a fortune as purveyor to the army and in speculations, and for ten years had lived a completely worldly life.

1. Letitia, 1750–1836.
2. Fesch, half brother of Letitia, 1763–1839.
3. Joseph, 1768–1844; Lucien, 1775–1840; Louis, 1778–1846; Jérôme, 1784–1860.
4. Élisa, 1777–1820; Pauline, 1780–1825; Caroline, 1792–1839.
5. Eugène and Hortense de Beauharnais, 1781–1824 and 1783–1837.

After the Concordat, the First Consul made him Archbishop of Lyons and put his name on a short list of prelates for whom he demanded cardinals' hats from the Pope. Cardinal Fesch now became the obvious instrument of his ecclesiastical policy – though the clerical member of the family, strangely enough, developed clerical tendencies, if not spiritual ones, which Napoleon sometimes found tiresome. I mentioned an instance of this in connexion with the Imperial catechism. As chairman of the Council in 1811, too, Fesch was not merely submissive and obedient.

For the brothers and sisters, or most of them, real greatness only came with the Empire, and at the same time some knotty problems arose. At once there was the question: how about the succession? The matter was all the more important, since Joséphine was bearing no children to Napoleon.

THE SUCCESSION: CLAIMS

For Masson, the Empire is an acceptable culmination of the Revolution. The people saw its own sovereignty embodied in the Emperor – this conception (which, as will be remembered, was also that of Thiers) is dear to the heart of Masson. But the hereditary succession, in particular as it was arranged with recognition of the brothers, seems to him reactionary. Indeed this idea made a particular appeal to the 'rallied' royalists, who in their hearts were not weaned from the *ancien régime*. With them Joseph intrigued merrily. In the end Napoleon gave in, conquered (such is the explanation offered by Masson) by his Corsican atavism, by that idea of the family with which he had been imbued as a child on his island; and Joseph and Louis (Lucien and Jérôme both being out of favour, owing to unsuitable marriages) were recognized as successors to the Emperor, failing a male successor in the direct line. Nevertheless Napoleon did not entirely divest himself of the true Revolutionary or, if one prefers, the strong, unsentimental, political, Roman conception, and left himself the possibility of adoption over the heads of his brothers, although his choice was to be restricted to their sons or grandsons.

This infringement of his claims roused the bitter indignation of Joseph. Disappointment one might have understood, but it was indignation he felt. Nothing is more remarkable than the ease with which the Bonapartes accustomed themselves to their grand position. I spoke just now of a dizzying ascent, but they did not in the least suffer from vertigo. They seemed never to realize that without their brother's genius they were nothing. Napoleon was sometimes capable of reminding them, bluntly and angrily. For instance, when Joseph tried to enforce his 'rights' by threatening to stay away from the imperial coronation, and attacked Napoleon in his most tender spot, his jealous sense of power.

Power is my mistress [he growled] and Joseph has been trying to flirt with her.

'If you stay away, you are my enemy,' he said to Joseph, 'and where is the army you can bring against me? You lack everything, and if it comes to that I shall destroy you.'[1] Joseph submitted, but how many times had Napoleon given in, and how often would he do so again, to his unreasoning weakness for his family – call it a Corsican trait or not. With regard to Jérôme, because he was the youngest, with regard to Joseph because he was the eldest (Masson lays great stress on the respect he felt, in spite of himself, for the rights of the eldest son), with regard to his sisters because Pauline was attractive and Élisa tenacious, or because Caroline was an intriguer and did not shrink from scenes.

What a picture, that family dinner,[2] a few months before the coronation, when Napoleon was present for the first time as Emperor and Joseph and Louis, with their wives, as Imperial Highnesses. Not only were they and the Emperor's mother affronted by the fact that Joséphine, as the Emperor's wife, took prededence of them, but the sisters – Élisa married to the nobody Bacciochi, and Caroline married to the dashing cavalry general Murat – were incensed because they had not been given titles. There were angry faces, tears, and even in the end a fainting-fit. There were excited recriminations. Napoleon worked himself up into a rage. It was then that he made that magnificent remark: 'They talk as if I had robbed them of their share of the late King our father's patrimony!' But he gave in. The ladies got their titles.

And they got more than titles. *Madame Mère* had written a threatening letter demanding a title also, and when she was allowed to call herself *Madame Mère* was not in the least satisfied, although Imperial Highness was tacked on to it: it should have been Empress-Mother and Majesty. (But then, they were none of them ever for one moment contented.) In any case, *Madame Mère*, who was notorious for her rapacity, had her monthly income of ten thousand francs rapidly increased, after repeated complaints and blackmail, to forty thousand francs, not counting a single grant of six hundred thousand; and I refrain from reporting other instances of largess.

As early as 1805 Élisa became duchess of the miniature state of Piombino, to which Lucca was soon added. She ruled (for her husband Felix I only carried the title) with much pomp and circumstance and also with devouring ambition and zeal. As Masson frequently remarks, of the whole family she most nearly resembled her great brother, a fact which though it inspired a certain esteem, did not make him feel any affection for her such as he did feel first for Louis, later for Jérôme, and for the third sister the pretty, frivolous, and non-political Pauline.

1. II, 448, 457.
2. Masson takes this (though he does not say so, as he unfortunately leaves out all references, see below, p. 192, note) from the memoirs of Mme de Rémusat.

Élisa fought the 'fanatical' priesthood – 'only base spirits allow themselves to be frightened by that foolish yelling'.[1] She stirred up trouble against her Spanish neighbour, the Bourbon Queen of Etruria, that is of Tuscany (another Napoleonic creation), whom Napoleon in the end dethroned, not for Élisa's benefit but in order to incorporate her country in the Empire; Élisa was given only the regency.

In 1806 Murat became Grand Duke of Berg, a frontier region made up of territories just handed over to Napoleon by Prussia and Bavaria, against compensation elsewhere. It embraced Wesel, Düsseldorf, and Clèves. Caroline and he were not satisfied – who would expect anything else of them! He was at once looking round for adjacent land to lay hands upon, and seemed to have nothing against a war with Prussia for that purpose – it was a question of a few abbeys and the territory of Mark. At that moment Napoleon was anxious to humour Prussia, but naturally this fresh trouble on her western frontier was making her even more suspicious and irritable than she already was inclined to be – suspicious and irritable, that is, about Napoleon. For while Murat was writing to Talleyrand (still Minister of Foreign Affairs) concerning the necessity of finally disposing of untrustworthy Prussia, treacherous as he was, and like Caroline full of envy of Napoleon, he sent a honeyed letter to the King of Prussia all about the latter's exemplary love of peace and how the policy he had pursued since 1795 had earned his country much more lasting benefit than the eternal, unappeasable war fever and land hunger of . . . others.[2]

LE GRAND EMPIRE AND THE BROTHERS

Piombino-Lucca; Berg, even when it was doubled in size; these were only trifles. They were only parts of a tremendous expansion of the Napoleonic system, of a Napoleonic reconstruction of Europe. At the end of 1805 what the First Consul had threatened Britain with had in fact happened. Napoleon had sallied forth, and by his victory at Austerlitz had laid the basis of a Western Empire. The Austrian ruler gave up his German imperial title, which had become a mockery, and in 1806 Napoleon not only created his Confederation of the Rhine from among the German princes, who kotowed to him, but he made Joseph King of Naples and Louis King of Holland. In 1807, after the downfall of Prussia and after Alexander had temporarily given up the struggle at Tilsit, Jérôme (relieved of his first wife, an American, and married to a Württemberg princess) was provided with a kingdom made up of portions of Prussia to the

1. III, 217.
2. III, 290 ff. He spoils the effect of this flattery by addressing the King as '*mon frère*'; his grand-ducal quality gave him no right to do this.

west of the Elbe, Hanover, and Hesse, and called Westphalia. It was unfortunate that Lucien continued obstinately to stick to his wife, in spite of year-long attempts to detach her from him with an eye to other combinations, a campaign in which the cardinal uncle assisted, only to receive a severe snub from the faithful husband.[1] It was also much to be regretted that Joseph and Louis were no longer free to marry princesses. Napoleon saw a way, nevertheless, of attaching Bavaria to himself by a marriage; the husband was his stepson Eugène, the Viceroy of Italy, whom he had adopted, though without giving him any prospect of the French succession. He also secured Baden by adopting a niece of Joséphine's, Stéphanie de Beauharnais, and marrying her off to the heir of the Grand duke of that German frontier state. Le Grand Empire had been created. A Family Statute, giving special rights to the Emperor in respect of all imperial princes and princesses, was to consolidate his hold on his vassals. And vassals they indeed were, these kings of his blood. They retained their positions as high dignitaries in France; Joseph, for example, was Grand Électeur. They remained French subjects, and the Emperor, who was to have so many disappointing experiences with them, imagined that their descendants would accept this position for ever.

One feels amazed at this conception. What is astonishing is that it comes from a man who was proud of his position as Emperor by the will of the French people, from a man who desired to be modern to his fingertips and who was accustomed to speak with contempt of the mummery of the old order in countries which had not been touched by the Revolution, from the man of order, reason, and enlightenment. Masson, who is keenly alive to this violation of revolutionary principles and is certainly not inclined, like Arthur-Lévy, either to gloss over it or to wrap it up in sentimentalities, always adduces the explanation that Napoleon was the slave of feelings brought with him from Corsica. But this contradiction permeates the whole figure of Napoleon, even where there is no question of an obsessive family sense. However proudly he might declare himself to be Emperor by the will of the French people, he still believed that these marriages with the old dynasties must be used to consolidate his position, and it was strange that to the last he attached so much importance to the papal consecration, for the same reason. The upshot showed how little all this was worth. He lived to see the same bishops who had bowed to him as the Lord's anointed address Louis XVIII in language no less submissive, no less flowery,

1. 'Vous avez donc oublié l'honneur et la religion. Ayez au moins assez de bon sens pour ne pas m'assimiler à Jérôme, et pour m'épargner la honte inutile de vos lâches conseils. En un mot, cessez de m'écrire jusqu'à ce que la religion, l'honneur que vous foulez aux pieds, aient dissipé votre aveuglement . . . Cachez au moins sous votre pourpre la bassesse de vos sentiments, et faites votre chemin en silence dans la grande route de l'ambition.' 6 October 1806; IV, 34.

while in 1813 not only did he appear to have overlooked the nations, but the rulers themselves left him in the lurch.

The link between these elements in Napoleon's mind is not to be found in Corsica. The fact of the matter is that though he was never unfaithful to the Revolution in some of its aspects, he was in other respects led into complete reaction by his profound suspicion of human nature and of the force of reason, egged on by counter-revolutionary forces of which he imagined he was in control. His policy shows a recrudescence of conceptions and conditions which the Revolution had by no means destroyed in the minds of men, and which indeed were still flourishing in the rest of Europe. It was really not in Corsica only that the family sense was strong under the *ancien régime*.[1] The zeal of the 'rallied' royalists for the undiluted principle of heredity was typical; no less was the promptitude with which Europe accepted not only Napoleon's royal state – his genius broke through all barriers – but the royal state of his relations. Even after the Emperor's fall this royal quality continued to envelop them in the eyes of the conquerors. It is true that by then they were in various ways related by marriage to the old royal houses. If that tipped the scale, it only proves once again how seriously the bonds of family were taken in the international circle of princes.

Nevertheless, it remains astonishing that the great man should not himself have perceived how little could be achieved with the unsuitable instruments provided him by his family. Of this unsuitability, resulting not only from incapacity but from frivolous conceit and unteachable intractability, Masson gives a compelling picture.

JOSEPH IN NAPLES

How was it possible, one wonders, that Napoleon could bring himself to place Joseph in Naples in 1806, after all that he had had to put up with from him? It is not only a question of the arrogant demands which he had so sharply refused in 1804. It is mainly that he could not possibly have held his eldest brother's capacities in high esteem. Joseph too has his legend. In this he is contrasted with his brother on account of his liberal ideas, of his gentle methods, and of his respect for the things of the mind. No doubt he was a well-meaning man. Mme de Staël had a high opinion of him, and for his part he tried to compose the feud between her and his brother. In 1803 it was well known that he favoured peace. As king he found nothing more pleasant than giving – at the expense of his

---

1. This comment, taken from Driault, was made by Dr J. Presser in his excellent article, 'The Bonaparte family in modern literature', *Tijdschrift voor Geschiedenis*, 1941, p. 156.

subjects – and forgiving, out of a helpless desire for popularity. He had long been surrounded by a circle of admirers, who now came to share in his royal fortunes. A certain spirit of opposition to Napoleon and his ruthless power policy reigned among them, and afterwards they still celebrated the wisdom and moderation of Joseph in their memoirs. As we have seen, those of Miot de Melito made a special impression.

Masson set out to probe Joseph thoroughly, and so indirectly to exonerate Napoleon. Apart from the fact that this was his intention, it must be remembered that he had from the start a prejudice against the liberal spirit. Nevertheless, although later on I shall have an opportunity for casting a somewhat more favourable light upon Joseph, Masson's presentation of him has an unmistakable touch of life about it. He contrasts his fine phrases with the way he profited from his position, the way he basked in his royal glory, his self-satisfied belief in a world created to make him rich and powerful. The contrast is undeniably damaging to the character of the man. Shocking as may be the coarse cynicism with which Napoleon was wont to rub in the fact that all Joseph's glory was but a reflection of his own, that his throne was shored up not by amiable intentions or dreams of mutual esteem and trust between people and ruler, but simply by the Emperor's power and the blood of French soldiers, Joseph's blindness did nothing to remedy these unpleasant truths. He emerges from Masson's sketch, pleasant and endowed with a certain talent for representation, but pompous and superficial, talkative and lazy.

Once again it strikes us as astonishing that Napoleon, who could so sharply upbraid him in his letters, can have imagined for one moment that this man, so completely untried, could dominate, pacify, and reform a newly conquered country whose banished king was still in Sicily under the protection of the British. Joseph was delighted with the expressions of loyalty showered on him when he arrived by *lazzaroni* and nobles alike. He devoted himself to the resuscitation of the theatre, and wrote long and detailed letters concerning the coat of arms he wished to possess and the orders he wished to found. But he left the French troops to deal with the war against the still active guerrillas, whom the British kept going with a landing here and there and with money and arms. Nor was this slackness, combined as it was with an unbelievable complacency, the worst. Like Louis in Holland, he took his kingly position extremely seriously. That is to say, in spite of the Family Statute and the duty encumbent upon him to remain a Frenchman, in spite, one might say, of the hard realities which tied him hand and foot to his powerful brother, in a spirit of extreme emulation he insisted upon his independence. He thought he ought to take into account Neapolitan sensitiveness in the first place, lest his popularity should suffer, and even taught the Frenchmen who held important posts in his court and government (a phenomenon unknown in Holland under Louis) to side with him rather than with the Emperor.

Naples, says Masson, became a well into which was poured French gold and French blood; if the peace with Britain which seemed possible in 1806 after the death of Pitt failed to materialize, it was owing to the claims which Napoleon made upon Sicily on Joseph's behalf. There is no need to assume that the decisive motive in this was brotherly love. In his utterances at any rate, Napoleon continued to make the sharpest distinction between private feelings and public interest. At the same time it is undeniable that by placing a member of his family in Naples he had pawned his prestige and limited his freedom of action. This was in any case a direct result of this system of governing through his brothers, which, where it was carried on, threatened to demoralize French officials and even high French military officers. Napoleon no longer always got the truth. Those who cherished their careers were chary of acting contrary to the wishes or views of the Emperor's brother. Many placed their hopes upon their immediate protector and were only conditionally loyal to Napoleon.

We have seen (p. 62) how much Thiers admired the statesmanlike qualities of Napoleon's letters to his brothers. In those to Joseph, it is true, one can see him sweeping away the web of illusions. 'What love,' he asked him,[1] 'do you suppose a people can have for you when you have done nothing to deserve it?' (Joseph had actually told a deputation from the French Senate that he was regarded by the Neapolitans in the same way that the Emperor was regarded by the French . . .)

You are among them by right of conquest [Napoleon continued] supported by forty to fifty thousand foreigners . . . As for me, I certainly do not need a foreign army to maintain myself in Paris. I observe to my sorrow that you are creating illusions for yourself, a dangerous occupation.

If one remembers how coolly Napoleon wished his brother a little local trouble in order that he might establish his authority, one is inclined to ask whether an attempt to build up a European domination on a basis of naked force could be called wise, and whether the idea that the truth could be hidden behind a show of fraternal royalty was not also a form of illusion. Even to throw away such wisdom as that contained in the letter previously quoted (p. 62) on so worthless a lad as Jérôme was in the end nothing else.

JÉRÔME IN WESTPHALIA

Jérôme, who became King of Westphalia in 1807, was a spoiled youngster of

1. III, 254.

twenty-four who had given proof of nothing save utter frivolity and instability of character. He had sworn solemn oaths to his American wife, but had nevertheless allowed himself to be robbed of her and of their unborn child. In the navy he had proved good for nothing; but when (after his marital adventure) he was sent on an expedition, with the strictest instructions to the commander to treat him as an ordinary subordinate, he could write quite freely about 'my squadron', just as even before he became king he could write to his brother Lucien, the *frondeur* of the family, about *'notre maison et celle des Bourbons'*. The following year he was commanding a German army corps in the campaign in east Germany, followed by a string of wagons, containing the most improbable luxuries, and a staff of flatterers and yes-men who pandered to his vanity. He made mistake after mistake, and his offences against army discipline were legion. What was the advantage of making Jérôme a king?

In a sense, nevertheless, it was from him that Napoleon received the greatest satisfaction. He too had begun with attacks of independence, and believed from time to time that his subjects worshipped him. Like Joseph, he had at first wanted his French officials to take the oath of allegiance to him. The idea of identification with 'his people' was very fine, but meant nothing save in the case of Louis, whom Masson persists in regarding as a neuropath and whose strangeness he certainly exaggerates. In Jérôme's case at any rate the inclination to maintain his independence against the brother who had made him king did not last long. The French officials and generals reformed, drilled, and made demands precisely as the Emperor instructed them, and Jérôme used his independence on the theatre, amusements, women, and building, none of it serious work, though as it cost a lot of money it hampered the work of others.

As for Napoleon, he would sometimes send him extremely curt admonitions, but at other times – carried away by his tenderness for the Benjamin who was so skilful in flattering him – he could not refrain from writing such a postscript as the following: 'Friend, I love you well, but you are outrageously young.'[1] Arthur-Lévy might exclaim about this being so human or so charming, but whatever one may call it, it is certainly far from wise.

ERRORS OF THE SYSTEM

The problem becomes still more puzzling when after two years' experience of this wretched system the Spanish Bourbons are removed from the throne and Napoleon proceeds to extend it. He begins by offering the Spanish throne to Louis, though this brother had opposed him most emphatically of all, and as

I. IV, 195.

Masson expresses it 'had become popular in Holland by making all the nation's grievances his own'.[1] Louis haughtily refused to be transferred or promoted like any official; he was a king, and knew only one loyalty. Joseph was not so particular. But what a choice! Napoleon's experiences with him had been no less unfortunate. And indeed, though he had allowed himself to be transferred, though he now had a new public for his performance, a new language, new historic formulas (the Catholic King, '*yo el rey*'), he once more began to go his own kingly way quite undeterred, until, when the tragic complications of the Spanish adventure became apparent, he showed himself ever more helpless, bewildered, and useless. And in Joseph's place, Murat with his Caroline now came to Naples. This coxcomb, as will be remembered (see p. 93), had prepared matters in Spain, as he fondly believed, for himself. His reports that the Spanish people would be delighted to receive a king from Napoleon had obscured the latter's view of the situation (Masson stresses this side of the case, without of course mentioning the forged letter – see p. 94 ff.). Now, egged on by his passionately ambitious wife, he was cut to the quick that he was 'only given Naples'.

I have called all this puzzling. Masson too asks himself, in a different connexion, how it was to be explained.

Only [he says] by assuming Napoleon not only to have been possessed with a blind tenderness for this brother [Jérôme] but to have been suffering from a kind of intoxication of family feeling which caused him to judge all those nearest to him by his own measure. Just as Joseph is destined to conduct negotiations and Lucien to preside over Parliaments, so Jérôme is to command fleets, as he himself leads armies. Disillusioned in respect of one, he clings the more desperately to another. Does he ever admit even for a moment that they are not equal to their tasks? No, it is their cussedness if they do not succeed. Whatever may have been their training or their start in life, it must be sufficient for them to turn their minds to anything in order to find within themselves all the abilities which *he* found. It must be sufficient that his name is theirs and that they are of the same blood: he touches them with his sceptre as with a magic wand, and they have genius.[2]

This seems more probable than the Corsican theory, until one thinks of Murat. Napoleon could not cherish these illusions with regard to him, and yet he used him for a position which was not only difficult but held the most dangerous temptations for an ambitious and unreliable man.[3]

1. IV, 196.   2. III, 107.
3. Looking back, Napoleon had no illusions about his brothers' suitability. The following extract from the *Mémorial* could have served as motto for Masson's book. There is no need to add that this view does not exonerate the Emperor from responsibility; on the contrary it implies a recognition of his own mistake.   [Cont. p. 183.

The whole system of the vassal kings was a mistake. There was an insoluble antinomy between the investing of a man with the old historic majesty of kingship, calculated to awaken expectations in his people and ambitions in himself, and the insistence that he remain a Frenchman, act upon Napoleon's slightest hints, and accept the offensive remarks to which the great man's impatience so easily led him. I would seek the source of this error (and here I am giving my own opinion, not that of Masson, though his narrative provides all the necessary data) in the pride which made it difficult for Napoleon to believe that anyone could set himself against his authority, and in his blindness – which again sprang from his pride – to the national feelings of nations, particularly of small nations, other than the French. Let them be given a good administration and the Code, suppress ruthlessly the first revolt, let them feel that they are powerless against the power of Napoleon, and they will seek their advantage in the only course left to them, surrender and submission. This is how Napoleon argued. The new Europe which he was shaping had nothing in common with a federation of nations each trying to further its own interests by friendly understanding with the other. Everything was to be for the greater glory of himself, or, as he put it, of France. Writers like Masson and Arthur-Lévy, who accept the identity of Napoleon and France as an article of faith, regard this policy of domination as perfectly natural.

Napoleon [writes the latter] when he took to himself the right to dispose of the throne of Spain according to his own good pleasure, was a great deal less concerned with that country's happiness than with the interest of France.[1]

The somewhat mocking tone accords with the writer's conviction that his French readers would find it as foolish as he would if Napoleon had thought differently. I shall not now discuss the aims and the pros and cons of Napoleon's policy of conquest. The only point which concerns us here is that this policy being what it was, Napoleon should have tried another means for imposing his will on the conquered peoples than that so outwardly impressive, so satisfying to his vanity, of the vassal kings.

In 1810 things were going the wrong way in Holland. Louis had been resisting Napoleon by leaning upon the independent spirit of a people with a strong

1. *Napoléon intime*, p. 254.

Je n'ai pas eu le bonheur de Gengis-Khan en ses quatre fils qui ne connaissaient d'autre rivalité que de le bien servir. Moi, nommais-je un roi? il se croyait aussitôt *par la grâce de dieu*. Ce n'était plus un lieutenant sur lequel je devais me reposer: c'était un ennemi de plus dont je devais m'occuper . . . Si, au lieu de cela, chacun d'eux eût imprimé une impulsion commune aux diverses masses que je leur avais confiées, nous eussions marché jusqu'aux poles; tout se fut abaissé devant nous; nous eussions changé la face du monde; l'Europe jouirait d'un système nouveau; nous serions bénis. . . .'

historical consciousness, whose instinct of independence had at the same time found support in Louis. Napoleon thought that by breaking his brother he would induce the Dutch to throw themselves into his arms. He broke him, with all the cunning, with all the disregard for the rights of others, which he could always summon to aid him in a conflict (see p. 63 ff.). Masson, though he emphasizes the strangeness and difficult temperament of Louis, nevertheless has to admit that the grievances put forward by Napoleon were in part pretexts. Louis was forced to a first surrender of territory by a threat to his personal freedom while he was in France. The rest was simply occupied, by an army which (as in Spain two years before) marched in without giving any explanation, till Louis left the country. What an overthrow, what a sensation in Europe, and what a shock for the other brothers! Masson, faithful to his system of personal or family explanations, connects the insecurity with which the thrones were suddenly threatened with Napoleon's second marriage and his hope of a family of his own. The development proceeds, however, from the deepest and most fundamental tendencies of the Emperor's power policy. Jérôme was not removed, but he had to shed a plume. A piece of his kingdom was taken away, another piece put on. Were these men kings? They were governors. How much better would it have suited the system had this reality been recognized from the first, and had Napoleon simply used officials who could be dismissed and who would obey.

JOSEPH IN SPAIN

Joseph in particular continued to be a source of worry. His position was, of course, unfortunate. It had all seemed so simple. The king and the heir had abdicated. Murat had sent a junta of francophil officials and nobles from Madrid to Bayonne, to pay homage to Joseph. With a very incomplete Cortes he had discussed and sworn a constitution drawn up under the eye of the Emperor. The most difficult problem had been provided by the abdication of the King of Naples in favour of Murat, in the arrangement of which Murat and his Caroline were beaten down both by Napoleon and by Joseph. At last, full of quiet confidence, the new king crossed the Bidassoa. News of resistance here and there in the provinces had made no impression at Bayonne. Indeed, only a minor French victory was needed, and it was soon forthcoming, to allow Joseph to enter his capital. However, before he arrived he was entirely disillusioned.

It is not quite fair of Masson not to refer to the letters written en route by Joseph to his brother, in which he warned him, on the grounds of the reception he was getting everywhere, that he had been misinformed, that he, Joseph, found himself entirely without supporters, and so on. He was scarcely a week in Madrid when the crushing news reached him that a French army corps under General

Dupont had capitulated to the rebels at Baylen, a good two hundred kilometres south of Madrid. He had to take headlong flight from Madrid, withdrawing towards Burgos two hundred kilometres to the north, and from there after a while to Vittoria, another two hundred kilometres nearer the French frontier. Here Napoleon found him in November, when he came to his assistance with a large French army. There was no other remedy. In his first dismay Joseph had wanted to go back to Naples. But was it possible to dispossess Murat and the ambitious Caroline of their new territory, when they had already moved there from Berg? It was no more possible, of course, than to leave Joseph without a kingdom.

So Spain had to be conquered methodically. Dispirited, aware of the fact that he was cutting an awkward figure, Joseph trailed behind the French army, and was in the end once more able to enter Madrid. Abashed though he felt, he was none the less jealous of his royal dignity. Napoleon could laugh about it, and about the fine constitution he had himself made, to which Joseph was now constantly appealing as though realities had not put it out of date. His position was entirely based on the presence of the French armies, who had to fight not only the rebels in their remote retreats but also the British forces, in order to protect him. Yet, surrounded by francophil, that is, generally speaking, anti-clerical ministers, he clung to the illusion that the Spanish people could be won over to his side by kindness, by a show of independence with regard to his brother, and by social reforms. He issued decrees of the utmost nobility which lacked nothing save execution, and meanwhile disputed with the French generals and tried to impose his authority on them.

In the end Napoleon determined on a measure which can be looked upon as a preliminary to annexation. Masson compares it with the gradual process carried out in Holland, beginning with the annexation of Zeeland and North Brabant. By a decree dated 8 February 1810, a considerable section of Joseph's kingdom adjacent to France, that is Catalonia, Arragon, Navarre, and Guipuzcoa, were organized in four military governments under completely French administration. Joseph, profoundly hurt, spoke of abdicating; there is no doubt that Napoleon wished to provoke Joseph to take just this step. France was losing blood rapidly from the Spanish wound, and Napoleon was willing if necessary to restore Ferdinand, if only he could count upon him to make common front against Britain. But when he made ready to take Joseph at his word, the latter had already changed his mind. Naturally he complained bitterly about the decree, and henceforth ascribed to it everything that went wrong in Spain. 'Only moral forces can carry through the affairs of Spain',[1] he affirms, while repressive military government and the attack on the country's unity could not but alienate men's

1. VI, 165.

minds. Striking words, but Masson shows their hollowness when he reveals that Joseph at the same time declared his readiness to abdicate if he might go back to Naples. In any case he wanted territorial compensation . . . The Spaniards could expect no more from such a king than could Napoleon. At the same time, as Masson states very plainly, the military administration of the four governments did have a most deplorable effect. The French generals, their former ideals long forgotten, thought of nothing else but lording it and feathering their own nests.

In every way the Spanish affair was a burden for Napoleon, an illness, a sore. One can understand that he would have liked to liquidate it. Why did he not force Joseph to abdicate? That is the problem. He openly declared that by continuing the war Britain forced him to subjugate the whole of Spain, but when Joseph, even more angry than hurt, came to France, he nevertheless obtained considerable concessions in a personal interview with the Emperor. The Emperor even made him his lieutenant in Spain and commander-in-chief of the French troops. When in 1812 the long-meditated campaign against Russia was at last begun, this position acquired real significance, with disastrous results, as might have been expected. Spain was in any case a training ground in disobedience for the marshals. With Joseph as commander-in-chief, the result was bound to be 'anarchy among the men, disunity among the commanders, inefficiency in the general staff, and sooner or later defeat and collapse'.[1] There was to be a long *via dolorosa* before that ending, but when the final disaster came in June 1813 at Vittoria – Joseph had once more been expelled from Madrid in July 1812 – it was accompanied by the most unsavoury incidents, a precipitous flight into French territory, and bitter recriminations against French commanders, who must bear the blame for the King's mistakes. And even in the gilded exile of Mortefontaine, Joseph still kept raising objections to Napoleon's plan, long overdue, seriously to undertake the liquidation of the Spanish venture and the restoration of Ferdinand. Joseph was determined to remain king, '*roi catholique, roi des Espagnes et des Indes*'.[2]

Masson's whole account is intended to show how foolish, clumsy, and self-centred Joseph was. The conclusion which he presses upon the reader is that it is really not fair to blame Napoleon for his impatience and rough handling of such a man, and that Joseph's utterances should not be produced in evidence against his powerful brother. Even Thiers had let himself be taken in by Joseph and his protagonists, and while recognizing that he was lacking in energy, believed in his insight, his '*sens*', his '*esprit juste*'. After the Vittoria disaster, he considered that instead of giving free rein to his wrath against Joseph and Marshal Jourdan, Napoleon ought to have remembered that it was to be imputed in the first place

1. VI, 347.   2. VIII, 259.

to his own mistakes.[1] But when Masson himself pictures Napoleon as 'a victim of the family sense, of the Corsican spirit, of primogeniture',[2] he hardly adds to his greatness as statesman. And if he is right in thinking that Thiers conceals Joseph's pretentiousness and glosses over his stupidities, thus giving a completely false picture of his true character,[3] Thiers's view that Napoleon ' with his penetrating genius and his perfect knowledge of affairs, was better able than anybody else to foresee everything, and with his undisputed power, to prevent it' is not thereby refuted.

We see here once more that Masson's judgement, as soon as it deals with Napoleon, cannot command unquestioning confidence. If we moreover remember that he preferred to set aside those shrewd observations of Joseph's which might seem to show up the Emperor's blindness, we shall at a later stage note with interest other comments upon the Spanish episode which put the eldest brother in a somewhat better light.

MURAT IN NAPLES

After the fall of Louis in 1810, the man who trembled most for his position was Murat. His fear led him into schemes which were nothing less than disloyal. He formed a party on which he could rely, to maintain himself in his kingdom should Napoleon try to take it away from him. Its components were dissatisfied Frenchmen and Italians whose thoughts reached beyond Naples. There was in particular a minister, Maghella, who pointed out to Murat how much support he might obtain from the rising Italian desire for unity. When disaster came, Murat put these lessons into practice.

He had accompanied Napoleon on the expedition to Russia. To whom should the Emperor confide the supreme command when he left the army to counteract in Paris the effect of the catastrophe?

The hierarchy which he had created [says Masson] hampers his freedom of action. He feels obliged to transfer the command, not to the one most worthy, not to the ablest or the most persevering, but to the one with the highest title . . . Murat is king, so Murat is to be the commander-in-chief. Napoleon believes in the prestige of that crown which he made with his own hands, like the savage who renders homage to the graven image which he has fashioned.[4]

Murat begins by making all sorts of conditions, political conditions, and gets satisfaction of a number of cherished wishes regarding Naples. In the ensuing weeks, however, his leadership was hesitating; he seemed to have lost his head.

1. *Histoire du consulat et de l'Empire*, v, 93a.   2. *Napoléon et sa famille*, VI, 347.
3. op. cit. VIII, 140 n.   4. VII, 339 ff.

His thoughts were not indeed with *la grande armée* but in Naples. On one occasion he gave vent to a fierce outburst against Napoleon in the presence of a number of marshals and generals.

Finally he, too, deserted the army in its desperate plight, and hurried to Naples, there to negotiate with the Austrians, who were still outwardly friendly to Napoleon but likely to be a force to reckon with in Italy if the Emperor should fall, and even with the British in Sicily, that he might save his throne from the shipwreck. Napoleon knew much and suspected more, but Murat's treachery remained concealed for a considerable time. Murat again fought at the side of the Emperor in the German campaign of 1813, but after the defeat of Leipzig he lost no time in making a pact with the Austrians. A few months later, Napoleon was expecting to see him come to his aid with a Neapolitan army, but when Murat moved north at the head of this army, he did so in consultation with the enemies of Napoleon and against him.

There is no need for me to describe Murat's further adventures, which brought him before an Austrian firing party a year and a half later. Nor need I say more about Jérôme, whose kingdom collapsed like a pack of cards with the change of fortune in Germany.

THE FAMILY AFTER THE COLLAPSE

The defeat of Napoleon opens up a new scene. It is with restrained bitterness that Masson tells in detail how each of his characters tried to save himself, his titles, and his possessions, seeing that he could not save his power, without bothering about Napoleon, who might be remembered in a few well-chosen words, if even that was not too much trouble. Eugène, the beloved stepson, always obedient and dutiful, whose conduct compared so favourably with that of the Bonaparte family, acted more prudently than Murat. He cut himself adrift in good time from Italian ambitions and French rights, that he might enjoy the undisturbed possession of his enormous fortune with his Bavarian princess in her own country. Joseph was still elegantly doing the honours at one or another of his mansions. That he might be spared trouble with the royal police, he did not scruple to enlarge to Talleyrand, now the King's minister, and to the ambassadors of Russia and Austria,[1] upon his complaints against his brother and his dislike of the latter's ungovernable ambition, for which he should not be regarded as responsible. Lucien, who had at least the excuse of years of opposition to the dictator, tried to retain his French senatorship under the Restoration. So did Bacciochi, the Prince of Lucca, Élisa's husband; and she herself moved heaven and earth to convince 'Europe' that compensation was due to her for her losses.

1. X, 220 ff.

Pauline alone, the family beauty, frivolous but not completely self-seeking, came to Elba to keep her brother company in his misfortune. *Madame Mère* was there too. In an appendix to his tenth volume, Masson refutes the charge of incest (to which, as we have seen – p. 136 – even Taine had given credence in a weak moment). He produces all the documents, and shows that the story was based on the mischievous gossip of a royalist police spy. As always when it is a question of human relationships, he here shows real understanding and a sense of measure. He outlines the figure of Pauline without sentimentality or embellishment, as the easy-living sensual woman she was. Coarse-grained she was not; indeed she was delicate and sensitive. But she was superficial, and Masson does not hide the fact that when her little son died in 1806 she did not allow the event to affect her participation in court functions. According to legend, she had watched at his bedside: Masson shows that the child in fact died alone in the family where she had boarded him out. Arthur-Lévy's account of Pauline gives the measure of the difference between these two writers. He does not conceal the lovers – in fact a French public would not expect him to – but he wraps it all up in a haze of conventional romanticism.

CONFLICTING ATTEMPTS AT SYNTHESIS

I began by saying that the impression of Napoleon left by Masson with the reader of his work is on the whole not favourable. It is impossible to view that tremendous career, the world-wide events, one might say, of those full and terrible fifteen years within the orbit of the Bonaparte family, without a sense of incongruousness, of disharmony. By his choice of subject alone, as a consequence of which we hear just so much of the diplomacy and the wars and the internal reorganizations and relations to religion and the Church as is necessary to understand family complications and preoccupations, Masson gives the impression that to Napoleon himself the latter were really what mattered. And the writer was the first to be influenced by stating his problem in this fashion. His attention was so entirely and so continually concentrated upon the personal side as to make him seek there the explanation, and the aims and motives, of his subject.

He was well aware that he was exposing himself to a dangerous temptation. This appears from his full introduction to the eighth volume, written in 1906. He says in so many words that the aim of his inquiry is to find out what influence upon Napoleon's 'plans, negotiations, and destiny' was exercised by his family sense. He says that though the family did contribute to the catastrophe, he is well aware that the true cause lies elsewhere. He then gives a sketch of international relationships as he sees them from 1799 to 1815, and also from the beginnings to 1906. Britain is the enemy throughout. Britain has always pursued her aim of world dominion with cold calculation and unrelenting pertinacity, and for this purpose, while roaming the seas and conquering territories, has had to keep the European continent divided. France has no enemy as inevitable as Britain. Napoleon tried to hit her, first by an invasion project, then by unifying the continent. But Britain continued to foment division and to promote the formation of coalitions against the dangerous rival. Hypocritical Britain, who begins to call the slave trade immoral once she has no further use for it, but knows that abolition will cause the French West Indies to languish, who fights with the aid of mercenaries, or better still by subsidizing rulers, who does not scruple to ally herself with Japan against the white race (we are now looking far beyond Napoleon), Britain on whose account unhappy France has allowed herself to be trapped (the *Entente cordiale* dated from 1904) into serving, with her blood and probably with her existence as a nation, against the new rival for world markets, Germany; this Britain it is who defeated Napoleon and with him the hope of a united Europe, and this Britain is for ever the enemy of France.

All this is appallingly crude. It is certainly only too characteristic of a particular French mentality, and it helps to explain by what ways Napoleon's imperial policy was able for so long to touch French hearts; but as history it is childish. Nor does this introduction fit organically into the work as a whole,[1] and the writer was unable to make the ideas he expressed in it into the flesh and bones of his great work. Indeed, international history is not really his affair. His domain is personal and family relationships, and so in spite of himself he succumbs, as I have said, to the temptation to overestimate their significance as factors in history.

This is shown clearly in a number of cases. For example, he dates the change in the relations between Napoleon and Pius VII from the latter's refusal of the Emperor's request to declare invalid Jérôme's first marriage (with the American, who was, as Napoleon stressed, a Protestant). The request was in fact more of a

---

[1]. So much so that Pierre Muret entirely overlooks it in his important article in the *Revue d'histoire moderne et contemporaine*, XVIII (1913), on '*La politique étrangère de Napoléon Ier*', and writes: '... M. Frédéric Masson a conçu une politique de Napoléon toute pénétrée de ses sentiments et de ses passions personnelles, révélant chez lui la volonté de plier l'histoire à ses conceptions au lieu de se laisser entraîner par des courants antérieurement formés.' In the Introduction to volume VIII this is exactly what Masson tries to argue. And which, according to Muret, are the sentiments and passions indicated in Masson's book as the true motives of Napoleonic policy? Family feeling, centred in the first instance on his brothers and sisters ('Les royautés vassales, que les historiens avaient jusqu'alors considérées comme un moyen de gouverner l'empire, deviennent une des raisons, peut-être la principale, de la conquête de cet empire') and next on his son ('la naissance du roi de Rome, parce qu'elle a modifié la conception impériale de Napoléon et de ses sentiments les plus intimes, est un événement plus gros de conséquences que nombre de batailles ou d'annexions').

demand, and Masson (who is quite indifferent to Pope or to Christendom) was well aware of the extreme tactlessness of Napoleon's letter and remarks neatly that the refusal 'annoyed him as an act of insubordination'.[1] There was so much that was difficult in this relationship, and it was more Napoleon's unbridled obsession with power than his special family sentiment which made the break inevitable. Again, Masson maintains that Joseph's reluctance to quit his shaky Spanish throne in 1812 was the only obstacle to a settlement with Britain. It adds a dramatic touch in his whole picture of Napoleon's enslavement to the family, this suggestion that the Emperor threw away his last chance of avoiding final catastrophe, out of deference to Joseph. But this time every detail is wrong.[2] That Napoleon's proposals to Britain were not intended seriously, and that he did not dream of giving up his Russian adventure whatever happened, are facts as solidly established as any can be in history.

But even if one does not follow Masson in the exaggerations and errors to which his one-sidedness leads him, his presentation of the story forces upon one the conclusion that the family factor, the pride and self-conceit extended to include the family, did all too often influence Napoleon's political action, so much so that his clear-sightedness, his sense of reality and balance, indeed his feeling of responsibility for the French people and for humanity in general were disastrously affected.

It is, as I have said, most remarkable that Masson's ecstatic admiration for Napoleon is in no way diminished. He never falters in his view of Napoleon as not only a character of unequalled greatness, an admirable human being, but also throughout as the man of the people, the son of the Revolution. His cause is that of the nations, and with his fall the freedom of the peoples went too. To this view, surprising to Dutch or British readers but far from unusual in French historiography, I shall be returning. In any case, as regards France, it will now be understood that in Masson's view it was the Liberator who returned in 1815, and that like Houssaye he regarded the Chamber's demand that Napoleon should abdicate after Waterloo as 'a coup d'état against national sovereignty', as 'a crime against the fatherland'.[3]

1. III, 157; see also p. 103 above.

2. VII, 280 ff. Compare for example VANDAL, *Napoléon et Alexandre Ier*, II, 386 and HOLLAND ROSE, *Napoleon*, II, 238 note. Masson certainly says that the seriousness of Napoleon's proposal has been doubted, but he began by calling it moderate and to describe it as an attempt to preserve the peace with Russia; in fact, if Napoleon intended anything at all, he intended to safeguard himself on the English side in preparation for his attack on Russia. The passage is typical of the light-heartedness with which Masson disposes of international questions.

3. XI, 164, 335.

FINAL IMPRESSIONS

To his twelfth volume Masson added yet another introduction, written in November 1918. The old man – he was seventy-one – imagines that it was the spirit of Napoleon which had won the war. It would be interesting to know how he reconciled this view with his introduction of twelve years previously, in which he declared that defence against a Britain eternally and unchangeably hostile was the essence of Napoleon's policy, linking it with French tradition. But we must not go to Masson for strict logic or consistency. He has now discovered a new enemy, emerging from the victory itself, that is the League of Nations, and attacks the profiteers of victory who have not taken part in the fight.

According to Thibaudet, shrewd and (it must be added) leftist historian of modern French literature, Masson's work had taken the place of Thiers's on the bookshelves of the generation before the First World War. The fact makes it difficult to be very proud of belonging to that generation, he comments sadly.[1] I can understand this comment if it refers to the mistake of looking to Masson for the authentic story of Napoleon. But Masson himself had pointed out that he intended to give something different, even though in practice he sometimes finds it difficult to separate the history of the man Napoleon from history proper. Certainly his introductions are enough to put on the defensive anyone who expects a balanced outlook from historians.

What a hothead the man is! His emotions and his feelings jostle his ideas; in the general confusion the goal is left behind. But the historical impulse derives inspiration from many sources. I find it pleasing to observe how diverse opinions and heterogeneous temperaments may assist in disclosing truth. In spite of all his exaggerations and shortcomings, Masson has certainly made a contribution to the understanding of Napoleon, by his intense and persevering interest and his sharp eye for character and human relationships.[2]

1. A. THIBAUDET, *Histoire de la littérature française de 1789 à nos jours* (1936), p. 271.
2. This was immediately recognized, and this in spite of the fact that Masson clung obstinately to his pernicious habit of not giving his sources. See, for example, the article by P. CARON on volumes V and VI in the *Revue d'histoire moderne et contemporaine*, V, 556 ff. (1903–04).

5 Count Albert Vandal

THE WRITER AND HIS IDEAS

WE pass to a writer very different from any of those with whom I have placed him in this section. The contrast with Masson is particularly striking. Count Vandal is as controlled and conventional as Masson is excitable and eccentric. Masson's style has something direct, not too polished; he pours out his animated story, now interrupting it to make a slashing attack or to shrug his shoulders in an angry aside, now flying off into rhetorical eloquence. Vandal on the contrary, for all his colourful descriptions and his far from charitable judgements, remains composed and urbane, and his work, though lively and varied, preserves a conscious poise.

The introduction to the first of the two great works he left, written in 1890, announces the spirit in which he intends to approach Napoleon. The subject was the relations between Napoleon and Alexander of Russia from 1807 to 1812, that is, the foreign policy from the period of greatest power to the beginning of the disaster. For Vandal there was something fascinating and imposing about the gigantic historical figure in itself, something which silences criticism. With Pozzo di Borgo, 'one of the men who hated and admired Bonaparte most', he says that 'to judge him would be like judging the universe'. This expression of respect and of awe, when confronted with fact, with power, certainly takes us far from Lanfrey with his ethical rejection and his obstinate refusal to see any-thing great in the figure of Napoleon. It is certain that such respect and awe form a pre-eminently fruitful element in the historical mind, and that their absence explains the unfavourable impression left by Lanfrey's work on Napoleon, in spite of all its merits.

But it would be a mistake to believe that historians who talk so much about awe do not therefore hold opinions of their own. To write history without introducing opinion is unthinkable. Vandal takes his standards from Napoleon himself, and from the interest of France as conceived by Napoleon. He adopts no ethical, freedom-loving, internationalist standards, or any others independent of Napoleon. Such an attitude has, I repeat, advantages for the practice of histori-ography, but in its turn it leaves the independent critical mind unsatisfied. In any case it does contain a judgement, involving acceptance, admiration, and identi-fication.

We are far now from Lanfrey or Mme de Staël. But with Vandal we are also far removed from Houssaye or Masson. He does not greet Napoleon as the man who fulfilled the Revolution, the idol of the people. Far from it; he shudders at the excessive. As a Frenchman, he feels oppressed by the triumphant spectacle in which the morrow was ever left uncertain, and he looks back wistfully on former periods in French history

when she combined a serene temper with strength, faith in the future with a complete possession of the present, and with the advantage of virile virtues that of ancient traditions, when she had not yet suffered the misfortune, of all that can befall a country the least easy to repair, the loss of a tutelary dynasty consecrated by the centuries.

With the reservation implied in this royalist and anti-revolutionary profession of faith, he still feels admiration

for the genius which carried out or inspired amazing deeds, whose magical power raised to their highest pitch those qualities of honour, audacity [*bravoure*], obedience, and dedication which are peculiar to our people, for him who, having reconciled our nation with itself, created from it an army of heroes and for a time lifted the Frenchman above mankind.

Much was spoken about honour in the days of Napoleon, but was the honour of a people drilled to fulfil the purpose of a dictator, their freedom of expression hampered, was that indeed the highest honour that may be conceived? Is *bravoure* the highest form of courage? Is not obedience, in this context, a polite word for submissiveness or even servility? Is dedication a virtue in itself? Finally, are these qualities typical of the Frenchman particularly? We may take this as a warning that we shall find Vandal concerned with other values than – let us say once more – Mme de Staël. We are warned, as well, that he is capable of a remarkable idealization of the past under the impact of his political prejudice. The 'serene temper' with which Louis XIV expelled the Huguenots, with which Louis XV gave himself up to dissipation, leaving himself just sufficient time to intrigue against his own ministers; France's 'strength', her 'faith in the future', her 'complete possession of the present', when Louis XIV brought her to the brink of disaster in the War of the Spanish Succession, or when Louis XV gambled away her colonial possessions in the Seven Years War – reflections like these put us on our guard against Vandal's judgement.

For the moment I am leaving *Napoléon et Alexandre Ier*, from the introduction to which these quotations have been taken. It will be glanced at again when I come to deal with Napoleon's foreign policy. I shall pass now to *L'avènement de*

Bonaparte, which appeared in 1903 and has since been generally and rightly recognized as a show piece of Napoleonic literature.

L'AVENEMENT: SPIRIT AND TENDENCY

Among the books I have discussed so far, the only works comparable are Houssaye's *1814* and *1815*. There is no survey or recapitulation of the whole career, no discussion, no argument, but simply a thorough and detailed study of a very short period. Houssaye takes the tragic final phase, Vandal the radiant début. From a historical as well as stylistic point of view, his work is of a higher quality. Indeed it is extremely fine. His documentation is no less circumstantial and careful, but the joins in the jig-saw puzzle are not so obvious, he has succeeded in building from his material a picture which is more vivid, more alive. He keeps his hero even less to the fore than Houssaye; indeed, the value and the attraction of his book reside in the broad treatment of the conditions and circumstances which made possible the rise of the dictator. Possible – and desirable.

For that is the conclusion which the writer underlines; the skill and forcefulness of his presentation are such that the reader almost believes he has reached it unaided. Something had to happen. Such was the confusion, that one might almost call it a society in dissolution. There was royalist resistance, backed by the British, in various districts all along the periphery of France, and here and there assuming the form of chronic banditry. There was the Church broken up by the *Constitution civile*, even when it was declared no longer valid; the majority of priests regarded as dangerous to the state and treated as such, while the loyal minority was despised by the faithful. The army, badly equipped and shabby, was in retreat on all the frontiers, while rascally army purveyors made fortunes. In Paris the members of a revolutionary rump, the relic of many murderous quarrels, were still concerned solely with the thought of staying in power, a kind of parliamentary oligarchy, suspicious of democratic pressure after all they had been through, averse to social revolution, and regarding revolutionary freedom as freedom for the upper middle class. Their heads, it is true, were still filled with revolutionary phrases conveying abhorrence of kings and the Church, and with these they teased the masses (who had expected something quite different from the Revolution) and governed, or rather failed to govern, by the aid of special decrees and arbitrary measures. The windbags of that quasi parliamentary régime appear in Vandal's pages little less hideous than the bloodthirsty Jacobins whom they had put out of office, but who – to the annoyance and terror of the ordinary people, whose only prayer was for peace and quiet – rose once more from their hiding-places. Could one be sure that they had been put down for good?

A sigh of relief goes up when at last a man appears who knows what he wants and who understands authority and order, a realist who does not care a rap for high-sounding principles which serve no other purpose than to worry the people or provide the so-called government with a façade of fine phrases. A man who though at first he is played off by some of those windbags against others, soon sweeps them all aside and takes power to himself. The reader feels relief, and understands the relief felt by the people of France. And next, seeing Bonaparte at work, with that amazing certainty of touch, he cannot help understanding the ascendance he exercised, the approval he won, and how it was possible that he could throw off in a few years the last vestiges of control which the parliamentarians had been able to include in the new constitution.

And at the same time one begins to wonder whether the irregularities he permitted himself before and after the 18th Brumaire in order to get rid of the intellectuals and the bourgeoisie, to tame them or break them, should be judged so in the abstract, as moral questions, so entirely apart from the circumstances, as we have seen done by the writers under Napoleon III, themselves typical opposition liberals. Vandal is not so particular. It is not that he flatters the motives and methods of the First Consul. He is quite liberal with such words as *cupidité* and *astuce*. But with him the balance is different. From his account of persecutions and deportations of political opponents under the Directorate (the worst cases were after the *coup d'état* of Fructidor 1797), or of its ambition to use the educational system to obtain uniformity of public opinion, we are forced to conclude – though this is never explicitly stated – that Bonaparte was at least not worse than his immediate predecessors. The only difference was that whereas he acted efficiently and purposively, they provided the depressing spectacle of a crude impotence. There is one passage in which Vandal attacks with a certain vehemence the point of view of what I might call for simplicity's sake the liberal school:

Among the legends which have found acceptance about the 18th Brumaire, none is more completely erroneous than that of the Assassination of Liberty. It was long a historical commonplace to represent Bonaparte as shattering with one blow of his sword a truly lawful state of affairs, and in the *Orangerie* of St Cloud [where the Five Hundred had been summoned for the *coup d'état*] stifling with the roll of his drums the last groans of French liberty. It is no longer permissible to repeat that solemn absurdity. Bonaparte can be blamed for not having founded Liberty, he cannot be accused of having overthrown it, for the excellent reason that he nowhere found it in being on his return to France.[1]

The plea is a striking one. Yet if one remembers what I have said of Quinet and Lanfrey's views, the objection can be raised that neither of them had overlooked these two points that liberty had been undermined before 18th Brumaire

1. I, 26.

and that the crimes of the Directorate had paved the way for the dictator. Quinet's lamentation, already mentioned (p. 77), is none the less justified:

As long as there had been a civilian government, and a constitution, and a republic, there were at least the roots from which liberty might spring to blossom once more; now there came, with the sword, a régime on principle opposed to liberty.

Apart from all this, the critical reader will from time to time get the impression that Vandal is trying to take him farther than the facts warrant. Again and again it becomes only too clear that the writer feels himself at home under a dictatorship. Strong government means more to him than freedom. This appears throughout in his comments and evaluations. The people's blind surrender, always the strength of a dictator in his first phase, he regards as instinctive wisdom. He takes an obvious pleasure in the bewilderment of the 'ideologists' who discover too late that they have given themselves a master. Would he have described the Parliamentarians of the Five Hundred and the 'lawyers' of the Directorate and their civil agents so scornfully, would he have belittled them so systematically, were he not hostile to parliamentarianism in general?

Vain and declamatory world, coarsely gesticulating, devoid of that external decency which, in times of monarchy, covers the ugly side of politics.

Directorial anarchy, parliamentary noise, these things were becoming abhorrent to the generals. This régime of impotent babblers revolted their manliness; their gorge rose at last with disgust against the malodorous untidiness of the revolutionaries.[1]

It will be noticed how unconditionally the writer takes sides in the eternal conflict between 'the generals' and 'the politicians', in which a different conception of history will hardly attribute all the wrongs so exclusively to the latter. Elsewhere we are struck by the strong moral disapproval he displays in judging one of the Directorate's proscriptive measures, designed indeed to remain inoperative, 'this cowardly and barbarous deed'.[2] One reflects that he never treats Bonaparte so harshly. It is true that in passing (for the story of 'the infernal machine' lies outside the scheme of his book) he calls the proscription of 'the general staff of the Jacobins' 'a cruel and arbitrary measure'; but this qualification is as it were hidden among explanatory and adulatory comments.[3]

One begins after a while to wonder whether the Directorate and commissioners were really so entirely ruled by low motives, selfishness, petty fanaticism as Vandal insists. Is not the whole background, against which Bonaparte stands out as a figure of light, painted in too sombre colours? I do no more now than put the question. We shall see that later writers have faced it, and I shall have something to tell of the answers they propose.

1. I, 75, 114.   2. I, 183   3. II, 452.

COUP D'ÉTAT OF BRUMAIRE

But is it not possible, without the aid of these other writers and without any original research of our own, solely by careful and discriminating reading, to arrive at more positive conclusions? Let us go more thoroughly into Vandal's account of the *coup d'état*. A comparison with Lanfrey's older version, so contemptible in the eyes of Napoleon's eulogists, will prove to be quite useful.

As a historical narrative, as the evocation of an important event in all its particulars, the lengthy passage in Vandal is infinitely more successful. It is a piece of artistry which it would be difficult to match. It is more true to life, less superficial, less ornate too, than Motley; has more mobility and vitality than Fruin; is more subtly shaded, more colourful, and yet more direct and clearer than Treitschke. A round hundred large-size pages are devoted to the two days, the 18th and 19th Brumaire, during which the *coup d'état* was accomplished.

A conspiracy was hatched between Bonaparte, who had just returned from Egypt and had immediately been hailed by the public as France's saviour from the threat of war, and Sieyès, who had recently become a Director and who had even before that been cogitating a thorough and if necessary revolutionary change in the constitution. The intention was to profit by the divisions in the ruling bodies themselves. The majority in the assembly of the Ancients was in favour of the change. It was now, making use of its constitutional powers, to move to St Cloud the less tractable Five Hundred, in which the Jacobins were strong, and at the same time – this was really already going outside the constitution – to entrust Bonaparte with the command of all troops in and around Paris. The purpose of it all was simply to fix on a firm basis the shift to the right in the republican régime. So it was thought; so at least Sieyès imagined. Bonaparte had his own views about the aim.

The *coup d'état* was carried out in two *tempi*.

THE 18TH BRUMAIRE

On the morning of the 18th, the Ancients decided on the removal of the Five Hundred to St Cloud and the handing over of the command to Bonaparte. Unreliable elements had not been asked to the assembly; they might have put awkward questions about the reason given, a Jacobin conspiracy which was indeed an invention and necessitated the use of big words to take the place of names and particulars. At the same time, Bonaparte had invited a large number of generals and high-ranking officers to his house. Guessing what was on foot, they talked excitedly and in a state of cheerful anticipation, until Bonaparte received the decree and was able to ask for their support to save the Republic. The noisy group accompanied him enthusiastically to the Tuileries, where he began by taking the oath in the assembly of Ancients, without however mentioning the constitution, and then set up his headquarters.

It was here that Bonaparte revealed that he was aiming at the Directorate. Barras, who personified corruption among the Directors, and who had been Bonaparte's protector a year or two before, sent his secretary to find out how the land lay, and it was to this obscure and trembling personage that the general made his famous outburst, the echo of which we heard even in Balzac's story:

What have you done with that France which I left so bright in your hands? [He was referring to his departure for Egypt.] I had left you peace, I found war; I left you victories, I found defeats! I left you Italy's millions, I found nothing but predatory laws and poverty. What have you done with the hundred thousand Frenchmen whom I knew, who were my comrades in glory? They are dead.

That eloquent charge was carefully rehearsed, and it had scarcely been declaimed when Bonaparte whispered to the secretary that Barras himself need not take it to heart.

Meanwhile, the Five Hundred had to wait for the following day before they could meet at St Cloud, and as a result were reduced to silence; but the conspirators were losing no time in seizing the Directors whom they wished to get rid of. These were three out of the five (Sieyès and a friend of his being in the plot, as we know). Of the three, Barras signed the high-sounding offer of resignation which was presented to him by Talleyrand, Bonaparte's admirer and follower since the Italian campaign. The two others, who refused to sign, were placed under supervision. The revolution had begun. The true test did not come until the meeting with the Five Hundred the following day. Sieyès wanted to weaken the assembly beforehand by taking into preventive custody their strongest Jacobin spokesman. But Bonaparte thought he could tackle them without this precaution.

THE 19TH BRUMAIRE

But on the 19th Brumaire things nearly went wrong, and brute force, which Bonaparte in his desire for public approval would have liked to keep in the background, had to be used publicly. It was a mistake to spread the whole affair over two days. The opponents had time to consult each other; many of the supporters, particularly the mere hangers-on, began to hesitate. The partial revelation of Bonaparte's true intention, and the prominent part taken by the military element in the *coup d'état*, contributed greatly to this development. In

St Cloud, whither Bonaparte went surrounded by generals, the Ancients were now meeting in the palace, while the Orangery was being prepared for the Five Hundred. These latter were in a pugnacious mood, and when in the afternoon their hall was at last ready, they began by once more swearing allegiance to the constitution.

Bonaparte, compelled to wait aimlessly, found himself in an extremely awkward position, and there were worried faces and anxious whispers among his following. His own nervousness appeared when, in order to hurry on the business, he came down to the assembly of Ancients and made an incoherent speech in which self-justification alternated with threats and bombast, the whole interspersed with insinuations and insults against the Five Hundred. In spite of the efforts of his supporters, he was unable to overcome the hesitation of the assembly. From there he went straight to the Orangery. The rumour of his violent words in the other place had preceded him, and members were in a state of angry excitement. His entry was the signal for a frightful uproar. 'Down with the dictator! Down with the tyrant! Outlaw him!' That last phrase, *hors la loi!*, had an ominous sound. It was with these words that the Convention had brought about the fall of Robespierre and doomed him to the guillotine. A few members laid hands on the intruder; officers and soldiers rushed to his assistance. But Bonaparte had completely lost his head and was carried away from the brawl in a half-fainting condition.

Within the hall there was now a move to turn the cry of 'outlaw him' into a decree, and it was fortunate that Lucien Bonaparte was chairman. With amazing coolness, he acted his part so skilfully that he managed to create confusion in the maddened assembly and to delay proceedings until finally, at his wits' end, he was able to get outside, more or less by surprise. Here Bonaparte, once more in control of himself, and alarmed by the report that the decree of outlawry had already been passed, had called *aux armes* through the windows, but the grenadiers who acted as guard for the assembly hesitated to take orders from him. In the garden the regular troops were drawn up, eager for action; these Bonaparte might if necessary march against the Five Hundred. Beside himself, he was already denouncing the assembly as sold to Britain, and accusing it of a murderous attempt on himself. But a tussle with the grenadiers would have made an unhappy impression. It now became Lucien's task to persuade the grenadiers. He used all his authority as president of the Five Hundred to implore them to bring to reason those traitorous representatives who had drawn their daggers against the suppressor of the Jacobin plot. When the grenadiers still hesitated, he sent for a sword, placed its point against his brother's breast, and swore he would be the first to kill him should he ever assail the freedom of France. This worked. The drums sounded a roll. The doors flew open, and in marched the grenadiers with lowered bayonets. The deputies admonished them, but the drums drowned their protests, the bayonets advanced, and the deputies fell back and fled. Bonaparte had won the battle of St Cloud.

EXAMINATION OF THE NARRATIVE

To a high degree graphic and dramatic Vandal's story undoubtedly is, but his comments and the way he lays his emphasis are sometimes surprising. Of Bonaparte's impressive outburst to Barras's secretary he says:

These words, in which the inaccuracy of individual points is wiped out by the overwhelming veracity of the whole, have echoed through a century and have for ever put a mark of shame on the Directorate.

A very different judgement is possible. Cannot the crafty mixture of truth and untruth be regarded as typical of the demagogue's art and in the eye of history incapable of imposing marks of shame?

To take the insinuation that the government had failed to maintain Bonaparte's peace, the historian must surely ask whether the war new had not risen from the seeds sown by him in the treaty of Campo Formio, from his Italian policy, from his Egyptian expedition (see p. 221). And there is a good deal more. Lanfrey, less impressed by 'this fine piece of rhetoric', underlines the words, which I did not quote, that this state of affairs, if allowed to continue, *would bring a despotism upon us within three years*. Likewise, an hour earlier, in taking the oath in the assembly of Ancients, Bonaparte had said: 'We want a republic based *on liberty*, on equality, *on the sacred principles of national representation.*' But once he had carried the day with the aid of his bayonets, to the consternation of many of his adherents (particularly Sieyès) he established a constitution in which all power fell to him as First of three Consuls, while the so-called representative bodies were simply nominated and moreover were left very little say in affairs. The members of the liquidated bodies, in so far as they had taken part in the enterprise, were enrolled in the new organs by way of reward – following precedents from the later years of the Revolution, for which these purifiers had been using the strongest terms of condemnation.

There is about this a duplicity which indeed pervades the events of those two days, and which the historian cannot dispose of in Vandal's easy way. With reference to the famous 'What have you done with this France?' he sighs: 'Why must the greatest scenes of history have their petty sides and their prosaic undercurrent?'[1] And he reveals that in his high flight Bonaparte was being carried on borrowed wings and was repeating an address just sent him by a provincial club.

1. I, 316.

As if there were nothing worse! Worse is the deception, sustained and many-sided, premeditated, and declaimed with all an actor's skill. Vandal is full of admiration for Lucien. As far as his strength of mind goes, his resourcefulness, his impudence, I can indeed see the point. But I am startled by his comment on Lucien's role on the 19th Brumaire, when he worked upon the soldiers with his lie about the daggers and swore to kill his brother should he threaten freedom. All he says is: 'His demeanour was there truly extraordinary and fine.'[1] Do all great historical events possess those petty aspects, do they all rest upon a basis of ruse and deception?'*With that man* everything was calculated,' says Lanfrey (when telling how Bonaparte held forth to Barras's secretary and then reassured him in a whisper), 'even his rage.'[2] Does not this come nearer the truth? Was it not more particularly in the case of Napoleon and of the Bonapartes that these great scenes had always an undercurrent of disingenuousness?

This question goes deeper than one might at first imagine. Vandal derives a malicious pleasure from the *dénouement*, when the deputies take flight, in their red robes. 'These petticoated folk', he calls them, with somewhat too easy scorn. And he has the nerve to write that

moral strength was now on the side of the bayonets, and nothing remained to the Revolution, succumbing to her errors and excesses, but to shelter under the hand of Power, essentially the dispenser of order and of discipline.[3]

That the errors and excesses of the Revolution were destroying it cannot be denied. Nothing weakened the Five Hundred at that critical moment so much as the memory of the *coups d'état* and the acts of violence in which they themselves had taken part. To this Lanfrey adds (though he is probably wrong in thinking it was the prime reason) that all the most eminent personalities had lost their lives in the Terror, in the proscriptions which followed it, or in the war. However this may be, Vandal's argument that 'moral force' was entirely on the side of the bayonets seems contradicted by his own laudably candid story. However frequently he produces statements or indications to show that the troops felt they had 'France' or 'the nation' behind them, he cannot make me believe in this unanimity. Indifference or exhaustion, of which other historians speak, seem more likely factors to me. And without undertaking an inquiry into the validity or worth of the evidence, I think we are entitled to quote as principal argument against Vandal's theory those very lies and those fraudulent assurances and false promises which Bonaparte and his accomplices found necessary to dispel the soldiers' hesitations and to win over the public.

The French people confirmed the result of the *coup d'état* in a plebiscite – this became the system favoured by the new Caesar. There was no longer to be an

1. I, 316.   2. *Histoire de Napoléon*, I, 459.   3. I, 389.

elected parliament, which would represent some power to balance his own, but there was to be direct consultation of the people. They confirmed – and did so by an overwhelming majority. Does this reveal the new ruler's 'moral force'? Apart from the way in which the plebiscite was held,[1] only the official version of the events of the two days was published; and the accomplished fact has a peculiar persuasive force. Moreover, the masses undoubtedly hailed Bonaparte first and foremost as the man who would protect his country against the advancing invader, and did not realize the consequences of his rise to power and the manner in which it was accomplished.

That is precisely what Vandal's circumstantial story enables us to do. It makes us feel that Bonaparte's appearance not only brought 'power as the dispenser of order and discipline' to France, but also, however beneficial his grasp of realities, his assurance, his independence of internecine party feelings might be at the outset, power that contained the germs of an insatiable militarism and a crushing despotism. The parliamentarians and lawyers who had turned to Bonaparte because they were impatient at the shortcomings of the existing constitution and the Directors, and because they were frightened of the Jacobins – though these served as bogy for the man in the street[2] – began to have an inkling of the alarming future even before the *coup d'état* was completed. They were warned by the clatter of sabres which accompanied it and by Bonaparte's incautious utterances. 'No more factions' – the future dictator considered every party as a faction – 'I will have none, I shall tolerate none', was a typical one. As the affair dragged on, several people asked themselves whether it might not be possible to find a better solution after all.

In a striking passage, the wider implications of which Vandal himself I think fails to grasp, he says that

the existence of Bonaparte was never anything else but a struggle against the most tragic vicissitudes of politics and of war, and his most perspicacious supporters were therefore almost continuously intent on having an alternative government ready behind his back, which could step from behind the scenes and throw itself suddenly on to the stage in case of a catastrophe. At times it is possible to recognize and get hold of that thread. The historians have pointed it out in 1809, after the warning of Essling; in 1808, after the first reverses of the Spanish war; nay, even as early as 1800, during the campaign of Marengo. As more light is thrown on the inner history of the Napoleonic period, one realizes that the first appearance of that precautionary attitude has to be set back and back; it is to be found on the morning of 19th Brumaire itself.[3]

1. Vandal says nothing about this, but we shall hear more of it later, pp. 278 and 320.
2. This comment, first made by Mme de Staël, is of course not to be found in Vandal, but is very common in later historical literature; see for example below, pp. 327, 331.
3. I, 347.

How is it possible for a man who is able so clearly to perceive the insecurity of this régime to regard it as a blessing for his country? The contradiction can only be explained by his profound hatred of the Revolution, which in his view it brought to a close, and of parliamentarianism, which it destroyed.

'ORDER, JUSTICE . . . MODERATION'

The *coup d'état*'s unattractive aspects must not prevent us from considering with an unprejudiced mind the constructive work undertaken by Bonaparte as First Consul. It is not only by contrast with the previous régime that Vandal extols his hero. Against the background of muddle and folly evoked by his picture of the Directorate, he draws a loving and in its way impressive picture of the dispenser of order, the lawgiver, the state-builder.

What were Bonaparte's aims? Let us peruse the draft of the proclamation which he addressed to the French people after his *coup d'état*. He wanted, he says here, in the first place to 'consolidate the Republic'.[1]

To consolidate the Republic, it is necessary that the laws should be based upon moderation, order, and justice.

Moderation is the basis of ethics and man's first virtue. Without it, man is but a wild beast. Without it factions may exist, but never a national government.

Order in income and expenditure: such order can be achieved only through stability in administrative, legal, and military organization . . . The lack of order in financial matters has caused the monarchy to perish and has endangered freedom. . . .

Justice is the true gift of equality, as civic freedom is that of political liberty. Without it, nothing governs the relations between citizens, and its absence causes the rise of factions.

Stable and strong government alone can guarantee impartial justice.

Vandal unearthed this document from the memoirs of Roederer, the Councillor of State whose job it was to turn the splendid 'simplicity' and 'precision' of Bonaparte's hastily scribbled words into the emphatic and declamatory style which the period demanded. This is how he introduces it:

As the frontispiece of his government, Bonaparte sets these words: order, justice, stability, power; and this word first of all: moderation.

Vandal accepts these words as truly characteristic. In his own description of Bonaparte's government during these first few years he makes few reservations, and none that temper his satisfaction at the spectacle. What most delights him is the reconciliation and unity through which the ruler seeks to solve the contrasts. A man who is entirely hostile to the Revolution and its ideological orbit is not

1. I, 542.

likely to inquire how far Bonaparte sacrificed the principles of 1789 in reaching that synthesis. There is here however no point that is not controversial and for which other French historians could not be found to oppose Vandal's opinions. Two of these points I shall now consider a little more closely. The one is the question of the centralization of administration carried out in Year VIII, and the other is the Concordat. Other matters, such as the question of whether the methods used by the First Consul to pacify the Vendée were not needlessly brutal, or whether his methods of restoring and maintaining order were not in general too reminiscent of terrorism, the question of his share in the drawing up of the *code civil*, and its merits, will be discussed later in connexion with other writers.

THE ADMINISTRATIVE LAW OF *PLUVIÔSE AN VIII*

Vandal gives a detailed and lucid description of the origin and the working of the administrative law of '*28 Pluviôse an VIII*'. As to its origin, it seems clear that it was the work of the experts in the Council of State, except as regards the central idea, that of the establishment of the prefects, which is supposed to have come from Sieyès. The First Consul was not immediately concerned, but it so closely represented his thought that at later stages he had only to consolidate and strengthen its tendencies. Vandal's conclusions are as follows:[1]

The system of Year VIII constitutes the most powerful mechanism ever devised to allow the ruler's will to penetrate from above into all parts of the social structure, the will which acts, directs, decides, impels, stimulates, and represses.[2] Everything is connected, and moves in unison. Ninety-eight prefects[3] act simultaneously and in the same direction under the pressure of the central motive force; they secure by decrees the execution of general laws, and issue ordinances of local interest. Through four hundred and twenty *sous-préfets*[4] they control thirty thousand mayors and municipal councils.[5] All municipal action is subjected to them; it is they who start it or approve, supervise, verify, and modify it. By successive transmissions, through channels regularly disposed, the motive power descends from the top down to the broad foundations, and spreads without losing its force.

1. II, 194.
2. This is how Thorbecke, the great Liberal statesman of mid nineteenth-century Holland, described the state mechanism, for the most part derived from the French occupation, which he was intending to alter by his revision of the constitution in 1848: 'Our institutions demand above all another and much greater participation on the part of the citizens than has existed hitherto. The Constitution excluded the people's strength; this it must now allow to flow through every vein of the State.'
3. One for each *département*.
4. One for each *arrondissement*, section of a *département*.
5. *Maires* and *conseils municipaux* all instituted by the First Consul or in less important places by the prefect.

Vandal does not attempt to deny the evil of this system, which does away with all local initiative. This is so obvious, he says, that it needs no demonstration. He merely denies that 'this masterpiece of centralization' was still weighing on France, as was so often idly asserted. 'From 1830 on, all our successive governments have introduced elements of liberty, of local life, and of true representation.' Even so, these reforms have often borne no fruit, owing to the lack of a favourable soil. And thus there comes the admission:

Even today the spirit of Year VIII still exists, both among the administrators and the administered, and the Act of Pluviôse rules us, morally rather than materially.

But now an explanation of this phenomenon is advanced which must silence all complaints against the men of Year VIII, and against the dictator who (at the least) made their work possible and took advantage of it:

That organization not only answered the needs of a period sick of anarchy and yearning for order; it answered the permanent and traditional aspirations of the French, the fatalities of their temperament and of their history.

To justify this statement, the writer goes on to maintain that the reforms which the French people had desired on the eve of the Revolution were simply those that would have strengthened royal authority, the source of order and law, which would have freed it from the excrescences of bureaucratic arbitrariness and have brought it closer to the people.

The nation desired not so much to govern itself as to feel the touch of a government, and especially of an administration, acting in accordance with fixed rules.

The Revolution, however, fell into the hands of 'the philosophers and their following, the deputies imbued with their doctrines, the thinkers, the dreamers, the ambitious, and the rebellious', and these were the men who had attempted 'to organize liberty and to extend it to excess'. That is how the constitution of 1791 and 1794 came into being, which had introduced an impracticable decentralization, a crazy hypertrophy of local autonomy, in reality 'a crawling sanguinary chaos'. No wonder, then, that

France of her own will adapted herself to the consular administrative system, authoritarian and too rigid, but organized, and based on simple, clear, uniform, and logical laws.

And so on.

The delicacy and ingenuity of this plea are admirable. It permits Vandal to call Bonaparte 'the most awe-inspiring despot that France has ever known', if a 'regularizing despot', and yet to free him from all blame, indeed to greet him with cheers. But if, discounting for a moment his personal liking for strong government and dictatorships – though this indeed inspired his eloquence on the subject – we follow his line of thought as far as possible, we shall see that everything turns on the view that France on the eve of the Revolution 'desired not so much to govern itself as to feel the touch of a government, and especially of an administration acting in accordance with fixed rules'.

WAS THE REVOLUTION BEGUN FOR THE SAKE OF LIBERTY?
FAGUET, MATHIEZ, AULARD

In asking this question Vandal refers (an unusual step for him) to a few books which had just appeared, Champion, *La France d'après les cahiers de 1789*, and a study of it by Émile Faguet, principally known for his literary criticism. I shall not follow him in taking the debate back to an earlier period, that of the Revolution, or even the years preceding it. It is enough to point out that Champion's interpretation, which became even more positive in the hands of Faguet, was immediately and most decisively rejected by other historians. In the *Revue d'histoire moderne et contemporaine* of 1904 is to be found an article by Mathiez: an equally fervent supporter of the principles of the Revolution, he was soon to oust Aulard as the great expert on its history. The article has the unequivocal title '*Une conception fausse de la Révolution française.*'

What had Faguet made of Champion's exposition of the Revolution?

The French Revolution, in the aims of the men who started it as well as in the results it achieved in the end, is a purely economic and administrative revolution.

According to Faguet, the *cahiers* prove that the men of 1789 were thinking neither of Liberty nor of Equality, that they did not dream of a parliamentary system, in short, that they had no general principles. 'The principles of 1789? They never existed.'

Paradoxes, says Mathiez; and from a *cahier* which had just been unearthed he quotes desires which are indeed in total conflict with Faguet's formulas. But what makes such untenable theories find support? Mathiez has no hesitation in explaining the fact by the political preoccupations of the writers. There are those who hope by this means to defend the Revolution against 'Taine and the reactionaries', according to whom it was nothing but an epidemic of violence and incapable of anything save abstract futility. But there are also those – the 'pseudo-liberals, the consular republicans' – who try to hide their recantation of the principles of 1789 by denying that such principles exist.

It will have been noticed that this is an old debate, and one which touches the core of the problem concerning the true meaning of Napoleon's work as a statesman. How fiercely Quinet or Barni protested against this view that the French had been concerned only with 'civic liberty' (see pp. 74, 78), as though they were indifferent to political rights and Napoleon had therefore in fact safeguarded all that was most valuable in the Revolution. This assertion, which in their day expressed no more than a purely personal or political assessment, was now given historical foundation in such a way as to exclude from the Revolution, as it were, the Quinets and the Barnis, the liberals and parliamentarians, deprived of their most cherished slogan, '1789'.

It is not surprising that Vandal took over the thesis of Champion and Faguet with such enthusiasm. Who really was entitled to claim the Revolution left him as completely indifferent as did the Revolution itself, but he must have been pleased to see the great tradition of 1789 so thoroughly undermined. The contention that the French people had never been interested in anything save order and prosperity (except of course power and glory) must have given him the flattering sensation that his own ideas were the only truly French, national, and traditional ideas, and this was at the same time the best defence for the imputations made against his hero that he had done violence to the French people and that he had changed the true course of French history.

Let us also note that Mathiez's protest was not unusual or merely personal. He was here in complete agreement with Aulard, however sharply he was soon to differ from him in the evaluation of revolutionary phenomena and characters. Along with the resurrected cult of Napoleon (we have already heard a Catholic voice raised against it) there continued to coexist the tradition of hostility on republican or liberal grounds, and it dominated education. We shall return to this tendency later.

THE CONCORDAT

'The Concordat', writes Vandal, 'was a consequence of Marengo.' He means that it was Marengo (14 June 1800) which first gave the Consul the popularity he needed to carry out his programme of reconciliation and bridging of conflicts in the face of intellectual and doctrinal opposition. He is again at his best in the fine description of the homecoming after the victory; his detailed picture of the festivities is colourful and significant. In the midst of the excitement and the glamour, one sees the quiet, small, unadorned figure of the triumphant hero, romantic in its simplicity and in the mystery of its brooding meditating stillness.[1] And even more fascinating is the description of Napoleon's impatience, of his excited longing for unfettered activity. In his view the Tribunate is now wholly

1. II, 442, 444 ff.

redundant. He is irritated by the opposition of all these talkers. Opposition to a king is all very well, but opposition to him, the people's choice, is an attempt on the people's sovereignty. In this frame of mind, he undertakes his 'cruelly arbitrary'[1] measure against the Jacobins and makes short shrift of the rebels in the West. 'To destroy the leaders and treat the masses kindly', such is his system. In Vandal's view all this is justified by the lofty purposes of his policy. And of these the religious pacification forms a significant part.

'The most politic as well as the bravest deed in his life'[2] is how Vandal describes the Concordat.

It answered to his immediate ambition, to the necessities of his pacification policy, to the needs of the time; and in truth, when he attempted to solve the religious problem from which France was suffering, he could not do otherwise.

The argument, as it goes on, is mainly directed against that of d'Haussonville (who is not, however, mentioned). According to d'Haussonville, as we know (p. 107 ff.), the forging of these new and galling bonds between Church and State was an error, and the desired toleration and free development of ecclesiastical life and of religion might much better have been assured under the already prevailing system of separation of Church and State. This is contested by Vandal.

At the beginning of his work he had already emphasized that the régime of separation introduced in 1795, when the bankruptcy of the *Constitution civile* had to be recognized, had hitherto been used by those in power to destroy the Church. For the new State recognized no association, no corporation: only citizens in juxtaposition. According to this doctrine, the Church had no existence unless guaranteed by a special regulation, and that State needed no other means to interfere in a hundred ways with the work of the priests.[3] Now a greater benevolence was shown. Apart from the *constitutionnels*, who still formed as it were a separate Church, a section of the former *réfractaires* – but a section only – had made a promise of obedience to the consular régime. Was that sufficient? Vandal regards the division of Catholics into three groups as an evil in itself, to which the State could not remain indifferent. But above all, this *modus vivendi* of the promise did not do away with two important factors, which remained a source of unrest.

First there was the episcopate, for the most part in exile and systematically counter-revolutionary. Even the most peaceful non-constitutional priests remained sensitive to the instructions and exhortations of their *émigré* bishops.

1. I have already quoted this characterization; see p. 197.
2. II, 460.   3. I, 26.

Besides, these priests were irreconcilably opposed on principle to certain of the arrangements made in the Revolution, accepted irrevocably not only by the French State but by French society as well: to name only the most important, the expropriation of ecclesiastical property (now in private hands) and civil marriage.

What France needed, and what Bonaparte needed, however, was a satisfied priesthood, recalled to unity, strictly Catholic, and on that account trusted by the people, but sincerely 'rallied' to or at least ready to acquiesce in the new institutions.

To such an attitude the Government could not by itself convert the priests; it needed the collaboration of the Pope.

'And so the imperious despot applied to the white-robed pontiff.' Can this somewhat artificial emotionalism and sentiment, to which Vandal has recourse upon occasion, hide the strictly practical and mundane nature of his conclusion? He does not attempt to disguise the fact that such was Bonaparte's attitude. Bonaparte, he writes, realized that with all his genius, his power, his glorious armies, his generals, prefects, lawyers, commissioners, and gendarmes, he could not hope to drill men's consciences . . . And he worked out in figures the moral strength possessed by the shepherd of souls at Rome. 'How must I treat him?' asked his first envoy to the Holy See. 'Treat him as if he had two hundred thousand men.'[1]

Do these considerations dispose of d'Haussonville? No: they run parallel, without touching his argument. But they fill in the picture, and help us to see Bonaparte's problem as he himself saw it. That in general is the great merit of Vandal's work, that he recreated the period as it were from within. But judgement should not therefore abdicate. Later we shall be considering another criticism of Bonaparte's actions in his ecclesiastical policy, a criticism which also proceeded from a standpoint other than that of immediate expediency, and we shall see then that our insight into the problem and the character can be still further enriched.

CONCLUSION

'The standpoint of immediate expediency' is perhaps a less sympathetic way of styling Vandal's attitude to his problems than he deserves. A moment ago I also spoke of 'recreating the period from within', and at the beginning of this chapter I referred to Vandal's 'awe when confronted with fact'.

It must be said, however, that as in the case of Houssaye's work, the impression gained from *L'avènement de Bonaparte* depends much on the narrow time limits of the subject matter within which the conception is worked out. We see Bona-

1. II, 470 ff.

parte rising above the confusion and corruption in which, according to the writer, the many-headed administration of the five Directors and the two Councils was so hopelessly involved. Afterwards we see him only in those first days when the task of reform and of construction satisfied his devouring desire for action. Even the violent discarding, after Marengo, of the limitations to which his power was still subject is dealt with only very briefly, while Vandal has nothing to say on the further career of Emperor, dictator, and conqueror. We also get hardly a glimpse of Bonaparte before his return from Egypt. Other writers, on the contrary, interpret the *coup d'état* of Brumaire by the light of what went before, in particular Fructidor. The war which he, in his demagogic manner, laid at the door of the Directorate, they connect, as I have already hinted, with his own conduct in Italy, with the peace treaty of Campo Formio, and with the bargaining away of Venice.

There is, however, more to it than this purely external question of time limits. Vandal's view of history is entirely governed by his tendency to accept what has happened, and contemptuously to brush aside every postulate of principle or ideal, and criticisms dictated by reason. He says somewhere that what the situation in 1799 demanded was 'a government that was truly reconstructive, tolerant, open to all, superior to party, and broadly national'[1]. If it had been suggested to him that this ideal was not permanently realized by Bonaparte, and that his hero's unbridled lust for power, which took the form of despotism internally and of conquest externally, must inevitably lead to its ruin, he would not have demurred. He might have replied indirectly by the passage with which his book closes:

That illustrious war chief became the pacifier of France: he restored the country's national cohesion; that is his glory, his incontestable glory, against which nothing will prevail. Could he have achieved through liberty that pacification which he accomplished by authority? Supposing that this great winner of victories had been able to triumph over himself, could he at least have granted to the French certain political rights, have allowed some control, have called the nation to exercise certain liberties, have prepared her for a more intimate knowledge of affairs, thus helping her on the way to a more normal destiny? Did such an attempt hold out any prospect of success, could it even be undertaken, on the morrow of unheard-of convulsions, at a time when the parties of violence were under control rather than exterminated, when so few Frenchmen had acquired any feeling and any taste for legality, at a time especially when France, triumphant though she was within her extended frontiers and in the wide development of her offensive and defensive fronts, nevertheless remained a vast fortress besieged by Europe? If Bonaparte in that crisis had made a beginning with the founding of liberty, he would have proved himself superior to his age, superior to himself. It is impossible to say whether the undertaking would have surpassed his genius; it was certainly above

1. I, 81.

the reach of his character. But while not attempting *this*, he devoted the respite left him by his truce with Europe to proceeding with his work of interior reconstruction and to reinfusing order and greatness into all parts of the commonwealth.

There is no doubt that Vandal means that order and greatness which the *ancien régime* had possessed but which the Revolution had destroyed, and that he is not even thinking of liberty. It is praise in which other admirers of Napoleon, who admired the Revolution also, could never wholeheartedly join. In any case we are thus reminded on the last page of something which was to be learnt from the introduction to *Napoléon et Alexandre* and which was anyhow on general grounds to be expected, that the attitude implied by acceptance of fact, and by impatience of those ideas which have not managed to impose themselves, goes with a very distinct political tendency.

Part 5

The Problem of Foreign Policy

1 Old Acquaintances

How far was Napoleon responsible for the wars waged by France under his leadership? What was the aim of his foreign policy? Had he any aim at all? These are questions which arise with any examination of his character and period. We have already repeatedly had to touch on them in dealing with the works so far discussed. At the turn of the century they were given much attention in historical literature; indeed, the whole discussion concerning Napoleon seemed to be revolving round them. Without doing too much violence to the chronological pattern of my survey, I can assemble a number of writers (with some of whom I have already dealt, while others will be new to us) in connexion with the problem of foreign policy, of the wars and their object.

BIGNON, ARMAND LEFEBVRE, THIERS, AND LANFREY AGAIN

Let me just recall what older writers thought on these matters. There was agreement between Bignon, Armand Lefebvre, and Thiers in so far as all three stressed the unsoundness of the system, which was outgrowing its strength; yet each had his own way of looking at things.

Bignon gives enthusiastic approval to the first stage of this gigantic growth. All breaches of the peace are laid to the account of foreign powers. It is in 1807 that he begins to have enough. Thiers is even more concerned than he is to prove how peace-loving Bonaparte was in his rise, but the date at which Bonaparte began to overreach himself he puts somewhat earlier, after Austerlitz. In discussing the breaches of peace of 1803 and 1805, Thiers follows the broad outlines of Napoleon's own presentation. He sees him in a defensive attitude, and what he has to defend is France's power position as built up by the Republic and entrusted to him, that is France within her natural frontiers the Rhine and the Alps, and outside these boundaries the spheres of influence necessary for her protection. I leave on one side for a moment the fact that neither frontiers nor power position can seem so 'natural' to those who are not French as they were to Frenchmen even a century later. (A Dutchman cannot help thinking of Flanders, including Zeeland-Flanders and Limburg, all of them incorporated into France, and of the military occupation of the Batavian Republic.) I will merely remark that Thiers takes leave of the Napoleonic presentation when he sees the effect of intoxication induced by success, after Austerlitz, in the overthrow of Prussia and the construction of a Germany under French hegemony or worse. From that point onwards, according to his view – and we have found Bignon making the same contrast – Napoleon no longer followed the good French policy, but an exaggerated and untenable one of his own. Even then it might perhaps have been possible to maintain in existence the tremendous edifice of a Germany completely subjugated to France, by taking all precautions and with the new Tilsit friendship with Alexander of Russia. But Napoleon, in his irresistible obsession with power, immediately overburdened the structure with the Spanish adventure. From that time on, no further triumphs could prevent the final collapse. The dividing line is thus brought forward after all from December 1805 to 1807, and the agreement with Bignon is complete.

Armand Lefebvre, on the contrary, estimated that Napoleon's foreign policy became untenable after the peace of Lunéville in 1801. In his view everything is dominated by the struggle against Britain. Napoleon himself was of course never tired of expressing this view, and for Bignon and Thiers also Britain is the principal enemy. Lefebvre, however, went much further than they in giving shape and system to the idea. According to him, the First Consul should have concentrated all his efforts on that aspect, and should for that purpose have sought friendship with Austria, even at the price of the position won in Italy. The question of personal responsibility, however, comes less to the fore in Lefebvre's treatment. Bonaparte was war-minded, but the French people too were drunk with glory and sense of power. No one dreamt of giving up Italy. And in any case the other powers were always treacherous, or greedy, or so weak as not to be worth mentioning (here Bignon and Thiers took much the same view). The long-drawn-out struggle, at least after Lunéville, was inescapable. Peace had become an impossibility, and owing to the position of the irreconcilable and impregnable Britain, the outcome was bound to be a disaster for France. Such a theory makes it possible to follow Napoleon's career without feeling shocked by the spectacle of the incorrigible war-monger: it compels fascinated attention for his energy, for his triumphs; and though regret at the approaching doom may be bitter, there is no blame for the hero. Lefebvre was not able to deal with the defeat, any more than Bignon, but he certainly would not have subscribed to Bignon's contention that Napoleon, had he wished, could have obtained peace on tolerable terms in 1813. Thiers, as we know, blamed Napoleon's conduct during that year. We shall see that a generation followed in whose eyes Bignon and Thiers were far too ready to desert the Emperor.

Lanfrey, on the contrary, is much more critical in his judgement of Napoleon's foreign policy than these older writers. There is no question with him of any fatalistic theory such as would eliminate personal responsibility. But he differs on principle from Bignon, and Thiers too, in that he draws no line and chooses no date before which he can approve and after which he condemns. In his view Napoleon never sincerely wanted peace. His whole career, even before he became First Consul, and before in that capacity he gave France these ardently desired but totally deceptive peace treaties of Lunéville and Amiens, shows him as uncontrollably ambitious, as a man living for power and to obtain more power, as one who would not rest while anything or anybody remained standing beside him. The war with Britain in 1803 was willed by Bonaparte; he only wished to give the French people the impression that he had wanted to avoid it. In 1805 he as it were deliberately exacerbated the feelings of Austria and Russia, especially by the threat to Naples. That restless extension in peacetime of France's sphere of influence at the expense of the small states was unbearable to the Great Powers. And in the end it was with real joy that Napoleon led to the Danube the army which had for so long been encamped near Boulogne. His British invasion scheme had revealed itself as increasingly impracticable as time went on, and now Trafalgar had made it finally hopeless. A continental war was for him a welcome way out of an awkward situation. And so time and again, down to the final disaster, Napoleon's wars were his own wars, made inevitable by his measureless greed for power, wars which never served the interests of France, wars for which the deceived and all too patient nation paid with the blood of its sons and in the end with the territorial gains won by the Republic.

ONCE MORE ALBERT VANDAL

The first important contribution to the problem made in the nineties – important because it was a detailed and thorough study of one important diplomatic episode, based on original research in the archives – was Vandal's book *Napoléon et Alexandre Ier*. To outline this, or even to summarize his story, would carry me far beyond the scope of my work. I have already (p. 86) used his book to correct Lanfrey's picture of a practically unsuspicious Alexander attacked in 1812 by Napoleon. Here I am concerned only with the general conclusions which the writer draws from his study – or which inspired him in it – and which are to be found in his introduction or scattered through the bulky volumes (there are three, each of five hundred large pages). The very first sentence of the introduction aroused controversy when the book appeared.[1] It was indeed challenging.

Throughout the whole of his reign Napoleon pursued one unchanging objective in his foreign policy: to secure, by a genuine peace with England, stability for his achievement, the greatness of France, and the peace of the world.

In one spring we are back in the Napoleonic legend. Thiers was much more

[1]. Sorel says this in his *Lectures historiques*, p. 172.

independent and critical of it, and even Lefebvre, though he brings Britain no less to the fore, does not take the fine phrases about peace too seriously. No doubt peace is always the object of war – the only question is what sort of peace. Some settlements are productive of nothing but more wars; Napoleon's vision of a world order based on the supremacy of France was such a peace. (Though I am prepared to accept the reality of this vision in the dreamer's mind, I cannot admit that it was the real motive force of his restless activity and daemonic struggle. Indeed I regard it rather as the subsequent justification and rationalization of that elemental urge.) Vandal too realizes that not everything in Napoleon's methods was suitable for winning Europe over to his ideal. When Alexander at Erfurt was already showing a certain reserve towards the friend on whom he lavished admiration in public, Vandal reflects that Napoleon was here paying for his dictatorial action of the preceding year, for the violence with which he had attacked princes and peoples (this refers, of course, to Bayonne). This 'cast a veil over the ultimate justice and grandeur of his aim, world pacification'.[1]

World pacification – to be obtained first and foremost by applying every means to make Britain accept a peace (that is by bringing Britain to her knees). Every means! First of all this requires an ally, a reliable ally, 'who could secure the obedience of the continent so that he might give his mind to the naval struggle'. He sought this ally everywhere, 'and everywhere he met only disloyalty'. By disloyalty, if we look closely, the writer means the reluctance to acquiesce in the conquests which France 'had obtained by fifteen years of battle and heroic courage'.[2] He thought he had found him in Alexander, and he imagined he could attach the Tsar to himself by holding out the prospect of a share in the spoils of the ramshackle Ottoman Empire, whose falling to pieces he now anticipated, though he had got it on his side *against* Russia not long before by exhorting it to fight for its future and its faith. This was the purpose to be achieved with the help of Alexander. But when Alexander became suspicious, not without reason, and no longer wholeheartedly took part in the blockade of Britain, it was once more to be fulfilled by turning *against* Alexander; Russia, too, was to be subjected. In thus working for 'world pacification', he treated the rest of Europe with even less ceremony. It had to take its chance. Holland was put under one brother, and when he proved disobedient, was annexed. Poland was lured with promises of freedom, or once more suppressed, because Russia so desired. Italy, Germany . . . But is it necessary seriously to demonstrate the folly of the view that a peaceful world might be constructed in this manner? Only a narrow nationalism, without imagination where the feelings of other peoples are concerned, or else a blind belief in the miraculous effects of power, can

1. I, 439.   2. I, 46.

have enabled anyone to advance such extreme opinions as late as the year 1890.[1]

But in the end Vandal does not hide from himself the fact that all these great schemes 'are but the outcome of the necessities of the Emperor's struggle with Britain'. We cannot share the view which Napoleon (and his admirer) had of Britain, that is of a mischievous extra-European power from which must be wrested the peace which it grudges our continent.[2] Given, however, that irreconcilable struggle, whatever one's views of its rights or wrongs, there is something striking about this idea that the whole policy of Napoleon was shaped by its necessities.

The government of Napoleon has been nothing less than a twelve-year battle fought all over the world against the English. His campaigns were no isolated and independent actions, after the conclusion of which he might have hammered in the boundary stakes of his domain and put a stop to the bloodshed. They formed the indissolubly connected parts of a single whole, of one and the same war, in which our nation finally fell, trampled on by Europe, after having swept into and reconstructed it, a war in which France was defeated but in which the French idea was victorious.

I do not intend to give more from Vandal's first work than this suggestion. It was not of course original. It too harks back to Napoleon's own propaganda. Nor was Vandal the first to have formulated it in historical terms. In spite of his inner contradictions, Lefebvre might be called a forerunner. But no less a person than Ranke, towards the end of his life, wrote in this same strain in an essay where with the typically conservative annoyance at the arrogance of a radical intellectual he tried to defend Napoleon when Lanfrey accused him of being bellicose and animated by a conqueror's greed. We shall meet the suggestion again as the *leitmotiv* of the great work of Sorel which I shall presently examine.

1. It deserves to be noted that in Napoleon's own time his 'universalist' aims were certainly taken seriously, even in Germany, or one might say particularly in Germany, a Germany not yet become nationalistic. Thus a German philosopher, Krause, in 1811 – just in time – constructed an entire theory concerning the development of history and of humanity upon this. See J. B. MANGER, *Thorbecke en de historie*, p. 28.

2. 'Pour arracher la paix à l'Angleterre et la donner au monde, il sentait le besoin ...' I, iv.

2 Émile Bourgeois

BEFORE Sorel had given his ideas on Napoleon their full form, however, a very different note was sounded in the *Manuel de politique étrangère* by Émile Bourgeois,[1] the relevant volume of which (the second) appeared in 1898, and which to this day has found numbers of readers for its many editions. The book is more than its title indicates, it is more than a handbook, being based on original research and presenting its own view of the development and significance of the events described.

Bourgeois will have none of that historical necessity to which Vandal sees Napoleon subjugated, and which for him determines both his tragic greatness and his indissoluble connexion with the French people. In Bourgeois's account the young conqueror, from the moment when as a plain general in Italy he took the control of foreign policy out of the hands of the Directorate, appears as a personal and an amazingly dynamic factor – from the French point of view a disturbing factor.

Even before he became First Consul, according to this theory, Bonaparte's tempestuous will, fed by his quite personal and fantastic ambition, forced history off its normal course. The Italian conquests gave him the chance to make a great position for himself. The bartering of Venice, where he had fostered riots that he might strike it down, was to assure temporarily the acquiescence of Austria. By the *coup d'état* of Fructidor (see pp. 77, 89) he broke all resistance in Paris against his self-willed conduct and his incalculable plans. And indeed in the meantime his real purpose had taken on body, the dream of his life had begun to stir, when by occupying Ancona (in the Papal States) and the Ionian Islands (Venetian territory), he set foot on the Adriatic (see p. 88) and saw within his grasp the east, the extensive, ramshackle and half-decomposed Ottoman Empire.[2] 'In the Orient alone are great empires possible today,' he said to his boyhood friend Bourrienne. The Egyptian expedition of the following year was truly his own undertaking, though when it went wrong it suited his purpose to make it appear

1. Member of the *Institut*, Professor of Modern and Contemporary History at the University of Paris, Professor at *L'École libre des Sciences politiques*.
2. *Manuel*, II, 164 ff.

as if the 'lawyers' of the Directorate had sent him there to get rid of him, even at the expense of France. This is the account in the *Mémorial*[1] and we have already had an echo in Balzac's story for the peasants.

A reckless adventure, this expedition, not only because it deprived France of an army which she needed badly when faced with the Second Coalition, but also because that emergency was itself provoked by it: it was that stirring up of the eastern basin of the Mediterranean which drove Russia to side with Britain.

The First Consul did not relinquish the eastern ambitions of General Bonaparte. The peace of Amiens, on which the French people built such joyful hopes, was never regarded by him as anything but a truce.[2] Wilfully, deliberately, for the sake of Malta (and that meant Egypt), Bonaparte moved towards a renewal of the war. But he could not show his hand to the people of France. What was the use of Egypt to them, and what did they care about it?

At this decisive moment, when France out of gratitude for the peace threw herself into his arms, it was his requital to drag her under false pretences into war. Nobody ever understood better the art of making men's passions serve his personal aims. The higher – patriotism, love of glory – he abused; the lower – hatred, pride, vanity – he excited. He will take good care not to incur the blame for a useless war as did the Directors, a war against tradition for the possession of Egypt. Incessantly he points out England to the French as the false and faithless enemy, enemy of their new institutions and of their peace. He will manage to have England declare war on him, in order to be able to pose before the French as the champion of national independence and greatness. So well did he succeed in persuading them of this, that to this day more than one historian remains convinced of the arguments which he dished up to our ancestors.

Bonaparte, as Bourgeois expresses it in an old-fashioned term, has his 'secret'. It was something very different from that 'world pacification' towards which Vandal sees him striving. According to Bourgeois, he follows his eastern plan with unfailing pertinacity, meanwhile telling the French one story or another. His camp at Boulogne was certainly more than a feint, yet his thoughts were with the occupation (which he set in train at the same time) of Tarento, Otranto, and Brindisi as ports from which to attack Turkey. The German secularizations which had meanwhile materialized as a result of the peace of Lunéville were popular with the French. It suggested a continuation of Louis XIV's tradition, this demolition of Austrian-Habsburg influence in Germany and this creation of French ties. Bonaparte's imperial title too seemed a victory over the Habsburgs. It was in this way that Napoleon carried the French with him in his policy of adventurism. Already in May 1804 the Prussian ambassador had observed that the new Emperor wanted war *on the continent*, in other words that he wanted to be rid of Boulogne and the hopeless invasion scheme.

The French [Bourgeois writes], whom he needed as tools, he tempted by the offer of Germany through an imperial title consecrated by the Pope. His own share was the completion of Italian unity [through the attack on the Kingdom of Naples], intended to put him in a better position for driving the English from Malta and the Russians from Corfu.[1]

And indeed, by his activities and mischief-making in Italy and his preparations for a further thrust to the east, he obtained his wish of shifting the theatre of war. The Austro-Russian alliance, entirely brought into existence by Napoleon's provocations, laid down that Russia was to guarantee Austria's position in Italy, while Austria guaranteed the integrity of Turkey for the benefit of Russia. It was not Germany, concludes Bourgeois, that was at stake in the war of 1805, it was Constantinople.

PRESSBURG AND TILSIT

Napoleon moved with lightning rapidity against his new enemies. Before the Russians and Austrians had joined up, he had encircled a Russian army at Ulm and forced it to capitulate. Even before he had followed this up by winning his most famous battle, that of Austerlitz, on 2 December, against the now united Emperors of Russia and Austria, Talleyrand sent him a note from Strasbourg on 17 October 1805 pressing him to offer peace to Austria without further humiliation or defeat, so as to draw her away from Russia and make her join hands with him to defend Europe against 'the barbarians'. After Austerlitz he again urged that action should be taken on the lines of his note. His advice has Bourgeois's fullest sympathy. Talleyrand appeared, he says, at that juncture as 'the interpreter of the nation's wishes and as advocate of her interests'.[2] This famous Strasbourg note is not always so whole-heartedly appreciated. In any case it is a fact that Talleyrand did not make any impression on Napoleon. How could it be otherwise? argues Bourgeois. For the means proposed by Talleyrand to persuade Austria to acquiesce in the loss of Italy, and to break her connexion with Russia, was to offer her the mouths of the Danube (Moldavia and Wallachia), in other words to lead her on upon the road to the east which Napoleon wished above all to keep for himself. Thus the peace of Pressburg, to which Austria had to agree – while Alexander, having escaped with his badly battered army back to Russian soil, continued the war – took on an entirely different character. This peace was calculated to reduce Austria to impotence. She was excluded not only from

1. *Manuel*, II, 253.　　　2. II, 257.

Germany and Italy, but by the loss of Istria and Dalmatia she was also prevented from closing the Adriatic and kept away from the gate to the east.

In the peace of Pressburg French opinion saw chiefly the final victory over the Habsburgs in Germany. This flattered French pride, all the more when by the establishment of the Confederation of the Rhine it was followed by the complete subjugation of Germany to France. Prussia remained for the moment outside this arrangement, but Prussia too – which in increasing fear of Napoleon's apparently unlimited ambitions had been on the point of siding with Russia and Austria – was forced by threats and the consolation prize of British Hanover into a new alliance which left her little independence. But here too Bourgeois sees Napoleon's ultimate purpose as the east, and we begin to suspect Bourgeois of being the slave of his system. According to him, the most important demand made of Prussia was not the closing of her coast to the British but the promise of help in maintaining the integrity of Turkey. This polite formula really covered intentions *against* Turkey, whose impending dissolution was admitted by all; and by involving Prussia, Russia was to be completely isolated.[1] At the same time – another pointer towards the east – immediately after the peace of Pressburg the continental portion of the Kingdom of Naples, hitherto protected by Russia and Britain, was completely occupied.

After his incredible achievements, and with France so much impressed that she was willing to swallow even the establishment of the Family Empire and of the Venetian and Neapolitan mayoralties for his generals and officials, Napoleon could imagine himself to be in a position to realize his dream.[2]

That dream was not, as has been asserted, a complete revenge on England. Nor was it world empire, a vague ambition unsuited to his exact and matter-of-fact mind. In the camp of Boulogne, during the first advance of the *Grande Armée*, at Austerlitz, and in the negotiations of Pressburg and of Schoenbrunn, when he incites the French against England, the Habsburgs, Russia, always the Emperor has his *secret*, to extend his Italian conquests, acquired in the service of France, down to the Adriatic, whose coast he has occupied, under the same cover, but always for himself alone, in order to get closer to the Near East, which he cannot reach by sea any more, since his reverse in Egypt and the loss of Malta.

At that moment when Napoleon's power was evolving in so fantastic a fashion, in 1806, Britain and Russia sent negotiators to Paris to discuss peace terms, simultaneously but independently. Bourgeois brings out what an important part the integrity of Turkey once more played in these extraordinarily involved negotiations. The complications were equalled by the bad faith. Napoleon offered Britain Hanover, which he had just given to Prussia. The Balearics, belonging to another ally, Spain, he used without notifying her as a prospective

1. II, 270 ff.   2. II, 265 ff.

compensation to the Neapolitan Bourbons for Sicily, should Russia agree to allow them to be deprived of that territory as well. It all came to nothing. Anxious Prussia secretly sought protection from Russia, and when the British, whom Napoleon had let slip in hope of reaching agreement with Russia, informed her of Napoleon's offer of Hanover, Prussia, in a mixture of panic and fury, threw herself definitely on the side of Alexander. Perhaps Alexander had never taken seriously the treaty already signed in his name in Paris. In any case he did not ratify it now; and Napoleon, with all his deception rudely torn asunder – for even Spain heard what her mighty ally had been plotting – had nothing left save his sword, which indeed he handled with consummate mastery. In a few weeks Prussia was beaten and he was victorious in Berlin.

But the King had sought sanctuary with Alexander, and as long as Alexander continued the war, nothing had been achieved. By appeals and fine protestations in oriental style ('Fate has chosen me to save the Ottoman Empire' is only one example of this), Napoleon actually succeeded in getting Selim, Sultan of Turkey, to take action against Russia. He even went to work on Persia. He flattered the Poles by playing on the theme of their recently lost national independence, though ready quite shamelessly to betray them to Prussia or to Russia if the need arose. It was proving a hard winter for the French army in the distant, cold, and barren land of east Prussia. The battle of Eylau, in February 1807, in which the losses were exceptionally heavy, remained in fact indecisive. Napoleon kept an anxious eye on France. What were the people thinking of this latest and unforeseen adventure? He pleaded that he had never wanted the war with Prussia, which in the narrowest sense was true. But had he not created the atmosphere of greed and suspicion from which it arose? He did his best to turn attention to Britain. The blockade of Britain, established in November 1806 in Berlin, was (still according to Bourgeois) intended to explain the necessity of his lording it along the Baltic coast. The colonies were to be reconquered from Britain on the Oder.[1] But finally the Emperor allowed Talleyrand to explain to the Senate that it was all about the integrity of Turkey. Bourgeois comments:

> After having dragged the nation along by means of her hatred of England and of the glory resulting from the conquest of the natural frontiers and of the imperial title once belonging to Habsburg alone, Napoleon fixes on the Vistula a new objective for her patriotism: the maintenance of the Ottoman Empire. He pictures that policy to her as vital for the preservation of her southern trade and even for the safety of her frontiers. The Russians in Constantinople would mean before long 'Those fanatics, those barbarians in our provinces . . .'

The Press received precise instructions to write on these lines. Napoleon was

1. II, 285.

in a tense and restless mood. As in Paris in 1806, he still wanted a compromise with Alexander. After Eylau he even made a great show of horror at the frightfulness of the battlefield: 'His soul', as Vandal writes, 'was sincerely moved . . .'[1] There was, however, no evidence of this sincere compassion in June 1807, after Friedland, when he was finally able to beat Alexander completely.

Then came the sudden change, the romantic meeting between the two Emperors on a raft on the Niemen at Tilsit, and the friendship which was to dominate the world. In spite of all the demonstrations of affection, in spite of a mutual show of spontaneous enjoyment of each other's company, it was a friendship full of reserves. The unfortunate King of Prussia had to give up all his territories west of the Elbe, as well as his newly acquired Polish lands. The Grand duchy of Warsaw which was thus established was also a possible weapon against Alexander.

But the friendship was to be crowned by grandiose schemes concerning the East. Selim's fall, as a result of a rising of the Janissaries, eased Napoleon's conscience with regard to the ally (Vandal says this without irony)[2] whom he had so recently assured that he regarded himself as ordained by Fate to save the Ottoman Empire. He now exclaimed to the Tsar, as if carried away by this news (though it was already known to him, he had the report given him, and received it as a surprise, in the other's presence): 'This is a decree of Providence [the word 'fate', though suitable for Constantinople, might here have sounded rather unchristian], it tells me that the Ottoman Empire can no longer exist.'[3] Vandal describes Alexander as hanging on Napoleon's lips and fired by Napoleon's imaginative eloquence to fresh dreams of eastern expansion.[4] Once more 'the barbarians' were the enemy, but this time they were the Turks.

Vandal's view of these matters is very different from that of Bourgeois. According to him, as we know, Napoleon was the instrument of France's destiny, and he rejects any assumption of an individual and un-French imperial policy. Thus he considers that Napoleon's mind had not been governed by eastern ambitions save during his Egyptian expedition. Since then he had used the East only 'by way of diversion or compromise; it was on that terrain that he hoped to divide our enemies, to break up the coalition by depriving it of one of its members, by drawing to himself one of the major powers, no matter which, and so finally to forge that great alliance which he needed in order to dominate the continent and conquer England.'[5] Not only was the coalition against France, which Britain again and again had sought to establish, broken by the Tilsit friendship, but Prussia and Austria were forced and Russia prevailed upon to act against Britain.

1. *Napoléon et Alexandre Ier*, I, 37.   2. ibid, I, 73.   3. *Manuel*, II, 292.
4. *Napoléon et Alexandre Ier*, I, 3.   5. *Manuel*, II, 293.

It cannot be denied that this was the result of Tilsit, but it need hardly be said that Bourgeois does not for a moment hesitate to declare Napoleon's ultimate and real aim to be conquests in the east: Constantinople, which he was not in any case going to leave to his new friend; Egypt; India ... Only he was not yet ready for these far-reaching schemes. First he had to strengthen his naval position in the Mediterranean, and place Spain under a trustworthy administration – a mere trifle, this last item! It was tiresome, meanwhile, that Alexander was impatient and had to be held back. When it became obvious that Spain was no trifle but a miscalculation which once more gave courage to humiliated Austria, the rift in the friendship with Alexander became wider just at the moment when it should have held firm. Erfurt did not heal it. In the new war with Austria in 1809 Napoleon was practically left in the lurch by his ally.

After stupendous efforts, he was victorious once more. And what did he demand at the peace? Illyria, that is Carinthia and Croatia south of the Save. Dalmatia, Istria, and the islands (acquired at Pressburg in 1805) were not enough for his schemes. He had to have a wide and safe land route to the Ottoman Empire, one which was not too liable to be cut by Austria.[1]

1812–13

Again, therefore, according to Bourgeois's interpretation, the lure of the east! But in the years immediately following it was still not possible to take the road thither which had just been opened. There was Spain, and in particular there were the relations with Alexander, which kept deteriorating. The danger of a resurrected Poland hostile to himself made the Tsar doubly distrustful. Finally the moment came when Napoleon made ready to take up his tried sword, always his last resort, against his opponent the sometime Tilsit friend, blocking the route to the east. The Poles must play their part.

To awaken the national fibre of that nation, to carry it with me ... I like the Poles on the battlefield: they furnish it well ...[2]

Poland was only a means. Moscow was to open the door to his life's dream, Asia, the Balkans; and if he had to give up Poland to the Tsar, after initial victories, or use it to buy the good will of his refractory ally Austria, why not?

Thus to the very last Bourgeois shows Napoleon as dominated by that single idea, the east. Even after the disaster of 1812, during the negotiations with Metternich in the summer of 1813, when Austria, having resumed its freedom of action, has to be prevented from aligning itself irrevocably with the coalition of Russia, Prussia, and Britain, Napoleon cannot bring himself to restore Illyria, and thus

1. *Manuel*, II, 430.   2. *Manuel*, II, 495 ff.

throws away his last chance and with it the last chance of France to retain the power with which she had entrusted herself to the First Consul.

He pictures Metternich as an agent of England; it is his theme and, to the last, his pretext. To hand over to Austria Illyria, perhaps Venice, his share of dreams and of ambition – never! Sooner ask France, while exploiting her, to make a last sacrifice: 'A man like me is hardly concerned about a million lives.'[1] [Words which Napoleon is alleged to have spoken in his last conversation with Metternich.]

The passages in which Bourgeois emphasizes Napoleon's eastern ambitions and the way in which he hoodwinked the French people, I have picked out from his narrative, which in so doing I have perhaps made to appear unduly simplified and emphatic. Nevertheless he stated his views without ambiguity. No reader of his book can for a moment be in doubt what he ascribed to Napoleon and what he blamed him for. Napoleon abused the trust placed in him by the French people, he was responsible for the war and the disasters, and his motive was not any concern for French interests, however eloquently he spoke about them, but his own personal fantastic longing for the east. I shall not now discuss this interpretation of Napoleon's foreign policy. When I come shortly to expound the systems of Sorel and of Driault, it will inevitably be tested.

1. *Manuel*, II, 520.

3 Two More Old Acquaintances

BEFORE I come to Sorel, I must recall the conceptions of Masson, and deal briefly with a book, in which the author of *Napoléon intime*, ten years after the appearance of that work, set himself to deal with the problem of Napoleon's foreign policy.

MASSON: BRITAIN THE ENEMY, NAPOLEON THE LIBERATOR OF THE NATIONS

We already know (see p. 189 ff.) that Masson had dealt at length with foreign policy in volumes III and IV of his *Napoléon et sa famille*, and that he gave his own interpretations, which do not agree too well with one another. It is possible to gather from those thirteen volumes that the true motive force of Napoleon's European policy was his family sense. On this showing, the Emperor did not so much use his brothers to administer *le Grand Empire*; he undertook his wars, and founded the empire on the fruits of his victories, in order to provide thrones for his brothers. The idea will be remembered from Balzac's story (p. 28); it seems somewhat in conflict with more authentic versions of the Napoleonic legend, although Balzac's veteran and his peasant audience found in it nothing to offend them. But in the introduction to his eighth volume (published in 1906) Masson takes the completely different viewpoint advanced by Vandal. Napoleon's policy and his wars are no longer determined by his omnipotent will. The Emperor and France are prisoners of the iron necessity of the struggle with Britain. Probably it was under the influence not of Vandal but of Sorel that Masson wrote in this strain. No one else at any rate worked up the theme of the implacable conflict between France and Britain to such a hymn of hate, even though his outburst can certainly be regarded as typical of feelings which no doubt Napoleon found in existence but which he subsequently fanned so successfully that even at the present day they have not lost their hold on the French mind.

But there is another aspect of Masson's view of Napoleon as a European figure, to which I have only referred in passing when dealing with his work but which deserves more emphasis here. He sees in him the liberator of the nations.

When Napoleon returns from Elba and Louis XVIII is forced to flee, Europe – still assembled at Vienna – has no thought of recognizing the Emperor. It excommunicates him, and at the same time, according to Masson (who, however, is quite wrong here), the sovereigns declare themselves ready to afford assistance to each government for the maintenance of the threatened order of things.[1]

Thus [Masson continues] his worst enemies enunciated, more eloquently than his most faithful friends could have done, this truth with respect to Napoleon, that his cause is the nation's cause; if he should fail, no nation will have the right to dispose of itself; each nation belongs to its sovereign . . .; all the principles proclaimed by the Revolution, popular sovereignty and national independence, will be compromised by his fall, saved by his triumph. The doctrine of the Holy Alliance is here already fully expressed, and the oppression of the peoples depends on whether Napoleon will vanquish or be defeated.

This view forms an integral part of the Napoleonic legend. For half a century after the Congress of Vienna it continued to exert an influence in Europe. Even in more recent times it can be traced in the work of French historians.[2] Yet the Dutchman, who remembers what happened to his countrymen under Napoleon, will find it difficult even to understand how such an idea could ever be formed. And indeed, one has to think of other parts of Europe – of Poland, of Italy, even of west and south Germany. And if here, too, objections crowd upon one's mind, one has to look at the period after the fall of Napoleon, a period of bitter disillusionment for all these peoples, of longing for a change, for liberation, and for national unity. The legend then becomes at least intelligible.

I shall be dealing with the problems which arise in connexion with this when I come to another writer, Driault.

ARTHUR-LÉVY ON NAPOLEON AND THE PEACE

In 1902 Arthur-Lévy published a second book, *Napoléon et la paix*. Much more ambitious than *Napoléon intime*, it was not nearly so successful an achievement. The writer's blind partiality and lack of critical acumen are even more in evidence here. The book is in fact only an extremely detailed study (of 650 pages) of diplomatic relations with Prussia in the years 1806 and 1807, although presented to the reader as a demonstration of the truth that throughout his career Napoleon pursued no other aim but peace. Arthur-Lévy expresses this idea in an even more provocative way than Vandal:

During the whole of his reign his sole aim was to arrive at a just and lasting peace which would ensure to France that status to which she is entitled.

1. *Napoléon et sa famille*, XI, 22; see remark at the end of note on p. 189 ff. above.
2. See e.g. in LAVISSE, *Histoire de la France contemporaine*, volume on *La Restauration* (1924), by Charléty, p. 76: 'Vainqueurs avec la France pendant vingt-cinq ans, la Révolution et les peuples étaient vaincus par sa défaite.'

Of course one feels at once prompted to ask, to what status is France entitled? How far should the interests of other nations be subordinated to French claims? Writers of other nationalities are likely to disagree with Napoleon and with Arthur-Lévy as to the answer, though fortunately there have been French writers too who realized that this is indeed the crux of the matter and that a statement such as the one quoted has no meaning.[1]

Arthur-Lévy continues:

England's unchanging rivalry, the terror of ancient thrones at the spectacle of a dynasty sprung up overnight, the hope of throwing up a dam against the spread of libertarian ideas, and the secret appetites of all, those were the elements out of which the successive coalitions were forged and against which Napoleon's pacific attempts were ever in vain.

Arthur-Lévy really attempts no more than to confirm by means of the facts the statements of the great man himself. The *Mémorial* is his bible. What did Napoleon say at St Helena?

All my victories and all my conquests were won in self-defence. This is a truth which time will render every day more evident. Europe never ceased from warring against France, against French principles, and against me, so we had to strike down in order not to be struck down. The coalition continued without interruption, be it open or in secret, admitted or denied; it was there in permanence. It depended solely on the allies to give us peace.[2]

So in his book the writer is concerned to show how false and untrustworthy were the Prussians (whom he disliked even more than he did the British, although they too are roughly handled). His task in this was not a difficult one, for the Prussians were greedy for their own advancement and at the same time were in an extremely dangerous position in 1806, which made them wriggle desperately from one side to the other. But next he sets himself to bring out that Napoleon was the kindest, most easy-going, and gentlest creature alive. This too was not difficult to justify, for in his public speeches and even in his correspondence the Emperor liked to show himself in this guise, and whatever he says is trustingly accepted by his eulogist, who at the same time does not take the least notice of circumstances which might excuse a contrary opinion. In the end, with all his long narrative and his emphatic statements and moralizing, he has not proved a thing.

It is amusing to notice that here too, as in *Napoléon intime* with regard to the ministers and the marshals, he laments feelingly on the damage Napoleon did

1. P. CARON expresses this view in a review of the book in the *Revue d'histoire moderne et contemporaine*, IV, 121.
2. Quoted in *Napoléon et la paix*, p. 257.

himself by his excessive tolerance. Tolerance, he means, towards the old dynasties, for which Napoleon cherished an ineradicable respect. The writer even ventures to chide his god for not annihilating once and for all the monarchies which victory laid at his feet, as he should have done, had he understood better the interest of France. How many princes could he not have sent to distant islands, as they sent him in the hour of his defeat? Had he done this, the coalitions would not have been renewed against him every four years.[1] Such a conception of international policy is of course childish. As if, even as it was, Napoleon had not extended his empire beyond his power, and as if 'annihilation', banishment, extirpation, and annexation were a sufficient cure for all diseases and disasters.

One is tempted to accuse the writer of out-Napoleoning Napoleon. But no! Here too he finds confirmation from St Helena.

I may [says Napoleon to Las Cases, and Arthur-Lévy concludes his book with the quotation[2]] I may in the name of the sovereigns have been called 'a modern Attila' and 'a Robespierre on horseback'; if they would but search their hearts they would know better. Had I been such, perhaps I should be reigning still, but so much is certain – *they* would long since have ceased to reign.

1. p. 161.   2. p. 653.

4 Albert Sorel

HIS GENERAL ATTITUDE

ALBERT SOREL was a great figure as a historian, and the influence he exercised is considerable. His chief work, *l'Europe et la Révolution française*, began to appear in 1885 with an introductory volume reviewing the tendency, spirit, and methods of French and European foreign policy under the *ancien régime*, and this reveals the author's reading and his impressive powers of constructive imagination. By 1892 three further volumes had appeared. These gave a detailed diplomatic history of the *Constituante*, the *Législative*, and the *Convention*, covering the years from 1789 to 1795. A close organic link was maintained with the general development of the Revolution, and in particular with its ideas and its spirit. After ten years' silence, four volumes appeared at brief intervals in 1903 and 1904. Under the same title, *l'Europe et la Révolution française*, these dealt for the most part with the foreign policy of Napoleon.

Sorel had joined the Ministry of Foreign Affairs just before 1870. A young and promising lawyer, his experiences there had an abiding influence on him and his work, although after a few years, and in spite of tempting offers from Gambetta, he chose a professorial career.[1] He developed consciously and with conviction into the exponent not of this or that party but of tradition and of the *raison d'État*. A highly cultured man, subtly sensitive to ideas and to form, a brilliant stylist who like his venerated senior and friend, Taine, combined a passion for system and synthesis with great powers of plastic expression and creation, he saw forces at work in history other than those of the mind, impersonal forces which cared not for the mind, which indeed used it for their ends. The spectacle did not rouse his soul to opposition. For him true statesmanship consisted in the recognition of these forces and alliance with them.

This attitude had made it possible for him (how unlike Taine!) to consider the Revolution *sine ira ac studio*, and to perceive that its foreign policy formed no breach with the past, that those humanitarian impulses which would have meant such a breach stopped short at words, and that the longing for natural frontiers which took the place of these impulses had deep roots in the methods and outlook of the monarchy. In that famous first volume, he displayed a wealth

1. But it should be noticed that he was Professor at the *École libre des Sciences politiques*, that is to say, not under the auspices of the University.

of precedents from the monarchy for everything which the violent years of the *Législative* and the *Convention* were to bring forth, for the most revolutionary-sounding slogans, for all the brutalities, for all the encroachments on European international law, which its contemporaries so bitterly blamed the French Republic for. Conversely, in the later volumes, he was continually at pains to show how great a role was played during the Revolution by the *légistes*, the lawyers, a class of men always regarded as typical of the methods of the *ancien régime*, and how much use was made of their juridical arguments and hair-splittings. In thus bringing out the continuity of French history – in representing the Revolution as merely quickening tendencies and strivings which had determined the life of the French nation under the monarchy too, as having been slowly prepared under those totally different auspices – Sorel is doing for foreign policy what Tocqueville, in his surprisingly perceptive book published as early as 1856, had done for social and administrative conditions.[1]

From what has been said concerning his attitude to mental forces in relation to *raison d'État* and tradition, concerning his realism, it will be readily understood that he did not share the objections of Mme de Staël and of Taine. He gave sketches of both authors, sparkling with sympathy and understanding, but rejected the judgement of each on Napoleon, and for the same reason.

The crisis that was beginning [he says in his short study of Mme de Staël] was not a matter of wit, eloquence, or *cabales*; it was a matter of state, the most formidable ever witnessed, and it needed not those vain Pompeys and Ciceros whom Mme de Staël never ceased to worship, but some of those Sullas and Caesars whom she always abhorred . . . Her conscience was too fair, her heart too full of pity, her soul of delicacy; she was capable neither of leading men, nor of exploiting their weaknesses and utilizing their vices. To spare someone suffering seemed to her the acme of human activity. Reason of state seemed to her a blasphemy. The word State in itself contained something harsh and tyrannical which repelled her . . . She loved nothing but freedom. . . .[2]

Mme de Staël, he wrote somewhat farther on, was less able than most to recognize the Caesar to whom France was about to give birth.

There is a fundamental error in her judgement concerning the Revolution . . . Of the two aims of the Revolution that matter, civil liberty and political liberty, the reformation of society and of the State, she was moved only by the second, while the great majority of Frenchmen were excited only by the first.[3]

(Here we have already a pronouncement on this problem, and we know that it was not for Sorel that Quinet had written. He includes in this judgement the

1. *L'ancien Régime et la Révolution.*
2. In *Les grands écrivains français*, 1890, p. 33.
3. ibid. p. 38.

entire party of 'Mme de Staël and her friends', the liberals, and this, according to him, is the reason why this party, 'distinguished though it was', never came into power.

They did not understand that France, left to her own devices, was transforming herself into a democracy in accordance with her instincts, impelled by her past and by the education she had received from her kings. The Roman liberty of the members of the Convention, the civic liberty of the Consulate, the people's obedience to the *Comité de salut public*, Bonaparte's popularity and his omnipotence, all this remained to the end inexplicable to those noble and ingenious thinkers. They proceeded with the development of their theories, while round them France moved forward on the course mapped out by her history.

I spoke of Vandal's respect for fact and for power. In the case of Sorel, this respect has been erected into a system. As for reason, with all his acute intelligence he forces it to abdicate as far as the State is concerned, or merely permits it to lose itself in the mystic creed of historical fatalism. This is what he says about Taine when, on joining the Academy, he has to pay tribute to his memory:

Until then [until the writing of that sensational portrait of Napoleon] whenever he measured himself with a thinker, a poet, an artist, Taine, himself a thinker and a poet, was able, when faced with the irreducible element, when passing from the formula to life, to supplement the impotence of analysis by the divination of his own genius. But here this divination failed him. He had said it himself in connexion with Guizot's work on Oliver Cromwell: 'In order to write political history one has to have experience of affairs of state. The literary man, the psychologist, the artist, are out of their depths.' The State was to Taine the last of the scholastic monsters which he had resolved to annihilate; he was absolutely allergic to the *raison d'État*. That is why, as in former days the *Comité de salut public* [Sorel, great admirer of Danton, also objected strongly to certain aspects of *La Révolution*], Napoleon remained a mystery to him.[1]

Nevertheless, it might be imagined that in spite of his admiration for Napoleon the statesman, Sorel recoiled before the appearance of Napoleon not as lawgiver and administrator but as soldier and conqueror, as Thiers had done after 1805; one might expect him to follow the example of Talleyrand, like Bourgeois and so many other writers, in making a distinction between the traditional French policy of moderation and the personal policy of the Consul-Emperor, which by its excesses disregarded the true interests of France. But this is not the case. Long before he came to deal with the Napoleonic period, Sorel had made it clear in what light he regarded Napoleon, that is as the inevitable product of circumstances determined by the Revolutionary government which preceded him.

1. *Nouveaux essais d'histoire et de critique*, 1898, p. 138 ff.

He had, for example, argued at the end of the fourth volume of his great work that all thoughts of a peace between Europe and a France extended to her 'natural frontiers' were no more than a chimera. Britain could never accept the possession of Belgium by France. Had France renounced the Rhineland, she might have prevented Britain from finding allies on the continent, but her dual conquest inevitably aroused the European coalition against her. This had happened before Bonaparte came to power. The natural frontiers were an article of faith for the new régime in France; the oath on the constitution included them. Bonaparte, in accepting the government, had also had to accept the task of defending them. This involved the whole drama of his career up to the catastrophe of 1814–15.

The only peace consistent with the Roman conception of Gaul [it will be remembered that in Roman times Gaul extended as far as 'the natural frontiers'] lay in an Empire in the Roman fashion, that is to say, England subjugated and France supreme in Europe.[1]

Lefebvre assigned a certain freedom of choice to Bonaparte in his early years, but considered that the decision of Lunéville bound him irrevocably to his destiny. Sorel leaves him no freedom at all. The fateful decision, itself determined by the previous history of France, had been taken when the Convention annexed Belgium and the Rhineland. In it were present, as the fruit in the seed, the wars, the further conquests, the Empire, despotism, and finally the catastrophe. Like Vandal and Arthur-Lévy, Sorel accepts Napoleon's own view that he had never sought anything but peace – peace. and the natural frontiers, of course – and that was an illusion.

BONAPARTE ET LE DIRECTOIRE (VOLUME V)

In the fifth volume, in which Bonaparte as army commander in Italy and Egypt already plays an important part, he does not yet seem to be entirely subjected to this idea. It is with a real pleasure that Sorel pictures him at work in his Italian pro-consulate, as he tellingly calls it, but he stresses the point that the ambitious general is carrying out his own policy and dragging the *Directoire* willy-nilly after him. The conquest and reorganization of Italy are at first exclusively Bonaparte's own affair, and tend to divert attention from the Rhine.

But soon the Directors were vying with their teacher in their eagerness for conquest and especially for the plunder of Italy. Sorel is as contemptuous of their interventions in foreign affairs as Vandal of their internal administration. They were inefficient and clumsy, but whenever the army's victories gave them the chance they became supercilious, exacting, and greedy. So can Sorel's judgement

1. *L'Europe et la Révolution française*, IV, 469.

of them throughout his fifth volume be summarized. In comparison, like Hoche on the Rhine, Bonaparte appears as the liberator, the protector, the master-builder.

It is the fatality of that age that through the folly and the corruption of civil power, the military power appears everywhere as the restoring factor, as the only one able to accomplish the task of order without which the nations cannot live, and the work of justice which the nations expect from the Revolution.[1]

How little does this tally with the story, as told by Sorel himself, of the sub-jugation of Venice, so specifically Bonaparte's personal achievement. But he tells it without a word of repugnance or reprehension. The trick played on the Venetian democrats, first encouraged to undermine their government and then, when they had served their turn, sold along with it, is scandalous indeed. But Sorel has previously referred to the precedent of the partition of Poland by Austria, Prussia, and Russia, and with subtle irony but apparently to the satis-faction of his conscience has placed the matter outside moral categories. When the Austrians, in their first peace talks with the general, inquired how he intended to carry out his offer of Venetian territory (the Republic of Venice being at that moment still neutral)

he needed only to quote the precedents of the Polish partition to release himself from the obligation of explaining how a state can be brought to agree to its own dismemberment. But he was anxious to show himself at home in the best circles, and acquainted with the ways of courts, and versed in all the tricks of the trade. France, he said, has a quarrel with the Venetian Republic, and her grievances will provide the excuse for a declaration of war, which will put us right with inter-national law.[2]

This matter does not prevent Sorel from surrendering whole-heartedly to the charm of Bonaparte's appearance at Mombello. The young hero, with his Joséphine, radiant with success and genius, and the young men about him, a veritable court, thoroughly enjoyed their good fortune. As yet they were hardly ambitious, thinking only of their duties and their pleasures (as one of them recollected later), while Bonaparte himself was flattered by Italian poets and intellectuals (one brought him his Italian translation of Ossian), who cele-brated in him their liberator from the Austrian yoke, from clerical tyranny, the bringer of life, the bringer of peace.

What is more natural [exclaims Sorel] in those days of universal illusion, than for all lovers of liberty to acclaim this young man, who seemed to be restoring the peoples and reanimating men's souls? Had not Europe allowed herself to be fascinated by rulers like Frederick of Prussia and Catherine of Russia, who were after all no more than builders of empires and destroyers of nations? For those who lived through

1. v, 168.   2. v, 156.

them, these were unforgettable days, of that intensity which makes one wish the course of life could be suspended; but life does not stand still, and Bonaparte, far from holding back events, was the very man to hasten them on.[1]

History so romanticized reminds one of Vandal, although this most unusual mixture of romanticism and refined intellectual scepticism is peculiar to Sorel. As in Vandal, so here, the radiance of the hero stands out against the dark background of impotence and trickery which is the 'lawyer's government' of the Directorate as described by Sorel. I shall shortly give an account of some of the arguments advanced against this presentation by other French historians. First, however, I will summarize the pages in which Sorel, after his sketch of the proconsul enjoying his triumph and letting himself be worshipped, goes on to consider the political figure, already pregnant with so marvellous a future, in all its peculiarities and in relation to the circumstances of France and of Europe at that time. They are splendid pages, and remarkable if only for the skill with which he as it were transfers to a higher plane factors which till then had been regarded as the proper working tools of the writers hostile to Napoleon – the ambition, the foreignness, even the unscrupulousness. The whole of Sorel's philosophy of history is here seen in action, the unreserved acceptance of fact, argued with such wit as to acquire a grace of its own. So irresistible does the stream of history appear, with the irresistibility of a divine power – nay, *the* divine power, the only one – that submission is seen to be virtue, the only virtue.

'Not the general of a republic now, but a conqueror in his own right,' was the description given in May 1797 by a diplomat. Sorel agrees with that judgement. Bonaparte learned statesmanship in all its aspects. Is it surprising, when he compares his rule with that pitiable misgovernment in France, that he prefers to put his triumphs at the service of something other than the greater glory of the lawyers of the Directorate?[2]

Everywhere he discerns interests and passions, and men who can be led by these passions and these interests, by desire, by ambition, by fear; be they the oligarchs of Genoa or those of Venice, the princeling of Sardinia [Savoy-Piedmont], the German Emperor, or the Pope himself. How much more so the Directorate!

The Directors crawl before him, he is in fact already the master. Nor did he need a very profound knowledge of history to remember the Pope's reply, more than a thousand years ago, to the envoys of Pepin the Short: 'It is better that he who wields the power should be given the royal title.' It was not the title that worried him, however. Director, Consul (like Caesar), Protector (like Cromwell) – he cared not for the word, but for the matter.

1. V, 178.
2. Remark of Bonaparte himself, noted by Miot de Melito: in SOREL, V, 178.

From the early days of the French Revolution political prophets had been foretelling that this revolution would find its embodiment in a man, who, through it, would subdue France and govern her with a power greater than that which had been Louis XIV's. Bonaparte saw it, as it had been divined by Mirabeau and Catherine, but with his Roman vision of history he had a clearer conception of it than the others. He more particularly *feels* it, since this history, which is revealed to his intellect, lives in him and seems to be living for his sake. He does not analyse it, he finds no subtle delectation in it; he goes for it, clearing away one obstacle after another; he sets out for the Empire after the fashion of Columbus, who reached the new world while imagining that he was encircling the old. The others are fearing, expecting, or blindly seeking the predicted and inevitable 'Man'. He knows him, for he will be that man. He reveals to himself his ambition, as his destiny finds its explanation in history.[1]

In a certain sense he takes the place in Europe of Catherine and of Frederick. These had dominated public opinion with the help of the French mind, lured from its allegiance to the imbecile rulers of France.

The Revolution had impetuously won back that 'magistrature' for France. It is to be personified in Bonaparte. If Frederick was the Philosopher King, he will be the Revolutionary Emperor. He will say so and believe what he is saying, and for long the French and the peoples of Europe will say and believe it with him. And in fact he owes all his strength to the Revolution. He absorbs the Revolution, he appropriates it, he shares its elemental passions; in his own person he welds together that spirit of national expansion and that spirit of royal magnificence which are so strangely mixed in the popular imagination. He will continue, with the large majority of Frenchmen, to proclaim: whatever is conquered for France is won for liberty. And he will think: I am France.

But nevertheless France remains for him a conquered country. He is no product of the soil; he comes from without. He is the son of foreigners. The French language is not his mother tongue, it is for him the acquired language of civilization, the European language. France is not the unexcelled, the sacred plot where his ancestors are buried; it can be extended to wherever his charger will carry him and his Roman eagles will perch . . . Therein lies his strength. Sufficiently imbued with the French spirit to understand the popular way of thinking, and be understood by the people; sufficiently peculiar, in his own genius, to remain separate from the rest while yet being one with them as part of the army and the people, this Corsican seized France, and identifies the French Revolution with himself . . .[2]

He admires Frederick and has made a study of him, but he does not allow himself to be dazzled, far less taken in. And indeed what a contrast does the patient, stoical, measured Frederick present, struggling with his narrow and poverty-stricken circumstances, counting on nobody but himself.

1. v, 179 ff.   2. v, 180 ff.

As for Bonaparte, he was from the first moment carried along with the current, the most vehement which history ever saw let loose, the richest in human force; it was the French Revolution, spreading through a generous and exalted nation the passions, the ambitions, the dreams of greatness, accumulated within the State by a monarchy of eight centuries, than which no monarchy has lasted longer. Those growing pains of France, these enthusiastic armies, that is what has made Bonaparte, through that he is everything, without it, in spite of his genius, he would be nothing but a prodigious and powerless individual.[1]

Bonaparte himself was conscious of being carried on by that current, and tended more and more to profess the historical fatalism which, even though Sorel describes it with a touch of irony, is fundamentally his own.

Events open up so broad a highway for him, he always manages to be so ready to put them to his advantage, he finds the history of Europe and the prodigious adventure of his life linked up so curiously and so constantly, that he comes to look upon his destiny as a kind of law of nature, of which he is the executor.[2] 'I declare [says Napoleon at the zenith of his power] that I am the greatest slave among men, my master has no entrails, and that master is the nature of things.'

Returning to the Bonaparte of 1797, Sorel shows him surveying all Europe and sometimes letting his gaze rest far beyond. The thoughts that stir within him, though he keeps them to himself, are always thoughts that live in the French peoples and emerge from their history.

France he sees peopled by men, Italy by children, Holland by pot-bellied merchants, Germany by herds enclosed within fences which their masters shift at will.[3]

The obstacle is Britain, or rather the British oligarchy; for, says Sorel, he makes the same mistakes as the Convention and separates the people of Britain from their government. Britain must be overthrown, for otherwise the new order in France cannot survive, and then . . . Europe is ours, and then for the Mediterranean Sea, Egypt . . .

The dream [comments Sorel, once more connecting these ambitions with the tradition], the dream which has fired French imaginations since the crusades. . . .

It is in this volume that Sorel lays, as it were, the foundation for his treatment of Napoleon as ruler of France, while from time to time casting a glance towards those later years. I shall give one more quotation from it. It is well known that Hoche, who was commander-in-chief of the army of the Rhine in 1797, was

1. v, 183.   2. v, 185.   3. v, 188.

the only general whose personality and prestige stamped him as a possible competitor for Bonaparte should a military government become unavoidable. He died in September 1797, just after the *coup d'état* of Fructidor (which was originally to have taken place under his direction), at the age of thirty-four. He has gone down to history as a true republican, a sincere lover of liberty. Sorel, with a respect through which pierces a scarcely veiled scepticism, refers to *le noble culte* devoted to Hoche's memory by republican France.

Hoche benefited from the immense deception to which the Empire was to give rise . . . France embellishes him with all her retrospective illusions and imagines that, if he had lived, she might with his help have broken her cruel destiny . . . The least Italian, the least Anglo-Saxon of men, neither puritan nor Machiavellian, as little familiar with the Bible as with the Digests, but a reader of Sully, whose chimeras of a Europe pacified by the Franks appealed to his imagination, while Bonaparte on the other hand nourished his mind with the maxims and the State realism of Frederick. The most completely and most fundamentally French of all the heroes of the Revolution . . . Would he have been strong enough to control himself and the victorious nation, to curb the lust for conquest, and, once the conquest was achieved, to win, by his use of it, the forgiveness of Europe for France's supremacy? Would he have been able to mollify that Europe which refused to ratify French conquests, being loath to undergo French supremacy? . . . Could he have compelled England to accept and to respect the Roman peace of the Republic? England alone, tough, inaccessible on her island and irreconcilable in her age-long rivalry, is enough to discourage all hypothetical conclusions . . . But the French will go on pursuing, with the shade of Hoche, the chimera pursued in vain by their fathers, renewing, against the evidence of the facts, and against the written documents of the past, the struggle sustained by their fathers against the nature of European reality, the hereditary tendencies of the French nation, and the necessities of the Revolution; so beautiful was this desire to reconcile, without in any way sacrificing one to the other, these three ideals, which a century ago mutually destroyed one another's liberty, the Republic, and the Rhine frontier.[1]

I said that Sorel's scepticism was scarcely veiled, but I might have put it more strongly still. For though at first he appears to be considering Hoche's possibilities with an open mind, his respect for what has happened, for the unshakeable historical fact, increases as he writes, and thus brings him to an eloquent expression of that fatalistic view of history which is to dominate the following volumes of his work.

CRITICISM FROM GUYOT AND MURET

The fifth volume of *l'Europe et la Révolution française*, which appeared after so long an interruption of the great work, made a great impression in France and

1. v, 224 ff.

elsewhere. The colourfulness and vivacity of its descriptions, of which my quotations give little idea, set within a scheme which for all its compass hangs together remarkably well, were bound to fascinate and impress its readers. Houssaye, Masson, and even Vandal (to say nothing of Arthur-Lévy), who hardly gave a more favourable picture of Napoleon than Sorel, laid themselves much more open to the charge of partisanship. Sorel appeared to view the fray from serene heights, and to deliver his judgements in the name of history alone. But the professional historians had many objections.

In the *Revue d'histoire moderne et contemporaine* for the same years, 1903-4, there appeared an article by Raymond Guyot and Pierre Muret, 'Étude critique sur *Bonaparte et le Directoire* par M. Albert Sorel', which ran to some fifty large pages. The writers begin by mentioning the general praise which the work was receiving. They consider it superfluous to add their own tribute of admiration, but deem it highly necessary to warn readers against the opinion, here and there expressed, that Sorel had said the last word on the problems of foreign policy under the Directorate. 'After this attempt at synthesis,' they conclude, 'there is still room for numerous and important studies of the subject.' Indeed one of them, Guyot, was to present a thesis of about nine hundred pages to the Faculty of Letters in the University of Paris, entitled *Le Directoire et la paix de l'Europe*.[1]

They begin with a minutely detailed analysis of Sorel's documentation. No history of foreign politics, they assert, is satisfactory which does not take into account records of other governments. Now here Sorel fell seriously short. Where published sources were not available, he had undertaken no archive research, yet such research was essential, particularly in Berlin, London, Spain, and Italy. But even the French archives were used in a perfunctory manner. The result is an excessive number of gaps and misapprehensions, which the reader, charmed by the flawless presentation and beguiled by the writer's assured tone, fails to notice, although they undermine the foundations of the book. The liveliest episodes, the most striking judgements, and the broadest conclusions, turn out to be built on a quite insufficient factual basis. This is all the more dangerous because Sorel is so much inclined to see history in the guise of a system, or to force it into a system. Conversely, the critics find in this passion for system an explanation of the insufficiency of factual material.

Did not M. Sorel [they inquire] to a certain extent, and of course unconsciously,

1. It is known that in France more is expected from a *thèse* than from the doctoral dissertation in Holland (or in Great Britain). It is written by older students, its scope is greater, and it takes a considerable place among the productions of scholarship.

distort his facts, if only by the way in which he narrated them, and did he not frequently allow his attention to be diverted from the critical study of facts to that imposing edifice of ideas which he was proposing to build?

They argue that on two important points, both of which influenced his view of Napoleon, the facts not only fail to justify Sorel's 'system' but actually contradict it. The first point concerns the peace negotiations with Britain in 1796 and again in 1797. It is true that General Bonaparte in Italy had little direct hand in this, but Sorel's whole theory concerning his career and his place in French history rests, as we have seen, on the hypothesis that there could be no end to the war with Britain, as long as France did not renounce the natural frontiers conquered since 1793, and especially the southern Netherlands.

And indeed of both these negotiations Sorel maintains that they were not seriously meant. Pitt entered into them merely to demonstrate to an uneasy public that France would not be prepared to give up the southern Netherlands. That he would never have considered making peace while the French were still in Antwerp is a proposition which Sorel thinks it hardly necessary to argue. British historians have tried to show that Pitt's attempts to conclude peace were sincere. Bourgeois was convinced of this. As a matter of fact Austria's defection from the coalition and her readiness to accept Venice in exchange for the southern Netherlands had been most discouraging to Britain. Just because it was of such importance for Sorel's whole argument to show not only that these negotiations had failed but that they could not have succeeded, it might have been expected that he would have gone thoroughly into the matter. But here too his documentation is totally inadequate, and he makes statements concerning instructions and intentions which, when the documents are examined, are seen to be wide of the mark.

The second point concerns the contrast consistently shown between the Directorate and the commander-in-chief in Italy, and which in Sorel's book no less than in Vandal's turns out so much to the advantage of the latter. Sorel's picture of Bonaparte as the liberator, the state-builder, in Italy, is matched by a presentation of the Directorate as concerned with nothing but robbery, intent upon squeezing the inhabitants dry, and indifferent as to the régime to be set up after the Austrians had been driven out. It was Bonaparte and the military in general who had to protect the Italians against the greed of the self-seeking commissioners appointed by the Directorate. It was Bonaparte who saw the importance of spreading revolutionary principles.

The critics show in detail the inaccuracy of all this. I can only select a few out of their many observations based upon very precise data. To begin with, Sorel exaggerates not a little the independence of Bonaparte's conduct and the fear he inspired among the Directors. In one case he is shown to have kept to their instructions, though Sorel stated that he exceeded them. In another, where he did exceed his instructions, the Directors did not hesitate to rebuke him. But in particular it is shown to be untrue that the Directorate had forgotten revolutionary principles. If they delayed in setting up republican régimes, it was as a result of reports received from their agents concerning the disinclination and immaturity of the inhabitants. As soon as a change in this attitude develops, the government in Paris proceeds with the republicanizing, without having to be spurred on by Bonaparte. Sorel praises Bonaparte for having considered the possibility of a religious pacification through the medium of the Pope – a foreshadowing of the Concordat policy – while in Paris men still clung to the blind intolerance of Convention days. The documents, however, show that the Directorate itself had already laid down the main lines of the policy.

As regards the sucking dry of the inhabitants and the personal corruption of civil agents in particular, Sorel's assertions and distribution of blame are indeed reckless. He neglects to distinguish between different kinds of commissioners. For example he assumes that one well-known personality had misappropriated funds (as according to him they all did), when in fact this man was a political commissioner, direct representative of the Directorate, and, having nothing whatever to do with finances, provisioning the army or taxation, he did not have any funds at his disposal. But, and this is important for the right understanding of the relationships, according to the two critics there is no ground for this belief in the nobility of the military and the depravity of the civil agents and authorities. I have already quoted (p. 236) a passage from Sorel which shows what far-reaching conclusions he based on this belief. Sorel writes as if the Directorate either ordered or at least approved all violence or extortion at the expense of the Italian population, while generals and the few honest agents, who wished to spare the people, protect religion, and curb looting, were suspected in Paris of *modérantisme*, of weakness, if not of intelligence with the enemy.

He gives as example the case of General Championnet. 'This rough soldier loved order – he was, as an Italian testified, a righteous man.' The commissioners came to Naples, where Championnet was in command, and their doings drove the inhabitants to despair. Sternly Championnet dismissed the troublemakers and sent them away. Whereupon the Directorate had him up before a court martial; and that was the end of order and justice in Naples. The whole anecdote seems to have been taken from memoirs, always a source to be used with caution. In this case the writer from whom most of the story is taken was an officer, a furious supporter of Championnet and critic of the commissioners. . . .

Guyot and Muret expound a general theory which is the opposite of Sorel's. Those who abused their power and were most greedy for money were the military, acting in connivance with corrupt agents. The Directorate's civil agents had their work cut out tracking down and suppressing these activities, and they did so at the instruction of the Directorate and with its support. The critics give one example, that of 'the notorious Haller', a banker and a jobber of military contributions. Repeatedly accused of corrupt practices, he was protected first by Bonaparte and afterwards by General Brune, till he was finally expelled from Italy in 1799 at the insistence of a political agent.[1]

Guyot and Muret do not refer to Vandal, but the reader will perhaps have noticed that their corrections of Sorel also affect the picture presented in *L'avènement de Bonaparte*.

But let me confine myself to Sorel. The criticism of his work cuts deep, and appears to me to be irrefutable. As regards actual diplomatic history the fifth volume is unsatisfactory, and we shall have to take account of similar criticism of later volumes. (It should be noticed in passing that for volumes two to four, dealing with the Revolution itself, the documentation is much more solid.) The thesis so dear to the writer, so often repeated and examined from different angles, has certainly not been proven. His work does indeed provide us with a striking example of the historian who approaches history with his opinions ready made, and who seeks only those facts necessary to support them.

There is no need for me to remark that such a method is open to serious objections. It is certainly not an ideal way of writing history, to construct theories without the most careful examination of the facts and without testing them all the time against what can be established as objective historical reality. But it should not for that reason be assumed that Sorel's work, or its last four volumes, is worthless. Not even Guyot and Muret suggest that. They merely conclude that

the work seems to us lacking, not in value, to be sure, but in solidity. M. Sorel's work, whatever has been said about it, is not 'definitive'. His judgement is not a 'verdict'.

This is absolutely true. Scarcely more than that can be expected from critics who, while the air around them resounds with praise, have been spending weeks or months studying the shortcomings, superficialities, mistakes, and omissions of the work in question. I could only have wished that these two excellent historians could have suppressed a certain spitefulness to be detected in their remarks concerning 'the agreeable style of M. Sorel', as if it were the sole cause of his popularity.

1. I merely note that a later and very extensive work, J. GODECHOT, *Les Commissaires aux armées sous le Directoire*, 1941, reaches conclusions which entirely justify the theory of Guyot and Muret. Cf. also in *Tijdschrift voor Geschiedenis*, 1941, Bartstra's thorough and instructive article: 'Nieuwe inzichten in de geschiedenis van het *Directoire*-tijdvak.'

Sorel, indeed, remains great for all his shortcomings, and in this fifth volume, too, not only as stylist but as historian. In historical writing, imagination and constructive powers must be kept severely subdued to critical judgement, but they are nevertheless qualities belonging to the great historian. Sorel possessed them to a high degree. We must not accept his views passively, but his statement of the problem never lacks importance. Even where he only stimulates disagreement, the reader's understanding is deepened. Nor do we get the untenable thesis all the time; facts do not always have to be twisted to suit it, and the untenable itself has its relative truth. Here are striking observations, amazingly apposite parallels, glimpses of unexpected connexions, in short, the reader is introduced to a rich and lively mind, and he will have to beware lest he be swept away. Yet some advantage will be gained from considering a little more closely the volumes that follow.

THE PEACE OF AMIENS (VOLUME VI)

It is only in Volume VI that the thesis constructed by Sorel as he was dealing with the history of the first revolutionary wars; and outlined above, comes to rule supreme. He certainly had not lost sight of it in Volume V, but it appeared as if the figure of Bonaparte might to a certain extent escape from it. The proconsul who imposed his policy on the Directorate, and had a quite individual and special interest in Italy, could easily have been presented as an unexpected element in the situation. But Sorel never did so explicitly. Now, and until the very end, the First Consul and Emperor is subjected to what Sorel seems to regard as an iron law of nature, the thesis that an enduring peace, especially with Britain, but also with Austria, and even with Prussia and Russia, was impossible while France continued in possession of her natural frontiers, that is of the Rhineland, Savoy, and above all the southern Netherlands, conquered in the first flush of revolutionary enthusiasm and declared inalienable parts of the one and indivisible state by a decree of 1795 which possessed constitutional authority.[1]

From this point of view the violation of the peace of Amiens was not, as I previously called it (p. 59), the turning-point in Napoleon's career as ruler of France. The fatal change had taken place before Bonaparte entered the political arena. Amiens could be no more than a truce, and it was not the First Consul but (as he called it) 'the nature of things' (see p. 239) which drew France into the new conflict, which was to end only with 1814–15 and the fall of France.

Quite different interpretations and explanations, however, had been given to account for the course of events. Bourgeois's view (p. 221 ff.) will be recalled. There was also an article by Martin Philippson which had appeared shortly before

1. *L'Europe et la Révolution française*, IV, 431.

in the *Revue historique*,[1] and in which, after a careful analysis of the data, the blame for the violation of the peace was ascribed to Bonaparte. A view existed that Britain in 1802, exhausted and discouraged by the second collapse of the continental coalition and the defection of Austria and Russia, was undoubtedly ready to allow France to retain the Rhineland and even Belgium. To justify his thesis, therefore, it was incumbent on Sorel to devote particular attention to the treaty of Amiens and its failure; nor did he omit to do so. His discussion of this problem forms an important part of his sixth volume.

The preliminaries for an Anglo-French peace were completed in London at the beginning of October 1801. It was not till 25 March of the following year that the final treaty was signed at Amiens.

Sorel is not so naïve as to attempt, like Thiers (see p. 59), to present Bonaparte as seriously inclined for peace. The peace, he says, was a move in his game. The French public, which he was at the same time wooing with the Concordat, expected it of him. He never regarded the settlement as anything other than a truce, but it was to strengthen his internal position and win time for him to consolidate his newly won mastery of Germany and Italy. He would be able to renew the fight with all the more vigour later.

The London Government (Pitt had resigned a few months before, and Addington's ministry was in office) was 'inclined, for similar reasons, and with the same undeclared motives' to accept a breathing space.[2] Britain had been left to face France alone. In this isolation invasion was an unpleasant possibility, and it was moreover feared that Bonaparte would close the whole continent to British trade. In case of a settlement, connexions could once more be resumed with the former allies. Both Austria and Russia seemed to offer possibilities. Moreover the British confidently expected to make a clever trade treaty and restore British finances at the cost of France herself. It is true that most of Pitt's former colleagues raised objections, but Pitt supported the idea, expecting that disappointments arising from the peace would make a renewal of the war acceptable to public opinion, and that meanwhile the 'truce' would give an opportunity for the necessary internal reforms.

This is, to begin with, an astonishing passage. Sorel, as he often does, begins by giving a long list of sources and contemporary literature of which he has made use. He fails, however, to account for his assertions individually, a bad

1. 'La paix d'Amiens et la politique de Napoléon Ier', *Revue Historique*, vols, LXXV and LXXVI. Martin Philippson, professor in Brussels, who has done much useful work mostly on sixteenth- and seventeenth-century history, writing in both French and in German, was not a Frenchman. For which reason I do not intend to cite his conclusions further. (They were most decisively in support of the view that Napoleon provoked the war.)

2. VI, 157.

habit already condemned by the contemporary usage of scholars. It is thus not made clear how he was able to probe the souls of the Addington ministry and of Pitt so confidently. Certainly the older French writers – Bignon, Armand Lefebvre, and Thiers – all give a similar interpretation. Data from the British side, however, all show not only that the public at large was relieved that the endless war was over, but that the government had given up the continent as lost and placed their hope for the future in the strengthening of their extra-European position, that in other words they were willing to give the peace a trial, provided Bonaparte did not make it too difficult for them. As for Pitt, he defended the peace in the House of Commons as an honourable settlement, not lacking in advantage, and expressed himself in similar terms in such of his letters as have come down to us. A few of his former colleagues disagreed, but Sorel's statement that this was true of most of them is incorrect.

I shall not analyse Sorel's account of the difficult negotiations which dragged on for six months before the peace treaty was signed. The scorn with which he speaks of Joseph,[1] who with Talleyrand was the official negotiator at Amiens, who gathered all the liberal and faint-hearted elements of the political world round him by blaming the warlike proclivities of his brother, and who was so blind as to believe Britain to be sincere in her desire of peace – and himself to be able to administer France better than Napoleon – the animosity with which he constantly accuses the British government and its negotiators of tricks, evasions, and obstructions; all this is intended to create an atmosphere in which the reader will accept his conclusion that the British were never serious about the peace. But our suspicions have been aroused by the passage quoted previously, and we now notice quite distinctly that not a single action of the British government is mentioned, not an utterance by any of its statesmen quoted, which would justify the accusation of bad faith.

It is certainly true that even before the peace was signed opinion in Britain had grown much less optimistic. Sorel would have us think that France's amazing recovery under Bonaparte had aroused envy and anxiety among the British. He describes the surprise of those who visited France after the cessation of hostilities and who found a country very different from what they had expected.[2]

Instead of wanton excess in the midst of devastation and impoverishment, they found cultivated lands; plentiful, abundant, and well cared-for cattle; neat cottages; factories under construction; everywhere order, people working, contentment, returning prosperity, a nation growing like a healthy body with powerful organs cheerfully functioning . . . And instead of a successful military

1. It is worth while noting that he here quotes Masson.
2. VI, 241 ff.

adventurer, they saw a statesman, and one of the most impressive bearing. Those who were most favourably inclined expected something like a cross between Cromwell and Washington; the most cultivated and the most ingenious [every-body will notice the indirect thrust at Taine] had amused themselves by giving the petty squire from Corsica the features of an Italian *condottiere* of the fourteenth century, changed, by the strangest conjuring trick, into the dictator of a revolution born of Jean-Jacques, Diderot, and Voltaire. What they in fact discovered – an infinitely more natural spectacle for France – was the *génie d'État* of the eternal rival revived in a single man, who was, for the greater glory of the *grande nation*, reconstituting the State of Louis XIV.

It is worth our while once more to note how completely Sorel accepts Bonaparte as the personification of the French State idea. His views concerning Mme de Staël and Taine had prepared us for this. But let us stick to the problem of the renewed war with Britain. It is not impossible that the spectacle described by Sorel may have caused some Britons to regret a peace which suited France so well. Nevertheless, it is more natural to attribute the rising scepticism about a policy of reconciliation in the main to the blunt manner in which, even before the final treaty, Bonaparte revealed the ambitions at the back of his mind. Although the treaty with Austria had guaranteed the independence of both the Batavian and the Cisalpine Republics, the First Consul strengthened his hold on both in the first months of 1802. Moreover, he immediately sent a strong expedition to conquer San Domingo, which was to all intents and purposes independent under its Negro ruler Toussaint L'Ouverture. He purchased Louisiana from Spain. Worst of all, perhaps, he turned a deaf ear to the British suggestions for a trade treaty, and even closed his Italian vassal states to British goods. Sorel, as much under the sway of protectionist views as was the First Consul himself, may write as though a trade treaty could only result in the enrichment of Britain at the expense of France; it is clear, however, that these measures in their totality must crush British expectations of any real slackening of the tension. And yet even so they allowed themselves to be pressed into signing a peace treaty without any of the concessions which they had tried to obtain.

Before going on to deal with the subsequent events which led to the expiration of the peace little more than a year later, Sorel pronounced its funeral oration. It is a passage of remarkable eloquence, and a happy sample of his skill in decking out his thesis with all the power and splendour of his philosophical ingenuity and his broad historical outlook.

Glorious though the peace might be for the Consular Republic, it was no more than a show piece, an illusion.

Later on Napoleon said: 'At Amiens I imagined in all good faith that I had settled France's destiny and my own . . . I was planning to devote myself exclusively to the administration of France, and I believe that I could have worked wonders. I might have achieved the moral conquest of Europe, just as I have been on the verge of accomplishing it by arms.'

If one compares this with what Thiers has to say about Amiens, (see p. 59) it will be seen that here too he did no more than follow Napoleon himself. Sorel is more subtle.

It was on St Helena that he spoke in this way [he continues] where he fought his lost battles over again, Leipzig and Waterloo, winning them, and fashioning his life according to his exile's dreams.

I remark in passing that the sincerity of Napoleon's statement is here accepted. It is also possible to see in it the conscious creation of a legend, for the sake of his good name with posterity and for the future of his son. Sorel continues:

Thus the people, eternal dreamer and poet of its own legend, pictures the history of its past in the likeness of what it would have wished it to be, and moulds its own destiny to its desires. It divests itself of its passions, which it no longer understands, and sets up cardboard scenery along the way, as was done for Catherine the Great when she went to see the lands conquered for her by Potemkin. No doubt the hour was a lovely and a brilliant one; but while that might be a motive for wishing it to last, it was hardly to be expected that Nature should interrupt her march and the miracle of Joshua be repeated. Bonaparte attempted – impelled by his interest – to maintain the continent in the state of submission to which he had reduced it, and to make use of the freedom of action he had obtained for himself to seek in India and in America for advantages from the peace. He made the attempt; but it was that very effort to stand on the peace of Amiens in Europe, and to develop it in France by trade and industry and by colonial expansion, which caused England to decide on the rupture. [I shall in a moment recall the occasion of the resumption of hostilities. It will then be seen whether this can with reason be described as 'standing on the peace of Amiens in Europe and developing it in France'] . . . The treaty of Amiens, like so many others, proved a precarious achievement, an edifice of clay built on shifting sands. To judge it, one must put it in its perspective, between its causes and its consequences, which latter were but the continuation of its causes . . . It is enough to have followed the negotiations [I have, however, indicated how difficult it is to do so in Sorel's account] to discern how this peace came to be shattered. All the avenues by which it had approached its conclusion were prolonged into so many ways of escape, down which it disappeared.

To make the peace of Amiens a lasting one, Europe should have attributed to it a character possessed by none of the preceding treaties, neither by that of Nymegen nor by those of Ryswyk, Utrecht, Aix-la-Chapelle, Paris, or even by the latest, Campo Formio and Lunéville. Europe, three times leagued against Louis XIV because that king had cast ambitious eyes on part only of the conquests of 1802, once more leagued in 1792 to throw back a France judged too powerful and in the words of an Austrian statesman to break the spring of that formidable State machine, should have accepted as a fixed arrangement what as a plan and as an attempt she had detested like the very monster Leviathan and had fought consistently.

There should have been a France who checked herself in the full rush of her revolutionary ardours, appeasing the passions which had for the last ten years urged her on to spread out over Europe and which had brought her to this triumphant moment; there should have been a France who turned her enthusiasm into common sense, her pride into modesty, her impetuosity into caution; who thought of nothing but how to enjoy within her magnificent territory the boons of liberty, the products of the labour and the genius of her people, to enrich herself, to create masterpieces; she would even have had to give up her interest in colonial conquests, and surrender Egypt, India, the Antilles, the Mediterranean, in order not to give umbrage to the English; she would, by a commercial treaty, have had to open her market to their industry at the risk of ruining her own, in order to console them for the loss of Antwerp and Cologne, abandoning her arsenals, calling back her fleets, retreating before the English on every ocean; she would have had to retreat before Austria in Italy and restore Lombardy to her, before Prussia in Germany; she would have had to allow to Russia the supremacy in the Holy Empire and tutelage over the Ottoman Empire. And, what is even more improbable, there should have been a Europe which, fascinated by so much moderation, would refrain from pushing on as France retreated; a France preserving enough prestige and a Europe enough self-control to permit French Republicans and Kings in coalition against the Revolution to put by their arms, each on their bank of the Rhine, and to respect the marks of 'nature' as the Convention had indicated them.

There should have been an Austria which did not regret Belgium, nor pretend to the supremacy in Italy; a non-covetous Prussia without any thoughts of supremacy in Germany; a Russia turning away from Europe in order to occupy herself with Asia solely; and, most paradoxical of all these metamorphoses, an England ceasing to be English, exclusive and ferocious, in order to find happiness in cosmopolitanism, no longer out for the control of the Mediterranean nor for the sovereignty of the seas; a creeping paralysis would have had to seize that England in the abundance of her strength and activity, with her traditions, her passions, her pride, her banks, her mines, her furnaces, her thousands of emigrants, her fleets, her merchants, her trading City, her howling 'mob', her Parliament demanding war to the bitter end, her inexhaustible credit, her contraband trade as lucrative as the legitimate, her untameable pertinacity, her genius for enterprise and for alliances; the England of the Hundred Years War, of William the Third, of Chatham, of Pitt.[1] That is to say, there ought to have been another Europe, another France, other peoples, other governments; the history of our Europe would have to have swerved from the course it had followed ever since the fourteenth century, and the French Revolution must have turned back on its steps.

1. The elder Pitt, minister during the Seven Years War.

And finally let us add to this the man Bonaparte, whose person and character count for as much at this juncture as those of Pitt in England or of Alexander in Russia, and who can no more be left out of account in future events than in those which went before: the Italian campaigns, the Egyptian expedition, Marengo and the treaty of Lunéville. The lovers of speculation, who dispose of his genius so light-heartedly, require a manifestation of that genius more prodigious than all he ever vouchsafed to the world: not only that he should transform himself, but that he should modify the nature of things, that he should become another man in another Europe . . . Later, and from afar [undoubtedly once more from St Helena] he said: 'I may have conceived a good many plans, but I was never free to execute one of them. For all that I held the rudder, and with so strong a hand, the waves were a good deal stronger. I never was in truth my own master; I was always governed by circumstances.'[1]

One may estimate the element of apology in this utterance of Napoleon's as highly as one likes. One may detect in Sorel's dissertation other weaknesses than those I have pointed out. One may in the end reject his conclusion, and continue to hold the view that Napoleon did have a choice at this juncture, and chose war – not because all the forces of the present and the past within and without France drove him to it, but because he cherished plans and ambitions, he, Napoleon Bonaparte, which could only be realized through war. Yet even then one is obliged to take account of a whole class of factors, a whole chain of ideas, which correct an over-simplified view of Napoleon's responsibility.

CRITICISM OF SOREL'S CONCEPTION

Let me not, however, refrain from criticism on that account. Sorel, repeating Napoleon, refers to 'the nature of things'. But I have already shown how much, in the case of Britain, the writer adapted the nature of things to suit his own purpose. The decline in Britain's enthusiasm for war, the timid acquiescence of the new government, even Pitt's concurrence in the peace policy – all these factors he either ignores or disguises. That Parliament of his imagination, clamouring for war, actually passed the preliminaries and even the peace treaty with an overwhelming majority and amid the applause of that 'howling mob'. And as for France, is it really necessary to imagine another France, in order to see a people sick of war and anxious to dedicate itself to peaceful activities?

It will be remembered that according to Bourgeois, Bonaparte was compelled, in order to get his war, to throw sand in the eyes of the French, hiding his real objectives in Egypt and the East, while seizing hold of everything that would revive the old distrust and rivalry towards Britain; in that way he hoped at the

I. VI, 202–5.

same time to rouse the British to such a state of irritation that they would declare the war and thus provide him with the excuse he needed for the benefit of the French public.

When one reads an account of these events (several have been touched upon already) in a large textbook or say in the article of Martin Philippson, the interpretation that Bonaparte exercised deliberate provocation is bound to arise in one's mind. The First Consul continued to expand his power in Italy, for instance by the annexation of Piedmont – clearly outside the natural frontiers – while in Switzerland he established his influence by military intervention. No wonder that all this caused anxiety in Britain. The worst, however, was the provocative tone in which Bonaparte dismissed all British queries about these matters or about whatever increase of power on the Continent he permitted himself.[1] The Treaty of Amiens had stipulated nothing about all this and therefore Britain had not the right to meddle. In the end he even used the unheard of threat that the objections of the British Government could only excite his appetite for conquests and induce him to establish that empire of the west they feared so much (see p. 60). Then there was not only the refusal of a commercial treaty, but also a number of economic and even financial measures discriminating against the British. Finally there was the publication in the *Moniteur* of Sebastiani's amazing report about Egypt (see p. 60) – the most amazing thing about it was the fact of its publication! However desirous of avoiding a conflict, the British Government now refused to continue conversations about the evacuation of Malta which it had undertaken at Amiens unless the First Consul was prepared to give explanations about Piedmont and Switzerland – 'trivialities', exclaimed Bonaparte to Lord Whitworth – as well as about Egypt. Gradually, and not least as the result of the public scene which he soon made against Whitworth (see p. 59), the patience of the weak London Government became exhausted, while the protests of the anti-French party grew louder – for undoubtedly there was such a party; the friends of Pitt had never ceased to proclaim the view that propitiatory words and soft manners were not the treatment for the Corsican. So at last the breach came.

Of course Sorel, too, mentions all these questions and incidents. Why then, one might ask, does not his account lead irresistibly to the conclusion that an exhausted and hesitating Britain was roused to fresh efforts by the irrepressible turbulence of this dictatorial conqueror? History makes a choice from the infinite multiplicity and diversity of life. A review such as I have given by no means exhausts the possibilities. Sorel finds many other aspects, utterances, and

1. I refrain from drawing parallels between these events and those of our own time; they are obvious. I must, nevertheless, recall how after the Munich Agreement Hitler took the line that Britain and France had no say in the affairs of eastern Europe.

events which he brings to the fore. It appears certain that Bonaparte did not think the British would dare throw themselves so quickly into another war. In the spring of 1803 he was himself not entirely ready, and therefore repeatedly expressed his desire to preserve the peace. On the other hand it would be foolish to imagine that the body of British public opinion, apart from that section of it which opposed war on various grounds, was only concerned with the fate of those small continental states which had been subjugated by Bonaparte, and was in no way influenced by hatred of the French, fear of the Revolution, or commercial imperialism. I have already (p. 247) quoted the passage in which Sorel describes the impression made on English travellers by the new France, and I emphasized that he did not omit to add[1] that they not only admired but were full of consternation. France was not only becoming too powerful; she was too prosperous and too industrious.

And England puts herself on her guard, determined to apply in industrial strife the same system as in the struggle for colonies: preventive war.

Seen in the framework of such tendentious observations, interspersed with facts and opinions of quite different tenor, the arguments which I brought together to support the view of Bonaparte as provoker of the war of 1803 lose much of their force. Perhaps it will have to be called a subjective judgement, but I am inclined to suggest that Sorel's presentation, his selection of this rather than that factor, was decided in the first place by his French nationalism, which made him fiercely anti-British (it must not be forgotten that he was writing under the recent impression of Fashoda and of the Boer War), and secondly by his enslavement to his thesis, itself born not without the assistance of that same French nationalism, to that historical fatalism to which it was his ambition to subject not only this particular critical problem but the whole of his great work from the first page to the last.

This judgement, it should be added, was immediately formulated by French historians as well. The *Revue d'histoire moderne et contemporaine*[2] again had a very detailed study by Muret. The Frenchman does not speak of French nationalism as motivating sentiment, but places all the more stress upon historical determinism. In contradistinction to the article written in collaboration with Guyot, he now pays generous tribute to the great qualities of the author, but he still has serious criticisms to make on his method and technique. In connexion with the problem of the peace and its breach in 1802 and 1803, of which he too recognizes the central importance, he is not convinced by Sorel's interpretation. The thesis, he considers, is most forcefully propounded, but in dealing with

1. VI, 242.   2. VI, 724-42.

specific problems the author leaves one too often unsatisfied. He takes no notice of the arguments of Bourgeois and Martin Philippson. Finally:

M. Sorel's views are not sufficiently supported by facts and the critical method behind them is not sound enough to permit of their unreserved acceptance.[1]

SOREL AND DRIAULT ON THE THIRD COALITION (1805) (VOLUME VI)

The story in Volume VI of the failure of the peace of Amiens, and the argument that Britain never took the peace seriously, are essential in the construction of Sorel's work, but equally important in his account of the completion and the purpose of the Third Coalition (Russia, Austria, and Britain, 1805), particularly the Anglo-Russian alliance of 11 April 1805. His presentation, however, is so distorted, that I propose, for the orientation of the reader, to give a short summary of the facts as set out by another writer, Edouard Driault, with whom I shall be dealing in more detail later. In his *Napoléon et l'Europe* Driault went over the whole ground covered by Sorel some years later. His second volume, with which we are concerned here, dates from 1912.

Napoleon had been at war with Britain since 1803. As we already know, instead of concentrating all his attention on the proposed Channel expedition, he had simultaneously pursued his Italian ambitions, thereby alarming and irritating both Russia and Austria, Russia by his occupation of Tarento in Naples in 1803 (Russia's interest in the eastern shores of the Mediterranean made her always sensitive here), and Austria by making the Cisalpine Republic into a kingdom with himself as king, in defiance of the treaty of Lunéville which guaranteed its independence. To make matters worse, he took the title of King of Italy, which gave rise to suspicion of the most far-reaching plans. Announced March 1805, the coronation took place at Milan in May of the same year. Europe was even more agitated by the subsequent annexation of Genoa (the Ligurian Republic) to the French Empire. The annexation of Piedmont in 1802, the first

---

1. I must note here a little book which appeared in 1904, shortly after Sorel's sixth volume: *Napoléon et l'Angleterre, 1803-1813*, by P. COQUELLE. It disputes Sorel's theory (which was also that of Bignon, Armand Lefebvre, and Thiers, as the writer points out) concerning the breach of the peace of 1803, on the grounds of new data from French and British archives. Coquelle depicts Napoleon as quite consciously shaping his course for war, because he expected to get his Imperial crown through war; he considers that the English showed remarkable patience under his rudeness and provocations, and that the annexation of Holland was the chief factor which made them decide on war. Coquelle was not a University historian (see p. 315 below). In various places he expresses himself quite sharply concerning Napoleon, but in the Introduction – this is typical of his period – he thinks it necessary more or less to apologize for this.

definite step taken outside the natural frontiers, had discredited the peace of Amiens in the eyes of the British public and so contributed to the renewal of the war. Since then, Napoleon had solemnly declared that the period of annexations was over. The anxiety and suspicion over this new action in Prussia as well as in Austria were all the greater.

That the elements were present here for the restoration of the coalition twice broken by French victories needs no argument. Yet it still proved a difficult business. Britain and Russia distrusted one another's ambitions in the basin of the eastern Mediterranean little less than both distrusted those of France. Austria hardly dared put her military strength to a third test, particularly if Prussia persisted in her neutrality. After abortive discussions in London between Novosiltsov and Pitt, who had returned to office shortly after the renewal of hostilities, an Anglo-Russian alliance was completed on 11 April 1805 at St Petersburg. Not until August, after the Milan coronation and the annexation of Genoa, was this enlarged to include Austria, though still with many reservations and merely through the exchange of notes in St Petersburg. Without waiting for the new coalition to be given a more secure form, Austria in her negotiations with France now took a tone which savoured of an ultimatum. Napoleon did not need pressing, and there followed that lightning switch from Boulogne to the Rhine, to the Danube, to Ulm and Austerlitz.

Anyone who approaches Sorel's account of these preliminaries to the new continental war with some knowledge of the facts will find it surprising reading. We know that he regards all Napoleon's wars as having no ultimate purpose other than the maintenance of those 'natural frontiers' inherited by the First Consul from the Directorate. How does he manage to justify that thesis here?

One of his methods is to make appear as innocent as possible those abuses of power on the part of Napoleon which gave Europe the impression of unbridled aggressiveness. He does not, for instance, so much as mention the fact that the independence of the Cisalpine Republic had been guaranteed by the treaty of Lunéville.[1] His account of the new settlement begins thus:

The Italian Republic,[2] the object of Austria's covetousness [so ugly a word as *convoitise* he would not easily bring himself to use for Napoleon] the aim of her armies, was the fortress of French domination in Italy.

He does not actually say that this justification covers everything, but that is the implication. He writes in the same way about the annexation of Genoa:

Napoleon deemed Genoa as essential on the seaward side as Piedmont on the land.

1. VI, 427.
2. This was the name given to the Cisalpine Republic even before it was turned into a kingdom.

The English in Genoa [not, of course, that they actually were in that town] meant a threat to Provence. Moreover he needed trained seamen.[1]

And that is all.

On the other hand, the attention of the reader is constantly drawn not only to the 'covetousness' but also to the cunning, deceitfulness, and treachery of the other powers. Earlier in the chapter *La Coalition*, the defensive nature of Napoleon's activities is deliberately brought into relief:

The entire policy, all the military preparations of Napoleon, turned on two aims: either to prevent or to retard the coalition, keeping Europe in suspense, now with *coups de prestige*, then again with promises, until the day of his crossing to England; or, if the crossing proved impossible and he judged himself to be threatened on the continent, to throw himself upon Germany and establish his control there, to crush Austria before the arrival of the Russians, thus making any coalition against France for ever impossible, and since he had been unable to annihilate English power in London, to reduce them to their island and to turn the coalition against them.[2]

Should the Italian crown and the annexation of Genoa come under the heading of innocent *coups de prestige*? Or are they already to be numbered among the defensive measures taken by a Napoleon who feels himself threatened? And would not a mention of the fact that other powers felt themselves threatened have been relevant?

But when he deals with the agreements of April and August 1805, which at last brought Britain, Russia, and Austria more or less in accord with one another, Sorel sees only one thing, and that he tries to impress upon his readers with all the force of his strong dialectical powers and his stylistic art. 'Europe' is uniting in order to fall upon France, and under fair pretexts and to the accompaniment of fine-sounding slogans to thrust her back behind her old frontiers. The instructions given to Novosiltsov, on the occasion of his abortive mission to London in 1804, according to Sorel, betray the fundamental, the real aims of Russia. The fine sentiments with which Alexander was so free – indeed the views of his French tutor, a typical *philosophe*, had made a lifelong impression on him – were entirely mendacious. He wanted, so ran the document given to Novosiltsov, to deprive the French of their strongest weapon, the general opinion that they were fighting for the liberty of the peoples, and to turn that weapon against them. The purpose of the war was to liberate France as well as the rest of Europe from the yoke of Napoleon. France was in no way to be forced back into the *ancien régime* and its abuses. It was this fine talk, says Sorel, by which the French liberals were actually ensnared in 1814. The French will be told, so run the cunning instructions of Alexander for his emissary, that they can retain the

1. VI, 435.   2. VI, 378.

Rhine frontier, but among themselves the Allies will agree that France's frontiers are to be limited by 'the Alps and the Rhine to a certain height'. There, exclaims Sorel, you have *tout le fin* [all the finesse] *de l'affaire*. The French will think that this means a frontier from Basle to the mouth of the Rhine, but once victory is gained, they will be told that a frontier from Basle to the Lauter was actually intended[1] – that is, one that includes Alsace and Lorraine but excludes the Rhineland, Belgium, North Brabant, and Zeeland. This Sorel appears to regard as an unendurable and humiliating situation.

The Anglo-Russian treaty is concluded in April. And now Sorel is firmly convinced – the instructions given to Novosiltsov proved it – that *la pensée derrière la tête* of the contracting parties, the idea 'which dominates the remainder of the agreement and through which it is to be elucidated', is that the war is to be carried on, in order to push France back behind her old frontiers. This idea was maintained to the very end, and in particular in 1813; we shall later see how debatable it is even as regards 1813. But it might be objected that this idea is not to be found in the treaty. Not in so many words, Sorel admits. 'It was not deemed expedient, it was even considered dangerous to insert it into the treaty.'[2] He gives not a single proof, not a single quotation either from Russian or British sources, to back his assertion.

The most subtle trick, according to Sorel, in this thoroughly cunning and treacherous treaty, is the provision that a congress is to be held after the war and that Russia and Britain will not make peace with France without the agreement of all the allied powers, the members of the alliance. The purpose of this ('not obvious, but juridically certain') is that if one of the allies has persuaded Napoleon to negotiate, another can demand the congress, so that Napoleon could not begin the war afresh without bringing about his own destruction.[3]

The argument really becomes too far-fetched here. It is not surprising that Driault considers this one of the passages in which Sorel's thesis 'is most exposed to criticism'.[4] Driault's sober and matter-of-fact account, in the course of which he more than once directly joins issue with Sorel, is by comparison refreshing.

When he in his turn analyses Novosiltsov's instructions, he points out that there is no need to discover a snare in the reassurances which were to be given to the French concerning the new régime, and their freedom to make a choice. Alexander tried to carry out his 'republican' ideas in his domestic policy also.[5] As regards the article concerning 'the Rhine to a certain point',

1. VI, 390. 2. VI, 416. 3. VI, 419.
4. *Napoléon et l'Europe*, II, 198 note.
5. *Napoléon et l'Europe*, II, 124. It goes without saying that much more could be said about the aims of Alexander and of Britain concerning France. One could point to the pertinacity with which both, though their points of view were so entirely different (in contrast to the stubborn attachment of the melancholy and unbalanced Tsar to his idea

this formula also need not be regarded as evidence of deep-laid wicked schemes of Machiavellian intent. It is merely an instance of the inexactitude which marks the whole document. Russia leaves to England, as being more interested in Western Europe, the task of more exact formulation.

Nothing is more natural than the desire of reducing France to its old frontiers in the case of 'a successful war'. In view of the fact that successful war had to be waited for till 1813-14, it is obvious that what happened then corresponds with the plans made in 1804-05 for this eventuality.

But one is not entitled to deduce from this that before this successful war Napoleon would have been unable to consolidate once and for all the new territorial greatness of France.

If only he had known how to moderate his ambitions just enough to prevent agreement between his potential enemies![1] Indeed, how difficult it was, even so, to establish this coalition of 1805, which does not even deserve the name of coalition. All this talk about 'Europe' which grudged France its power, and of 'Europe' which followed its aim with cunning determination, misses the mark: 'Was there a Europe?' [2] Even Napoleon's 'indefatigable activity' was hardly enough to remove the difficulties.[3] The treaty of 11 April 1805, which Sorel takes so tragically, which caused Armand Lefebvre to foam at the mouth – 'let us keep calm', says Driault after quoting the latter[4] – this treaty, 'full of high-sounding phrases, of which some were in the conditional' is in Driault's opinion mainly a proof of the mutual rivalries and suspicions against which the would-be allies had to struggle. In any case, he says:

It is a sophistry to allege that the conditions to be imposed upon a defeated France were intended for the glorious France of 1805, and that the Emperor was therefore compelled to fight against an eternal coalition [?] for the protection of France's new frontiers.[5]

Indeed, even if one looks more closely at the secret articles intended for the situation resulting from 'a successful war', one will see that there is no question

1. 'Combien il eût été facile à Napoléon de rompre cette coalition si fragile! Il lui eût fallu seulement quelque modération' (op. cit. p. 219).

2. op. cit. p. 113.   3. op. cit. p. 194.   4. op. cit. p. 198.   5. op. cit. p. 201.

of a united Europe, there was Britain's sober calculation concerning national sovereignty, for herself but also for others), resisted in 1814-15 the desire for annexation of great and small German powers, which might have cost France a good deal more than the natural frontiers won at the Revolution. See for example the suggestive book by W. ALISON PHILLIPS, *The Confederation of Europe* (1914).

of depriving France of the Rhineland or the former Austrian Netherlands. It was only the country north of the line Antwerp-Maastricht that was to have been added to a Dutch State under the restored House of Orange.

Perhaps the main point made clear by Driault is that the coalition was the product of the provocations of Napoleon.

By crowning himself King of Italy, Napoleon provided a sufficient reason for the formation of the Third Coalition; it remained surest foundation. The annexation of Genoa supplied the immediate occasion.[1]

The Russian Minister of Foreign Affairs, on receiving this piece of news, wrote exultingly of 'Bonaparte's latest folly'.

Driault deals somewhat ironically with Napoleon's excuses in the case of the royal crown of Lombardy. The Emperor began by offering this crown to Joseph. As though this were a particularly virtuous and self-denying action, he announced it at once to the Emperor of Austria, who was of course an interested party owing to the Treaty of Lunéville. Needless to say, the offer was looked upon in a somewhat different light in Vienna, but matters became much worse when it was known that Joseph had refused the crown and Napoleon pretended that he now had no option but to take the burden upon himself. Sorel puts all the blame upon Joseph, who is said to have placed the Emperor in an awkward position. Driault, however, is convinced that Napoleon had foreseen Joseph's refusal and what is more had provoked it by putting unacceptable conditions. One feels a momentary surprise when reading Driault's conclusion that indeed

only Napoleon the Emperor could be King of Italy. The iron crown of the Lombard kings could belong only to the possessor of the crown of Charlemagne. To give it to anyone else would have been an absurdity in the light of history and a political blunder which it was impossible for him to commit.[2]

In other places, too, we are struck by expressions of generous admiration for the policy of war and expansion which is at the same time described with so much frankness. These are some of the author's idiosyncrasies which will find their place in the picture I shall give at a later stage of him and his work. Here I have only drawn attention to the passages where he dispels the apologetic fog of defensive intentions with which Sorel tried to cover the history of Napoleon.

As for Sorel, we can already foresee how he will be going to treat 1813 and 1814. All attempts to sunder the French nation and its dictator will be deception, all inclination to fall in with it will be treason. For all their apparently moderate peace offers, the Allies will have one purpose only, that of breaking French resistance, and Napoleon's sole duty will be to resist to the bitter end.

1. op. cit. p. 212.   2. op. cit. p. 163.

LE GRAND EMPIRE, 1806-12 (VOLUME VII)

I have pointed out that unlike Thiers, who draws the line at Napoleon's wars after 1805, Sorel tries to explain as defensive the whole apparently excessive policy right down to the catastrophe. Faithful to his thesis, in the years described in his seventh volume he sees Napoleon involved in a tragic struggle to preserve and to consolidate the position of power which France had acquired as early as the days of the Convention, the position within her natural frontiers, even though these had been further and further left behind. A tragic struggle, because he was always victorious and every victory made his position more untenable, in a Europe subjected but not reconciled, a Europe which no doubt underwent the influence of France and of the Revolution represented by Napoleon and became profoundly transformed by it, but only to turn the spirit thus roused against the conqueror and oppressor himself. This development, which appeared first in Spain, then in Germany, surprised Napoleon. He never learnt to understand it, unless perhaps when looking back from St Helena.

Sorel has no illusions about this lack of understanding.

By now there are Germans in Germany [it will be remembered (see p. 239 ff.) how he described Bonaparte as seeing only 'herds' there] and perhaps the most peculiar thing about the French supremacy is that it has discovered them to the Germans themselves, most certainly without Napoleon's knowledge and against all his calculations. Dalberg, the most grovelling courtier of them all, Prince Primate, and the last survivor of the ecclesiastical princes,[1] even Dalberg would have liked to see a new Germany spring from the Confederation of the Rhine. 'Rubbish,' Napoleon said, 'I have made short work of these fancies . . . In Germany the common people want to be protected against the great ones; the great ones want to govern at their pleasure; now since I do not desire anything from the Confederation but troops and money, and it is the great ones and not the common people who can supply me with both, I let the great ones alone, and the others will have to manage as best they can.'[2]

No wonder Chateaubriand ('who took a more distant and a higher view', as Sorel puts it) judged the Confederation of the Rhine, originally a profound conception, to have degenerated rapidly into a fiscal and military machine: 'The tax-collector and the recruiting sergeant took the place of the great man.'

But, for all its gross materialism [continues Sorel], the system is there, and it has far-reaching effects. Napoleon deals with taxable material and cannon fodder, but that material is human flesh, it is human labour, and the process produces a con-

1. Archbishop of Mayence.   2. VII, 486.

sciousness and a soul. Human beings spring from the clay that has been turned up, dug, and ploughed ... Napoleon thought that by effacing so many frontiers and drawing all these strategic roads he was merely tracing the way from his barracks; in fact he was opening the roads to a fatherland.

The rights of Man, the dignity of Man, preached by Rousseau – the effectiveness of will-power and the need for action, displayed by the French Revolution – these things are discovered at last by the Germans under the whip of the conqueror. They too want to be a nation, and they exchange their dissolvent cosmopolitanism for patriotic selfishness. Such are the unforeseen shapes into which the ideas spread by Napoleon are translated.

Meanwhile in France the dynamism of these ideas has weakened. France has become an empire of Diocletian. Napoleon himself used the comparison in referring to his domination after 1810. Sorel writes:

It is a Diocletian's empire in respect of the administration, the codes, the entire apparatus of government, the barbarians employed in military service, the fortified frontier provinces, and furthermore, outside, the mystery of the forests and of the limitless plains, of the Scythians, the Sarmates, and the Slavs.[1]

Sorel admires that organization for its fitness, as shown by its durability. Successive régimes have been able to make it serve, with slight adaptions; and it continues to exist, freshly painted and given a new dress at every revolution.[2] That under Napoleon no liberty was left, our great realist admits with as it were a shrug of the shoulders. Political freedom had been abused, and people were content with civil freedom.

National pride and political servitude – that is what the Convention and its committees had educated the French people up to. This French people, proud of its Revolution, though above all happy to have got it over, still looked upon itself as being the most enlightened people of the Universe, a torch among the nations, the lord of the world; and this, too, is after all a conception, and a very Roman one, of liberty.[3]

Sorel, however, is perfectly aware of the fact that this conception no longer possessed the impulse by which Napoleon in his early days had felt himself propelled (see p. 260). Nevertheless he puts every emphasis upon the fact that the Emperor and the Empire were still popular, and particularly with those classes which bore the heaviest burdens of the war, the peasants and the workers. And in fact, there was much material well-being in France; the Continental System was not as yet a burden to the French. But an opposition did exist, and it was serious, however hidden and secret; it was found among the high officers,

1. VII, 462.
2. We have seen Vandal give another account (p. 206 above).   3. VII, 462.

the court dignitaries, the senators; and among the officials, especially those of the higher ranks. Needless to look to Sorel for much sympathy towards these people's point of view. He is sure to have read Mme de Rémusat with scepticism. The explanation of the phenomenon he finds in the fact that Napoleon, 'after his coronation as Emperor, and more and more as he ceased to be the Emperor of the Republic in order to become a sovereign like the others', began to draw his higher personnel from among the royalist *ralliés*.[1] This was a grave mistake. There was nothing to attach these men to the Revolution or consequently to an Emperor who had emerged from the Revolution.

After having got everything they could out of the imperial régime, it became their care to preserve their spoils in titles and goods under the new régime [which they felt coming, and their relations to which they were already preparing] . . . Down to 1806, a royalist restoration would have roused to resistance all the interests in the country, all the prejudices of the men in whose hands, in that centralized state, rested power . . . After 1810, it could count on all possible facilities . . . It was not disobedience or insubordination; it was a treacherous readiness to do without the Emperor, to wish silently for his disappearance, to acquiesce in it beforehand . . . Peace within contracted frontiers and 'the Empire without the Emperor'.

While revolutionary dynamism was thus weakened in France, new feelings and passions were aroused in the defeated peoples by the principles of the Revolution and even by their very subjugation. Towards the end of the book this change is made visible graphically in the form of a striking contrast. Napoleon is staying at Dresden, surrounded by the throng of his vassals, before he starts upon his last enterprise, the expedition to Moscow, which is at last going to lead him to a fixed point of rest. At the same time, in the environment of Alexander, who is at Vilna awaiting the shock, tense excitement prevails.

Everyone working in Europe against Napoleon hurried to that court . . . If Napoleon had secured the services of the rulers, Alexander summoned the peoples. He concluded an agreement with the delegate of the national Cortes of Spain. He built up a general staff, a secret chancellery, of enemies of France, a proselytizing agency to rouse the nations of Europe, equally dangerous, but even more deceptive, than had been Jacobin proselytism formerly. There you have the great proscript Stein,[2] together with English agents and agents of the Neapolitan Bourbons; then there are the news-writers, the declared enemies, indiscriminately, of Napoleon, of *la grande nation*, and of the French Revolution . . . Even the failures of desertion

1. VII, 468; 'soit pour les rallier, soit qu'il les juge plus dociles'; 'peu dociles' must be a misprint in my edition. The remark of Napoleon is well known: 'Ce ne sont que ces gens-là qui savent servir.'

2. The great minister of Prussia, whose reformist policy was intended to raise the country after the disaster of 1806, but who was dismissed by the King at Napoleon's orders.

and plotting are called to the rescue, Dumouriez, for instance,[1] and especially that successful Dumouriez, that Dumouriez already very nearly crowned, Bernadotte[2] ... To rouse Poland with the deceptive bait of independence, Germany with that of greatness, France with that of liberty 'within the natural frontiers',[3] Spain with that of liberation from alien rule and of a free government – these are the aims for which they all work with equal zest, some falsely, others in good faith, all for the benefit of Alexander. They woo him for the support of his strong arm, they stir him up to the crusade, as in 1791 at Pilnitz the French *émigrés* incited the King of Bohemia and of Hungary[4] and the King of Prussia to go and crush *l'infâme*, the French Revolution. But the course of events had been reversed. French emigration in 1791 went against the current of the time; aristocratic, a caste movement, anti-national, summoning the foreigner to take arms against the French people's independence, it went under in the maelstrom. The *émigrés* surrounding Alexander were members of what were essentially national movements; each of those exiles spoke on behalf of his nation, and together they were stirring up so many national revolutions; they represented the independence and the liberty of their respective peoples. The effect of their action, favoured by tide and wind, was bound to be formidable. The prestige and power of the French Revolution had resided in the dual character which was also noticeable in the revolution preached by these exiles; for the prestige, a cosmopolitan, completely ideal programme, which would make it possible to unite the various peoples in one war; for the power, a patriotic and national plan, differing for each of the allies.

While Alexander, transformed into a liberator of nations, was holding that singular congress of subjected nations in Vilna, at Dresden Napoleon, the Emperor of the Republic, was collecting about him – and here was a still more surprising change – a court of monarchs ... He received his father-in-law the Emperor, his ally on parchment, but in whose soul lurked defection; and the King of Prussia, faithful in words, a traitor in his heart[5] ... The Kings of Bavaria and of Württemberg were obsequious and servile. But Napoleon divines the treason in the heart of kings, he has a presentiment of the resistance of the peoples ... At moments the infirmity of his system is apparent to him. ...[6]

1. The general, who conquered the Austrian Netherlands in 1792, but who, having joined the opposition during the Terror, entered into negotiations with the enemy and had finally to go over without his army.

2. General Bernadotte, brother-in-law of Joseph, had always been somewhat reserved towards Napoleon. Nevertheless he had been made Marshal and Prince of Ponte Corvo. In 1810 Sweden chose him as heir to the crown, and since he refused to promise Napoleon that he would never take arms against France, his princedom was taken away from him.

3. Deceptive bait (*leurre*), because Sorel considers that it was from the beginning intended to drive France back to her old frontiers; nor would the Spaniards get a 'free government'.

4. Leopold II, still not crowned Emperor of the German Empire.

5. *Féal* and *félon*: both terms in feudal law.

6. VII, 571–3.

A truly grandiose conception provides the basis of this volume, and it has been carried out with a master's hand: strong, fresh, vivacious, and witty, and with surprising insight.

The integrating factor is the recurring representation of the 'natural frontiers' as the purpose of the wars and as the real motive of the conquests. This does not reduce the work's dimensions; though if one takes historical acceptability as the test, it is the weak point. In this volume the argumentation becomes almost paradoxical.

I have pointed out (p. 86 ff.) that Lanfrey – one among many – presented Alexander's attitude in the gradually increasing tension before the crisis all too innocently. As Vandal has established, Alexander had taken considerable military measures. But it is quite another thing to conclude from this that he was preparing an attack, or even that he had not the slightest reason for being afraid of the continued expansion of Napoleon's power. When Caulaincourt, Napoleon's ambassador with Alexander, arrives in Paris in 1811, he beseeches his master not to embark upon the crazy adventure of a Russian campaign. Caulaincourt was one of the very few who dared maintain an attitude of their own against the master; he was a man of unfaltering loyalty and a man of character. Napoleon angrily reproached him for having been won over by Alexander, the trickster. But through Caulaincourt, Sorel remarks bitterly, the Tsar was able to convince his contemporaries and the historians that Napoleon alone had willed the war and prepared it.

Napoleon looked upon that war as inevitable; he thought so and he said so, but there was no one to believe him any more. He was struggling against his own fate and against posterity in that dramatic conversation with Caulaincourt.[1]

Caulaincourt warned him that Alexander was feeling concerned about Napoleon's plans for Poland. Napoleon objected that he had merely taken measures which must deprive the British of all hope and compel them to make peace.

Thus [speculates Sorel] matters were reduced to the state in which they had stood after the peace of Amiens and before Austerlitz. Then Holland and Italy had been at stake, of which countries Russia demanded the evacuation. The result of six years of war, of Jena, of Friedland, of Wagram, was to transplant the dispute to Poland; but the dispute remains the same. Holland had to be taken, in order to secure Belgium; Germany to be overthrown and dominated, for the retention of the left bank of the Rhine; Naples to be subjected, Rome to be annexed, so that Piedmont, Lombardy, and Venetia might be kept; the conquest of Spain was dictated by the need to have forces free to deal with Austria, that of Poland by the requirements of the war in Spain; the annihilation of Prussia was necessary for the securing of one of the Empire's flanks, the enslavement of Austria for that of the other. Napoleon

1. VII, 538.

fears that as soon as he loosens his hold on Poland, the Russians will advance in Germany, and that Prussia, seeing him retreat, and the Spaniards, thinking his position to be endangered, will at once take the offensive; Austria, which has all the time been playing for safety, will then also take a hand; he, Napoleon, will be obliged to summon his troops out of Italy, and, Italy once evacuated, the Mediterranean will belong to the English. The coalition will automatically be revived, history will turn back in its course: after the evacuation of Poland, that of Germany will be demanded; after Germany, Italy and Holland; after Italy and Holland, Belgium and the left bank of the Rhine. That is to say, in 1811 he guesses at the secret plans revolved by Alexander in 1804, which in 1813 and 1814 are to be translated only too faithfully into the deeds of the Coalition.[1]

It would be possible to make a criticism of this interpretation similar to that of Driault on Sorel's account of the completion of the coalition in 1805. In fact Sorel is doing no more than follow Napoleon's own presentation of events.[2] At the very time when he was arming himself against Russia, Napoleon spoke in public about the war 'against Carthage'. The Continental System, which Bourgeois sees as a piece of propaganda to divert attention from the Emperor's real plans, was taken by Napoleon in deadly earnest, according to Sorel. He believed that by it he could subjugate Britain, and it was his grim determination to carry out his plan that led him from one annexation to another, on the shores of the Baltic, the North Sea, the Mediterranean. It was, says Sorel in summing up, 'the *raison d'être* of his *grand empire*'.[3] Tilsit, which Bourgeois connects with the oriental schemes, is summarized by Sorel as:

War to the death against England, that is Tilsit; and to pay for this war, war against Turkey.[4]

Driault discussed this seventh volume in the *Revue d'histoire moderne et contemporaine*. While expressing the greatest admiration, he pointed out the obvious exaggeration of which Sorel is guilty in these passages. He too argues the connexion between the South Italian and Dalmatian conquests and eastern schemes which cannot possibly be counted among the defensive measures against Britain. Not that he tried, like Bourgeois, to explain everything by the eastern factor: the German settlements explained themselves. As to the overriding preoccupation with the war against Britain, which Sorel finds everywhere and which can in practice be traced back to a determination to hold the Low Countries in spite of Britain, Driault makes a comment which we have (pp. 221, 224) already heard from Bourgeois.

No doubt England is incessantly mentioned in Napoleon's correspondence, and particularly in his *Bulletins de la grande Armée*, in his *Messages au Sénat*, in his most

1. VII, 541.   2. VII, 114.   3. VII, 504.   4. VII, 187.

impressive proclamations. Was not this for him the only way to win popular approval for his insatiably bellicose policy, to justify it at least to a certain extent, to place himself in the right with public opinion and later on with the opinion of historians? It was essential to put forward some explanation of that mad ten years' chase across Europe. England was unwilling to disarm: there you had an excuse for all enterprises, against whomsoever they might be directed.[1]

THE NEGOTIATIONS OF THE SUMMER 1813 (VOLUME VIII)

The last volume of *L'Europe et la Révolution française* is the weakest of the eight. This is because the thesis has to be defended from beginning to end, against overwhelming odds in the shape of facts and probability. Nowhere else in the whole work does the thesis rule so supreme, and nowhere else is it so untenable. As we saw from the last quotation from Volume VII, and as we already knew (see p. 256), Sorel believed that the sole aim of the allies in 1813 and 1814 was to deprive France of all her conquests, including the 'natural frontiers'. Indeed, according to his view, they had cherished this ambition for twenty years, coalition or no coalition, in war or in peace. It goes without saying, therefore, that after the Russian disaster they prepared to make good their opportunity. Now the fact is that during the last year and a half there were continual negotiations in the interludes between the military operations. Sorel argues that Napoleon never had a chance to obtain peace without sacrificing the 'natural frontiers' for which he had fought for so many years in Italy and in Spain, in Austria and in Prussia, on the Vistula and the Beresina, and to which his 'new *départements*' (Holland and the north-west corner of Germany, 'the Hansa towns', the west of north and central Italy and the Illyrian provinces), his Confederation of the Rhine, his vassal kingdoms, his Duchy of Warsaw, were but the outer defences. Thus it was not Napoleon's blind obstinacy which upset the negotiations, brought war at last to French soil and to Paris, and swept him to Fontainebleau and Elba, but the unreasonableness of 'Europe', which grudged France the Rhineland and Belgium.

Such was not the current view, even in France. As we have already seen, both Bignon and Thiers considered that in the summer of 1813 Napoleon wantonly neglected the chance of an honourable peace (p. 216). We have seen Prince Napoleon place the blame on Metternich (p. 149). But Bourgeois, as we have seen (p. 226) once more looked for an explanation in Napoleon's obstinate refusal to give up Illyria, his gate to the east, thus sacrificing France to his personal ambition.

The culminating point of the negotiations was reached, as a matter of fact,

1. *Revue d'histoire moderne et contemporaine,* VII, 223.

at the Congress of Prague in July and August 1813, where what mattered was the attitude of Austria. This was Metternich's great moment. In describing the circumstances, I shall have recourse not only to Sorel's account but to the memoirs of Metternich and of Caulaincourt, and in particular to an article by Driault in which he reviewed this eighth volume, at the same time giving an account of events based on his own research.[1] I must add that this account, though extremely interesting, seems to me somewhat simplified and for that reason too positive in places.

Before his expedition against Russia, Napoleon had concluded alliances with both Austria and Prussia; if pressure had been needed in the case of the former, downright compulsion had to be applied to Prussia. We have seen (p. 263) how scathingly Sorel writes of the princes who came to grace the Emperor's court. Is there not more occasion for amazement at the shortsightedness of Napoleon, who imagined that the rancour caused by his mad misuse of power could be overcome with 'parchment' arrangements? Prussia deserted in the midst of the retreat from Russia, and in a short time Russia and Prussia concluded an alliance at Kalisch. The spirit which had inspired the French Revolution was now busy on the other side, and the signatories addressed a stirring call to the German people. The new Allies also tried to detach the French people from Napoleonic policy, in accordance, it will be noticed, with the ideas which Alexander had expounded to Novosiltsov in 1804. Austria too began to go her own way. That Austrian marriage, at the very moment when Napoleon expected it to work miracles, proved powerless to cast a spell on policy.

As early as 16 December 1812 the Emperor Francis offered his mediation, a role very different from that prescribed by his obligations as ally. Metternich saw a chance to restore Austria's position. He soon let it be known on what grounds he considered peace to be possible. Prussia would have to be strengthened with at least the return of her Polish territory (this implied the sacrifice of the Grand duchy of Warsaw, already indeed occupied by the Russians). France would have to forgo her recent German annexations, that is, the 'Hansa towns', as well as the protectorate of the Rhine Confederation. She would moreover have to return Illyria to Austria. To all this Napoleon answered with the most emphatic refusal to relinquish any territory annexed by a *sénatus consulte*. He actually bound himself to this not very conciliatory attitude by public statements. The repercussions in Germany of the call to arms from Kalisch, the unmistakable war-weariness in France itself and in his own immediate circle – nothing induced him to hesitate. The fight must be fought to a finish. As his new ambassador in Vienna, Narbonne (whose predecessor Otto had been

1. *Revue d'histoire moderne et contemporaine*, VIII: 'Napoléon et la paix en 1813, à propos du dernier volume d'Albert Sorel.'

recalled because like Caulaincourt he was too much in favour of peace), wrote to the Minister of Foreign Affairs, Maret, Duke of Bassano:

The Emperor will, I am sure, clear up everything with his magic wand, which for the moment can but be his sword . . . So please ask him, were it but to lighten my task here, that he win me speedily one of those battles of Marengo, Austerlitz, or Jena. More I do not desire of him, to reduce everything to peace and to render the universe happy.

'Here we have the authentic tone of Napoleonic diplomacy', comments Driault.[1] One will look in vain for this passage among the quotations from Narbonne's correspondence in Sorel.

But the magic wand had lost its power. Luetzen and Bautzen (in May) cost the lives of tens of thousands of the young men France had been obliged to provide, and though the latter battle was proclaimed a victory, it was in no sense decisive. This was all the more dangerous because Austria was using the delay to make preparations for war.

Mediation had become armed mediation, and the idea of having to yield to the threats of his false ally filled Napoleon with bitter and fierce anger. Nevertheless fear of Austria was a contributory factor in making him agree to a truce, which he intended to use to make his battered army once more fit for the field. The Russians, the Prussians, and the Austrians, however, were equally ready to put a couple of weeks to good use. It has often been considered since that the conclusion of the truce was the proof of his declining power even as a military leader.

What certainly had weakened was the spirit around him. Not only did the army consist to far too great an extent of hastily trained conscripts called up before their time, but the marshals themselves were tired. They were pining for rest, they grumbled and muttered among themselves. Even Maret – previously a fierce believer in Napoleon and his power policy, and accustomed to carry out the wishes of his master with a certain impetuousness as behests of the divine law – wavered and with much caution and courteous respect allowed the unpleasant word 'peace' to escape him, and the still more unpleasant reference to 'confidence shaken'.[2] But Napoleon thought of nothing but a fresh test of arms. He was in any case determined not to submit to the Austrian yoke. Rather would he seek for a direct understanding with Russia. But he had no idea of the obstinacy with which Alexander was now determined on his downfall, a mistake which is perhaps partly to be attributed to the influence of Caulaincourt, who longed passionately for peace and cherished illusions concerning

1. *Revue d'histoire moderne et contemporaine*, VIII, 186.
2. SOREL VIII, 125.

his friend the Tsar. Meanwhile, Napoleon's gamble on coming events, or rather his unconcealed annoyance at the mediation, drove Austria further and further in the direction of Russia and Prussia, who had now reached agreement with Britain too.

In Sorel's reading of the situation, these four had really been in agreement from the outset, and all Metternich's negotiations had had no other aim than to win time and to put Napoleon in the wrong with Europe and with France. One has only to look at the realities of Austrian conditions and of Metternich's policy to understand that the mediation was meant seriously, at any rate at first. The Kalisch manifesto had shocked the conservatism of Metternich as much as that of his master Francis II. The popular enthusiasm in Germany made them feel thoroughly uncomfortable. They were uneasy moreover at the thought of the influence which Russia stood to gain in Europe from the fall of Napoleon, and they particularly disliked Alexander's Polish plans. So true is this, that at the end of the war which they did after all fight together, the antagonism came to light once more: it will be remembered that in 1815 it was touch and go whether a war by Austria supported by France (which then meant Talleyrand) and by Britain against Russia and Prussia would not put an untimely end to the Congress of Vienna. How obvious it would have been for Napoleon in his distressed situation of the summer of 1813 – with Hamburg in revolt, supported by Sweden, and with the most deplorable news, Vittoria, soon to come from Spain – to accept Austria's overtures. But he could not do it.

The truce was to last till 10 August. On 26 July Napoleon received Metternich at Dresden. Already then matters had assumed a sterner aspect. In conversations with the Prussians and the Russians at Reichenbach, Metternich had prepared a treaty in which it was agreed that Austria would declare war on France if her agreement to certain peace proposals had not been obtained by 10 August.

This Dresden meeting has become famous.[1] We possess two versions of it, one from each of the two antagonists; and there was no witness present, to tell us which was correct. According to his own memoirs, Metternich was considerably more eloquent than he is made out to be in the note which Napoleon had made, according to which he scarcely said a word. Metternich tells us that Marshal Berthier, Prince of Neufchâtel, chief of the general staff, while ushering him in to the audience, anxiously asked whether he was bringing peace, and told him that France and Europe had need of it. Here we also find the story of Napoleon's angry outburst, provoked by a remark concerning the youthful appearance of his troops, in which he declared that Metternich did not understand a soldier's spirit, that he had never learnt to hold his own life cheap or that of others.

1. cf. Fruin's rectoral address, 1878: *Verspr. Geschr.* IX, 356.

A man such as I cares little for the lives of a million men ...

Metternich, if we are to believe him, replied that they ought to throw open the doors and the windows so that all Europe might hear. Whereupon Napoleon climbed down a little and said that of the 300,000 men he had lost in Russia, less than a tenth were French. To spare the French he had sacrificed Poles and Germans. To this Metternich replied: 'You forget, Sire, that you are addressing a German.'

From Napoleon's own report, too, it appears that the meeting was a stormy one. The Emperor began straight away with the most bitter reproaches. Austria had gone over to his enemies. 'Without your ill-omened intervention, peace with Russia and Prussia would have been restored.' What did Austria ask in return for neutrality? Would she be satisfied with Illyria?

It seems to me that the basis of Napoleon's policy reveals itself for one moment in these questions. He was ready to buy off Austria, if she would no longer concern herself with Russia and Prussia. What infuriated him was the idea of mediation. Mediation would inevitably lead to and had already gone a long way in the direction of collaboration between Austria and his enemies, and might well produce a settlement guaranteed by all of them against him. On the other hand, should the first possibility materialize, he would begin by disposing of Russia and Prussia – 'my army is quite sufficient to make the Russians and the Prussians see reason' – and would then be able to turn against Austria herself once more and recover what he had paid. In his outburst against Metternich, Napoleon summed up what he imagined would be the result of acceding to the collective demands, to the following effect:

If Austria (on these terms) got Illyria, she would not be content with that, but would want Italy too. Russia would want Poland, Sweden would want Norway, Prussia would demand Saxony, and Britain would put in a claim for Holland and Belgium. They wanted to tear the French Empire to pieces. And he, still in possession of half Europe, was expected meekly to withdraw his forces! What sort of a figure did they mean to make him out before the French people?

'Oh, Metternich, how much has England given you to decide you to play this role against me?' At these words (Metternich always denied that they were spoken) Napoleon's three-cornered hat, which he had under his arm, fell to the ground, and in the course of his angry outbursts he kept kicking it away, while Metternich, who also mentions the incident, did not deign to pick it up for him. According to Metternich, Napoleon's last words were an infuriated threat: 'Ah, you persist, you still want to dictate to me. All right then, war! But *au revoir*, in Vienna!' And when, at his leaving, after an interview which had lasted for hours, Berthier hurried up to ask if he was satisfied, Metternich according to his own report answered: 'Yes, he has made everything abundantly clear. It is all up with him.'

Immediately afterwards, Napoleon felt that he had handled the affair unwisely. In a second conversation he was amiability itself, and arrangements were made for a congress at Prague, where peace would be discussed under the now recognized armed mediation of Austria. But is it to be wondered that Metternich, already in a sceptical frame of mind after months of shilly-shallying and boasting, could now no longer believe in the possibility of an agreement? Even then Napoleon did nothing which bore witness to any desire for peace. Quite the opposite – the opportunity offered by the congress was allowed to pass. As Maret wrote to Narbonne on 17 June (the other French plenipotentiary Caulaincourt was to keep the conference waiting till 28 July) Napoleon wanted to draw out the negotiations if possible till 20 August, because by then the harvest would be in, which would be an advantage for the new campaign. He hoped, moreover, that time would allay the ardours of Prussia and Russia, and that Austria too would think again when she saw the tremendous forces he was collecting both here and in Italy. The cause of the unfruitfulness of the Prague Congress has often been sought; it is sought by Sorel in the ill will of the allies. But is not, asks Driault,[1] this letter explanation enough? It was not Caulaincourt's fault that he stayed away so long. He had tried every means to avoid leaving for Prague, if he was to be sent with evasive instructions; but at the same time he did his very best to move Napoleon to a more conciliatory mood. He urged giving up the new German *départements* and the Confederation of the Rhine. In return he got angry answers, doors were slammed on him, reproaches heaped on his head.[2] After days wasted in this way, he did obtain a promise, but to his disappointment it was followed by a perfectly useless instruction.

So, once at Prague, he could not refrain from going beyond his instructions in bringing pressure to bear on Metternich. He even did it in a way which according to French historians[3] verges on treason, though it can also be said that his action is only another proof of the disapproval, not to say despair, with which Frenchmen with any sense of responsibility regarded the Emperor's line of conduct.

Look on me [said Caulaincourt, who now sought comfort no longer from Russia but from Austria] as the representative not of the Emperor's whims, but of his and France's true interests. I am, in the questions now at issue, as good a European as

1. *Revue d'histoire moderne et contemporaine*, VII, 190.
2. This all from Caulaincourt himself: *Mémoires du général de Caulaincourt, Duc de Vicence*, Introduction . . . par Jean Hanoteau, 1933, I, 153.
3. op. cit. p. 156.

you are. Promote our return to France, be it by peace or war, and you will earn the blessings of the entire French people and of all the Emperor's sensible servants and friends.[1]

Metternich now uttered a grave warning that Austria had pledged herself to declare war on France if nothing had been obtained by 10 August. The transmission of 'that threat' earned Caulaincourt a reprimand, but at any rate Napoleon now allowed him to ask for the conditions. More days were lost owing to an undoubtedly obstructive absence of the Emperor from Dresden. His question was dated 5 August. The conditions Metternich laid down were: another partition of Poland between the neighbouring states; restoration of Hamburg and Lübeck, and abandonment in principle of the rest of the new German *départements* and of the protectorate over the Confederation of the Rhine; restoration of Prussia, with a tenable frontier on the Elbe (which meant that the former territories of Prussia in the west, now part of the Kingdom of Westphalia and of the French realm, were not demanded back); Illyria was to return to Austria; all the powers, great and small, were mutually to guarantee their possessions.

Caulaincourt sent the document to the Emperor, together with an impassioned appeal.

No doubt Your Majesty will see in this ultimatum some sacrifice of *amour-propre*, but there will be no real sacrifice for France . . . I beseech you, Sire, let all the chances of war be weighed in the balance with peace; have regard to the irritation in men's hearts, the state into which Germany will be thrown when Austria declares herself, France's fatigue, her noble devotion, the sacrifices she made after the Russian disasters; listen to the prayers of this same France for peace, to the prayers of your faithful servants, true Frenchmen, who like myself are bound to tell you that Europe's fever must be allayed.[2]

But Napoleon's answer, which could only be conveyed after the fatal term, 11 August, was on the usual lines. It consisted of two counter-proposals, the second of which was to be put forward only in case of necessity. Sorel does not consider it necessary to state the first; yet it is important enough. In return for the partitioning of Warsaw (which he 'did not mind' in itself),[3] Napoleon wanted compensation for the Grand duke, the king of Saxony, and that in the form of Prussian and Austrian territory. In the Prussian territory, Berlin was included . . . Prussia would thus become in the main a Slav state.[4] Metternich's remark that this did not give the impression that the Emperor wanted a

1. SOREL VIII, 165.
2. SOREL VIII, 173, and CAULAINCOURT I, 157.
3. CAULAINCOURT I, 151.
4. *Revue de l'histoire moderne et contemporaine*, VIII, 193.

durable peace is only too understandable. And even in the second proposal he still tried to bargain. Napoleon refused, for example, to let Hamburg and Trieste go; there was still mention of compensation for Saxony, at the expense of Prussia and Austria. The negotiations were broken off. War was left, and war not only with Russia and Prussia but with Austria also. At Leipzig, Napoleon was to find out what that meant.

Sorel, who has been at pains throughout his account to show that Metternich's sole purpose was to reach active cooperation with Russia and Prussia (and I have already pointed out that he neglects very important factors), makes no comment upon Caulaincourt's appeal to Napoleon, other than to say that it was naïve of him to believe that the Emperor's affirmative could have brought peace. At the eleventh hour, no doubt, everything had gone too far for the process to be arrested by one word. But is not Caulaincourt's complaint (in a letter to Maret) that this affair had been so badly handled completely justified?

The cause of our disappointments is in the refusal to make timely concessions, and it will end by ruining us completely.

Napoleon had had the most splendid chances to divide his opponents. The Dutch – or let me say all good Europeans – may well be glad that he neglected to use them, and that Metternich almost in spite of himself became the hero of Europe's liberation. But the whole story brings out Napoleon's uncontrollable pride, his gambling propensities, his complete indifference to human life, his blindness to moral factors such as the national ferment in the subjugated territories and the exhaustion of France.

This is not to suggest that the good European ought to close his eyes to the selfishness of the powers who finally encompassed Napoleon's fall. The Europe they resurrected or built anew was no perfect construction, and all of them strove, some with more success than others, to realize their own ambitions in the field of power politics, and thus – in some cases more than in others – brought about fresh injustice, fresh oppression. That is a point of view which Sorel is very ready to bring into prominence.[1] It is as if land-hunger and despotism appeared primarily on the coalition side, so bitterly does he harp on Alexander's unlimited greed for power, the maritime and colonial imperialism of the British, the avidity

1. Thus he underlines, for example, in the bitter letter in which Louis XVIII protested from exile against the imperial coronation, the phrase: 'Jamais on n'opposa le droit au crime . . . la Légitimité à la Révolution'. And he adds on his own account: 'Rendre la Pologne aux Polonais, restaurer la république à Venise, restituer les Légations au pape, les évêchés et abbayes d'Allemagne aux princes ecclésiastiques étaient des pensées qui n'entraient dans l'esprit ni du tsar, restaurateur de la justice, ni des augustes assesseurs de son tribunal, le roi de Prusse et l'empereur d'Autriche.' VI, 409.

and the hatred of France shown by the Prussians, and the immovable conservatism of Austria, which was again going to stifle Italy and a large part of Germany. In all such comments there is some truth. What is unacceptable is that
they should be brought forward as part of a system of apology in which, at the
same time, the fact that the entire public opinion of contemporary Europe
groaned under Napoleonic oppression and was weary of the Emperor's eternal
restlessness is passed over.

This is Sorel's conclusion concerning the abortive negotiations.

So the war began again, the war without end which had been going on ever since
1792, and it began again for the same reasons which had caused its twenty years'
duration and its extension into the farthest corners of Europe . . . What the coalition
wants is the destruction of the *grand empire*, the overthrow of the French supremacy,
the repulsion of France within her old frontiers. What Napoleon is in reality
defending on the Elbe, what he is inevitably bound to lose in case of his being
beaten back, are those bridgeheads, those advance posts, which the *Comité de salut*
public and the Directorate had marked on the map, and which were essential for
the conquest and for the retention of the natural frontiers.

How is it possible? is Driault's comment on this passage.[1] The reasoning is
indeed such as to make one rub one's eyes. Driault queries 'the old frontiers',
and it will have been noticed how far even now the demands of the allies fell
short of them. As Caulaincourt and others had warned Napoleon, it was only
owing to the war that the 'natural frontiers' were brought into question. I am
not going to discuss the rest of Sorel's book, but Driault points out that even
in 1814, had Napoleon only been content with what was attainable, there were
still possibilities of dividing the allies and saving the 'natural frontiers'. But
Sorel passes over these possibilities too, because they do not fit into his thesis.

THE OBSESSION WITH THE 'NATURAL FRONTIERS'

The criticism of professional historians has not been able to deprive Sorel's
arguments of their authority. Let me repeat that they are stimulating to the
historical imagination and must be considered as an enrichment of Napoleonic
literature. They cry out for criticism, however, and a good deal must be rejected.
Yet they have been swallowed whole in numbers of French and even non-French
books.[2] Many thousands of readers have met them, a generation later, in Jacques

1. *Revue d'histoire moderne et contemporaine*, VIII, 194.
2. As example of the latter I would only take MAX LENZ, *Napoleon*, in the illustrated
Monographien zur Weltgeschichte by Velhagen and Klasing. This book, which appeared in
1908, and from which many Dutchmen have derived their idea of Napoleon, is entirely
influenced by Sorel. In his introduction he praises Sorel and Vandal for their 'Ruhe des
Orteils', and at the same time appeals to Ranke and his 'Unbefangenheit der Betrachtung'
(see p. 219 above) to find a patron for the idea that 'the historical world was no clay in

Bainville's biography of Napoleon, of which I shall shortly have something to say.

There is something in this whole trend of reasoning which charms French chauvinism. The disaster of 1814-15, the loss of the Rhineland and of Belgium, have been sore points for a century or more. Talk of the bad faith of the allies, of their covetousness, of Prussian hate, of British selfishness, has been indulged in for its alleviating effect. And I need not repeat that the liberators of Europe did have other motives apart from those given in the Kalisch manifesto. All these are reasons why the Napoleonic legend has been able to strike such profound roots in French thought.

It is true that the Frenchman can oppose Napoleon on that very ground of the 'natural frontiers'. If it is accepted that Europe could easily have been reconciled to those French acquisitions, the conclusion follows that it was only the excessive policy of Napoleon which irritated European opinion, and in the end brought about the loss of the 'natural frontiers'. That is more or less how Bignon, Thiers, and Bourgeois reasoned, as we have seen; Driault and Georges Lefebvre will be found to say the same. This school, therefore, is not less convinced of the plausibility of the annexation of the Rhineland, Belgium, and North Brabant. A careful reading of Sorel leads one on the contrary to ask oneself whether he was not exceptionally reasonable and moderate in this respect.

If one follows his argument – that the Rhine frontier, including both German and Dutch territories, was bound to bring in both Britain and Germany, that this policy could therefore only be carried out by establishing a zone of dependent states through new conquests, which would indeed involve a life and death struggle with Europe, an endless series of wars, and thus would not permit of a peaceful republic but would demand the establishment of an empire on Roman lines – if one takes in all this, then the Convention decree concerning the 'natural frontiers' cannot but appear extravagant, as a measure completely outside European realities. It may be possible thus to exonerate Napoleon, who was saddled with this policy from the beginning, but the whole period becomes stamped with the character of a tremendous effort doomed beforehand to failure; however grandiose, it becomes a paroxysm of energy, showing all the tendencies of the normal French expansionism in an exaggerated form, and incapable of

---

the hands of the Titan, whose actions must be interpreted in the light of French and European history and the connexion of centuries'. And who would not assent to this? But the critical point from which Lenz deduces his argument is that in 1803 it was not Napoleon but Britain which wanted war, and he decides all other problems in accordance with this. He himself regards his view as a victory of objectivity over the hate-ridden tendentiousness of German nationalists such as Treitschke and von Sybel. Much might be said about this.

achieving anything more than that amazing spectacle.[1] But is it perhaps Sorel's intention in his great work to preach the wisdom of remaining within the old and more modest frontiers, and to warn his public that a renewed struggle for the Rhine would once more lead to nothing else than a heroic but in the end fatal clash with Europe?[2]

As a rule, it must be admitted, he makes quite a different impression. An explicit affirmation of France's right to the 'natural frontiers' will not, it is true, be found in his work. The whole idea of right in international relationships left him too sceptical for that. But he does repeatedly counter charges by the other European states against France's insatiable expansionism by pointing to their own practice. It is particularly the partitioning of Poland of which Russia, Prussia, and Austria had been making themselves guilty that he uses against them. The French governments were already in the habit of doing this, and not only with the idea of silencing criticism on moral grounds; they considered that the territorial expansion of the three Eastern Powers gave them a title to compensation. Now Sorel shows that this idea of compensation was part of the current European conception of public law, and considers that expansion to the Rhine was in no sense an exaggerated claim for the avoidance of a disturbance of the balance. He never mentions the fact that national differences made the annexation of the Rhineland and of Flanders unsuitable. In fact the principle of nationality leaves him cold.

No, Sorel did not erect his system into a warning against the policy of the 'natural frontiers' on account of its train of fatal consequences. Rather does it serve him constantly to identify himself with Napoleon. While he refers throughout to 'Europe's' envy and 'Europe's' desire to divide France, to throw her into confusion, to weaken her, he defends or extenuates everything done by Napoleon, since he was merely following the direction already laid down for France.

He is thus able to write as if Napoleon, who could not give up the smallest fragment of one of his conquests without bringing everything, including the early Republican acquisitions, into danger, was justified in his obstinate refusal

1. The final judgement at the end of Volume VIII is indeed only an extension of this idea.

2. The clearest example I have noted of Sorel's dislike of the Natural Frontier policy occurs towards the end of Volume IV, p. 477, that is to say, before he treated, after a pause of ten years, the period of the Directorate and Napoleon. 'Only the victories of Bonaparte,' he says there, 'made the realization of the conception of the natural frontiers possible' (let me remark in passing that this is a curious way of expressing it; the natural frontiers had been reached before the victories; Sorel means that the victories were necessary to consolidate them) 'and by speeding up the course of events, his policy brought to light the fundamental error of the system and made the inevitable collapse more disastrous.'

to accept what were on the face of it very fair peace proposals, and in his 'war to the death'.[1] Indeed, his defence of Napoleon and his condemnation of men like Talleyrand and Caulaincourt create the impression that far from uttering a warning against a policy of conquest, he found it quite in order for a great country to turn the whole of Europe upside down for the sake of what it regarded as its 'natural frontiers'. He seems to think that France, in order to keep Belgium and the Rhineland in her power, had a right to Holland and Germany and Italy, that she was free to liberate Poland or barter it away again as circumstances dictated, and to put Spain under tutelage. Napoleon actually did reason thus, when he found it useful to reason, and if another line of argument (for he had several) did not happen to suit him better. But to find an echo a century later in the works of a scholar, and one of so remarkable a mind as Sorel, remains somewhat surprising.

Let me conclude on ground which is more specifically historical. Driault thought Sorel's portrait of Napoleon was out of drawing, and he protested not so much against the whitewashing as against the belittling of the figure. That powerful personality – which had set its mark on Europe, whose own outlook and dynamic will shaped the destiny and the institutions of the western hemisphere – transformed into the slave of Destiny, with all its endeavours determined by the previous policy of the kings and of the *Comité de salut public*! Anyone putting the problem like this, and considering that insufficient justice is done to Napoleon's greatness, shows that he is himself possessed by a particular conception. Here is matter for debate, which many will be inclined to decide by the most general and *a priori* notions about the free will of the individual or about the compelling power of impersonal forces and tendencies in history. I have deemed it sufficient to treat the problem historically, and to show how much can be advanced against Sorel's system from this point of view, and to what a distortion of the facts it led him.

1. 'Il fallait, comme en 1795, comme en 1798, comme en 1800, comme en 1805, 1806, 1809, choisir entre une lutte à mort et le retour pur et simple de la France à ses anciennes limites. C'est du Grand Empire que l'on prétend l'exproprier d'abord, puis de l'Empire même et des conquêtes de la République.' VII, 118.

5 Édouard Driault

A SCHOOL TEXTBOOK

AMONG the writers I have discussed, only a small minority are professional historians, products of the University and teachers under its auspices. Apart from Bourgeois, Driault is the most important of that description. The work by which he first made his name was a history of the Eastern Question covering several centuries. He followed this with a school textbook. In 1903 he wrote the section dealing with 1789–1815, *Révolution et Empire*, in the *Cours complet d'histoire* edited by Gabriel Monod. He was then *professeur agrégé d'histoire . . . au Lycée de Versailles*. It is worth while glancing at this book, which as far as Napoleon is concerned belongs unmistakably to the democratic hostile school.

There is, for example, the emphasis placed on the loss of freedom which the *coup d'état* of Brumaire implied for the French people. After a description of the constitution of Year VIII, there follows the statement that 'France of the *ancien régime* had possessed more liberties'. Nor is a reminder lacking of how little the plebiscite to which the constitution was submitted had in common with a genuine consultation of the people. The constitution had already been put into operation. Voting was by writing and public . . . The writer has no more respect for the 'organic' laws which the First Consul introduced. Bonaparte, it is true, respected the great social achievements of the Revolution, but in every way he did away with liberty,

under the pretext of saving France from anarchy and 'of ending the Revolution'.

his administrative law killed practically all local freedom: the municipalities became 'minors'; the State exercised administrative guardianship over them.

Towards the end Driault writes that the Emperor's renown cost France more than it brought her, and that in a certain sense she was the victim of the great role he made her play. 'Caesarism only displayed its power and its glory by exhausting the country's resources.' That is what the scholars at republican colleges must be made to realize. The horrors of conscription, of the rounding-up of absconding conscripts (the *réfractaires*) are told, as also the suppression of all representative bodies (that of the Tribunate after Tilsit), of all free expression of opinion (the censorship), the oppression of the Catholic Church. The passage leads up to a quotation from the memoirs of Mme de Rémusat (characteristic choice !):

278

'The egoist Napoleon, thinking of nothing save himself, killed the Empire.' Dissatisfaction in Italy, ferment in Germany, war in Spain. . . .

The opinions of Driault in 1903 would not, however, be fully known, if no account were taken of his treatment of the events of 1813 and 1814. He had then apparently not yet investigated the negotiations of Prague independently, and he put all the blame for the failure on the bad faith of Metternich (a very different story, therefore, from that [see p. 267] told in 1907). But his indignation only reaches its height when he comes to describe the manifesto of 1 December 1813 and the congress of Châtillon in February and March 1814. The action of the allies in holding up Napoleon to the French people as the man responsible for the withdrawal of their offer of a peace leaving the 'natural frontiers' intact he regards as rank hypocrisy, and when, having reached French soil, they reduce their proposals to the frontiers of 1792, he like Houssaye simply sees Napoleon as the hero defending France's holy right to the Rhine frontier and to Belgium with the courage of despair, and he glories in the fact that the French people did not back Talleyrand in his 'treachery'. Here the non-French reader is struck by the crass contradiction with the writer's other views. I draw attention to it because we can perhaps find the explanation here of the change which Driault's appreciation of the whole figure of Napoleon was to undergo, which would otherwise remain a psychological puzzle. But first let us turn to his original contributions, prior to the change.

REJECTION OF EARLIER INTERPRETATIONS

The books from which we can obtain data consist in the first place of two monographs dated 1904 and 1906, entitled respectively *La politique orientale de Napoléon 1806–08* and *Napoléon en Italie 1800–12*. What strikes one in both is that the writer used them to develop theories about the policy of Napoleon in general, about the aims that were shaping in his mind. It is thus not to be wondered at that Driault next embarked on a great work entitled *Napoléon et l'Europe*, which appeared between the years 1910 and 1927, in five volumes. It is this work that has given him his important place in Napoleonic historiography. Nevertheless, in setting forth his ideas I shall chiefly use the two earlier monographs and one or two articles, and of the larger work I shall quote only from the earlier volumes. The reason for this will appear in the course of my survey.

We have already seen how forcefully and how positively Driault let himself be heard in the debate on Sorel's theories. He rejected the conception of Napoleon as driven by the impersonal forces of the history of France and of Europe; Napoleon exercised his own personal influence on the course of history. Sorel's theory distorts and belittles him. It does so not only by reason of its historical fatalism, which subordinates personality to the course of events, but also, and even chiefly, because of the interpretation given of this compelling development itself: that it was all done solely for the sake of the retention and security of the 'natural frontiers' already achieved, that Napoleon did nothing more than continue the work of the *Comité de salut public* and of the Directorate, which for their part continued the work of the monarchy. Driault will have none of this. Thus far he is in agreement with Masson and Bourgeois, who likewise discover a strong new personal factor in Napoleon's policy by which French history was forced from its normal traditional paths.[1] But Driault is satisfied neither by the explanation that Napoleon's family feeling (first for his brothers and then for his son) was the true motivating force, nor by the idea that his eastern dream was behind everything.

As for Napoleon having his secret, as Bourgeois called it, that to Driault is beyond question. Thus he feels urged to offer another hypothesis. Napoleon had an aim. His clear mind could not remain satisfied with a vague longing for world domination. There must have been something more precise, something that can be defined and described.[2] The uncertainty results only from the fact that Napoleon was indeed a secretive person. He gave no one his confidence, he hid his inmost mind. His correspondence is certainly an invaluable source, but

it is not always frank. He does not display all his ambitions, he never admits himself to have been wrong. He throws on his enemies, particularly England, the responsibility for the long wars by which he exhausted France. It appears as though he was always in a lawful state of self-defence, and that nobody possessed the virtue of moderation to the extent that he did. It is not incumbent on anybody to take him at his word.[3]

As, I would add, Arthur-Lévy and Sorel believed him, in his correspondence and even in the utterances from St Helena.

Britain, which Napoleon so much likes to bring up as an excuse, is important in Sorel's presentation not only for that reason but also because, as the most obstinate fighter for the independence of the Low Countries, it did seem to bear out the theory of the outstanding importance of the natural frontiers. Vandal, as we have seen (p. 217 ff.), was even more positive in his view of Britain as *the* enemy, never for one moment out of Napoleon's thoughts. Without mentioning him, Driault joins issue with a British historian, Seeley. This writer, endowed

1. I follow here the interesting survey of MURET in the *Revue d'histoire moderne et contemporaine*, XVIII (1913), 'Une nouvelle conception de la politique étrangère de Napoléon' (pp. 177–200, 353–80), written after the appearance of the second volume of DRIAULT's *Napoléon et l'Europe*.

2. *La politique orientale de Napoléon*, p. 375.

3. *Napoléon en Italie*, p. 1.

with vision and attracted by great subjects,[1] wrote a striking biography of Napoleon in which he pointed to the subjection of Britain as the real aim of Napoleonic policy; and this, it should be added, chiefly for the purpose of obtaining room for economic and colonial expansion.

What? [Driault exclaims] When he made himself King of Italy, it was to strike at England? When he destroyed the Holy Roman Empire of the German nation, when he founded the Confederation of the Rhine, when he resuscitated Poland, when he added the Illyrian provinces to his empire, when he set out for Moscow, it was to strike at England? That is indeed hard to believe.

True – he found Britain constantly in his way, she resisted him, she fought him, and finally brought him down.

England was his obstacle, but not his aim. If he had only wished to beat down England, why did he not attack her directly? Had he spent at sea one tenth of the effort which he undertook for the conquest of Europe, he would have stood a better chance of settling accounts with his everlasting enemy. But on the contrary, if he was defeated by England, it was because he gave no sufficient attention to her, because he turned his back on her most of the time, digging himself in in the east.[2]

This view of Britain the enemy as a slogan with which to deceive, this reference to the east, are both reminiscent of Bourgeois. And indeed Driault admits that much of the latter's explanation is attractive, and that it has shown him his direction a good part of the way. But it is too limited, too one-sided. In particular, he cannot agree with the reading of Tilsit which postulates Napoleon's willingness to share the Turkish empire with Alexander. On the contrary, he used Tilsit to keep the Tsar's attention occupied, and at the right moment to lay hands on the entire inheritance of the Sultan. But the chief difference is that Driault is unable to explain everything by the hypothesis of eastern ambitions as Bourgeois does. What have these to do with the Confederation of the Rhine, or with the annexation of Spain and Portugal, or with the crushing of Prussia? 'Prussia certainly did not bar Napoleon's way to the east.'[3]

It was not the 'natural frontiers', then, not Britain, not – or not only – the east. Nor was it dynastic feeling. In a review of Masson, Driault wrote: 'One must not attach greater importance to that intimate family history of Napoleon's than it deserves.' Napoleon did not allow his policy to be decided by his relatives, he used them for his policy:

1. His best known work is still, perhaps, *The Expansion of England*.
2. *La politique orientale de Napoléon*, p. 376.
3. *La politique orientale de Napoléon*, p. 377; cf. Bourgeois on this subject, p. 223 above.

He gave them such thrones as suited him, took them back at his pleasure, and hardly allowed the incessant demands of that insatiable band to trouble him.

NAPOLEON A ROMAN EMPEROR

What then?

Napoleon, says Driault, 'was a Roman Emperor'.[1] Or rather, he became one, he wanted to be one. His command in Italy – Driault takes this idea gratefully from Sorel – was his preparation for the Imperial office, as the campaigns in Gaul had been for Caesar. But at first the forms and tradition of Emperorship which gave shape to his policy were those of Charlemagne.

One of the most remarkable traits of Napoleon Bonaparte's mind was his instinctive but eminently picturesque feeling for the scenery of the past and for the historical significance of his own times and career. He carefully measured the symbolic importance of the imperial title, with one bold leap of the imagination he lifted himself up to Charlemagne, to Rome itself, and was immediately at home in that apparently archaic role: there was in his behaviour no trace of the upstart.[2]

Charlemagne: this, then, was for the time being to be the figure he wished to embody. Even before the coronation in Notre Dame, this was made clear during a visit to Aix-la-Chapelle, the ancient capital of the Frankish Emperor. There, in September 1804, he received the new Austrian ambassador in solemn state: 'That already suggested the abdication of the head of the Holy Roman Empire making room for the new Emperor of the West.' Indeed Francis II was not to carry that title much longer. He was to lay it down in 1806, after the territorial reorganization of Germany. It was from Mayence – surely there was irony in the choice of the ecclesiastical capital of the moribund Empire – that Napoleon sent his congratulations on the new title of Emperor of Austria, which Francis had taken beforehand. After Aix-la-Chapelle and Paris, Milan. For Charlemagne, too, the iron crown of Lombardy had been the necessary completion to the Imperial crown which the Pope had placed on his head. As in Notre Dame, Napoleon in Milan Cathedral himself placed the crown on his head. In his title, King of Italy, claims to the whole peninsula were implicit.

But to his contemporaries, the imperial title was eloquent enough.

There could be only one Emperor really, the Emperor was the sovereign, the sole master of the other princes. That was the classic tradition, handed down through the centuries from the Roman Emperors.[3]

1. *Napoléon en Italie*, p. 30.
2. *Napoléon et Italie*, p. 294.
3. *La politique orientale de Napoléon*, p. 394.

This imperial title, the imperial character of Napoleon's power – therein is contained the explanation of the new coalition which was formed against him, and which he broke up at Austerlitz.[1] But Austerlitz and Jena extended reality beyond the Charlemagne dream. Italy and Germany, with France, now formed the basis of a truly imperial and supra-national power. In all directions he sent out kings of his blood, to govern the conquered peoples and to assure to the imperial idea as many firm supports. Other vassal kings he bound to himself by marriage. The Holy Roman Empire whose shade he had so recently annihilated lived again, with its centre of gravity in France.

But is it not obvious that there could be no arrest at this juncture? Napoleon desired, and he had been aware of his desire at an early stage, the dominion over the Mediterranean. That sufficed to break through the form of the western Empire. Automatically the idea grew and became a resurrected Roman Empire before the split, when it included both east and west. The system of vassal states had to give way before the system of unity. In 1806 Napoleon had written to the Pope saying that he was Emperor of Rome (see p. 103), but in 1809 he went further and annexed Rome. The expectation and soon the birth of an heir strengthened this tradition. And then not only Rome, but Constantinople! The Holy Roman Empire of the German nation had so easily been shattered with a couple of sword thrusts; could the tottering Ottoman Empire give more trouble? Rather the opposite. 'Napoleon, the successor of Charlemagne, can also be the successor of Constantine. Only then would he in truth be Emperor.'[2]

That the imperial idea in its full classical import became for Napoleon a compelling law of life – nothing could be more natural, in Driault's view.

By his birth, by his origins, by all the characteristics of his genius, penetrated with the feeling for order, with the passion for unity, he was in truth a Roman. And that inclination was strengthened by his circumstances. The generation to which he belonged was permeated with the classical spirit. It applied it in everything, in literature, in art, in politics, in the very forms of the language. Palaces, columns, triumphal arches were built after the Roman fashion. From the Romans were taken the noblest motifs in sculpture and in painting; the Sabines were pictured, the oath of the Horatii. In his painting of the imperial consecration David hid the Gothic forms of Notre Dame behind Classic colonnades and tapestries. The terms of Tribunate, Senate, Consuls, were revised; a new Rome was built on the ruins of the Revolution. Follow that line, and it leads to Imperial Rome. The Consulate was succeeded by the Empire, and to the Romans the Empire meant unity of power secured by the military prestige of the eagles. The *Imperator*, that was the conqueror mounted on the Capitol, the top of the world. Napoleon clasped the imperial diadem round his temples, and in his brain was born the ambition to undertake

1. *Napoléon en Italie*, p. 304; see p. 255 ff. above.
2. *La politique orientale de Napoléon*, p. 394.

the complete imperial function. With his clear-cut profile, his obstinate chin, his haughty look, his smooth-shaven face, and hair cut short, he was the very image of an Emperor. He wanted to *be* the Emperor.

And in so far as it was possible in modern times, Driault continues, he actually did become the Emperor. At Austerlitz he defeated the two other Emperors.

He overthrew the eight-centuries-old Holy Roman Empire, and took possession of his inheritance. He conquered Italy, and like Charlemagne came to own the iron crown of the Lombard kings. For a time he spared the Pope. Like Charlemagne, he was already extending his empire as far as the Adriatic and the Ionian Sea. He conquered Germany, and became the patron of the Confederation of the Rhine, whose frontiers he brought down to the Elbe. He crushed Prussia, which had dared to oppose his imperial destiny. He restored Poland, under the name of Grand duchy of Warsaw, and made it into a military frontier of his empire: had not the ancient Western Empire possessed marches on the confines of the barbaric world? He did not call the Polish nation into being again: he took no notice of the rights of the nationalities, which he wanted to pound to pieces in an imperial unity. He stood apart from his period: that is why he himself was bound in the end to be broken.

Being a Roman Emperor, he wanted to rule over the Mediterranean, which had once been a Roman lake . . . For that reason he coveted the East. Aix-la-Chapelle he had; Constantinople he wanted to have. Only then would he be the Emperor, and not simply an emperor. At the same time, to crown his ambition, he coveted Rome, which he took. From then on he surpassed Charlemagne, who had left the Pope at Rome. He dispossessed the Pope, he had the papal archives carried to Paris. In the days of Constantine the Pope was a humble servant of the Emperor, by whom he used to be confirmed as such, so that he could not encroach with his claims on the majestic unity of the Empire . . . His son, the King of Rome, was an Emperor's son, and the grandson of an Emperor.

Permeated with those ideas taken from antiquity but brilliantly rejuvenated in his mind, he did nothing directly against England. England had no place within the sphere of imperial policy. In that aspect he stood apart from his period and was doomed to defeat.

How could he [Driault concludes, thus coming back to the subject of the book in which these reflections are to be found] how could he have shared the Ottoman Empire with Russia? The Ottoman Empire was his, he had staked it for his domain: for it was the Eastern Empire. How could he have established a sincere and durable alliance with the Tsar, who also wanted to be the Emperor of the East?[1]

On the contrary, he was obliged to oppose this ambition. That message to the Senate in the spring of 1807, sent from east Prussia, when the war in Germany had enticed him ever further east against the Slav hordes, before Tilsit; that message in which he warned the French against the disasters which would arise

1. *La politique orientale de Napoléon*, p. 396.

from the barbarian Russians' domination of Constantinople – it will be remembered perhaps that Bourgeois (see p. 224) regarded it simply as a piece of propaganda inspired by an awkward situation, but for Driault it enshrines Napoleon's most profound convictions.[1] Thus, after attempts to subjugate Spain properly, after having forced Austria into his system, the great undertaking at the end becomes a real culminating point. All the peoples of Europe, jumbled together for a moment in the Empire, were led by him, in order to throw Russia back into Asia.

It had been the task of the Roman Emperors to control the barbarians, to protect civilization under the laws of a single authority organized on a grand scale. Once he had beaten Russia, he could settle matters in the eastern world once and for all. . . .

In practice this meant a dynamic foreign policy which turned out to be a great misfortune for France, and Driault is not blind to the fact. In 1805-6, an alliance with Prussia was within Napoleon's reach, if only he would moderate his German policy and return to the tradition of remaining entrenched behind the 'natural frontiers' and seeking beyond them nothing save influence.[2] Tilsit might have been a real peace with Russia, had Napoleon been prepared to open for Alexander the way to the east, as the Tsar had expected, and as he had in fact been promised. In that case no one could have taken away from Napoleon Italy or Spain or the Confederation of the Rhine. But

he was less concerned to safeguard France's security behind her natural frontiers than to conquer the Empire for himself.

Indeed, Driault remarks,[3] the whole notion of alliance was alien to the imperial idea. The Emperor could not share, the Emperor could not recognize conditions, the Emperor scorned the basis of equality, the only basis on which alliance can exist. He knew only vassals, he desired only obedience, he took all advantages for himself.

THE PROPHET OF THE REVOLUTION IN EUROPE

But, Driault pronounces, the last word should not be with the Frenchman, resentfully considering the loss of the Rhineland and of Belgium as a result of this over-ambitious policy, or impatient at the stifling centralization which Napoleon's institutions fastened on his people for so long. He should also have an eye for the greatness of the work done in Europe. However transitory may have been the structure of the Napoleonic empire, its influence makes it one of

1. *Napoléon en Italie*, p. 674.   2. *Napoléon et l'Europe*, II, 445 ff.
3. op. cit. I, 471; II, 448.

the most fruitful, one of the most profound forces in world history. Napoleon – and this it is which constitutes his greatness – was

often unintentionally the agent of the Revolution. On entering upon the First Consulship, he declared the Revolution to be at an end. As regards France that was certainly so, but for Europe it had only just begun. Napoleon's victories were victories for the Revolution.

We have already met with this view (see p. 37 ff.) in Mignet, who could see in Napoleon's work in France nothing but reaction, but who would not deny him praise as the propagator of the principles of 1789 in Europe. Driault quotes a passage, dated about 1840, from the socialist philosopher Pierre Leroux – a man so little inclined to autocracy that after the *coup d'état* of Louis Napoleon in 1851 he was obliged to seek refuge in England:

The great events of the Empire and of the march of humanity would become totally unintelligible if one were to see in Napoleon nothing but a fascinating despot or an ostentatious conqueror, and tried to put it all down to his personal ambition and superhuman pride . . . Wherever he ruled or placed his rulers, the Inquisition, feudal rights, all exclusive privileges were abolished, the number of monasteries was reduced, customs barriers between provinces thrown down . . . Viewed in that light, it was he, and he alone, who carried through the Revolution. Feudalism, priest rule, barriers isolating the nations, social prejudices which divided humanity into castes, all sorts of inequalities – he took up his sword to cut those Gordian knots of mankind. At every step forward that he made, his Code smoothed out everything in his rear. That Code was the conqueror's gospel: his victories expanded its domain, and it presented him with armies.[1]

Vandal, the conservative Vandal, whose attitude to the principles of 1789 was indifferent if not downright hostile, would certainly have marked this eloquent passage with a good many queries. Yet he too claims for Napoleon the honour of having guided the peoples of Europe along new paths; there is no doubt that he was thinking not so much of the principle of equality and its blessings as of the growing national consciousness of the oppressed. It will be remembered (see p. 229) that Masson too considered that the fall of Napoleon in 1815 was the fall of the 'liberator' not only of France but of 'the nations' as well. In the introduction to his *Napoléon et Alexander Ier*, Vandal puts it as follows:

It was his dream to be Charlemagne. He wanted to bring unity to the scattered states of the west, and, seizing the peoples and snatching them away from their memories and traditions, to subject them to an authority which rejuvenated them for all that it was imposed, he tried to impel them violently on the course of their future destinies.

1. cf. QUACK, *De Socialisten*, III, 333.

The idea is almost a commonplace in French historiography. There is for example the striking passage from Sorel which I quoted above (p. 260 ff.) about the stirring up of the European soil for a new harvest, a passage which Driault was eager to quote.

Thus the idea was by no means new when Driault took it up, neither in the form in which Napoleon was regarded as being the propagator of the social reforms of the Revolution, nor in that in which Napoleon was seen as the liberator, in the name of the Revolution, of the nationalities; indeed it is part of the inheritance of St Helena. But in the importance Driault attached to it in his presentation as a whole there was an element of novelty. Vandal, after the passage just quoted, says that these conceptions do not spring spontaneously from Napoleon's mind:

They only appeared there, so to speak, as reflexes, occasioned by the necessities of his struggle against England.

Sorel, who looks for the source of Napoleon's strength in the impetus of the Revolution, certainly relates the propagation of Revolutionary principles more closely and more organically to his policy. His emphasis, however, falls so much on the purpose of protecting the 'natural frontiers' that he cannot do justice to the other idea – no more than Masson, who was fundamentally too narrow and too exclusively the French nationalist. Now this is what Driault set out to do, and his main thesis gave him the necessary latitude. For Charlemagne and the Roman Emperors had something to carry out; they too had a European task.

Towards the close of antiquity [writes Driault[1]] the Roman Empire gave to the world the political unity needed for the propagation of those principles of moral and religious unity which classic philosophy had been slowly maturing and which were now represented by Christianity. At the close of what we call the *ancien régime*, the Emperor Napoleon gave for a while to the historical world the unity needed for the propagation of those principles of a political and social revolution which had been announced by eighteenth-century philosophy and which have not ceased ever since to change the face of Europe. There you have the whole of the historic significance of the Emperor's role, and it suffices for his greatness. He was the prophet of the new age.

One's immediate reaction to this passage is to say that the writer has greatly overrated the significance of the transition from *ancien régime* to modern times, but it becomes historically more questionable when he attributes this conception to Napoleon himself and uses it to measure the stature of the statesman.

Having described how the First Consul plunged France into the renewed war with Britain, how he aroused the ancient hatred for Britain, and with it the old

1. *La politique orientale de Napoléon*, p. 399.

ambition and fighting spirit necessary to defeat Britain in Europe and help him to build the Gallic Empire, Driault asks whether we have on that account to condemn Bonaparte.[1] 'History,' he answers, 'is not ethics; the task of understanding and portraying him already demands quite enough of us.' Indeed, Napoleon could not do anything else:

He was victory itself, the genius of war ... And above all, after the Convention and the Directorate he had to follow another career, which they had indicated to him. For a secret instinct called him, as it did France herself at that time, to represent the Revolution in all its power of expansion, as Charlemagne had represented Christianity at the moment when it was definitely spread over the Continent of Europe.

The Revolution produced Napoleon. With its immeasurable force of destruction, he was able to overthrow the whole of Europe so that there might be room for new political and social reforms. His labours were favoured by the weakness and decrepitude of the *ancien régime*, as well as by the youthful energy of the revolutionary spirit ... What a progress had been made since Brumaire! Then France was still threatened in her natural frontiers ... Now the old thrones have to think of their own defence; the old Europe feels death approaching. It is the Revolution in the service of the conqueror, the conqueror in the service of the Revolution. Napoleonic conquest is the Revolution on the march: the Revolution is aggressive by nature.

What was it he did?[2]

He crushed the kings. In particular did he break down the crumbling edifice of the Holy Roman Empire, he freed the peoples from old despotisms, he awakened nationalities which had been slumbering for centuries. 'The whole of Poland mounted on horseback' and took service in the *Grande Armée*. Illyria ... Servia ... but above all Italy ... It is owing to Napoleon that Italy began to be something more than a geographical expression. No other European nation is so much in his debt ... Wherever he passed, the marks of his activity can be shown. In Spain he destroyed the Inquisition, and called into being the liberal party who were at first called the *Josephinos* and who have never ceased to labour for the resuscitation of the country. Even in Russia, who can tell if Year XII [1804] has not contributed to the rise of that great liberal party which is so actively undermining autocracy? [It should be borne in mind that this was written in 1906, when the first Duma was in session in St Petersburg.] In all the countries over which Napoleon has reigned, however briefly, new institutions based on the equality of classes and on liberty of conscience initiated that revolutionary transformation which shook the entire nineteenth century.

He was as it were the prophet of the new nationalities ... How great would he

1. *Napoléon et l'Europe*, 1 (*La politique extérieure du Premier Consul*), p. 473.
2. The passage is from *Napoléon en Italie*, pp. 667–70.

have been, if he had kept on serving the Revolution instead of making use of it for his own ends, if he had omitted to make of liberty a means to power, if after rousing the Italians and his other peoples to independence he had not kept them under the yoke, if he had not violated his promises. But has any conqueror in history ever been known to let go of his conquest? He was never willing to do anything in order to free the nations over which he ruled ... He was afraid, and certainly not without reason, to see them rise against him. He tried to melt Europe down in the great revolutionary unity which was the *grand empire*.

No doubt he could find ground for the reassurance of his conscience. Perhaps he looked upon the work of his hands as 'providential'. At least he could sincerely believe that the countries he had conquered would, if left to themselves, immediately revert to the forces of the past. The whole of Europe had not gone through the philosophic education which had been the lot of France, and even in that exceptionally developed France it was possible after him for the Restoration to try and restore the *ancien régime*. He could well believe that he alone had the strength needed to establish and to maintain everywhere the Revolution, and that his retreat would be the signal for the reaction. It was by the aggressive nature of revolutionary propaganda rather than the need for lawful self-defence against the coalition of the kings that he was dragged into his incessant wars. And as a matter of fact these terms are not mutually exclusive.

So he was in a state of lawful self-defence after all?

CRITICISM OF THE IMPERIAL IDEA

Driault's views concerning the general tendencies of Napoleonic policy are, as far as this study is concerned, the most important part of his work, but they are also the most open to criticism. Before letting criticism have its say, I would point out that there is a great deal more to be found in his monographs and in his great history of Napoleonic foreign policy. His account of diplomatic negotiations, his analysis of political situations at this or that critical moment, are all based on substantial research (though he too has been charged with having neglected foreign archives), and apart from that his narrative is sound, acute, sober, and to the point, generally not without a pleasant matter-of-fact flavour. He certainly managed to find firm support for part of his thesis from his own investigations. The legend of the peace-loving Napoleon with no thought for anything but the 'natural frontiers' he has shorn of much of its plausibility – we already noticed that when I compared Sorel's account of the origin of the coalition of 1804–05 with that of Driault in his second volume. Likewise, it is more difficult, having read Driault, to maintain that Napoleon only thought of Britain, or of Egypt and Syria, or of his family.

Especially interesting is his independence of the anti-British prejudice so noticeable in many of the French writers. What tirades have we not already heard about the wickedness of the 'English oligarchy'.

In discussing Pitt's return to office after the resumption of the war in 1803, and the coincidence of this with the plots against Bonaparte's life, Driault points out that the latter did not neglect to hold forth on the complicity of the British agents on the continent, who were in fact stimulated to greater activity by Pitt.

This was his most precious means for the influencing of public opinion, the one which therefore he used most frequently. '*L'or anglais*' – that was the customary theme of the proclamations with which he kept the fires of French patriotism burning. '*La perfide Albion.*' A century later French hearts still thrill to that phrase, and feel the throb of anger; long before Waterloo, Napoleon made a cult of it.[1]

Driault, at least the Driault of those days, would have nothing to do with the anti-British tradition which was so strong among his contemporaries such as Sorel, Vandal, Masson.

His attempts at constructive argument, however, are less convincing.

In the first place, what are we to think of this imperial idea, of these recollections of Charlemagne, gradually superseded by recollections of ancient Rome, as affording the true explanation of that tremendous career and the motivating force of that restless spirit of enterprise? It is certain that Napoleon's mind – and the thought of his time – was permeated with images and ideas, with terms and phrases, taken from Roman antiquity. Nothing is more plausible than the argument that in the reaction against enthusiasm for Republican memories, men turned to imperial times. It is striking to find this pointed out time and again in Napoleon's ideas, in his deliberate showing off as well as in his more intimate utterances; moreover Driault has independently elaborated the parallel in point after point, sometimes with telling effect. But is it more? Is it more than an artistic illusion, a superficial frame superimposed loosely on great events which were hardly moulded by its discipline? Just as when Quinet tried to see in Napoleon a Constantine reborn through the mysterious workings of atavism, I find myself inclined to write 'far fetched'. The comparison is exciting, and awakens all kinds of slumbering notions; I am even prepared to admit that Napoleon's mind was occasionally set going in this fashion, and driven into a certain course. But can it be the real explanation? Even with regard to his ecclesiastical policy, where the influence was perhaps the strongest, this seems to me entirely unacceptable. And as for its being the motive for the wars, the decisive factor in directing the ambition, the true reason why, for example, Britain remained outside Napoleon's active interest while Constantinople drew him, I cannot bring myself to believe this. I believe rather that the Western

1. *Napoléon et l'Europe*, II, 114; see p. 159 for another example

Empire, and afterwards the Empire in its wider sense, Charlemagne, Constantine, and Diocletian, were names with which to adorn the untameable urge for action, the insatiable lust for power, and each new object of conquest as it appeared on the horizon. In other words I believe that the interpretation which Driault rejected, as being too vague for so precise and definite a mind, is the right one – the desire for world domination ('*une domination universelle*').

But let me rather relate what another French historian has to say on this point. Muret, whom we know already as a critic of Sorel, published in the *Revue d'histoire moderne et contemporaine* of 1913 an elaborate argument (see p. 280) in which he compared all the different hypotheses presented in the course of the last few years about the meaning and the purpose of Napoleon's foreign policy. He assigned a central position in that article to Driault's 'new conception'. Muret, by the way, limited himself to criticism in the domain of Napoleonic study, and this is a pity. I know nothing more penetrating, more cogent, and more balanced on the subject.

Muret has much praise for Driault's work. He looks upon it as a contribution of outstanding importance which sweeps away a number of misconceptions and one-sided views and brings new light. The main attraction of this interpretation to him is its breadth. For the explanation must cover a conquest and a domination which did not cease to expand in all directions. This requirement was certainly satisfied by the conception of an irreconcilable Europe which compelled France to conquer ceaselessly in order to preserve (Sorel), but since the study of the documents is leading historians ever further from this view, Driault's thesis of imperial ambitions becomes tempting.

Nevertheless it is imperative that one should be clear as to what one means by it. 'The word *empire* is a vague term.' (It is amusing to find Muret here turning against Driault the qualification with which the latter set aside '*domination universelle*'.) 'And as soon as one tries to be more precise, the question arises whether M. Driault does not draw excessive conclusions from a single word.'

The word *empire* can be connected either with the extent of the territories to which Napoleon's ambitions were directed or with the nature of the power which he desired to exercise.

If territorial extent be considered, the word *empire* must be called exceedingly vague. The empire of which Napoleon may have 'dreamt' has no analogy with any of the great empires mentioned by history. No doubt it may be roughly said that he reached at first more or less the boundaries of Charlemagne's empire, that then, through domination of Germany and Italy, he approached the extent of the Germanic Holy Roman Empire, and that finally he seemed to strive, by appropriation of part of the Mediterranean lands, and by aiming at the east, towards a restoration of the Roman Empire. But would he have found his limit there?

Already in 1812 the French Empire extended along the course of the Elbe and the Vistula into regions never dominated by the Romans. But above all, at the point it had reached, the Napoleonic Empire must in 1812 involve the ruin of two great empires: the continental Russian and the maritime and colonial English. Suppose [and Muret is able to justify the activity of his imagination with the example of the 'dream'[1] with which Driault credited Napoleon just before the catastrophe of December 1812, when at Moscow he deluded himself into thinking that he had the Russian Empire at his feet] suppose that Napoleon had remained victorious in 1812. According to M. Driault, he would in that case not only have occupied Constantinople but have thrown back the Russians for good and all towards the north of Asia. That is to say, he would have restored Poland, he might even have taken away the Baltic provinces. Suppose further that as a result of the establishment of Napoleonic domination over the whole European continent, England were compelled to make peace. Would not Napoleon then have thought of India, where he did actually plan more than once to strike at the English? Once in control of Constantinople and of India, would he have suffered the continued existence of the Persian Empire, another territory with which he had already meddled in 1806 and 1807? What would have become of the old Spanish colonial empire? Since we are now launched on the wide waters of supposition, I am beginning to wonder whether we are justified in saying that Napoleon would have halted in Constantinople or at the eastern basin of the Mediterranean, or at the Atlantic coast. Can one not imagine a vast empire, outside the bounds of the old Roman Empire, down to the far corners of Iran, down to Ceylon, across the Indian Ocean, and covering Central and South America? What does all this mean, if not that it is impossible to confine the Napoleonic dream and to draw an arbitrary limit which his ambitions would not have crossed? Applied to the extent of territory, the word *empire* has no sense unless it means world domination.[2]

Muret is thus led to ask whether the search for the aim of Napoleon's policy in which all the recent authors had joined had any object at all. 'Had this policy an aim? Was there a great Napoleonic plan capable of definition?' Was there a *secret*?

To speak of an aim is to speak of choice, is to speak of subjecting all other objects to a definite plan of disciplined activity. Now Napoleon – *this is at least the impression which we have gathered from the writings of M. Driault* [my italics] – was never willing to choose. He carried on simultaneously and in all directions the most varied enterprises . . . Napoleon could never bring himself to sacrifice certain ambitions for the better success of others. No mind was ever less capable of understanding the necessity of compromises [*transactions*]. This does not mean that he could not in certain circumstances be an accomplished diplomat, or that he did not in certain cases voluntarily reduce his claims. But – and M. Driault has proved it with abun-

---

1. *Napoléon en Italie*, p. 675 ff.   2. p. 375 ff.

dant evidence – he never consented to moderate his claims otherwise than temporarily, never without the thought at the back of his mind that he would soon leave behind him the signpost at which he was halting. Never was he willing to take into account the interests or the ambitions of others.[1]

The conclusion to which Muret is led by his argument[2] is that 'the Napoleonic policy is to be explained not by a definite plan but by a state of mind'. It is as though we were back with Taine, or with the entire school of Mme de Staël.

Meanwhile Muret has also been arguing that the word *empire* applied to the *nature* of Napoleon's power is no more capable of precise definition. No doubt analogies can be noted.

The creation of vassal states, the family connexions, characterize the Napoleonic Empire as belonging to a type of medieval dominance; later on the idea of unity seems to make it approach the Roman form. But how small is the significance of these analogies when we try to be a little more precise. At the origin of the Carolingian conception or of that of the Holy Roman Empire we find the Christian idea; and what remains of that in the Napoleonic conception?

Has not Driault himself written that Napoleon, who wanted to be a Constantine, could in the eyes of the Church be no other than a Diocletian, a persecutor? And rightly so. 'Napoleon, the Emperor of the Revolution,' says Muret, 'did not resemble, he was the opposite of Charlemagne, the Emperor of the Church.' Let us note, in fairness to Driault, that he did not try to establish an identification, but explicitly declared that Napoleon as Emperor brought another message than Charlemagne, to wit the message of the Revolution. But it was a message all the same, and thus far there was a resemblance. Yet it is also true that this made a radical difference at any rate in the attitude to the Church. But, Muret continues, Driault admits that Napoleon had more in common with the Roman Emperors.

In Rome too [so Driault had written] the Emperor's function was of popular origin and had been instituted in democratic fashion. Like Napoleon, the Caesars were the chosen of the people, so much so that they did not dare make their power hereditary. Reaching across the royal dynasties, which based their existence upon divine right and which were consecrated by the bishops, he recovered the antique conception of the supremacy of civil power, secularized political authority, and linked the doctrines of the Revolution with those of imperial Rome.

Muret does not contest the truth of this, but he judges nevertheless that there is an essential contradiction between the two systems. The rights of man, the idea of equality, which behind the imperial armies Napoleonic administrations brought to the nations, have no room in the Roman world of ideas. The revolutionary force which propelled Napoleon, and which is essentially French in origin, the national resistances which by themselves formed so strong an obstacle

1. p. 379.   2. v. 380.

that it was crushed against them, have created for Napoleonic activity circumstances which find no analogy among those in which the Roman Emperors had to work.

But what then is the significance of all these Carolingian or Roman formulas, which were not invented by M. Driault, which he did indeed find in the official literature of the Empire, but which he gives so unexpectedly important a part to play? In my opinion they were destined to strike the popular imagination; by evoking almost legendary figures or reminiscences, the public was to be made to feel the grandiose character of imperial enterprise ... One must not take for the aim of Napoleonic policy what was no more than a kind of symbol, an attempt to express it in the language which was most consonant with the mentality of contemporaries.[1]

'THE PROPHET OF THE REVOLUTION': CONTRADICTIONS

There is yet another aspect of Driault's theories which is also of essential significance in his system; I refer to his exaltation of Napoleon as the disseminator of the principles of the Revolution. We have seen that he introduces it into his development of the imperial idea and tries to establish an organic connexion between the two. From two points of view and in two manners, as we have also noted, he depicts the Emperor's activity. He shows him introducing social reforms in the conquered territories, and at the same time creating the spirit and the condition which will give rise among populations that are oppressed, or divided between several states, to a national consciousness and to modern national movements. Muret refers to this only in passing, yet in so doing he raises a question of essential importance. 'It is necessary,' he says, 'to distinguish between the aims of Napoleonic policy and its consequences.' And he wonders whether it is valid to conclude, from the fact that the Napoleonic conquest was favourable to the development of liberalism and of nationalities, that this advance animated the conquest and provided it with its purpose.[2]

There is no doubt that the latter opinion is sometimes expressed by Driault. When he has to admit that Napoleon did not liberate his subjected nations and did not even prepare their freedom, he is ready at once with the excuse – we have met it before (p.289) – that they, and Europe, were not yet ripe for freedom. It is true that in another place he frankly admits that Napoleon paid no attention to the rights of nationality, that he crushed the nations within the unity of his empire, and that therefore, as not belonging to his own time, he was broken himself (see p. 284).

Elsewhere, at a later stage of his work,[3] he describes Napoleon as 'the very

1. p. 377 ff.   2. *Revue d'histoire moderne et contemporaine*, XVIII, 378.
3. *Napoléon et l'Europe*, III; *Tilsit* (1917), p. 18.

conscious and determined agent of the expansion of revolutionary principles
... the most forceful apostle of social equality, which forms the kernel of the
French Revolution's doctrine'. He considers that the *Code civil* which Napoleon
'taught to and imposed upon the major part of Europe' rightly bore his name,
if only for a moment, and he even propounds the hypothesis (see p. 285) that
Napoleon fought Russia because this 'autocratic and still Asiatic' country was
felt by him to be the principal obstacle to the decisive forward step of civilization.

Yet, it is true, some ten years earlier[1] Driault had quoted the letter in which
Napoleon urged Joseph, only that moment appointed King of Naples, to introduce the Code forthwith. But why? Out of love for social equality and to make
civilization move a step forward?

Introduce the *Code civil* in Naples; then you will see all that is not devoted to you
melt away in a few years' time, and what you want to retain will be more firmly
established ... The Code will confirm your power, because it does away with
everything that is not protected by entails, and no great estates will remain except
such fiefs as you will found. [Those fiefs he wanted granted especially to Frenchmen, and soon there followed the establishment of duchies for his marshals and for
others who were to form, in Naples, Illyria, and elsewhere, a trustworthy French
nucleus.] This [Napoleon concludes] is what has made me preach the need of a
civil code and has persuaded me to introduce it.

The Driault of 1906 looked upon this as 'a curious admission', and judged that
one could hardly apply it to the action of the First Consul in France. This may
be, but as regards Naples this conception of the Code as an instrument of power
policy has nothing incredible.[2] The Driault of 1917, however, who saw Napoleon as the protector of social equality against Russia, had forgotten even the
pronouncement applied to Naples.

Contradictions like these are typical. Vandal (see p. 286) has told us already
that Napoleon '*tried* to propel the nations faster along the road of their destiny'.
Vandal, who (as appears from his book) knew as well as anybody the complete
lack of scruple, the exclusive preoccupation with the interests of his power policy,
which animated Napoleon in his dealings with the Poles; Vandal, who even
commits himself to the general statement that for Napoleon 'human beings are
first and foremost tools',[3] and who would hardly have thought of arguing that
he looked upon nations in another light! And when Masson laments the fall of

---

1. *Napoléon en Italie*, p. 463 ff.
2. The argument Napoleon uses to persuade Louis to introduce the Code in Holland
is similar in tendency. 'Cela resserre les liens des nations d'avoir les mêmes lois civiles et
les mêmes monnaies': in other words, not to introduce social equality among the Dutch,
but to bind Holland more closely to France.
3. *Napoléon et Alexandre Ier*, I, Foreword, p. vi.

Napoleon in 1815, as being at the same time the fall of the nations, need I mention how little he cares as a rule for the freedom or the well-being of non-French peoples?

Undoubtedly national pride is a motive force. Driault roundly admits that 'we', – we Frenchmen – in spite of the ill turns which Napoleon has done France, 'cherish a secret admiration for the glorious deeds performed by him at the head of the *Grande Armée*, when we realize that he, and we through him, prepared the revolutionary transformation of Europe'.[1]

Actually we are facing here the emotional factor which was going to animate Driault's main work, and which came more and more to dominate his judgement: pride at the spectacle of this Roman Emperor who did such great deeds with France. That instead of trying to conquer the whole of Europe, he might by following a more modest policy have secured the 'natural frontiers' for France, is admitted by Driault in so many words more than once. He rejects explicitly Sorel's opinion that 'Europe' would never have resigned itself to this.[2] 'In a hundred ways and on many occasions Napoleon might have consolidated the frontiers conquered by the Republic.' But however much the possession of the Rhineland and of Belgium may appear to him desirable and altogether suitable, after having studied the Emperor's policy for many years, Driault cannot find it in his heart to reproach Napoleon for his failure. His admiration for this imperial, this salutary activity is unbounded.

Perhaps [he speculates] he might have avoided the final disasters, if he had stopped there [that is in 1808, when having previously fought only with princes, he entered upon his struggle against the Spanish people]; if after having brought to life or resurrected the Italian, German, Spanish, Polish nationalities, he had only applied his genius to the completion of French nationality within its national frontiers [it should be noted in passing that the 'natural frontiers' have now become the *national* frontiers, and that this enthusiast for the idea of nationality thinks it perfectly reasonable for Napoleon to 'complete' French nationality with Rhineland Germans, Flemings, and Brabanders] and to the organization of the Europe of the nationalities, which had during the last century been endeavouring so painfully to come into existence. But a happy Napoleon would not have been as great as the Napoleon of Leipzig and of Waterloo.

Moreover: 'It is easy for those who are not heroes to preach moderation in victory.'[3]

When the Frenchman looks with such complacency upon Napoleon's policy of conquest, when he seeks Napoleon's glory, shared by the whole nation, in his

1. *La politique orientale de Napoléon*, p. 2.
2. For example *Napoléon et l'Europe*, III, 362.
3. III, 373 ff.

contribution to the propagation of the beneficial principles of 1789 and to the awakening of the consciousness of modern nations, it becomes highly relevant to examine how this actually took place, and as far as Napoleon is concerned what objective he pursued. Phrases like 'that it was his historical task' or 'that a secret instinct drove him', are, when all is said and done, no more than romantic or pseudo-philosophical fog, which hinders close matter-of-fact study of the historical problem. Before I show to what extent Driault lost his way in that fog, I want, with a few more or less arbitrarily chosen examples, to give a hearing to other French historians who in the course of detailed studies have expressed opinions about French domination in one or other of the occupied territories.

MADELIN'S SATIRE

Let me begin then with a somewhat lengthy quotation[1] from an early work of Louis Madelin (about whom we shall have more to say), *La Rome de Napoléon* (1906). It is doubly interesting because in the attitude of mind of the Napoleonic officers and officials as described by him there are aspects which one could easily apply, if maliciously inclined, to Driault and other enthusiastic authors.

In the Frenchman of 1809 there was something of the missionary as well as the victorious conqueror. Ever since 1791 he had been an apostle, and however para-doxical the claim may appear, under Napoleon he still looked upon himself as the great apostle of liberty. With the missionary he shares the belief in the excellence of the creed which he propagates and the pitying contempt for the heathen who has had to live without it for so long; he burns with zeal to impose it, and is borne along on a proud conviction that the savages whom he converts to his religion will in course of time appreciate the benefits it confers.

That creed, Liberty, relates, so Madelin goes on to explain, to 'Roman liberty', that is civil liberty, for the sake of which political liberties have had to be surren-dered; since 1792 this has become *French* liberty. Bonaparte, for all that since Brumaire he has suppressed the political liberties of the French,

is none the less in Europe the champion, the incarnation of liberty. He liberates the peoples while at the same time regenerating them.

Similarly every soldier is wanting to 'regenerate Europe with the breath of liberty', and so behind him is every French official. The one in his haversack, the other in his dispatch case, both bring liberty to the *citoyens* of Europe, and to their minds darkened by *obscurantism*, by priestly *superstition*, and by the *despotism* of tyrants, enlightenment.

He quotes Sorel ('the master of us all', as he calls him, for to him his book is

1. pp. 132–6.

dedicated), to characterize the Frenchman of that period: 'Let not the universe reject the regeneration which we offer it; to resist it is rebellion.'

The nation [Madelin continues] which has undertaken so great a task and has in part achieved it is *la Grande Nation*. It is a signal honour to be allowed to become, as is the case of the Spaniards and the Neapolitans, the vassals of the *Grande Nation*, to share the benefits of its code, to be ruled by its princes. But the greatest honour in the world is to become, like the Belgians, the Rhinelanders, the Lombards, the Illyrians, a part of the *Grande Nation*. Every general in his proclamations, every prefect in his circulars, will loudly assert this; more, they believe it in good faith, or, let me say, naïvely.

The *Grande Nation* has conquered a dozen countries for this unique 'French liberty' and the salvation it alone ensures, at the cost of a series of incredible victories; the French have grown used to laying down the law, in the most literal sense. Caesar's generals and pro-consuls combine the pride of the missionary with the superciliousness of the conqueror, and without admitting any comparison between the systems they have brushed aside from Amsterdam to Naples and that which they have substituted for them all, they consider themselves to be born masters of the universe.

Out of so proud a reliance upon his strength there springs in the Frenchman a contempt, tempered by an almost friendly condescension for those 'poor fellows' whom he has compulsorily liberated with his arms and whose eyes he has opened to the light with cannon fire.

On the whole the soldiers behaved well, discipline was strict. But the conquerors could not fail 'profoundly to humiliate the conquered by an incessant boasting of their superiority, which soon became insulting . . .'

Every people has its pride and suffers when this is offended every day. And it was offended by those confident assertions that the crying need of these people was to be civilized, liberated, and regenerated, and that in the meantime they were deserving of compassion. . . .

Another consequence of this French conceit is the wish of the majority of French administrators to substitute their laws, their institutions, and their regulations for those of the countries annexed, and even their spirit, their ways of living, their customs. Sometimes a prefect, more sensible than many others and realizing the undesirable effect of this line of conduct, would try to reconcile his instructions with local usage or would even set them aside in response to local aversion. Immediately he was called to order and reminded of the Napoleonic conception, the French tradition, the doctrine of centralization. Twice, in 1798 and in 1809 [that is to say, after the abduction of Pius VI by the Directorate and after that of Pius VII by the Emperor] French officials resented the spectacle of the clock of the Quirinal indicating the hour according to Roman instead of French time. Small as it is, the incident reveals a state of mind. The Imperial University with its programmes and its lecture hours; the clergy reduced to the unalterable rule of the Concordat; the administration supervised by the ministries in the Rue de Rivoli or the Quai Voltaire and working with its unvaryingly similar bureaus and its holy red tape on a strictly centralized pattern; the prefects making their tour of inspection from Amsterdam, Hamburg, Laybach, or Rome on the same date, the same tour of inspection which is at the same time performed by the prefect of Seine-et-Oise and by the prefect of the Bouches-du-Rhône; the courts of law from Haarlem to Naples under the auspices of the *Grand Juge* of the Place Vendôme applying the articles of the *Code Napoléon*: that was the dream, and for five years it was the reality. A cruel reality, because it offended and crushed local habits; malignant, because it corroded the desirable and charming variety of the peoples; mad, because it went against the nature of things, against the character of men, against the needs of the climate. At times it became ludicrous, as when – and this is but an instance – the French prefect at a distribution of prizes, whether at Laybach, the Hague, or Rome, addressed the scholars with the identical speech which he might have used for the *collégiens* of Arras or of Besançon.

This, it may be objected, smacks of the conservative, and it is an impression that will later be confirmed. But this does not prevent there being truth in Madelin's satire (for it deserves this name), and one need not be a conservative to smile at it and to learn from it at the same time.

GRANDMAISON, CONARD, PISANI, LANZAC DE LABORIE ABOUT SPAIN, DALMATIA, BELGIUM

Madelin is by no means singular among French historians, with his sceptical treatment of the policy of reform in the subjected territories. Take Grandmaison, from whom (p. 172) I have already given a quotation, and whose principal work deals with the relations between Napoleon and Spain. Naturally we know beforehand that the attitude of this Catholic author towards the problem will be different from that of Driault. He sees in the intervention in Spain nothing but the blindness of the despot, who, having found it possible to mould according to his whim that uprooted generation of Frenchmen prepared for despotism by Rousseau, imagined that every other nation would be equally powerless to resist. But in Spain he hit his head against the untameable resistance of an entire nation, and above all of the masses. (See, however, the remark in note 2, p. 301.)

It is not uninteresting to have an opportunity of observing Napoleon at work. Grandmaison describes his arrival in the little town, not far from the French border, where Joseph had taken refuge and where he was holding his court in November 1808 in expectation of being taken back to Madrid by his brother's army. This Spanish expedition came at a most inappropriate moment for Napoleon. Earlier in the year he had imagined that his *coup* at Bayonne would give him quiet in that direction and enable him to give the whole of his attention to eastern affairs. Since then he had met Alexander at Erfurt, where things had seemed bright enough on the surface. But although he was unaware exactly how far the inner estrangement had already proceeded under Talleyrand's encouragement, he had been acutely conscious that the Spanish contretemps had affected his prestige. Now to have to undertake a campaign in that country, which was in itself unimportant, and this while Austria, spurred on by the Spanish example, was on the lookout for a chance to get its own back, was dangerous, was costly, was an intolerable delay.

It was therefore with a bitter mind, with tingling nerves, with a worried look, and a mouth inclined to utter reproaches, that he crossed the Bidassoa.[1]

Without warning, he fell in with Joseph and his French and Spanish courtiers, and talked and talked. The need for a close unity between France and Spain was his theme; Spain must follow the French system step by step. Long faces among the Spaniards. But Napoleon took no notice of anything, and began to inveigh against the monks: he would dissolve every monastery. One Spaniard found the courage to tell him that these words, if they became known, would be worth an extra hundred thousand men to the rebels. Napoleon did not listen. On the previous day at Tolosa he had already snarled at the Capuchins who came to greet him: 'Messrs Monks, if you have the hardihood to meddle with our military affairs, I promise you I'll have your ears cut off.' And he went on and on in this tone.

As early as the beginning of December, Madrid had to capitulate. The hot-tempered population submitted to this with difficulty, but Napoleon was able to avoid an assault, and thereupon caused his propaganda machine to hand out the most sugary description of the attitude and the state of mind of the Madrileños. At the same time, however, he was already engaged upon reforms, and this without even consulting Joseph. Monasteries were dissolved, the tribunal of the Inquisition was abolished (Grandmaison sees no merit even in this, since this institution had become completely innocuous), and also seigneurial rights and tribunals; officials were dismissed ignominiously. The unrest continued, and the tone of the imperial bulletins grew sharper. All groups of the resistance were condemned in most offensive terms. The *corregidor*, accompanied by a number of deputies, had to listen to a speech by Napoleon which was a mixture of threats, reassurances, and boasts. His contemptuous remarks about bad conditions and about backwardness certainly contained more truth than Grandmaison is prepared to admit, but when one reads the text one readily understands that this was not the way to achieve anything with the Spaniards:

Your grandchildren will bless me as your *régénérateur*. The day when I appeared in

1. GRANDMAISON, *L'Espagne et Napoléon*, 1, 260.

your midst, they will count among the most memorable, and from that day Spain's prosperity will date its beginning.[1]

. Taken as a whole, Grandmaison's picture is undoubtedly partisan,[2] and thus in a sense unfavourable to Napoleon. Every measure taken against the Church is in his opinion reprehensible. But now take Pierre Conard, who in 1909 wrote a thesis about the French military government in Catalonia (February 1808 to January 1810).[3] He argues that it will not do, as has been repeatedly attempted, to put all excesses to the account of the generals. They acted on the strength of Napoleon's orders, and gained his approval. He held up their conduct as an example to Joseph, and the judgement of Conard, who shows no special tenderness towards the Church, is that

their measures did not seem in any way to aim at regeneration. Even those which were occasionally announced as preparatory for reforms or renovations in reality sprang from military or financial considerations.

In 1893 there appeared a work about the French administration in the regions along the east coast of the Adriatic. The author was an abbé.[4] He describes Dalmatia as a country which at the beginning of the nineteenth century was still in the middle ages. Its clergy were all-powerful, and yet the French authorities (Marmont, Duke of Ragusa, was for a time the governor) tried to govern without and against the clergy. French legislation was introduced, without any reference to the educational level of the population.

A people's legislation is the product of its habits, its traditions, its history, even of the nature of its soil. France was in those days too proud of its laws to be able to admit that they might not answer the needs of all times and all peoples ... The result ... was that this population was turned into rebels. Awaiting the call to arms, the Dalmatians kept as much as possible outside the administrative machinery, of which they did not and would not understand the mechanism. With an instinctive aversion they looked upon that formidable machine; their simple and narrow minds were able to discern these two of its functions only: conscription and taxation. All the legislator's great ideas, his wise, beneficial, and farsighted intentions were misunderstood.

1. op. cit. p. 483.
2. A more recent book on the same subject is that of A. FUGIER, *Napoléon et l'Espagne*, which rejects a presentation of the resistance as general, national, unhesitating, on account of this being a conventional or romantic presentation.
3. *La captivité de Barcelona*, p. 368 ff., 386.
4. The abbé PISANI, *La Dalmatie de 1797 to 1815*.

A third case is that of Belgium, about which Lanzac de Laborie, also a man of fairly conservative inclinations, wrote:

One can, of course, not say of Belgium that little was achieved there, because it was exposed too long to the systematic operation of French assimilation, and because the spread of the French language among the aristocracy and intellectuals at an earlier date made its influence felt during the twenty years of annexation. But what causes for irritation there were, and what aversion! The religious policy which as a result of the Concordat had for one moment taken a direction acceptable to Catholics, when Napoleon found himself at odds with the Pope, became repellent to the Belgians and particularly to the Flemings.

But in his conclusion Lanzac de Laborie speaks in quite general terms about 'the diffidence and hostile sentiments of the population', which in the end 'were the answer to the irksome meddling of the administration'.[1]

If one asks whether the result of the undoubtedly profound transformation of Belgium which resulted from this episode was salutary, one will at the very least have to take into account some darker aspects. The old administrative forms, which were cast aside without mercy, afforded protection to valuable social institutions. The new leading class which rose with the new administrative arrangements was in many respects – and in Flanders in particular, owing to the language – more remote from the population. The centralization was fatal to much that was characteristic and independent.

GERMANY: RAMBAUD

The most backward countries, Spain, Dalmatia, which were still most deeply immersed in feudal ways of living and of thinking, proved to be the least accessible to French reforms. It was not in the backward but in the enlightened part of Europe that these were readily accepted. In western Germany, in Italy, in Holland – but in Holland their effect was extremely limited[2] – there existed a civilization and a social consciousness which had certainly been stimulated by the French 'philosophy' but which was mainly nourished from currents and traditions that were both native and universally European. The French philosophy, after all,

1. *La domination française en Belgique* (1895), II, 335.
2. Dutch historiography is accustomed to emphasize the advantages of the annexation. It should be realized, however, that in taking this line Dutch historians have chiefly had in mind political reforms: the resolute imposition of unity, and an administration to match. From the social point of view, the French had no great contribution to make; the rule of privilege which they had had to overcome in France had been on the wane for centuries in Holland, and to a certain extent had vanished altogether. Owing to the Reformation, the problems of the monasteries, ecclesiastical property, and the attitude of the Catholic hierarchy to the State had ceased to exist in Holland. Thus French annexation of Holland did not involve a social revolution such as resulted from it in various other countries.

was by no means exclusively French. One has only to recall the British contribution. It was principally their political disruption which made it difficult for the nations mentioned to take the initiative for thorough reform, and it was the French conquest that helped them over this obstacle. Who dare say that if it had not taken place, civilization and progress might not have found another way, a better one, perhaps? There were indeed minds in those countries which could have taken the lead. We have already seen French writers who contrasted the German civilization of those days to its advantage with that of the French, as it had become under Napoleon. Before the French Revolution a number of European countries possessed reforming 'enlightened despots'. In Holland there was a highly promising middle-class agitation. Who will be able to weigh the speeding-up of the process of development, as a result of the violent interference by the French Revolution and Napoleon, against the disasters that resulted from it; against the clumsy mistakes, the violence, and the unnecessary breaches with the past; against the intensification of national antagonisms, in particular of the German hatred for France which has been a curse for Europe and most of all for France herself? Even the reaction about which Driault likes to expatiate – 'the Holy Alliance' of princes is a nightmare to him – might perhaps never have taken on such acute forms. It must be admitted anyhow that in most countries the reaction was not as bad as might have been expected. It turned only by exception against the civil liberties which had been everything for Napoleon. Against the political liberties, yes, and also against the freedom of nationalities like the Poles and the Italians, it was at its worst. But one must indulge in a good deal of crooked reasoning to presume to place Napoleon in shining contrast on these two points (although we have already seen a few French historians writing in this sense, and presently we shall see Driault doing it as well).

Let us look at one other well-known book which deals with the French domination in Germany. It appeared in 1897, and the author was Alfred Rambaud.[1] What do we read here about the case of Palm (see p. 43)? That Napoleon gave orders not only for the arrest but for the death sentence, including its justification; that the unfortunate bookseller of Nuremberg had done nothing very dreadful; that the deed caused profound emotion and indignation in Germany, and contributed mightily to the rise of the German sense of cohesion across the boundaries of the small states, and at the same time turned it intensely against the French – all this we are told uncompromisingly. The conclusion is, nevertheless, somewhat surprising in a historical work, in the work of a University scholar particularly.

1. *La domination française en Allemagne*. The second volume is called *L'Allemagne sous Napoléon Ier* (1804–11). The author was *Professeur à la Faculté des Lettres de Paris*.

The death of an innocent man, or if one prefers to put it so, a punishment so ill proportioned to the offence, is well calculated to bring about a revulsion of humane sentiments. But we must harden our hearts about such matters, we who have since [an allusion of course to the war of 1870] seen German generals threatening French towns with sack and bombardment for the sake of a newspaper article.[1]

When we see the dictator [says Rambaud in trying to draw up the balance] proclaiming in Westphalia, in Bavaria, in Poland, the liberation of the peasants, freedom of conscience, equality before the law, when we see the Code of the Constituent Assembly, which has become the *Code Napoléon*, get a footing on the Rhine and on the Vistula, we have the right to feel proud on behalf of the French Revolution which was made by the nation as a whole.[2]

It was only natural that the Germans of the Rhineland, who in 1792 had enthusiastically welcomed the French revolutionaries, should recognize in the Napoleonic measures the realization of part of their programme. But the eternal wars were not in accordance with the principles of 1789, they were the Emperor's personal policy.

It is no use saying that his victories were necessary for the propagation of the new principles. It needed no more than a France strong within her frontiers of Rhine and Alps, for the French principles to find their way in Europe. Thus the propaganda would have been slower but surer, and liberty and equality would not have been exposed to the vicissitudes of war, finally to succumb in Germany, after Leipzig, because a despot was beaten in the field by other despots. Western Germany, daily growing more like France, daily further outstripping eastern Germany in progress, would have recognized its friends and compatriots not in Berlin or Vienna, but in Paris. The period of national hatreds and of the terrible national wars could not have come upon us. Out of that great crisis would have been born not a Prussian Germany, for which we remain the hereditary enemies, but a French and democratic Germany, united with us in a common political faith, co-heir of the Revolution.

Napoleon accepted in the name of the Revolution as legislator but rejected as man of war; this is an entirely different conception again from that of Driault (see p. 288) with his 'the Revolution is aggressive by nature' and with his 'the nature of humanity is such that the sword is sometimes necessary for the triumph of ideas'.[3] But this well-meaning and pacific Rambaud deems it best, nevertheless, for the Rhinelanders to become French. And he views with regret, and, what is worse in a historian, without understanding, the national uprising of the German people against French domination.

Fichte, who welcomed the French Revolution in 1792, inveighed against

1. p. 33.   2. p. 471.   3. *La politique orientale de Napoléon*, p. 5.

Napoleon in his *Reden an die deutsche Nation*. 'To this evolution of the great philosopher corresponded that of the whole of liberal Germany, which no doubt acquitted itself dutifully in 1813. But what did it profit liberty?'[1] Thus Rambaud, and he opposes the current German view, which applies the national standard as a matter of course and sees good Germans only in those who took part against the conqueror, while it rejects those who supported him. 'There is nothing dishonourable to Germany in the fact of our hegemony', he declares; and he observes that the Napoleonic system was accepted by statesmen, rulers, scholars and men of letters, industrialists, and peasants. But one has only to read his own book, to understand how completely unacceptable that régime was. I have already mentioned the impression made by the execution of Palm. How could German opinion remain indifferent to the attempts at armed resistance in 1809? How could the Westphalians regard it as an honour to be governed by a playboy like Jérôme, whose sole virtue was to be the brother of the conqueror, who knew no German, in several of whose ministries all business was conducted in French, while at the head of the secret police was a Frenchman who also knew no German?[2]

If, having looked at the problem a few times from various angles, we now return to Driault, we are in a better position to understand how immensely simplified is his conception. No one will deny that the French Revolution and the French conquest under Napoleon gave a tremendous impulse to the development of new social and political forms in the rest of our continent. But Driault's antithesis between enlightened mature France and backward, simple-minded, and monarch-ridden 'Europe' bear witness to a somewhat naïve national self-conceit, and betray not only a lack of understanding for the feelings of other nations but also ignorance concerning their history. As I have already suggested, his view was more or less that of the imperial officials described by Madelin. And his increasing tendency to exalt Napoleon as the liberator of the nations, the prophet of their national sentiment, without asking himself whether this was a conscious endeavour, or the unintentional outcome of the oppression to which he subjected them, exposed his historical understanding to most surprising aberrations.

OVER THE BORDERLINE (VOLUME IV)

At the beginning of this chapter I said that I would try to reconstruct Driault's interpretation as much as possible from his earlier works. Even this has turned out to be a difficult enterprise, because while ceaselessly revolving the same conception he modifies the accents on each occasion. But although even then

1. p. 478.   2. pp. 264, 286.

this acute and critical mind displayed a tendency to lose itself in a Napoleonic mysticism, his friends of the *Revue d'histoire moderne et contemporaine* can hardly have foreseen, though they must now and then have shaken their heads over him, that gradually he would throw away all self-control, all judgement, for the Roman imperial fantasy, and end by writing books which are in flat contradiction to his first. Anyhow, he soon went his own way, and in 1911 he became the first chief editor of the *Revue des Études napoléoniennes*.

The third volume of his *Napoléon et l'Europe*, which appeared in 1917 in the midst of the war, is still on the borderline, although I have quoted passages which make an odd impression.[1] With the fourth volume, published in 1924, the borderline is definitely crossed. Driault has become the victim of the system which he had been constructing for years, and in the end proves unable to stand up to contact with Napoleon and his imperial dreams. But the shock which caused him to lose his balance was (as will become still clearer in the last chapter) the First World War.

The style, always a little disjointed, short of breath, colourless, but at the same time sharp and to the point, has now become impatient, staccato, nervous. The fourth volume opens with a recapitulation of the whole system, in which every characteristic is more strongly marked. I shall try to lift from a good thirty pages the most striking sentences.

The historical tradition of the imperial title.

History was severe to the first emperors, Tacitus and Suetonius dealt hardly with Tiberius and Nero and the rest. This is because they knew them only through their crimes and their despotism; they lived too near them – as we do to Napoleon – to be able to judge rightly of their historic function. [The reader is now warned that crimes and despotism will no longer disturb the author.] The imperial idea throughout the centuries was not an accident born of personal ambition; it was one of the fundamental laws of world history. This it still is, and will be for a long time, for ever ... This activating idea [*idée-force*] meets with contradiction, with obstacles. The conception of individual liberty does not square with it, at least so it seems. Nor does the conception of nationality – but perhaps that too is so only to the eye ... The universal, humanitarian revolution of 1789, with its new political creed, sprung from the teaching of Christianity, of the equality of all human beings before death and before God, will find its instrument, its conqueror. ...

The Roman Education of France.

Gaul was Rome's best pupil ... A Frankish Mediterranean Empire ... The Merovingians and Carolingians, barbarians as they still were, had imitated the laws of Rome with touching zeal ... Pan-Germanic historians have never ceased to exploit

1. pp. 294-7 above.

the Treaty of Verdun of 843 . . . The greater Lotharingia, created by this treaty, will ever mean death to France unless it becomes French. The Rhine frontier is indispensable for the normal life of France . . . Germania had nothing Roman . . . The Emperors were strangers in Rome, barbarians . . . France created the law of the balance of power, a refuge for the weak . . . As a form of political organization, however, the balance cannot compare with the empire. The empire is best for peace, because it imposes peace. . . . [Whether that really is the safest way for peace, everyone may judge for himself.]

Now follows the application to Napoleon. 'All that he touched at once took shape and became great in history.' Even in the controversy with the Pope, in which until that moment Driault had shown much understanding for the ecclesiastical point of view, he now takes sides with Napoleon; there *was* an Emperor of Rome! 'There was even a Roman Emperor.' Napoleon's benefactions to Italy are recalled. But his greatest benefaction was Austerlitz.

There at last he overthrew after ten centuries the Holy Roman Empire, the enemy of the nations, the Bastille of Europe, the barrier against the Revolution. There, without *perhaps expressly* [my italics] willing it, he pointed the way to the oppressed nationalities . . . Westphalia, a colony of the French spirit.

As Charlemagne once tried to introduce Germany into the civilized world through Christianity, so he – 'a second Charlemagne, with a clearer mind and greater genius' – tried to do the same through the doctrine of the Revolution, and in this way it will no doubt at last be a success! In passing, Lavisse, the great *universitaire* historian of that generation, is rapped over the knuckles because he had called Napoleon's empire 'an unbearable anachronism'. Driault, who in former days (see p. 284) had placed Napoleon outside his time, because of his lack of understanding of the nationalities and his neglect of Britain, now will have nothing of this. The unbearable anachronism is the Holy Roman Empire, which he destroyed:

In that way he assured the existence of the new nations; he calls them, he already allows them to live, to begin with under his guardianship, for they are still fragile, and by his fall their life will be jeopardized.

Need I say that while this is a profession of faith, it is not history?

The Emperor [says Lavisse with a truly satisfying sense of balance] clothes the Revolution in archaeological dress . . . but the Revolution is within him. It is the Revolution he serves, in spite of himself and against himself, when, oppressing Europe because such is his pleasure, he awakens the soul of the Spanish and of the German peoples.[1]

1. In the two pages which deal with Napoleon in his *Vue générale de l'histoire politique de l'Europe*, 1890.

In spite of himself and against himself – once upon a time Driault too knew this (see p. 294). Yet we are now presented with this coloured print of the Emperor fondling the nations. Pure legend of St Helena!

Later, when discussing European conditions in 1810, Driault defends the whole of the Emperor's unsound and shaky structure in Germany. The greatness of modern Germany originates with Napoleon. (Had he intended this too? It is not said in so many words, but it seems to be implied.) Yet, says the author, his German work was less successful than his Italian, one would almost say that his 'Latin genius' felt less at ease there. But he was interrupted in Germany – and with this apology the author allows himself to soar into dithyrambics on this account as well:

His Latin genius, given a little time, would have perfectly sufficed for the task. The Latin genius is sufficient for all organization; it is capable of bringing order into the worst chaos, even into the Germanic chaos.[1]

If, at the outset, Driault's treatment of the theme 'Prophet of the Revolution' still showed contradictions, these have now been solved. But how? Through admiration for the impressive phenomenon, carried away by remarkable and striking parallels (which are, after all, no more than parallels), the man who seemed to take position against Sorel's determinism, who saw Napóleon's greatness in the freedom, in the personal nature of his policy, has now slipped back into determinism himself. At first there were only passing references to the necessary, the providential, character of Napoleon's interventions in Europe, to his task as the agent of the greatest and most salutary revolution mankind has ever known, at any rate since that of Christianity. Napoleon may have acted consciously or unconsciously; this did not seem very clear to the author, and the worst is that he did not care. Now the system has been closed, Napoleon has become inviolable. To set oneself against him is to put oneself outside history. All liberal opposition within France, all national opposition without becomes senseless or, if it has a sense, reactionary. We are not to inquire too nicely into his mentality or his intentions; Napoleon has become the chosen champion of the goddess Revolution, of the French Idea, in other words of Enlightenment, Progress, and Civilization.

There remains one slight reservation as a relic of the author's past opinions: Napoleon perhaps did not *intend* all these beautiful things. Or rather, he did intend them, but *perhaps not explicitly* (see p. 307) . . . The fourth volume was not Driault's last. In the final volume even this reservation has been thrown to the winds.

1. IV, 168. Driault never consistently proclaims the true 'universalism' of Napoleon's aim, as Vandal does (see p. 217 and note to p. 219 above.)

THE CONVERT (VOLUME V); 'THE TRUE FACE'

In the fifth volume, *La Chute de l'Empire*, we turn with anticipation to the chapter on the Congress of Prague. What do we find? I note the title: *Le Congrès dérisoire*. It is a quotation from Napoleon's correspondence – that correspondence about which Driault had warned us twenty years earlier (see p. 280) that the Emperor never admitted himself to be in the wrong, that he always showed a pacific face, in short that one ought never to take him at his word. I also note the conclusion: 'War was indeed inevitable. The Allies wanted it, and Napoleon could not capitulate.' One would like to press into the author's hands the article he once wrote against Sorel – not that I consider that article to be the last word upon this matter.

1814, 1815 – the emotionalism and the distress of Houssaye, Arthur-Lévy, and Masson added together can scarcely equal the emotion with which Driault describes the downfall and the treason, the heroism and the steadfastness. But with the last chapter, 'The Legend of Napoleon', the author recovers all his courage, all his faith. He is like the veteran of whom Balzac tells (see p. 28) that he could not believe in the Emperor's death. Napoleon is still alive, Napoleon is the People personified for Action. He is Democracy, in the sense of popular authority. There exists in France, says Driault, an antithesis between the consular or imperial democracy and the parliamentary republic.

The University chose sides for the parliamentary régime; founded by Napoleon, it used the centralized force which he gave it to preach in all its divisions the doctrine of parliamentary liberties against authoritarian democracy.

Here, one would expect a *peccavi* from the author, since we saw how he had associated himself with this attitude in his textbook. But he contents himself with the conclusion that these are two sides of democracy which ought to agree. He has broken now with Mme de Staël, whom he once (see p. 159 n.) protected against her biographer Gautier. He mocks at the few ideologists, distant disciples of hers, to whom the long-dead Napoleon is still the bogy-man. France, he exclaims, knows better; France has not repudiated the glory of Arcole, and of Marengo, of Austerlitz, and of Jena, of Montmirail, and even of Waterloo. In the war – the First World War – Britain participated for the sake of destroying German trade. (One sees that Driault, who used to shrug his shoulders at the fashionable French anglophobia, now shares it as an accomplished Bonapartist.) America came in as late as possible, in order to be quite sure that its intervention would be good business . . . (The British; the Germans, naturally more than ever since 1914; the Russians, finally revealed as barbarians since 1917; and now apparently also the Americans – all are in the author's bad books. Only the French remain . . . or is it, perhaps, the Latins?)

In that war [Driault continues] it is the dead hero sleeping in the Invalides who when France wills it for her salvation and for her greatness compels the government to act. In the supreme moment of danger Gallieni[1] is put into office at Bordeaux.

Masson, too, it will be remembered, imagined that it was Napoleon who won the war of 1914 . . .

The fifth volume of *Napoléon et l'Europe*, which concluded the work in 1927, is not likely to have reached a wide public. In its inception it was aimed at the circle of those who have some historical training, even though such readers in perusing the last volume must at times have rubbed their eyes. But a few years later Driault published a popular work called *Le vrai visage de Napoléon*, which will nicely round off our study of the author.

Though written entirely for effect, and by no means without talent – unless this be the impression created by the inspiration borrowed from its subject – every page bears the mark of the well-informed scholar. All the problems are faced vigorously, and the points at issue handled with a sure touch. Only, it is in every respect the precise counterpart of the school book of 1903. Not a single word of criticism of the Consul-Emperor appears.

Brumaire, the unpleasant side of which had once been brought to the fore, is now greeted with jubilation, altogether in the manner of Vandal, except for that challenging declaration (obviously addressed to him, even though his name is not mentioned) that Brumaire, which saved the Revolution, was not a counter-revolutionary act.[2] Centralization, of which the deadening effect on intellectual life was once emphasized, and which is still a subject of grievance in *La politique orientale* of 1904, has now become one of the greatest creations of Bonaparte, ineradicable.

A Roman work, performed with good French material, backed by several centuries of experience and classical education; with the strong mason work of the First Consul's will, it seems to partake of eternity.[3]

The Concordat . . . but this deserves a digression, which will be the last.

In his book on *Napoléon en Italie* (1906) Driault made a remark about the policy of Bonaparte, which we have not yet met elsewhere and which is nevertheless sufficiently widespread in modern historiography to deserve our attention for a moment. Bonaparte wanted an understanding with the Church. But, advised by Talleyrand, he also wanted to uphold Gallican principles. What a mistake he made ! Thus Driault. For while he was holding forth on the doctrine of Bossuet,

1. V, 431.   2. p. 83.   3. p. III.

the arrangement he made with the Pope was its very denial. Indeed, the strength of Gallicanism resides in the independence it attributes to the Bishops and their councils. True, even under Louis XIV the State had tried to ally itself with this and to make use of it. (Driault might have pointed to the same phenomenon in Germany and in Austria, in the shape of Febronianism.) Yet its indispensable source had been the national theologians' conviction of the divine origin of the episcopate, which made the Pope appear as no more than *primus inter pares*. Bonaparte himself administered the death blow to Gallicanism when he agreed with the Pope that the latter's spiritual supremacy would be made to heal the schism born from the *Constitution civile*. The true Gallican method would have been to reach an agreement with the French bishops, to unite into a council and reconcile *constitutionels* and *anti-constitutionels*. 'Perhaps this would have been the way once and for all to found a national Catholic Church in France.' (The *perhaps* covers a great deal: it is easy to imagine how impertinent Vandal would have considered this criticism of the First Consul, since such a reconciliation between the *constitutionels*, whom the faithful abhorred as revolutionaries, and the *anti-constitutionels*, who were mostly *émigrés* and in whom the government saw dangerous counter-revolutionaries, must remain impossible without the intervention of the Supreme Head of the Church.) To compel both parties to resign their dignities into the hands of the Pope and to submit to be reinstituted by him, in so far as they could be employed – that in any case was a solution from which must result an ultramontane Church.

I have already indicated the grounds upon which one could attack this interpretation. Yet the failure of the Concordat, even in Napoleon's own time, and the increasingly ultramontane character of the French Church, are symptoms which justify a critical attitude towards the alleged wisdom of Bonaparte's policy. But in *Le vrai visage* no trace is left of the author's former insight, and everything done by the First Consul is well done.[1]

We are noticing all the time how strongly the repercussion of contemporary events makes itself felt in the work of historians. For the Driault of *Le vrai visage*, the Bolshevists are still the traitors of 1917, the destroyers of society; and the far-seeing genius of Napoleon receives all the more praise, for he it was who wanted to unite Europe in resistance to Slav barbarism.[2] Driault is obsessed by the war through which he has lived, by the brutality of the Germans and the beauty of the victories that have been won. The Marne is more beautiful than Austerlitz, more beautiful the heroism displayed by the nation, its soldiers greater still than those of the *Grande Armée*. He recalls the ceremony of 1921, a century after the death of the hero.

1. p. 112 ff.; for the whole question see p. 102 ff. above.
2. p. 230.

In the evening at the Invalides Marshal Foch, Generalissimo of the Allied Armies, holding in his hands the sword of Austerlitz, saluted, in his turn [after the Minister of War, Barthou, and the President of the Republic, Millerand] the great emperor reclining in front of him in his porphyry sarcophagus: 'Sire, sleep in peace. Even from the tomb you are still working for France.'

And so forth.

Indeed, the commemoration of 1921 fell into the hands of militarists and conservatives to such an extent that M. Herriot, the then President of the National Assembly of France, felt himself obliged to resign from the National Committee.

Part 6

The Antithesis at the End

Currents and Counter Currents

ANTI-MILITARISTIC TENDENCIES

WHEN I wrote (p. 172) that in the years before and after 1900 the chorus of admirers dominated, and mentioned the persistence with which a Catholic author kept on sounding an inharmonious note, I thought of the historical writing with literary pretensions, a genre which can at the same time possess historical originality and reach and influence a broad public. In reviewing the apologies and the glorifications, however, we have come across sharp and independent criticism from quite a number of writers apart from Grandmaison. I have mentioned pronouncements of that kind by Lavisse, Bourgeois, Rambaud, Muret, Guyot, Conard, Coquelle, Carron, Godechot. It is worth while underlining the fact that all these, with the exception of Coquelle, belong to the world of professional historians[1] from the *Université*. I shall try presently to show, from works which could not find a place in a section devoted to the problem of foreign policy, to what extent there prevailed in that world a conception of Napoleon different from that held by the Houssayes, the Massons, the Vandals, and the Sorels.

It was only in their circle – we may indeed say the circle of the *Académie*, and we may oppose to it the circle of the *Université*, even though the statement ought to be accompanied by a number of qualifications and restrictions – it was only in the circle of authors with literary pretensions, after Taine, that the 'detractors' were hardly heard any more. And indeed my attempts to account for the striking renewal of the legend by the circumstances of the time and the spiritual atmosphere[2] did not give the whole story. True though it undoubtedly is that in the nineties among men of letters and thinkers a conscious and systematic turn towards tradition, authority, and nationalism can be observed, which favoured the Napoleonic cult, there never lacked counter currents, which were swelled considerably as the result of the *Affaire Dreyfus*. Generally speaking, love and admiration have a greater creative capacity than hatred and aversion. In any case they more easily established contact with the reading public, and the

---

1. Translator's Note. The usual expression 'academic' historians cannot be used here since it would lead to confusion with historians belonging to the *Académie*.
2. p. 143 above.

interest in Napoleon – precisely at the moment when his figure was slipping away into the distance of time and the immediate political significance of the various ways of viewing him was perhaps weakening – became an interest in the *great* Napoleon, and demanded the absorbing, elevating, thrilling spectacle rather than the cool, matter-of-fact, destructive analysis.

Meanwhile the fact remains that the traditional connexion between French radicalism and military valour had grown weaker about the turn of the century. After the first defeats of 1870, this tradition had still shown itself personified in Gambetta. That it was not dead would soon appear in the person of Clemenceau, and the events of our own time prove its unshakeable vitality. But just at that moment there arose against it an anti-militaristic internationalist frame of mind, which contributed to strengthen the old liberal-humanist aversion to Napoleon. In the Dreyfus affair these currents joined for a moment, and in Anatole France, the sceptic, the mocker, who was suddenly and in spite of himself drawn into the struggle for offended right, we can see them united. Let us listen for a moment to what he, also an *académicien*, but a black sheep in that white flock, has to say about Napoleon.

ANATOLE FRANCE

One naturally turns first to his satirical history of France, *l'Île des Pingouins* (1908), and one will indeed find some amusing pages, although they do not amount to more than somewhat broad fun at the expense of the Napoleonic legend. A Malay traveller finds the island – not an *île* but an *insule*[1] – in a deplorable condition. The memory of a certain Trinco appears to be worshipped because he did a great deal of fighting, in which, the stranger reflects, he did not distinguish himself from the rest of mankind. But the Penguins cling to their pride in his victories, although they had to pay a terrible price for them: 'Glory is never won at too great a price,' they reply severely to the visitor's doubting questions.

In *La Révolte des Anges*, in 1914, however, there is a passage which cuts far more deeply. It occurs in the paganistic *Discours sur l'histoire universelle* of the fallen angel Nectaire-Aléciel, who surveys the fate of men with tender and pitying sympathy. The sketch of Napoleon, in its pregnant brevity, and for all its almost insolent one-sidedness, is wonderfully stimulating to the historical imagination.

What made him so eminently fit to dominate was that he lived entirely in the present moment and had no conception of anything except immediate and instant reality. His genius was vast and shallow; his intellect, immense in extent but

1. See p. 283 above – 'in the very forms of the language'.

CURRENTS AND COUNTER CURRENTS

common and vulgar, embraced humanity without rising above it. He thought what was thought by every grenadier of his army, but there was an incredible strength behind his thinking ... He was too clever not to use in his game old Jahveh, who was still a force in the affairs of this earth and who was not unlike him in his violent and overbearing disposition. He threatened, flattered, caressed, and intimidated him by turns. He imprisoned his vicar, whom he forced at the sword's point to give him the oil which is supposed, ever since Saul, to make kings strong. He restored the cult of the Demiurge [this is Aléciel's contemptuous description of Jahveh] chanted *Te Deums* in his honour, and had himself recognized by him as God on earth, in little catechisms distributed all over the empire. So did they join their thunders, and the noise was something wonderful.[1]

THE *UNIVERSITÉ* VERSUS THE *ACADÉMIE*

But let me stick to the historians. I have already opposed the *Université* to the *Académie*. As a matter of fact, among the admirers the *Université* had a bad reputation. We have noticed that after the lawyers and journalists and men of letters, Masson mentioned the professors as a third group of haters of Napoleon. Driault, who was in a position to know, declared that the *Université* fostered a tradition of anti-Napoleonic doctrines (see pp. 165. 309).

From the elementary school to the university [he adds] the teachers of youth used their ingenuity to tear up the finest pages of our history; the *bloc* of national unity was smashed. It was a wicked enterprise, it was an attempt to mutilate us, like the efforts made to blot out of our imagination the image of the Rhine [of Alsace Lorraine, and of the *revanche*, of the Rhineland].[2]

The past tense is connected with Driault's conviction that the denigration of Napoleon had made room for a better and more patriotic understanding – an illusion, as we shall see.

The historians of the *Université* did not fail to bear witness to their convictions. They produced a strong uninterrupted stream of scholarly studies, of monographs, and of textbooks. To avoid being overwhelmed by it, I shall limit myself to the more general works, and even there I shall have to make a choice. There is diversity of views in abundance, and yet there is striking agreement. The Napoleonic legend has no hold upon these authors from the *Université*. Of a Napoleon cult there is no trace. Generally speaking, these works are weaned from nationalistic or authoritarian *a priori* reasoning, and in stating this I am thinking of the whole period from the beginning of the century to the Second World War. The First World War, which seemed to create the conditions for

1. *La Révolte des Anges*, p. 249.
2. *Napoléon et l'Europe*, v, 421 (1927).

a new efflorescence of the cult, and which indeed was responsible in 1921 for a considerable output of excited prose (of which we have had a sample on p. 312), scarcely made itself felt in this literature. The sanity of a solitary Driault may have been affected by it, but the *Université* as a whole kept its balance. The historians do not dispose of Trinco as light-heartedly as Anatole France; but with every effort to evolve a positive appreciation of the Napoleonic episode, with all fine shades and distinctions, the opinion of the experts is not that of the enthusiasts.

The phenomenon will appear the more striking when after five *universitaires* – I am keeping a sixth for the conclusion – I place three *académiciens* under the magnifying glass. With the latter (even with Hanotaux, whose opinion after all is very independent, so much so that one might look upon it as a transition to the outlook of the *universitaires*) the tradition of Vandal and Sorel will still be found present in unimpaired vitality.

And yet, is it right to speak of 'the opinion of the experts'? I wish to safeguard myself against the misconception that in the case of the authors I am now going to discuss I had met with nothing but scholarly method and objectivity. The scholarliness of their method is certainly not something purely external; it disciplines their mental attitude as well. But it would be foolish to overlook the fact that these authors come to Napoleon with their own, different *a priori* ideas; that they measure him against standards of spiritual freedom, of culture, of humanity, of social progress; that politically they are as a rule of the left. With some of them anti-clericalism is predominant, with others liberalism or socialism. It is rare that upon close inspection one cannot fairly accurately 'place' an author.

1 Alphonse Aulard

THE ESTABLISHMENT OF DESPOTISM

AULARD, with whom I want to deal first, exercised great influence as an expert of the Revolution period, and founded a school. Appointed in 1886 as the first holder of a new chair in the History of the Revolution in the University of Paris, he produced in 1901, when he was over fifty, after many editions of sources and monographs, a great work of synthesis, *Histoire politique de la Révolution française*. The leader of the new historical tendency which claimed to study and appraise events in an objective scientific way, 'historically and not politically',[1] Aulard presented a conception which though based upon an impressive amount of factual material, strictly sifted and arranged, is in truth dominated by a rigid ideology, and that in a tyrannical manner. He follows the history of Bonaparte as far as the imperial coronation: this in his opinion brings the Revolution to a definitive end, a conception which already implies a judgement. Mignet went to 1815; Thiers saw in the solemnity at Notre Dame the coronation of the Revolution; while Quinet thought that it was its untimely conclusion.[2] In the eyes of Aulard, also, Napoleon is the man who arrested the Revolution, who even initiated a reaction towards the *ancien régime*, who abolished liberty and encroached upon equality. His chapters dealing with the Consulate give little else than the story of the derailment of the Revolution, of the gradual demolition of liberty, and the establishment of despotism.

The brutality with which force was used on the 19th Brumaire, says Aulard, was unintentional; and at first Bonaparte seemed to make himself as inconspicuous and innocent a figure as possible, in the hope of being forgiven. Public opinion indeed allowed itself to be reassured; but the means necessary to this end proved how little it desired what Bonaparte really was preparing. There were professions of undeviating republicanism, of immutable fidelity to the principles of the Revolution; the general put on civilian dress; his Minister of Police, Fouché, once more branded the *émigrés*. But the confidence gained in

1. According to a French critic: cf. G. KALFF, *De verklaring der Franse Revolutie bij haar voornaamste geschiedschrijvers* (a thesis, 1920), p. 176.

2. Carlyle, be it noted, thought the Revolution was finished by General Bonaparte's 'whiff of grapeshot' of 13 Vendémiaire (October 5th) 1795, and with this concluded his book.

this way he misused to press through a constitution which made him practically the sole master. The remark which I have already (p. 278) underlined in Driault's textbook, about the plebiscite for the approval of the constitution being a mere make-believe, may have been taken from Aulard's book, which was older by two years. The whole interpretation differs as sharply as is possible from Vandal's spontaneous popular enthusiasm pushing automatically in the direction of a dictatorship. Aulard had carefully checked the registers of the votes, which, as we know, had been given publicly and in writing. Among the 1562 opponents, he points out a few well-known ex-*Conventionnels*; but such were also to be found among the three million who voted 'yes', apart from 'almost the whole intellectual élite' of France. 'These republicans thought they were voting for the Revolution and the Republic, against the monarchy and the *ancien régime*.'[1]

The centralization of the law of 23 Pluviôse is, according to Aulard, an instrument of despotism, and the criticism made against it in the Tribunate has his full sympathy. Nevertheless he recognizes that the law had good results at first, thanks to the ability and the genius of Bonaparte. 'It was only little by little that it became brutal and despotic, as the master himself was being transformed from a good into a bad despot.'

The signs of this transformation are not long in appearing. At first there is no court. Busts of famous men adorn Bonaparte's dwelling: Demosthenes as well as Alexander, Brutus as well as Caesar; Frederick the Great; but also Washington, Mirabeau ... The daily entourage of the new potentate consisted of men of the Revolution, liberals, intellectuals of the *Institut*. But after he had acquired the Consulate for life, the Consul began to live in princely style, and already then he was bent upon filling his court with the old nobility, the 'rallied' royalists.

The muzzling of the Press, the expulsion of the opposition from the Tribunate, the establishment of extraordinary tribunals and military commissions – all these steps towards despotism, which we already know, are given the fullest attention by Aulard.

Of special interest is his explanation of the popularity which Bonaparte was meanwhile gaining with the Parisian working class. The liberal opposition with which the name of Mme de Staël is linked, full of abhorrence for that despotism to which it had so naïvely opened the way by welcoming the *coup d'état*,[2] an opposition of the salons and the legislative bodies, when it looked for support thought of the generals. For the generals (whom we involuntarily visualize in their later character as courtiers and marshals) were at that moment still good republicans. These liberals gave no thought to the labouring class, for it had averted its face from politics and the dictator had won its heart. Certainly not because he presented himself as 'a kind of democratic Caesar'.[3]

1. p. 711.   2. p. 761.   3. p. 765.

On the contrary. He always treated the working men as inferiors. By a law of Year XI and a decree of Year XII [1803 and 1804] he placed them under police supervision, prescribed for them the possession of an identity book without which they were liable to arrest as vagabonds, once more prohibited unions and strikes on pain of imprisonment, and charged the Prefect of Police with the settlement of wage disputes. It was a relapse into the *ancien régime* when the *Code Napoléon* laid down that in such disputes the word of the employers was to be taken. The plebiscite might be the foundation of a new régime, but here as in other cases Bonaparte gave evidence of an inclination to destroy equality and to divide French society into a politically and socially privileged bourgeois class and a subordinate plebeian class.

But the labourers made no complaint. They did not even notice the contradiction of the principles of 1789.

Their love for Bonaparte was aroused and maintained by means of material and moral benefits.

The former resulted from the care taken by the First Consul to have Paris well provided with food, and at a low price; for this purpose bakers and butchers were placed under control. Industry revived, there was work, and wages rose; later conscription sent them up even faster. As regards the moral benefits ('illusory, I should perhaps have said', adds the author, who has no liking for chauvinism),

Bonaparte acquired dazzling martial glory for France, and the Parisian working man's patriotism had taken on a markedly chauvinistic hue. He was at the same time passionately anti-royalist and saluted in Bonaparte the leader of the Revolution, the beneficent dictator predicted and invoked by Marat, the protector of the new France against the Bourbons.

We have heard little as yet about the working class. Aulard quotes from police reports to show how they remained deaf to all incitements on the part of the liberals, and allowed themselves in every circumstance to be carried away by Bonaparte's propaganda; against the conspirators, against the British, and finally for the Empire and the hereditary principle.

Aulard's conclusion is of importance for the right understanding of the history of the whole nineteenth century in France.

This meek and complete subjection of the Parisian working men to a master condemned the republican bourgeoisie to impotence, their opposition became nothing more than a childish *fronde de salon*. It is from that moment that the breach between the liberals and the people dates; for long years democracy and universal suffrage were to appear incompatible with liberty.

THE ECCLESIASTICAL QUESTION

No less important is Aulard's treatment of the ecclesiastical question. That his point of view is diametrically opposed to that of Vandal will be understood beforehand. But he also differs considerably from d'Haussonville. No doubt he considers, as does the latter, that the régime of separation of Church and State, as Bonaparte found it, might and should have been preserved. But d'Haussonville wanted this because only under that régime could religion and the Church really prosper, while Aulard considered it desirable because it prevented the Church from growing strong and from becoming a menace to State and society as they had been shaped by the Revolution. In his interpretation we recapture more exactly than in Quinet the spirit of the atheist intellectuals of the *Institut* and of the Council of State (where there was laughter at the more 'mystical' passages when the First Consul read the Concordat).

What was the situation of religion? Like Vandal, Aulard draws attention to the existing division: there was the former 'consitutional' Church, which most certainly did not muster the majority of the faithful, but which nevertheless – by the quality of its priests, among other things – was still a power. Then there was the former *réfractaire* Church, recently subdivided into the *ralliés* (who had given 'the promise') and the royalists. There were also the Protestants and the Jews, and finally the freethinkers and rationalists, among whom the cult of theo-philanthropy still subsisted. Already in 'the reaction following upon Marengo' the police were instructed no longer to protect them, while after an iconoclastic attack on a theo-philanthropic church 'probably carried out by Catholics' the cult was suppressed by a decree of 4 October 1801, even before the Concordat became operative. Fashion, says Aulard, no longer favoured free thought, but it was not the religiously-inclined souls like Chateaubriand and his admirers who wanted the altars of other confessions to be overthrown. 'It was only to the intransigent group of papist priests that the régime of separation seemed intolerable.' The author himself frankly calls the division among the Catholics an advantage. The Catholic Church was 'the most formidable power of the past against which the Revolution had to struggle', and now that the Revolution had succeeded in breaking it into three groups, the State (with secularized education) was secularized, free, and the master.

How was it that Bonaparte came to give up a régime so favourable to the State? It was not because there existed in public opinion an irresistible current in favour of a Concordat. On the contrary, had there been a free Press an almost universal opposition to the idea would have come to light. In the course of the long negotiations, the Press was forbidden to discuss religious questions of any kind. Nor was it because his own religious sentiment moved him in that direction. To prove that Napoleon lacked religious feeling, Aulard quotes the well known pronouncements:

For my part, I do not see in religion the mystery of transubstantiation but the mystery of social order.

Society cannot exist without inequality of property, an inequality which cannot be maintained without religion . . . It must be possible to tell the poor: 'It is God's will. There must be rich and poor in this world, but hereafter and for all eternity there will be a different distribution.'

Bonaparte's motives, then, were of a political nature. He wanted to dominate consciences through the Pope, and thus to realize his dreams of world domination. He also wanted to get rid of the Church of the former *constitutionels*, among whom the democratic tendency was too strong for his taste – he was especially suspicious of the elections which the *Constitution civile* had introduced. Also he wanted to deprive Louis XVIII of his last means of influencing French public opinion, and he wanted to pacify the Vendée.

Are we to believe, as d'Haussonville wants us to, that the Concordat brought no advantages to the Church? It restored the Church, even though this was not formally expressed, practically to the position of State Church. It healed the schism which had paralysed the Church's power to weigh upon the State and society. It provided the Church with considerable financial advantages, which the Consul-Emperor amply supplemented. In the sphere of education, too, as we already know, Napoleon went beyond the stipulations of the Concordat. In 1808 he did away with the secular principle and laid down 'the principles of the Catholic religion' as the basis of his newly founded *Université*. All this went against the spirit of the intellectuals and high officials, who after the *coup d'état* of 1799 had been his principal collaborators. But all such opposition he pushed impatiently aside as coming from 'ideologists'. It is significant that in 1803 he dissolved the class of 'moral and political sciences' at the *Institut* in order to deprive such opposition of a centre. And yet in the end his ecclesiastical policy proved a deception. After having immensely strengthened the Church's power in French society by his policy, he did not find it the willing tool he had imagined.

Viewing the whole work of demolition and reaction more or less consciously performed by Bonaparte [says Aulard in conclusion to this chapter] one sees the Concordat stand out as the counter-revolutionary act *par excellence*.[1]

1. p. 747.

2 A. L. Guérard

AT first sight one might ignore this author as not being typical. Guérard was a Frenchman, but he was half anglicized, wrote in English, and was professor at an American university. But the chapter 'Napoleon' in his *French Civilization in the Nineteenth Century*[1] is in its conciseness an excellent summary of what I may call the opposition point of view. It is sober in the good sense of the word, that is to say not clouded by romanticism or propaganda and advertisement, but penetrated with respect for humanistic and cultural values.

All the *motifs* already known to us – the love of war, the pride and exclusive faith in force, the spiritual compulsion through Concordat, *Université* and Press censorship, the undermining of independence by an excess of bureaucratic centralization, the reactionary tendencies in legislation and social reconstruction, the vulgar display and undignified snobbery in the improvised court – find their place in this sketch. And yet the picture is not, as are those of Lanfrey and of Taine, devoid of light. Guérard acknowledges that there is something beautiful in the first idea of the Consulate and in the constructive work then undertaken, though he sees at the same time the dangers threatening the whole venture.

Bonaparte's ambition knew no internal check: he had no scruples, a limited culture, and boundless contempt for 'ideology' and for 'imponderable' forces.

Nevertheless he ends with the remark that the character of the imperial period, as seen from the point of view of the historian of culture, is more complex than is generally assumed. Through the oppressive imitation classicism, there appear signs of a liberating aspiration after a new and higher existence. In this young romanticism the new Caesar is also a factor, 'in spite of his Italian ancestry, his classical features, his Roman aspirations, and the practical character of much of his work'.

The contrasts and dangers of his adventurous career; his constant hankerings after the elusive and gorgeous East; his fatalism and superstition; the gloom and isolation of omnipotence: all these were either the signs or the causes of a romantic turn of mind. And this would find expression in his love for Ossian, or better, in sudden outbursts of unacademic eloquence which give him a brilliant place in French literature.

1. A. L. GUÉRARD, *'Agrégé de l'Université'*. The book discussed was published in Britain in 1914.

3   G. Pariset

In the great history of France under the direction of Ernest Lavisse, one of those collective works which had become fashionable in historiography, there appeared in 1921 (as the third of the ten copious volumes in which contemporary history beginning with 1789 is surveyed) the volume of G. Pariset on Consulate and Empire. It is a textbook of high quality, sane, sober, and clear but by no means impersonal. It unhesitatingly presents an original conception. Let me illustrate the nature of this with a few of its main points.

FOREIGN POLICY

Bonaparte's victory at Marengo and that of Moreau near Hohenlinden led to the peace of Lunéville. Hohenlinden formed an indispensable element in this situation, and to that extent Bonaparte rejoiced at it, but the fact that it was Moreau's victory irked him: 'He could not forgive victorious generals.'[1] Anyhow, it was peace, and the joy that reigned in France was indescribable. Some people, however, were already afraid that the First Consul would use his success to expand his own power and to undertake new adventures. But even the most timid admonition in the Tribunate was apt to anger Bonaparte, and it is therefore difficult to find out how widespread this concern may have been.

This much is certain, that France was profoundly and decidedly pacific; never was she less militaristically inclined than immediately after his greatest successes in the field.

No doubt men take pride in the glorious character of the peace.

But the destinies of Holland, Switzerland, Italy, the German princes, touch the nation only indirectly. It is satisfied, now that the safety of France, for ever firmly established within her natural frontiers, is no longer threatened. It remains indifferent to Bonaparte's distant combinations. The nation was even more fatigued than in the days of the Directorate. It imagined that the object had now been attained, *its* object. But the man who was already the sole master of its foreign policy had no object, or at least he was continually shifting it, and further away every time.[2]

1. p. 51.   2. p. 55.

We have already learned that Pariset rejects the thesis of Sorel; that he looks at Bonaparte's personal policy for the source of the wars; and that he does not see this policy in the way Driault sees it, as an attempt to realize a grandiose but definite plan, but that like Muret he sees it as the effect of a particular mental attitude.

THE CONSULAR *TERREUR*

I continue to glance through his pages. There is the pacification of the West, of the Vendée. As Pariset sees it, General Hédouville, who had been sent there by the Directorate, was already working ably at this pacification and with a good chance of success. Then Bonaparte comes to power, and his 'strong manner' takes the place of the 'prudent and skilful manner' of Hédouville. He intervenes roughly. The execution of Frotté, leader of the *Chouans*, who thought he had surrendered upon terms, may not have taken place upon the explicit order of the First Consul. Bonaparte, in any case, now had what he wanted, 'a deed of sensational severity': 'disloyally, uselessly, and too late'.[1] This view of the incident, by the way, has no originality; I might have pointed to it before, in Lanfrey or in Aulard. But of course another interpretation is current as well.

Let us once more refer to Vandal. It is an instructive comparison, because the presentation of the facts is practically the same, and the divergence arises altogether from the mental attitude adopted towards them. Vandal does not deny that the execution of Frotté was a treacherous act, nor that it cannot be entirely cleared up, but he exerts himself to show the probability that the First Consul had absolutely no hand in it and that as he put it himself 'he had been deceived in this affair'.[2] Nor does Vandal attempt to hide Bonaparte's immediate conviction that peace could only be restored by an impressive example. He introduces his account with the remark that Hédouville acted in a 'conciliatory', perhaps too conciliatory manner. And how sympathetically does he deal with Bonaparte's 'strong manner'! 'The system of Bonaparte is always to make individual examples, and to make them frightful, while he rallies the masses with a generous gesture of pardon.'[3] In any case 'he wanted to destroy the remainder of the rebellion in such a way that the noise of destruction would resound within and beyond France'. But when further on he discusses the question of responsibility, Vandal fails to recall this.[4]

Pariset sees this deed of violence in connexion with so many others, and he detects a system. One reproaches the Directorate, he says, with the measures of

1. p. 59.   2. *L'avènement de Bonaparte*, II, 143.   3. op. cit. I, 488 ff.
4. Lanfrey is naturally convinced that Bonaparte was personally responsible for the condemnation of Frotté; II, 79.

proscription after Fructidor, and one talks about *la terreur fructidorienne*; one might equally talk about *la terreur consulaire*.[1] What Pariset has particularly in mind are the special tribunals which the First Consul insisted on establishing, against strong opposition from the Tribunate and the Legislative Body, in order to suppress resistance in disturbed *départements*. This institution did not disappear with the occasion that had brought it about. It was even extended, and continued to exist throughout the Consulate and the Empire.

As regards the case of the proscription after the attempt with the infernal machine, Pariset considers that the readiness of the public to believe in the guilt of the Jacobins is proof of the efficacy of Bonaparte's propaganda, which invariably aimed at making them out the wickedest malefactors imaginable while at the same time trying to tar the republicans with the same brush. 'Do you want me to deliver you up to the Jacobins?' is the saying which in Bonaparte's mouth must excuse all his arbitrary acts. I recall the fact that Mme de Staël had already observed that the Jacobins served as bogy-men to Bonaparte.

The ever-increasing restrictions on spiritual freedom, the cunning with which, little by little, to avoid giving too much offence to Revolutionary ideology, a new nobility was introduced between 1806 and 1808, the stifling centralization, all this and much more could be discussed to show the emphasis Pariset places upon all that is not only oppressive and harsh but also systematically anti-liberal and hostile to freedom, in the Napoleonic régime. Let me merely add something about the way in which he deals with the Code.

THE CODE: A COMPARISON WITH THIERS AND VANDAL

We have already heard so much of the Code, in particular from Driault, that it will not come amiss to point out that on this subject too the most divergent opinions have been expressed, both about the share of Bonaparte in the composition of the great work and about its tendency and contents.

This time I wish to go back even further than Vandal, and look once more at the work of Thiers. From him we hear a paean of praise. The Code itself is unsurpassed and could not be bettered. The work of able lawyers, 'led by a chief who might be a military man, but who was a superior mind and knew how to cut short their hesitations and to keep them at their work', it came to be a fine compendium of French law, cleansed of all feudal elements.

The very bad reception given the first project by the Tribunate excites nothing but contempt and mockery in Thiers.[2] These revolutionary dogmatists wanted to legislate as though for an entirely new country; these heroes of the letter, enamoured of new-fangled and original conceptions, imagined that they could

1. p. 77.   2. I, 327 ff.

teach a lesson to the lawyers. In reality, the spokesman of the Council of State, Portalis, was right when he argued that the old law could not be set aside, that it must be codified and at the same time adapted to the new conceptions and to the circumstances which arose from the Revolution. 'It was impossible', is Thiers's opinion, 'to do it otherwise or to do it better.' Certainly in this extensive work a word might be replaced by a better one here and there, a pastime of which assemblies are fond; but let 'these violent and ill-trained tribunes' loose upon these thousands of articles? It would soon sicken one of the whole job.

As regards the role of Bonaparte, it was the admiration with which it inspired Thiers that led him to write the passage already quoted (p. 57) about Bonaparte's glorious appearance at the beginning of his rule.

The First Consul, who attended each of the sittings devoted to this subject by the Council of State, displayed in his conduct from the chair a method, a lucidity, and frequently a depth of insight which were a surprise to everybody. Accustomed as he was to direct armies and to govern conquered provinces, there was nothing strange in it when he revealed himself as an administrator . . . But the fact that he possessed the quality of a legislator was a matter for astonishment.[1]

He had prepared himself by asking his fellow Consul, Cambacérès, for a few books on law, and

he had devoured them as he had done those books on religious controversy when he was occupying himself with the Concordat. Soon ordering in his head the general principles of civil law, and adding to these few rapidly collected notions his profound knowledge of the human race and his perfect clarity of mind, he proved himself able to direct those important labours and even to contribute to the discussion a good many sensible, new, and profound ideas. At times his imperfect knowledge of these matters led him to sustain somewhat peculiar ideas, but he soon allowed himself to be guided back on to the right track by the learned gentlemen who surrounded him. When the moment came to draw from the conflict of opposing opinions the most natural and the most reasonable conclusions, he was the master of them all.

On both these points, of the opposition of the Tribunate and of Bonaparte's share in the preparation, the views one gathers from Pariset are different indeed.

The tribunes said, and not without reason, that the drafts were ill-digested and insufficiently considered, and that it was necessary to revise them; but above all they said, and proved, that these drafts meant a retrogression compared with the laws of the Revolution, which were sacrificed to the conceptions of the *ancien régime*.

And this is his unenthusiastic comment on Bonaparte:

1. THIERS, I, 317a.

He presided over numerous sittings, and took part in the debates with passion. His mind ever alert, keen, and animated, he expounded his ideas on *la mort civile*, women, the family, divorce, adoption, illegitimacy, and all possible matters.[1]

And that is all.

His praise for the Code itself is in a much lower key, too. It had the pretension, says Pariset, to immobilize society, or at least to fix it for a very long time; but in reality it reflected the conditions of a transitional period, and with them it soon became out of date. Nevertheless he does not deny that it had great merit. He too finds in it the fusion established between traditional law and the new conceptions. 'It has secured some of the essential rights of the Revolution.' But the makers of the Code – Cambacérès, for instance – had in the course of ten years achieved greatness and wealth, and their ideals, which used to be dynamic in the revolutionary period, had become static. The Revolution was over. There were still people without property, but the Code was not made for them. The articles which concerned them were few in number, and never remarkable for good will. 'The Code safeguards civil equality and civil liberty; in so far as it is democratic.' But it has also an undemocratic side: 'It is the Code of the propertied classes.'

Clarity of division and of style is a great merit of the work. Harsh and incomplete though this old conception may appear to us, in the Western Europe of the early nineteenth century it meant an immense progress. One need only compare it with the Prussian Land Laws of 1794. Hence the significance which it was able to acquire in conquered territories. Thus Pariset.

We find here the expression of views which half a century after Thiers had become common property. This is apparent when they are found also in an author who is so far removed from Pariset as is Vandal.

A compromise between new law and old, between customary and written law, between the 'philosophical' and the legal mind, the Code occasionally sacrificed what was good in either system in order the more easily to combine the two. In some places it may make too large concessions to the spirit of the Revolution, in others it reacted against it too strongly. Nevertheless, in spite of its imperfections and lacunae, it contained the greatest sum of natural and rational equity which men had thus far found it possible to collect in their laws ... It does not create; it registers, fixes, and stabilizes progress. Red hot matter takes on in the Code firm and indelible shape; through it, in that respect, the Revolution becomes bronze and granite.

Essentially democratic, Vandal says in another passage, it was yet in many points bourgeois. This is exactly the view of Pariset.

1. p. 165.

At the same time it will have been noticed that Vandal, with all his reservations, keeps intact the admiration by which the whole of his book lives; and so, too, his judgement about the share of Bonaparte is different. (With his respect for results and his contempt for babblers, he does not even mention the opposition in the Tribunate.)

He notices first of all that Cambacérès was much more conservative than Bonaparte. Whereupon he says:

Taking it all together it was the great lawyers who did it, but they would not have done it without Bonaparte, who put them in a position to complete the work. It was he who inspired their labours, got them going, kept them on the move, and led them to the goal. The result was permeated with the spirit which he had imposed on his period, that is to say, with the idea of a fusion between different systems and with the determination to come together.

The reader will have recognized Vandal in my quotations: the general trend of ideas of his work reveals itself in all its parts, and his stylistic power suggests connexions inspired by a deeper insight. Personally I cannot help being struck by a contradiction, not to say a trace of insincerity, in his conclusion about the Code after the apparently generous concessions to criticism. On the other hand, his judgement about the contribution made by Bonaparte, although perhaps *more suo* a trifle embellished, appears to me fairer than the somewhat excessively grudging presentation of Pariset.

4 Jules Isaac

A SCHOOL-BOOK

THE school-book by Driault which I discussed in a former chapter was part of a *Cours complet d'histoire* composed 'in conformity with the programme of 31 May 1902' for the upper forms (*les classes de première*). I have before me a section of this *Cours complet*, composed 'in conformity with the official programmes of 3 June 1925'; it is dated 1929. The author is Jules Isaac, '*professeur agrégé d'histoire au Lycée St Louis*'. I will do no more than glance at a few passages to show that in its treatment of the figure and rule of Napoleon it is no milder than its predecessor, the book of Driault, so that it provides the best refutation of the later Driault's assertion (see p. 317) that French schoolboys no longer had the finest pages of the history of France mutilated by bad patriots.

The story of the *machine infernale* and its aftermath is told with a fair amount of detail.

Bonaparte made use of the opportunity to rid himself of the republicans . . . He paid little attention to the legal guarantees of individual freedom. It was like a revival of the revolutionary terror and of the monarchical *raison d'État*.

An illustration shows a print of the period in which a ragged fierce Jacobin lights the fuse that leads to a small barrel containing powder and shot. One can see from this, says the caption, that the government misled the public into believing that the attempt was a Jacobin plot.[1]

Napoleon and intellectual life; education.

Napoleon's only care was to have obedient subjects, and men efficient in their professions. He did not perceive in the slightest degree that intellectual life feeds on liberty, and at times he let this appear in the naïvest fashion: 'People complain that we have no literature; that is the fault of the Minister of the Interior.'[2]

From the small chapter about the Council of 1811, I need quote only the title: 'Religious Persecution.' Thiers would altogether fail to understand that matters could be presented in this way in a republican school. As for Masson, he would roar that one must indeed be a 'professeur' and a Jew to vomit such slander against the great Emperor. A few of Napoleon's coarsest letters, with orders concerning the treatment of the Pope in his prison, are given among the 'texts'.

1. p. 264 ff.   2. p. 287.

331

Napoleon's foreign policy; his responsibility for the wars. The thesis of Sorel is expounded, as well as its refutation. It is apparent that the author agrees with the critics, and it is in this spirit that the ensuing account of events is told. I merely note the negotiations of 1813, about which Isaac remarks that Napoleon thought of war more than of peace, and that the powers had not for one moment contemplated depriving France of her 'natural frontiers'. Driault is quoted here – but which Driault? Not the one who wrote *Napoléon et l'Europe*, Volume V, but the Driault of twenty years before, of the article in the *Revue d'histoire moderne et contemporaine*. Driault's shade might indeed sigh

> The evil that men do lives after them,
> The good is oft interred with their bones. . . .

One final remark before I pass to another author, which is that these schoolbooks, that of 1903 as well as that of 1929, give one a remarkably favourable impression of the standard of French historical teaching. It is particularly the courageous introduction of pupils to the discussion of historical problems that appears to me worthy of admiration.

5 Charles Seignobos

MATTER OF FACTNESS RAISED TO A SYSTEM

THE pages – not more than half a score – devoted by Seignobos to Napoleon's rule in his *Histoire sincère de la Nation française* are characteristic. Seignobos wrote this pleasing little book towards the end of his life, about 1930. He was a university professor in Paris, and had made a name for himself by his dry but able and independent history of civilization, and by his excellent volume about the period of Napoleon III in Lavisse's *Histoire de la France contemporaine.* 'Dry' is also the epithet one might apply to his *Histoire sincère*; it lacks every flight of imagination, and has neither colour nor warmth of style. Yet it is not the word which occurs to one in the presence of a work so unpretentious, in which a man with extensive knowledge and who has reflected much indicates the connexions and consequences which in the course of his study have gradually impressed themselves upon him as the essentials, a man, moreover, who without any straining for effect always calls things by their names.

It will appear in a moment that he starts from a definite philosophy of life, and also that judged by this philosophy Napoleon does not cut an advantageous figure. Even before introducing him upon the stage, Seignobos wonders whether the chaos in public life and in finances which is alleged to have existed in France under the Directorate has not, like the licentiousness, 'been exaggerated in order to enhance the importance of Bonaparte's work of reorganization'[1] As regards the administrative system – which, though it was introduced under the Consulate, cannot be considered as Bonaparte's work, because in those early days he had to leave such measures to the experts – Seignobos concludes his description with these words:

A centralized system of government agents, opposed to the régime of elective self-government created by the Revolution. The nation had no longer any share in the conduct of its affairs or in the choice of its local leaders. The French ceased to be citizens, to become once more subjects, no longer of the king, but of the government.

In his remarks about the Concordat we recognize the idea of Driault.[2] Bonaparte

1. p. 381.
2. See p. 310 ff. above; SEIGNOBOS, *Histoire sincère*, p. 387.

created the conditions which must make the French clergy ultramontane, although he wished to preserve its Gallicanism.

What, according to Seignobos, is there about Napoleon which explains the admiration, the enthusiasm, of so many adherents? It cannot be expressed more soberly:

His marvellous activity, his astonishing quickness of decision, his incredible memory for detail, the sureness of his practical judgement.

And what of the other side of the account?

His despotic nature tolerated no activity independent of his own. He abhorred the liberals, whom he called the ideologists. He had no conception of disinterested devotion to a cause, and ascribed all actions to self-interest or to vanity . . . Educated in Corsica before that country had been merged into a unified France, Napoleon never managed to feel a real Frenchman.

In support of this conception, which has by now become so well known to us, Seignobos adduces an argument that is novel. 'I wish', Napoleon wrote in his testament, 'that my ashes may rest on the banks of the Seine, amidst that French nation which I have loved so much.'

'It would have occurred to no Frenchman to express himself like that', says Seignobos. And the remark is strikingly true. Yet, as everyone knows, the sentence is inscribed on the wall of the crypt of the Invalides, and it has never failed to move the French.

His method of government [Seignobos continues] did not dovetail into French tradition. In his native island he had learned to know only clan solidarity, and this is why in France and elsewhere he failed to recognize the strength of national consciousness.

Restrained by no inner moral curb, he went on to the point where his power met with an insurmountable obstacle.

Armed force was the real basis of his domination, which was bound to collapse, when, one after another, his armies had been used up.

In the upshot, France retained nothing of his military achievements, and moreover she lost the conquests of the Republic. In Europe a profound distrust of the French remained; they were looked upon as a people fond of war, while France was left with the Napoleonic legend, which was a disturber of domestic peace and which in the end landed the nation in an adventurist foreign policy.

At the end of his small book, the author reverts to this idea and says that in the period behind us the misconception of a bellicose and fickle France, based on the wars of Louis XIV and of the two Napoleons and upon the Paris revolutions of the nineteenth century, is beginning to fade out in foreign countries.

'The French nation is beginning to be seen in its true nature as sensible, reasonable and peace-loving.'[1]

I doubt whether the French nation is more intelligent, more reasonable, and more peaceful than another. I should certainly not care to call it more bellicose or more fickle, but it has had its unintelligent unreasonable periods, when it was a worry to its neighbours. It was, to keep to our subject, a most willing tool in the hands of Napoleon, and after his death a credulous dupe of the legend. The thought which it repays our trouble to meditate, in this conclusion by Seignobos, seems to me to be that in the course of history a nation can assume many very different aspects.

THREE *ACADÉMICIENS*

I shall now, after the five *universitaires*, deal with three *académiciens*. The example of Anatole France has already proved that one can belong to the Academy without rating Napoleon particularly high. About Hanotaux, the third of the trio now under survey, it will soon be noticed that his admiration is by no means unmixed. To be sure, he strikes a different note from that of the *universitaires*, and one seems to feel that he has been in closer communion with Vandal and Sorel than they. Nevertheless, the true outlook of the *Académie* will be found rather in Bainville, and especially in Madelin, and I have therefore deemed it appropriate to deviate here from the chronological order and to deal with the work of Hanotaux after that of the other two. My last author, George Lefebvre, an unmistakable *universitaire* but who has absorbed much of the other conception, fits in too well with Hanotaux for me to part them from one another.

1. p. 491.

6 Jacques Bainville

THE AUTHOR AND THE *ACTION FRANÇAISE*

BAINVILLE'S *Napoléon*, of 1931, is probably the most read biography of Napoleon in our time. If only for a moment, the book confronts us with a difficulty which we have usually been spared. Ought we to classify the author as *for* or *aganist*? I have already mentioned him, in passing, among the admirers who achieved access to the *Académie*; but when one reads in his conclusion that 'apart from glory, apart from art' it would probably have been better if Napoleon had never lived,[1] one would be inclined to assume that we are dealing with one of the critics. The book, however, constantly strikes another note. By whatever point among those which usually give rise to disapproval we test it – the wars, centralization, terroristic methods, lack of spiritual freedom, the attempt to subject the Church – we shall meet either with apology or with complete indifference. But this negative test is not the only one we can apply. The whole book, leaving on one side approval or disapproval of political trends, is pervaded with admiration for the central figure. The greatness, the beauty of this figure, the satisfaction it gives to the spectator's 'artistic' sense, that is what gives Bainville's biography its positive content. Lanfrey and Quinet would have rejected the book with horror.

And indeed, the author was no Bonapartist; but he also was not in the least a liberal. He was a royalist. His leader was Maurras, who counts Barrès among his spiritual precursors, although the French tradition from which the *Action française*, like Barrès, wanted to extract all its strength was more exclusively attached to the old royalty. In consequence it was bound to reject Napoleon, in so far as it had to look upon him as an interruption or a deviation. But being little inclined to place emphasis upon moral norms in judging political or historical phenomena – and also since the slogans of spiritual freedom or justice meant less to it than those of Fatherland, power, order – it felt no qualm in surrendering to a foible for the strong man, for the great personality. Houssaye, Masson, or Driault would not have been satisfied with Bainville's book; but the dominant impression which the reader receives from it is undeniably such as to range it under the heading *For*.

The *Action française* was too extreme and its solution for all the ills of France,

1. p. 581.

Le Roi, too unreal for it to influence practical politics otherwise than by spreading suspicion and by bringing about public disorder. Nevertheless it struck chords in certain French prejudices and moods, and was thus able to nurture a state of mind far beyond its own small circle. For this purpose Bainville, popular author of great intellectual and stylistic gifts, was (next to Maurras) a force of considerable significance. Before *Napoléon* he had captured an immense following with his brief *Histoire de France*. Afterwards, when his *Napoléon* had opened the doors of the *Académie* for him, in 1935 shortly before his death there also appeared his history of *La troisième République*. This little book is of importance for our better knowledge of the author's mind. In his *Histoire de France* he had managed to deal with the Dreyfus affair without letting a word escape him about guilt or innocence. The chapter *La Révolution Dreyfusienne* in the latest book is less discreet. For those acquainted with the details of *l'Affaire* it makes amazing reading. The guilt of the Jewish officer is implied with the help of tendentious or half true statements, suppressions, distortions of the motives of the defenders; all this directly against the evidence of the facts which led in 1900 to the annulment of the sentence, strengthened as that evidence had been by the subsequently published testimony of the German military attaché Schwarzkoppen. As one reads the chapter one wonders – can this man be honest? But it is possible to put it less bluntly and perhaps more truly. Bainville, like Barrès (I have already – p. 145 – quoted the words in connexion with the latter), belonged to those for whom 'objective truth' means less than their own 'organic, inherited, passionate truth'. We must not forget it when reading his *Napoléon*.

TRAGIC GREATNESS IN THE GRIP OF FATE

Bainville's Napoleon has tragic grandeur. The element of tragedy arises from the conception of a man with unflinching energy and with unequalled talent struggling with an impossible task, a task beyond human and even beyond *his* capacity. Apparent success, dazzling even, but unsound and in the final account of no value whatever, accompanies him for many years in all his expeditions and enterprises, and heightens the effect of a cruel game which divine powers are playing on him. He must go on; he must struggle, he vanquishes and conquers, he subjects and cows, but throughout the spectator knows that the catastrophe is drawing nearer and he himself, for all his display of assurance and pride, unflagging in the performance of his incredible deeds, in his ingenious combinations to keep ahead of fate, he too is haunted by the fear that it is in vain and that it will all end in ruin.

From beginning to end the book is more a discussion supported and illustrated by particulars and quotations than a narrative built up from description and disquisition. What the author wishes all the time to convey is the brittleness of Napoleon's position, its uncommon and excessive quality, which dooms it to perpetual restlessness and causes it in the long run to be untenable.

It begins immediately after Brumaire. It should not be thought, says Bainville, with emphasis, that Bonaparte was now the master. Much patient labour, much management and wiliness were still necessary to achieve that consummation. When he is away on his campaign of Marengo, everything is at once unsettled. Behind his back in Paris, vast intrigues are on foot to produce another government in case he is defeated. He is aware of it, and in the midst of his triumphant return he has moments of bitterness and fierce contempt for humanity. But the triumph is colossal, and it grows more colossal when the following year, after Hohenlinden, the peace for which everyone has been longing is secured. Bainville contemplates the Consulate with enthusiasm, and without a single one of the reservations of which we know. On the contrary, we find in his book the familiar reasoning (see p. 207 ff.) by which the authoritarian régime established by Bonaparte can be linked up with the Revolution, and the Revolution itself be shorn of its liberalism so as to cease being troublesome to a conservative realist, who would rather exclude the friends of liberty and republicans from French tradition.

Had not the French of 1789 mistaken their desires? Was not what they really longed for – after equality, which came before everything – authority, rather than liberty?[1]

It is on the occasion of Bonaparte's choice of Lebrun as one of his two colleagues in the Consulate that Bainville makes this remark. This choice, with that of Cambacérès (a man of the Convention and a regicide), was characteristic of his programme; for Lebrun, no longer a young man (in 1810, when he became Governor-General of Holland, he was over seventy), had been secretary to the Chancellor Maupéou, who in the reign of Louis XV had abolished the *Parlements*, those privileged courts of law which stood in the way of a reformist monarchy. If this 'revolution', as it was called at the time, had not been unmade under Louis XVI, if Louis XVI had had the courage and the vision to continue along the road of enlightened despotism, instead of restoring the privileged members of the *noblesse de robe* to a position in which they could sabotage all radical measures, then perhaps the Revolution of 1789 would not have taken place. Through Lebrun, Bonaparte established a link with the tradition of eighteenth-century enlightened despotism, a tradition by no means yet forgotten: for the 'ideologists' from whom Bonaparte had not yet broken away, the intellectuals of the *Institut*, were tired of the whims of the masses, were

1. p. 158.

drifting away from democracy and – like their master Voltaire, Bainville might have added – were advocates of enlightened despotism.

So far the personality of the First Consul could not have been painted in more rosy colours; but what deprived him of a solid foundation, according to Bainville, was the international situation. Peace! Everything depended upon it. Bonaparte was in the eyes of the French the giver of this peace so ardently desired. He himself felt how much his popularity owed to this. He wanted peace. For a moment he shared the illusion that Amiens was meant seriously. How otherwise could one explain those colonial enterprises: San Domingo; Louisiana, which he acquired from Spain but which – this particularly is significant – he sold forthwith to the United States when the renewal of war appeared inevitable. War was inevitable, because Britain could not resign herself to France's possession of Belgium, of Antwerp; while on the other hand France, though wanting peace, wanted it to be accompanied by the 'natural frontiers', and no one was less in a position to give up the 'natural frontiers', since it was precisely to Bonaparte's good sword that men looked for their preservation.

Connected with this is the sense of insecurity which never left Napoleon concerning his internal policy as well. His experience at the time of Marengo was never forgotten. Least of all did he trust the generals, until recently his equals. At first he treated them with extreme caution, notwithstanding the tone of authority he sometimes adopted; if he took the imperial title, it was not in order to place himself above them – the ceremonial at the court was intended for this purpose, and in particular the care with which the civilian character of his dignity was underlined.

But even the imperial title was by no means sufficient.

Never [Balzac has written] could Napoleon quite convince of his sovereignty those whom he had had as his superiors or his equals; nor those for whom law took the first place. Nobody considered himself bound by the oath taken to him.

Napoleon himself declared at St Helena:

I had risen from the masses too suddenly. I felt my isolation. So I kept throwing out anchors for my salvation into the depths of the sea.

Anchors for his salvation? This it was, more than ostentation, or pride, or megalomania: anchors for salvation. This was to be the function of those brother kings (only they performed it very poorly). An anchor for salvation, also, was the consecration by the Pope. He sought the semblance of legitimacy; but if he won the Catholics thereby, he knew very well how much he was once more hurting the feelings of the men of the Revolution (although by the killing of Enghien earlier in the year he had hoped to obtain an undeniable claim to their confidence).

Hence those pinpricks, those insults, which he administered to the Pope during his sojourn; it was to restore the balance . . .[1]

But the fatal menace comes from outside.

Another ten years! [Bainville speculates, when discussing the elevation to the imperial dignity.] Hardly ten years have passed since he began to rise from obscurity, and in another ten years all will be finished. So it is decreed by the breathless rhythm of his life's destiny. A subaltern at twenty-five, he is, miracle of miracles, Emperor at thirty-five. Time has seized him by the shoulders and pushes him on. His days are counted. They will pass with the speed of a dream, marvellously full, broken by hardly any intervals or breathing space, as if impatient to reach the catastrophe more speedily, and charged at last with so many tremendous events, that his reigns, so brief in reality, will seem to have lasted a century.[2]

I give this quotation because it is characteristic; again and again Bainville inserts into his narrative passages like this, reminding us that only nine, only eight, only seven years are left . . . England has time. But, 'in London everything has already been calculated, everything is ordered, for the moment of his downfall'. Those famous discussions of the Russian envoy, Novosiltsov, with Pitt (see p. 256 ff.) – Bainville does not even mention the name, and does not bother about negotiations or precise details – are woven into the narrative for the sake of effect:

At a distance of nine years – for now only nine years are left, and since Senate and people elevated him to the imperial dignity, the brief respite allowed him by fate has shrunk once more – not only his defeat is foreseen, not only are the terms for France laid down, but the very method, this manoeuvre of gradual pressure, by which Napoleon will be compelled to abdicate, the whole of this policy has been traced beforehand, so that all that remains to be done in 1813 and 1814 will be the filling in of the outline of the sketch.[3]

The aim remains, as ever, to cheat France of her 'natural frontiers', but by now the psychology of the French nation has been grasped; the intention is no longer proclaimed, the fight is alleged to be against Napoleon and not against France, and all the cunning is directed towards creating misunderstandings over the frontiers.

It will be readily understood that in this interpretation Talleyrand's conduct at Erfurt is condemned. Bainville insists less upon the treason than upon the mistake. Talleyrand considered that he was doing a good work, even for Napoleon himself, by throwing obstacles in his way that would compel him to remain within 'the law of possibility'. As if Napoleon were free to remain moderate; as if, just as inside the country he was obliged to climb higher and higher in

1. pp. 241, 245.　　　　　2. p. 239.　　　　　3. pp. 253 ff.

order to make himself respected, he would not abroad have to go further and further for the sake of preserving these dear possessions of the French nation, the 'natural frontiers'! Talleyrand failed to realize the necessities of this unequal struggle with Britain, and the open or hidden determination of the powers to throw France back once more within her old frontiers. The game which he thought so clever was naïve. As for Napoleon, he left Erfurt deceived and betrayed, not quite clear in his mind as to what had happened to him, but still depressed, silent, and pensive. 'These accursed Spanish affairs are costing me dear,' he sighed.[1] And indeed, the Spanish mistake – Bainville does not deny that the Emperor had made an error by judging Spanish conditions and the Spanish people according to his eighteenth-century French notions, as what he aptly calls a genuine 'ideologist'[2] – this mistake had to be paid for very heavily. But it was not only that. Nobody has been betrayed so much and has punished so little, says Bainville. But why? 'Not that he was vulnerable, but his position was.'[3]

The expedition to Moscow, as we can already guess, was inevitable: Napoleon had no choice. But now his destiny is nearly accomplished. How loudly we now hear Bainville's often repeated motif. 'Everything I have accomplished is still very fragile,' he confesses to Caulaincourt in the sledge. And at the same time, with what greatness he bears himself in the disaster! The contempt which he feels more than ever for his ministers and for the Senate, because they hesitate; because they imagine that concessions can avert the disaster and make Britain give up its coveted prey, Belgium; because they believe, however shyly and half-heartedly, in this distinction which is being made between the Emperor and the country – Bainville clearly indicates that he thinks it is fully deserved.[4]

One would expect that Bainville's royalism, in his treatment of the years 1814 and 1815 if anywhere, would place him in opposition to Napoleon. In his *Histoire de France* this expectation is justified. There, Bainville praises the policy of Talleyrand and Louis XVIII, who managed to save so much from the *débâcle* into which Napoleon had led the country. The disappointment of the public at the loss of the 'natural frontiers' avenged itself on them by the amazing turn of 1815. The great adventurist arrived from Elba without any hope of reigning without a new war, and made his last desperate bid; the result, after the Hundred Days, a new and worse disaster for France.

All these events [Bainville wrote in 1924] have the colour of a novel, and their character is that of the human passions. They do not belong to the domain of

1. p. 357 ff.
2. p. 333. Note the contrast with Taine's conception of Napoleon, p. 128 above.
3. p. 368.
4. p. 469.

reason. A three months' folly brought back the foreigner in our country, and jeopardized everything that had been so painfully obtained in 1814.[1]

He counts up the territorial losses which were now inflicted on France and says:

France had brought those disasters on herself when, giving way to sentiment and moved by the memory of the days of glory, she forgot everything, to throw herself into the arms of the Emperor.

And yet the legend was hardly born; it grew and throve only with the martyrdom of St Helena.

This is not the language of an admirer. But in his *Napoléon*, Bainville refrains almost entirely from passing a political judgement on these events. 'He had not yet had his genuine fifth act,' he writes, 'there had been a false curtain at Fontainebleau.'[2] He then particularly emphasizes the necessity which Napoleon felt of flattering the revolutionaries and keeping on good terms with the liberals, and his hopelessly false position as a constitutional Emperor. He continues to look upon the course of affairs from the personal side. After Waterloo, when Napoleon wants to embark upon the British vessel, *Bellerophon*, and a French general asks whether he is to accompany him, the Emperor replies ('and how well it is put!' says Bainville): 'No, general. It must not be said that France has delivered me up to the English.' Bainville's comment is: 'An actor, but one who works only in the grand style.'[3]

READABLE BUT OUTSIDE THE HISTORICAL DISCUSSION

The reader will have recognized Vandal in the interpretation of the Consulate, but he will have been particularly reminded of Sorel. Indeed, the whole of Bainville's Napoleon – defender of the 'natural frontiers', prisoner of a system already settled before his time, victim of the determination of Britain and of Europe and of their astute deception of French public opinion – is the Napoleon of Sorel. The book brings no original vision. It is a popularization of the conceptions of others, and especially of one other. It makes exciting reading, and in its concentrated form it is dramatic; upon uncritical readers it exercises a high degree of persuasion. But it can hardly be called a contribution to the historical discussion of Napoleon.

As a matter of fact, those who are aware of the literature of the subject will be hardly less surprised at this than at the author's chapter about the Dreyfus affair in *La troisième République*. I have summarized the argument about the breach of the peace of Amiens. It may have been wondered what Bainville would have

1. *Histoire de France*, p. 439.   2. *Napoléon*, p. 525.
3. op. cit. p. 556.

to say about Sebastiani's report concerning Egypt and its publication in the *Moniteur*. The answer is, nothing: he does not mention it. In this way it is not difficult to put all the guilt upon Britain. And such throughout is Bainville's method. He passes in silence everything that does not fit into his system, and he takes no notice of the criticism aimed by the experts at his guides Vandal and Sorel. When one reads him, it is as though Guyot and Muret and Driault had not written. The Directorate is still uniformly contemptible; Bonaparte always provides a shining contrast. He alone knew that one should not plunder the Italian population, he alone understood that the Vendée ought to be pacified. And so forth. Napoleon's pronouncements about the British peril are taken without criticism as expressing his profoundest opinion, and no mention is made of the hesitations and differences of the powers. I could fill pages by adding up points which we have met in this discussion, on which one certainly cannot demand agreement from every subsequent author, but which Bainville brushes aside in a manner that is really somewhat too light-hearted. It is true that by thus placing oneself outside the discussion, and by keeping obstinately to a single leading idea, one can write an exceedingly readable book and get into the *Académie* as well; one can also serve one's own 'organic truth' by so doing. But as for objective truth – no.

ARTIST AND INTELLECTUAL

Is not this last observation so crushing that I must be thought illogical if I still give any further attention to Bainville's writing? It was not, however, my intention to demolish him, although I have made most serious reservations. His slavish dependence upon Sorel notwithstanding, one cannot deny him historical imagination. He has seen his Napoleon, and he has seen him in connexion with a broader picture (although again most daringly fashioned to fit his own particular conceptions) of the history of France. And in any case, what I am now going to discuss is his own invention, in greater degree than what precedes.

Apart from this insistence on Napoleon's subjection to fate, there is another idea which gives life to the book. As early as page 2 the author recalls Napoleon's own explanation at St Helena ('What a novel, anyhow, my life has been!') and thereby indicates a *leitmotiv* of his work. The striking aspect of his conception is not so much that he tried to bring into relief the novel-like character of the life he describes. Every author, unless too much absorbed by the moral or political significance of the events to pay much attention to the appearance, will be struck by the wonderful aspect of the career, and will try to communicate this impression to his readers. But Bainville has made Napoleon's capacity to be impressed

343

by his own life into a main characteristic of his personality. It had not escaped the attention of contemporaries. Mme de Rémusat notes the intense interest Napoleon felt for his own life story. Talleyrand, once or twice, realized that the great man was consciously at work on 'the novel of his life'. Chateaubriand, his enemy, called him – though not in the pamphlet of 1814 – 'a poet in action'.

Bainville has worked this up into the portrait of a man able to make a dichotomy of his ego, who can see himself live – the gift of the artist, of the intellectual. What a different basis is established here for the admiration of Napoleon the man than that presented by Arthur-Lévy, for whom he could not sufficiently resemble a good bourgeois! A third conception was that of Lanfrey, which though so very different from that of Arthur-Lévy – Napoleon the cold calculating egoist, the perfectly amoral adventurist – was from this point of view, as will be recalled (see p. 85), the diametrical opposite of Bainville's reading. For Lanfrey denied to Napoleon precisely this capacity of looking without prejudice and disinterestedly at his own personality, his own actions. The remarkable thing about these conceptions of the figure, however much each appears to exclude the other, is that all three of them make the reader feel he is brought in contact with 'a side of the personality'. That was how I put it (p. 164) in discussing *Napoléon intime*. The Napoleon of Lanfrey, who calculates his effects even when he appears to be most unselfconscious, is just as little a pure invention. But here Bainville, in bringing out this trait, at first sight incompatible, also carries conviction.

On the evening when he has occupied the Tuileries as First Consul, in itself an important decision, Bonaparte is supposed to have said to Joséphine: 'Come along, my little *créole*, go and lie down in the bed of your masters.' A famous phrase, and one which Bainville characterizes as among the most revealing of those that have been preserved.

The unforeseen, the fantastical, even the irony of the situation, are well conveyed by it; nothing of all that escapes this uncommonly mature young man, who can, when time allows, see himself live, who is capable of reflections on his destiny and on himself.[1]

Bonaparte has become Emperor.

One of his most remarkable traits [writes Bainville] which he owes to the predominance in his personality of the intellect, is his capacity for a dual vision. Nothing ever surprises him, of all the incredible things that happen to him . . . He lives on a footing of equality with his destiny. To reign comes perfectly naturally to him. It is a chapter of the novel in which he is a personage. Not that he forgets

1. p. 170.

where he comes from, whence he has risen, all that had to happen to make him possible, and how fragile is his rule. He knows it better than anybody, and without ever being troubled by it. Nor does greatness alter his mind or even his language. Majestic on solemn occasions, he remains what he was before in intimate and human intercourse, brusque, ironical, now distant, now familiar, amiable or blunt, and occasionally coarse. For himself he admits no compulsion, while he imposes on his surroundings the laws of a strict etiquette ... On the throne Napoleon is more at his ease than if he had been born to it, for even the traditions he revives in his court are calculated and a matter of will.[1]

Thus he remains to the very last. See him after the Russian disaster in the sledge with Caulaincourt.

That perilous journey is merely a striking new chapter in his adventurous life. Years earlier, indeed, Bonaparte had departed from Egypt in similar circumstances, trusting himself to fortune. Nothing amazes him. He has always been ready for anything to happen. During that journey, he discusses himself as one would a stranger, with that pleasure in seeing himself live by which the artist may be recognized. He has taken Caulaincourt with him as if he were anxious, or curious, to find himself alone with the man to whose counsel he had refused to listen ... One would almost say that Napoleon is having a rehearsal for the *Mémorial de St Hélène*; his way with Caulaincourt is already that with Las Cases later on.[2]

The same day on which he addressed the ironical remark to Joséphine – the wide divergence of mood covered by that mind is repeatedly pointed out by Bainville – Bonaparte walked with the State Councillor Roederer through the rooms of the old royal palace, and when Roederer, influenced by the memories it awakened, said to him '*Général, cela est triste,*' he replied: '*Oui, comme la gloire.*' Bainville comments: 'The upstart gave way to the literary man, to the poet, who felt things.' To the romantic, as he says elsewhere, and as Guérard had already remarked.

But it is not only in detached utterances, it is in his whole life, in the deeds and calculations of the statesman, that Bainville finds this intellectual and artistic quality. In the ambitious plans of the First Consul to begin with. The historical forms of which 'this powerful imagination' makes use, could only arise so naturally with an intellectual, *un cérébral*. This sense of historical greatness was prepared by the bold flights of mind to which the studious little officer had abandoned himself in his rooms at Auxonne. Greatness does not startle him nor make him ridiculous. It is a natural action for him to choose the cardinal

1. p. 239 ff.   2. p. 467.

archbishop, de Boisgelin, who twenty-five years earlier had delivered the sermon on the occasion of the consecration of Louis XVI, that in praising the Concordat he might compare its author to Pepin and Charlemagne.[1]

Or take the scene in Notre Dame, on 2 December 1804, when Napoleon, notwithstanding the most positive promises made to the Pope, forestalls him at the critical moment by taking the crown in his own hands and placing it on his head. We have heard authors who note above all the deceit; others in whose eyes the symbolic meaning of the act seemed to compensate for it. Bainville forgets it because of the fine gesture.

This gesture [with which he forestalled the mild-hearted Pius] which is described to us as at the same time imperious and calm, so studied that it looked spontaneous, inspired as by an indwelling genius – perhaps the genius of the Republic – this gesture he managed to make so noble and so great that all those present felt it belonged to history.[2]

The romantic, I said a moment ago: an unexpected combination with that appearance, with that display of impeccable Roman classicism, with that Latin clarity and precision, from which Bourgeois and Driault deduced their otherwise so different theories about the purpose of his foreign policy! If one has clearly envisaged the fact that Napoleon united in himself those contradictions, this alone explains the rich possibilities of widely divergent interpretations. But Bainville points out another trait, which, in combination with the others, strikes us as unexpected, and which actually leads us back to the Napoleon of Arthur-Lévy. 'Egypt', he writes, 'is in the career of the general what Atala was in that of Chateaubriand.' And he means the romantic pull of the exotic. But in that famous proclamation to the soldiers about 'the forty centuries' looking down upon them 'from the top of the Pyramids', he is irreverent enough to discern an attempt at the sublime which only its epic quality saves from being ridiculous. He smiles at 'this way of speaking at once oriental and bourgeois', these stylistic effects which flatter the Joseph Prud'homme in the Frenchman. Similarly of the scarcely less famous proclamation after Austerlitz – 'Soldats, je suis content de vous . . . Il vous suffira de dire: "J'étais à la bataille d'Austerlitz," pour que l'on réponde: voilà un brave' – he says:

Emphatic style, well suited to impress men's minds with the middle-class and popular romanticism, with that genre of surburban taste in ornaments for the mantelpiece of which Bonaparte had discovered the secret.[3]

Here there would still be room for a dispute about the question to what extent

1. p. 198.   2. p. 248.   3. p. 271.

this rhetoric, which was to suit Béranger so perfectly, bubbled up from the depth of Napoleon's soul, or whether it was an expression of conscious artistry, the technique of an actor who is master of his craft; or – a third possibility which would bring one into agreement with Lanfrey – whether it came from a calculating turn of mind and was directed towards aims that were strictly practical.

7   Louis Madelin

THE AUTHOR

LOUIS MADELIN may be counted among the professional historians, although he has never tried to make a career in the *Université*. He is a talented writer, he professes the correct conservative, religious, and patriotic sentiments. No wonder then that with a book about Fouché and a highly admired and unrevolutionary history of the French Revolution to his credit, he was elected to the *Académie*. But of the many 'immortals' whom we have met[1] he seems to me, for all his charm, learning, and productiveness, to be the least outstanding personality.

Madelin's *Fouché* goes back to the beginning of the century. I shall not enumerate his works (from one of his books I have already – p. 297 ff. – given a quotation). In 1932 and 1933 he published, in Funck Brentano's *Histoire de France racontée à tous*, in which twenty years earlier his *Révolution* had appeared, two volumes about *Consulat et Empire*. I shall limit myself mainly to these, although soon afterwards he began the publication of a much more detailed work in which the same subject matter was to be dealt with once more, but this time in twelve volumes, of which, however, only four had appeared at the outbreak of war.

From Madelin's somewhat sarcastic description of the self-opinionated Napoleonic officials outside France proper which I have quoted (p. 298), the reader may have formed the impression that his conservative attitude of mind is likely to make him critical of the activity and the personality of Napoleon. This is far from being the case. It is impossible to hesitate even for a moment about him, as one can about Bainville. He is an admirer; and while Bainville copies without further consideration from Vandal and Sorel, but yet adds something of his own, it can be said of Madelin that his work continues on the lines laid down by the two great Napoleonic historians. There is less uncritical copying, but also less that is original. As a result we do not find in his work important new points of view. On the main issues he treats us to an interpretation already familiar to us, and what characterizes him is not so much the dramatic

1. Chateaubriand, Mignet, Thiers, d'Haussonville, Taine, Houssaye, Vandal, Masson, Sorel, Lavisse, France, Barrès, Bainville, and presently Hanotaux.

and spirited presentation, as in the case of Bainville, as the clear, detailed, and able exposé. For this reason his twelve volumes will, when complete, form an important contribution. However strongly one may object to his conceptions, the controversies of recent times and the opposing views to which they have given rise have undeniably been utilized in his broad treatment. Moreover, the extensive annotation is highly instructive. But we are concerned here mainly with views, and these, as I said before, I intend to illustrate for the most part from the two-volume textbook.

PORTRAIT OF BONAPARTE IN 1799

Shortly after the beginning of *Le Consulat et l'Empire* the author gives a portrait of Bonaparte, or better of *'le Bonaparte de l'an VIII'*.[1] This occupies some highly interesting pages, which exactly reflect the spirit of the whole book.

'Bonaparte' (according to a phrase of Schopenhauer, who had met him) 'is the finest embodiment of human will power.' This is Madelin's point of departure. In matters of state, this characteristic leads Bonaparte to an authoritarian conception. But authority is for him merely a prerequisite for order. 'He had order in his blood.' Such a character, according to Madelin, even if directed by an ordinary spirit, would have been a blessing for the France of 1799,

but with a wonderfully gifted, organized, and powerful brain applied to regulating and instructing these tendencies, the blessing became immeasurable.

A broad and profound outlook, a mind inclined to study, well read, ever busy, hardworking: 'A passionate worker, Bonaparte was even more a man of mental labour than a man of action.' He was for ever in search of facts, facts, facts, which he arranged and meditated upon tirelessly. His powerful imagination did not work in a vacuum. His dreams were not purely visionary. 'They were transformed immediately into concrete acts, into practical measures. The fact is that he was extraordinarily realistic.' This is how with his common sense he was able, at the rise of the Consulate, 'to redress the evil wrought by the crazy ideology of the *Assemblées*'. Thus his policy was that of an opportunist. But it is particularly in his execution that he displayed his realism. He was able to extract everything possible from his collaborators and officials. Sometimes he worked them to death, but it was in the interest of '*la chose publique*'.

As regards the ideas of this unusual man, 'they fulfil the aspirations of the country'. They sprang 'from his own character, from his study of history and from the spectacle that presented itself to his eyes over the preceding ten years'.

I. I, 31–43.

He had been a supporter of the Revolution, almost a Jacobin; but now he recognized, though fully appreciating certain results of the Revolution, that there had been much good in the *ancien régime*.

He thought, and rightly so, that the movement of 1789 had aimed only at equality. 'Liberty,' he used to add, 'was no more than its pretext.'

What he saw besides in the Revolution (Madelin quotes the following from Vandal) was 'the military and martial side, the conquering and Roman quality'. Madelin continues in his own words to the following effect:

The natural frontiers acquired, French glory exalted, the way prepared for French hegemony, these, with all careers open to talent, were undoubtedly among the achievements of the Revolution those which seemed to him most beautiful.

Equality, the *tabula rasa* made by the abolition of the old provinces, now the basis upon which could be constructed that centralized state of which Colbert had dreamed but whose realization had been prevented by the kings; the 'natural frontiers' as the concern of the people. Looked at in this way, the Revolution seemed to Bonaparte a blessing, and he was willing to pass for 'the embodiment of the Revolution'. He wished to serve not a party but the nation. He loved France, and he loved her past. He felt a link between himself and his predecessors, with the *Comité de salut public* and with the kings. A man of authority, he disliked 'the assemblies' and the Press equally. But this is not to say that he wished to govern against the people.

On the contrary, it was his firm intention to base himself on *la démocratie*, against the oligarchies.

For the people of Paris he wanted an assured bread supply and amusements that would elevate the soul (see p. 321). Soon he was to grant the Legion of Honour to an honest miner while withholding it from the monied men.

None of the oligarchies he abhorred as much as he did that of the financiers, so influential under the Directorate.

He did not want a military oligarchy either, nor a domination of priests, nor the rule of lawyers.

A master, a chief: a sovereign arbiter, restorer, and preserver of order, who, freed from the pressure of social groups, was to prevent all possible excesses of parliamentary oratory, of the Press, of the electorate [in their *comices*] – such was the First Consul's conception of authority.

Next: 'The defence of the nation against Europe and the conquest of a glorious peace. Peace is what he wants.' But he also wishes to retain the 'natural frontiers', and he knows that Europe grudges them to France.

MARGINAL NOTES TO 'DEMOCRACY' AND 'REALIST': NAPOLEON
AND ROME

The outline invites a few remarks. It will have been noticed that there is no
shading to the picture. After the evil wrought by 'crazy ideology', a happy
period dawns of authority, order, and common sense. Madelin, who places
himself unmistakably to the right (with Vandal and Bainville) by his interpretation of the Revolution as indifferent to liberty, abhors parliamentarianism as
much as does his hero. For him it is the same as oligarchy, and he discredits it
still further by connecting it particularly with the moneyed oligarchy. *Tabula
rasa* through the disappearance of the historic division into provinces, and at
the same time through equality and the political impotence of all social groups.
It is amusing to see the author afraid that every one of these social groups, the
financiers, the lawyers, the priests, the generals, may come to exercise domination, but that he has not a word to say on the danger that the dictator who absorbs
all these different powers might himself at a given moment abuse his omnipotence. But why be afraid of Bonaparte! Bonaparte wanted peace, even though
it had to be a glorious peace with the 'natural frontiers' intact (these, by the way,
'Europe' was already leaving to him in 1801-2, but about this we shall hear
more from Madelin), and he rested his power on *la démocratie*.

Need I point out that the word democracy is not used here in its true significance? No free Press, no political discussion, but the people conciliated through
bread and amusements to elevate the soul (no serious popular education, however) and through a decoration for an honest miner – needless to point out, to
our generation, that this is not democracy.

One more point. 'Bonaparte was eminently a realist.' How is it possible to
assert this without reservation? I could contrast with the statement Bainville's
sketch of a Bonaparte concerned with artistic effects and working at the novel
of his life. But let me recall the remark made at an early date by the liberals that
Bonaparte's cynicism and his contempt for men (about which Madelin keeps
silent) blinded him to loftier motives, to disinterested convictions and idealism,
although these too can be realities in the case of individuals and of groups. I
recall the particular case of his blindness concerning the Spanish people, and in
general concerning the national movements which were to turn against him
in Europe at a later stage. Bainville, surely, was right when he wrote that Napoleon's Spanish mistake was the mistake of an ideologist. He overestimated the
universal power of attraction of the Revolution's reforming slogans with which
he approached the Spaniards. He also overestimated, as he did so frequently,
the miraculous effect of his military power and of intimidation. In short, he

acted according to general principles, instead of paying attention to the special circumstances of the Spanish affair: *that* would have been realism.

But finally I should like to place over against the realistic Napoleon of the portrait of 1932 the entirely different figure outlined by Madelin in 1906 in his *La Rome de Napoléon*. One would almost think that a lifelong study of Napoleon had affected the independence of Madelin's attitude towards the great man, though not so seriously as in the case of Driault.

By an uncommonly striking atavism this Corsican army commander had Rome in the marrow of his bones. His blood was Roman, his profile was Roman. From the ancient Roman he derived the relish for greatness, the passion to dominate, the extravagant imagination, at times allied with merciless realism. [The contrast with the later portrait is indeed striking.] Engraved in his brain he has Roman law; the Roman manner marks his decision, his style, his way of governing. Instinctively he feels Rome to be his ideal centre . . . In his imagination he has dwelt for ages on the Capitol. He was fed on Rome. Many years before he brought Caesar back to life, he made an impassioned study of Livy, Tacitus, and Plutarch and of all the works which the eighteenth century had produced on the subject of Rome. But his powerful intellect burst through the framework of that history, grandiose though it was, and he preferred the Rome of the great Corneille to that of the excellent Abbé Rollin: so great a subject seemed to him to belong exclusively to the domain of the poet of genius, 'whom I should create a prince if he were still alive'.[1]

For many pages Madelin then proceeds to show how, early and late, Napoleon was 'possessed' by Rome. At first, in his earlier years, it was Brutus and Scaevola, the Catos and the Gracchi. Then it is Caesar. In 1809 he conversed with Canova, who was modelling a statue of him.

What a great people were these Romans, especially down to the Second Punic War. But Caesar! Ah, Caesar! That was the great man!

And when the sculptor mentions Titus, Trajan, Marcus Aurelius, the Emperor exclaims: 'They were all great, all, down to Constantine!' Britain is Carthage. He compares his own government (as we already know – see p. 261) with that of Diocletian. He likes to put himself in the place of others who have been connected with Rome, of Charlemagne and of the Emperor Charles V (for, as Madelin remarks, Napoleon is an incorrigible dabbler in history, and for him past reigns are but the prelude to his own). But at bottom these men, even Constantine, are for him but

half emperors, because they have had the weakness to hand over Rome to that brood of priests, or to leave it to them. The figure which leaves him no rest is that

1. *La Rome de Napoléon*, p. 149.

of Augustus with his crown of laurels, who instead of the Rome of bricks which he found, leaves behind him one of marble.

The Rome of his own time is not even of brick; he looks upon it as a ruin, he waxes indignant at the bad government as well as at the neglect of old monuments. He makes magnificent plans for Rome, always in connexion with himself, or with a son of his. He cannot bear to leave it to anyone else. The difficulties with which he meets at Rome, the unwillingness of the Romans to be made happy in his manner, wound him profoundly.

And all this from a distance, for he has never been there. He has never been there, because he did not wish to come unless as the undisputed master, recognized by the dethroned Pope as well as by the population. Never was he able to renounce that dream, and to the last he hoped to force or to overawe the Pope.

But, and this is the point which matters, his dreams, his idealized Rome, the Rome of his reading and of his imagination, prevented him from discerning or understanding the real Rome.

The priests he took to be cowards and the Romans heroes, because he had read Rousseau and Plutarch.[1]

He shared the misconceptions of his time and of his country about the ancient and the modern Romans, but his personal sentiments added a particular vehemence. No Frenchman had a mind so stocked with errors on the score of Rome as had the Emperor.[2]

And this put its stamp upon his policy towards the city and towards the Papacy. At times it made him too impatient and too irascible, at times too yielding and too hesitant.

In short, in a political matter of the greatest importance he showed himself anything but a realist!

THE CONCORDAT

Is it necessary to analyse Madelin's treatment of the Concordat? One understands beforehand that neither the reservations of Quinet or d'Haussonville nor those of Aulard will be found in his work. In a little volume of essays, dated 1913, he had already given his view on the Concordat in dealing with a work by Cardinal Mathieu, which opposed to d'Haussonville the conventional Catholic conception. According to Madelin's interpretation, Bonaparte was led to take this measure against great opposition and countermoves, simply because the French nation wanted it. The French nation wanted its priests, its church bells,

1. op. cit. p. 161.　　2. op. cit. p. 148.

and peace with Rome; and he had enough insight and courage to grant it its wish. The fact that personally he had no faith makes his action all the more deserving in the eyes of Madelin.[1]

There is something naïve in this way of reasoning. The modern critics of the Concordat, and certainly those who agree with d'Haussonville, do not begrudge the French people their priests, their church bells, and their peace with Rome. The popular joy which greeted the proclamation is a fact, and a fact of importance. But is it not clear that the French people had no conception of what was the real significance of the arrangement in Bonaparte's calculating and self-seeking mind, and that what they longed for and rejoiced at could have been achieved in a different manner? That at least is the point in debate; but one must not expect Madelin to shed light upon it.

THE PAINFUL CASE OF VENICE

But I leave this matter and proceed to examine Madelin's view of the problems of the consular and imperial foreign policy.

First a minor point, which carries us back to the period of General Bonaparte. It concerns the treatment of Venice in 1797. We saw (p. 81) how scathingly Quinet rejects as a sophism the later assertion of Napoleon at St Helena that he had delivered the old Republic to Austria for the sake of strengthening the patriotism of the Venetians and educating them for their Italian future. Madelin sees it differently.

> In his heart it is painful to him to deliver up that fragment of Italy to the Austrians. We have evidence of this – slight perhaps, but still an indication – in the letter which he wrote to the French *chargé d'affaires* after the consummation of the sacrifice at Campo Formio; he was to counsel acquiescence to the citizens of Venice, but Bonaparte adds: '*Qu'ils ne désespèrent pas de leur patrie!*'

One can easily imagine how Lanfrey would have interpreted this advice, had he known of it – as being thoroughly characteristic of Bonaparte, who sells the Venetians to Austria, but at the same time already prepares against the eventuality of his finding himself once more at war with Austria, when he would be glad of their support. Thoroughly characteristic; especially on account of that utterly unprincipled game with the national idea, which he flatters at the very moment he treads it under foot. Madelin, on the other hand, takes the utterance quite seriously.

'*Qu'ils ne désespèrent pas*'; and on 26 December 1805 the treaty of Pressburg does

1. *France et Rome*, p. 351.

take Venice from Austria, to join it with the 'kingdom of Italy'. It is as if, as early as 1797, Bonaparte foresaw the future.[1]

This treatment of the undeniably rather 'painful' case of Venice goes to show what a benevolent judge the whole policy of Napoleon will find in Madelin. One can also conclude from it that he will endeavour to maintain this important component part of the legend, the belief in Napoleon's sincere feeling for national aspirations; and this against all evidence from the facts of his actual policy.

THE RUPTURE OF THE PEACE OF AMIENS

As regards the central problem of Napoleon's foreign policy, Madelin says explicitly that: 'The thesis of Albert Sorel – whatever Driault may have urged against it – appears to me after fresh study still to be in accordance with the facts.'[2] Thus we shall not, as I have already said, find anything new here, but it is worth while to follow up a few points and to see how this modern writer gets rid of objections which indeed do not all originate with Driault. In doing this, we shall once more notice an over-excited nationalism which I am inclined to ascribe, as in the case of the later Driault, to the influence of the First World War.

Bonaparte – to give a brief summary of Madelin's views about the rupture of the peace of Amiens – wanted peace. He expected the recently concluded peace would be lasting. Britain, on the other hand, envying France's renewed prosperity, wanted war. (This is exactly Sorel, as will be remembered – p. 247). The assertion that Bonaparte's advance on the continent (Holland, Switzerland, Piedmont) excused Britain's delay in evacuating Malta, is absurd. As Bonaparte himself observed (here I follow the large work of 1939):[3] 'All this is not mentioned in the treaty. I see in it only two names, Tarento, which I have evacuated, and Malta, which you are not evacuating.'

This sounds extremely cogent, but it takes no account of the British thesis, which, as I have already pointed out (p. 252 n.), was undoubtedly current in the international and public law of Europe at that time, and which the British Government formulated as follows, in its instructions to Lord Whitworth:

H.M. is determined never to forgo his right of interfering with the affairs of the continent on any occasion in which the interest of his own dominions or those of Europe in general may appear to him to require it.[4]

1. *Histoire du Consulat et de l'Empire*, II, *L'Ascension de Bonaparte* (1937), p. 375.
2. *Le Consulat et l'Empire*, I, 221. Note that he mentions only Driault; yet Muret's and Guyot's criticisms also deserve attention.
3. *Histoire du Consulat et de l'Empire*, VI, *Le Consulat*, p. 292.
4. J. HOLLAND ROSE, *Life of Napoleon I*, p. 403.

But Bonaparte, as Madelin says himself, would never have concluded the peace of Amiens if it was to have tied his hands in any way whatsoever.[1] Our author does not seem to realize to what extent, by these words, he qualifies his hero as an intractable and mischief-making element in Europe. He nevertheless takes the trouble to look at each of the three important continental expansions of power of the First Consul from this point of view. Piedmont and Switzerland are waved aside with a shrug of the shoulder, as being of no importance or nothing new. In the case of Holland, he recognizes that it must affect Britain, but he says: 'Who was ignorant of the fact that Holland had for the last two centuries been England's client in time of war as well as of peace?' And thus the occupation of Holland by France is justified, at any rate with a public which is as badly informed about Dutch history as is the author himself.[2]

Awkward facts, like the mission of Sebastiani and the publication of his report about Egypt in the *Moniteur*, or the philippic against Lord Whitworth, Madelin does not pass over in silence, as did Bainville; but he knows how to make them innocuous. He recognizes that they were mistakes. Sebastiani's mission, however, he discusses as something perfectly natural; it is only the publication which he admits was an error. Yet the mission had not remained a secret to the British, and had inspired them with concern about the First Consul's intentions. But these mistakes had been the result of provocation. It had been evil intention on the part of the British Government which made it choose Lord Whitworth in the autumn of 1802 to go to France. (Madelin, it may be noted in passing, persists in calling him *Withworth* in both his books.)

Instead of a diplomat who would have been disposed to pour oil on the troubled waters, they sent a representative of the English peerage, the element least inclined towards peace, a great lord who had sworn to disturb the peace while waiting till it could be broken, so that as far as was possible he could hamper the great work of the Consul.

Madelin, apparently, is as ignorant of British history as of Dutch. The separation he tries to make as to political inclination between the 'great lords' and the other British – an echo of those tirades against the British aristocracy or oligarchy to which Bonaparte himself was so much given – has no foundation in fact. The author anyhow produces no single proof in support of his view of Lord Whit-

1. *Histoire du Consulat et de l'Empire*, IV, 307.
2. 'The last two centuries'! In the seventeenth century therefore – in the time of unrestrained Anglo-Dutch rivalry, which gave rise to three wars! Even for the eighteenth century (in spite of Frederick the Great's well-known remark) the assertion is quite untenable. In 1787, not long after the fourth Anglo-Dutch war, it could be said that Holland was in the position of a client with respect to Great Britain, but this had lapsed as early as 1795, owing to the creation of the Batavian Republic.

worth's personal sentiments, and it is a fact that Whitworth had been chosen for his post at a moment when the British Government had still every hope of preserving the peace. But in the opinion of Madelin it was the attitude of 'this *grand seigneur*' with his phlegmatic arrogance which first irritated the First Consul and finally caused him to lose his self-command.

What a Withworth [*sic*] wanted, what those who had chosen him wanted, had come to pass: the First Consul, more and more exasperated, had committed mistakes.[1]

Without hesitation I call this a striking sample of history writing distorted by partisanship. We have repeatedly noticed how a desire to whitewash Napoleon, accompanied by anti-British sentiments, led French authors astray. But it strikes me doubly disagreeably in a book which is presented to the world as an attempt to summarize the whole of our modern knowledge of Napoleon, and this by a man who is not only an *académicien*, but a professional historian of long experience, working with learned and instructive notes, thoroughly familiar with the literature of the subject, and pretending to take part in the discussion.

'THE WHOLE OF THE QUESTION' OF 1814

One is thus left with little inclination to give much more attention to Madelin's views about the problem of war and peace in Napoleon's career. It is always Sorel. It is always the European coalition aiming at her 'natural frontiers' against which the Emperor has to defend France. I note in passing that Madelin calls the dethronement of the Spanish Bourbons and the occupation of Rome, to be followed inevitably by its annexation and the kidnapping of Pius VII, the cardinal errors, but also that for the first of these at any rate he has found a scapegoat in Talleyrand. It was Talleyrand who presented to the Emperor the dethronement as a link with the tradition of Louis XIV, even though it was the latter's descendant who would be the victim. As our author says: 'Talleyrand had the knack of giving to the worst of his transgressions – the arrest of the Duc d'Enghien had been a case in point – a colour of profound political thought.'[2] It is hard to fathom the intentions of that most dangerous of Napoleon's councillors, but Madelin undoubtedly implies that he wanted to bring about the Emperor's undoing.

I shall merely add a reflection about the way the year 1814 is dealt with.

The situation at the end of 1813 was a critical one. There was Leipzig, and the

1. *Histoire du Consulat et de l'Empire*, IV, 308 ff. See also p. 296; and HOLLAND ROSE, I, 403.
2. *Le Consulat et l'Empire* (1932), I, 361.

Russian catastrophe which had preceded it, and the protracted misery of Spain. On 4 November 1813 all that remained of the three hundred thousand men with whom in the spring Napoleon had entered Germany was concentrated at Mayence. There were 60,000 men, and with these the marshals were to try to hold the Rhine frontier while the Emperor went to Paris to conjure up another 300,000 men. It is true that almost 200,000 men were still dispersed in garrisons between the Vistula and the Elbe, and Napoleon did his utmost to get them back. But it was too late. They were cut off, and all now depended upon the new armies which he might be able to form.

Madelin pictures to himself [1]

the Emperor on his departure from Mayence, casting a glance heavy with thought on the splendid river, on that Rhine which the troops of the nation had crossed four times before him [1793, 1794, 1798, and 1799] and with himself at their head another four times [1805, 1806, 1809, 1812]. A hundred and five years were to elapse before the troops of the nation were once more to pass across the bridge of Kastel [in 1918]. As for Napoleon, he was not to see the Rhine again. Nothing was further from his expectation, for this amazing man was still confident that, supported by a nation like the French, he would be perfectly able, with his genius – for that at any rate showed no signs of fatigue – to wrench from Fortune what she, after so many favours, seemed for the last two years determined to refuse him.

Would the country respond to the trust reposed in it by its great leader? That was the whole question.

Whereupon Madelin begins to argue that the 'exhaustion' of France, after twenty-one years, was by no means so profound as historians have said and repeated. 'Those twenty-one years had cost her fewer losses than would four years of war a century later.' No doubt this is true, as is Madelin's remark that France was exhausted because she thought she was – in other words, that she was morally exhausted. He looks for the cause of this in the circumstance that the war has for so long been waged far away from the frontier, and that the people no longer had their hearts in it. He admits, further, that the people, though attached to the Emperor, had lost all initiative, as a result of the authoritarian régime, and could no longer as in the days of Danton answer with *élan* when there was a call for a *levée en masse*. Yet he has nothing but contempt for the *Assemblées*, which after so many years of servility suddenly discovered in themselves souls on the Brutus pattern, and for the whole bourgeoisie, which suddenly burned with the love of liberty.

For Madelin, as for Houssaye, and for so many others, 'the whole question' is whether the country will once more produce for 'its great chief' the necessary hundreds of thousands of young men. There is no further mention of Napoleon's

1. op. cit. ii, 234.

mistakes, and anyhow, if one agrees with Sorel that he had all the time b
compelled to defend France against an envious Europe, these mistakes are c
little significance. The interest of France is at this critical hour inseparably linked
up with that of Napoleon. People were indeed made to feel it after his abdication, when the new king had to sign the Peace of Paris. For this peace fell like
a blow. People had been sufficiently naïve to imagine that by sacrificing Napoleon they could escape from humiliating terms. Had the Allies not proclaimed
three times that they were not waging war against France? But France looked
upon the 'natural frontiers' as her right, as a part of herself; and of these, of
the whole Rhineland and of Belgium, the peace was now depriving her.

One feels in the whole description of these events by Madelin how much he
too takes to heart the loss of these territories. Talleyrand says of the peace: 'It
was a good and even rather a noble peace.'

The country [comments Madelin] thought the peace neither good nor noble. It
was still proud of the glory and of the conquests acquired by *La Grande Nation*. If all
this had to be given up, it had not been worth while to allow the sacrifice of the
Emperor. . . .

As an indication of the frame of mind which would soon prevail – in spite
of the satisfaction created at first by the *Charte* and the liberal régime which it
announced – which made possible the expulsion of the new king and the Hundred
Days, this is excellent. But I repeat that Madelin himself thinks of the 'natural
frontiers' in the same terms as did the most fiery supporter of the Convention's
decree of 1794, and this colours the whole of his interpretation of the parliamentary opposition to Napoleon, of Talleyrand, of Napoleon's own attitude.

THE WRITER

WE possess only a fragment by Hanotaux about Napoleon. It is to be found in a number of articles in the *Revue des Deux Mondes* in 1925 and 1926. These amount altogether to some 380 pages, but it seems that the author's interest or his strength failed him. He never finished the work, and it was never published as a book. This is a pity, for Napoleon is looked upon here from unusual aspects, and the resulting picture, in spite of a certain lack of cohesion and of smoothness, is one of the most striking in the whole gallery.

Hanotaux, who was trained as a historian, became an official at the Ministry of Foreign Affairs, and was himself Minister from 1894 to 1898. In this capacity he attempted to carry through the policy of expansion in Africa, at the risk of creating friction with Britain. No doubt he had the earnest intention of avoiding a war, but he was ready in the last instance to play the card of cooperation with Germany. The Fashoda incident was the result of this policy, but it occurred just as Hanotaux was resigning.

Apart from Thiers, no one among our authors played so weighty a part in affairs of state and at the same time left behind him such an important body of historical work. He differs from most of the others in not having concentrated mainly on Napoleon or the Napoleonic age. He reached Napoleon only when he was past seventy, after a monumental work on Richelieu and a large-scale history of the first ten years of the Third Republic in four large volumes. He also wrote about Joan of Arc, and on various modern subjects. All this is reflected in his work about Napoleon. It is especially the man with personal experience of high matters of state, and the man who spent many years in intimate commerce with Richelieu, whom we find in this work.

ANTITHETICAL PRESENTATION

Hanotaux's articles do not form a connected history. They deal with the tendencies of the régime, and with the characteristics and qualities of Napoleon. The first is called *Du Consulat à l'Empire*.

He accepts the Consulate as a necessary solution, and, taking everything into consideration, salutary. As soon as one does this the figure of Napoleon automatically takes a place among the greatest and most fruitful rulers of France, but what distinguishes Hanotaux from the true admirers is that he was by no means blind to the shortcomings of the statesman, nor to the mistakes that were inherent in the essence of his work and which must inevitably carry their penalty with them.

From a number of pronouncements and passages of Hanotaux an interpretation might be constructed which would lead the reader to exclaim: 'But this is Vandal!' No words are too strong to express his abhorrence of the misgovernment, the desperate confusion, the 'muddy pool' of the Directorate. He quotes Sir James Frazer on the lack of freedom of primitive societies. The slaves of the past, such are the 'natural men' whom demagogues and dreamers have described as being free; their society is a thing of inferior quality, marked especially by stagnation. But sometimes it happens that an unusual man achieves supreme power, and succeeds in carrying out reforms which would otherwise have required the work of many generations. And as soon as the tribe is no longer governed by the timid and often contradictory counsels of the ancients, but obeys the single direction of a powerful and determined mind, it becomes formidable to the neighbouring tribes and enters upon the road of expansion of power which promotes social, industrial, and intellectual progress. Hanotaux proceeds to apply this view to Bonaparte's appearance as First Consul. 'C'est l'heure du commandement.'[1] The great achievement of Bonaparte has been that into stagnant affairs he introduced the factor of decision.

His work consists in creating political institutions, as a result of which the decision – coming from the centre – will be transmitted without obstacle to the outer parts and will be obeyed without demur.[2]

But at the same time, to what great purposes did he not put this capacity for decision and this power! First there was Marengo and the prospect of peace, and after that it was nothing less than

miracles which administered to the cloudy revolutionary mixture the shock that was needed to bring about a stable and solid precipitation. It is the end of the Revolution and the remaking [la réfection] of France. Where the assemblies lost their heads because they were absorbed in hair-splitting arguments and in bloodshed, command sets to work. That man alone – and precisely because he was alone – is successful.[3]

The Code, the Concordat. . . .

One would almost think that this is another of autocracy's eulogists. Yet it is only a historian who recognizes that at a specific moment this manifestation

1. *Revue des Deux Mondes*, 1925, XXVI, 91.
2. p. 92.   3. p. 98.

was needed, and who can appreciate it within its framework and even enjoy its impressive air. He at once makes reservations of the kind one misses in Vandal, and as he proceeds with his observations the dark sides of the picture seem to oppress him more and more.

To begin with he remarks that this command must carry a martial character. 'This was fatal. People count on the new ruler for the safety and for the development of the national domain.' After this opening, one would expect the argument that Bonaparte was not personally responsible for the wars of his régime. Indeed, Hanotaux has other remarks tending in this direction.

No doubt [he says] the Emperor was inclined to war by his profession and by his genius, but in addition he was driven towards it by a force stronger than his will. Neither he himself nor France could stop where they were. They were on the move, and must go on to the end.[1]

But he never enters on an argument. If at moments he seems, like Sorel, to see an irreconcilable antagonism between France and Europe, he views it in an entirely different light. He sees first and foremost the contrast between the old feudal and the new egalitarian powers; the 'natural frontiers' he scarcely mentions. Britain's enmity was, he considers, inevitable for yet a number of other reasons, including, needless to say, British imperialism. But Hanotaux also sees that Bonaparte's pretension to a free hand in continental Europe and to the domination of the Mediterranean were factors in the renewal of the struggle. A trade agreement might perhaps have saved peace, but this was not to be expected from Bonaparte, since he lacked all economic insight – a great weakness, as Hanotaux insists, which made itself felt later also during the war with Britain.

'Napoleon,' he concluded, 'was vowed to war.'[2] And yet he was not without pacific impulses. 'But unhappily the statesman, when it came to a clash, was no match for the warrior.' And this leads him to the verdict that Napoleon overburdened his internal task, an enormous liquidation, with a merciless foreign struggle, with the adventitious enterprise of conquering the world. This pronouncement, implying as it does responsibility or partial responsibility of Napoleon for the wars, would find no place in Sorel's rigid system; and Vandal, with his glorification of the seeker for world peace, would also reject it.

One could point to inner contradictions in what I have quoted so far. Sometimes Hanotaux advances the wars as an excuse for the dictatorial character, basically military, of Napoleon's régime. He notes that nothing came of the guarantees for freedom promised at Napoleon's elevation to the imperial dignity, and admits that this was partly the result of Napoleon's nature, which could brook no contradiction: 'He did not want to.' But he goes on to say:

1. op. cit. XXIX, 267.   2. ibid. p. 275.

To be fair, one must recognize that the undeniable necessities of a fight to the finish against Europe drove the man in the same direction as his temperament.[1]

At another moment these wars themselves are represented as having been, at any rate partly, brought about by this temperament.

The Emperor's genius is, and remains, military... With a little less of this dangerous genius an energetic man might, without these risks and misfortunes, have put to much better advantage the introduction to the world's affairs given him by the Revolution. The problem of the general European restoration after the Revolution might perhaps have been solved.[2]

I shall not say that no more synthetic interpretation of Napoleon's policy is possible than this unsolved juxtaposition of *for* and *against*. Nevertheless, even this has something satisfying for those who have freed themselves from the powerful fascination of a system in appearance so cogent and strictly logical, in which everything is deduced from impersonal international forces, or in which on the contrary Napoleon appears as the autonomous disturber of tranquillity, a system in which he is merely the builder of a better state and a better society, or again only the cunning contriver of his own power and advantage.

A PORTRAIT OF BONAPARTE

In any case, the personality, the temperament, in the view of Hanotaux has its historical importance. So he too has tried to sketch a portrait of Bonaparte. It is a very striking portrait, incomparably more profound than that of Madelin, in my opinion, and more true to life.

Only half a Frenchman, begins Hanotaux: 'A Frenchman from abroad,' like Rousseau, with whom as a young man he becomes infatuated, and in whom Hanotaux sees one of those ardent souls,

unable to forgive France for her moderation, her wit, her reasonableness, instinctive enemies of France's classical turn of mind ... In them the age of 'philosophy' approaches that of romanticism.[3]

With this we are already far from the energetic realist, the formula in which Madelin thought he could shut up Napoleon. True, Hanotaux soon sees the emergence of a personality altogether different from 'the Werther, the René' of the beginning.

In his own sphere, that of war, he displays from the beginning an unparalleled and

1. XXIX, 281.   2. XXIX, 278.   3. XXVI, 68.

infallible force and exactness of mind . . . We see here a different Bonaparte indeed from the pupil of Rousseau and Raynal, a very different man from the dreamer steeped in Ossian. Let us say at once, however, that this original romantic inclination will never be quite corrected. When the spring slackens it will once more appear.[1]

Bonaparte's energy is not only a remarkable incidental.

Incessantly he keeps his eye and compasses on the map. His imagination is active all the time and works even in the abstract, if only to keep himself in training and exercise the elasticity and readiness of his reflexes. This complete immersion in his task is the ratio of his being, it is the whole of his life. This is what distinguishes these extraordinary natures. They obey a plan, a superior scheme of things. They 'act under God's orders'; they 'were born for this', as Joan of Arc expressed it. Their course has been *set* for them, they *follow* their star. A hundred times Napoleon referred to his dependence on a mysterious being . . . and what, if that necessity is considered, is one to call him and the others, the blood that is shed, women, and the masses? Tools, tools of Fate . . . This enjoyment of action, this passion for its results, this hunt for an ever more exalted and unattainable prey, this excitement felt in the mastering of life, of the past, and of the future, of the world, with powers infinitely extended, in short this superhuman existence, strains the spring till it breaks. Everybody will agree that these unusual beings are ambitious, for that is *what they were born for*. But what their nature wants to feed on is the subordination, the self-denial and sacrifice of others, and if they do not restore to them what they have taken, if they oppress them only to enjoy their own sense of power, their abuse of superiority becomes intolerable and tyrannical.

Hanotaux goes on to sketch Bonaparte's ambitious dreams and the unrest he suffered as a result of them. Richelieu was subject in his youth to fits of weeping: so Bonaparte had his moments of despair. He felt driven, he knew not where; the east tempted his imagination as an escape.

'La modération dans les conceptions fortes', therein the superior quality of the mind shows itself. The coiled spring, command over self, this is true greatness, this is what one should strive for above all . . . Napoleon betrays a lack of balance in the limitless nature of his aims.

In the long run his keen mind, his practical sense, his clear intellect become blurred; they lose themselves in an unbridled loquacity, in explosions of wild vehemence, in chimerical schemes which mean a return to the earlier romanticism, in that curious reluctance to discern or to recognize truth in which his imperious command is to lose sight of the right track. As he lies to others and to himself, so others will lie to him. He complains that he is being betrayed; he has betrayed himself. This failure of the richest natural gifts ever received by mortal man has a moral origin. Bonaparte's disposition was ever personal, not perhaps so much for himself as for

1. XXVI, 75.

his enterprise and for his family. As a true Corsican, he never lost sight of his following, of his clan. One never finds in his career that complete subordination to duty which is demanded by the public interest, nor is there a trace of that care for others, that humanity, that humility towards life, or that self-denial which are the only inexhaustible resources and which depend exclusively on man himself. He is for ever looking out for advantage and gain, and too often calculates the immediate interest without taking into account more distant consequences.[1]

What is remarkable about this portrait is that Hanotaux, while fully recognizing the greatness of his deeds for France, at any rate at the beginning, yet sees in Napoleon himself the origins of his downfall and of the partial failure of his achievement. A secondary cause – but one which can also be referred to the faults of Napoleon's character, to his impatience, to his inability to wait before embarking upon the *coup d'état* – Hanotaux considers to be his dependence on the vilest relics of the period to which he was putting an end, on Fouché and Talleyrand.

It must be admitted that the drama, *le roman de sa vie*, gains from this abominable complication a more moving and a more human aspect. So he too is human after all!...

THE CONCORDAT

Nevertheless Hanotaux is full of admiration for the achievements of the ruler, at any rate till 1807. For then there is a turn; then the foreign task, the war effort, begin to dominate to such an extent, to exercise such pressure upon everything, that the fruits of the régime are squandered and his finest projects spoiled and demolished by their great initiator himself.

To begin with, the Concordat. Hanotaux discusses it as a believing Catholic. So did d'Haussonville, but Hanotaux has none of the reserves made by the earlier author. Yet his attitude is also not that of Madelin. That the people wanted the Concordat is not the whole story for Hanotaux. There is also the reconciliation of France with its past, and although Bonaparte certainly saw in the Concordat 'a source of power' (there were 40,000 priests who were henceforth going to support his authority – and who in particular were going to protect him from possible attack from the generals), Hanotaux does not, like Madelin, take pleasure in the thought that it was the purely political act of a man personally indifferent to religion. On the contrary, 'nothing is more honourable to this superhuman man than his anxiety to find a rule which transcends man. The restlessness about divine things possessed him till his death.' It is when dealing with the regulation of education that Hanotaux says this, but he sees Bonaparte, the maker of the Concordat, in the same light.

1. XXVI, 81 ff.

As to the significance of the Concordat, Hanotaux is prepared to look for it in the revival of the religious sense which others – d'Haussonville as well as Aulard, in their different ways – also noticed, but which according to their opinion did not need the Concordat, or was even impeded or perverted by it.

From a conception like this, notions arise which are irreconcilable with those of men starting from different basic ideas. In the opinion of Hanotaux, the rationalism and sensualism of Voltaire and Condillac, followers of Locke, are so 'painful' and 'irritating'[1] that he cannot look upon them as a component of the national spirit, but only as a dissolvent. The reaction against these theories had its origins before the Revolution: see Rousseau, Swedenborg, and St Martin. In other words, it was originally not dogmatically Catholic but only religious, 'mystical'. But when the time is ripe, to continue Hanotaux's argument, all this finds its traditional form.

Religion is a policy . . . Man in general and the Frenchman in particular is not a metaphysical being.[2]

So when people began to put questions about God, the reply was:

But this is *our* God. Nothing can be simpler. 'I am of the religion of my fathers' – a word of sturdy common sense.

And thus the Concordat not only provided Bonaparte with the support of those 40,000 priests, but the maximum possible cooperation was obtained from all the spiritual and material forces, that the nation might become *la Grande Nation*.

Why [sighs our author] was the man who benefited from this practical unanimity to take it upon himself to destroy it? On the day Napoleon entered on his struggle with the Pope, he smashed with his own hands both unity and Empire, so delicate is the problem of faith, which is both the foundation of modern society and the rock on which it can be shipwrecked.[3]

From all this it may be gathered that Hanotaux can see national unity realized only in Catholicism. French and Catholic are for him inseparable terms. It is a conception which Protestants, Jews, and freethinkers will for ever reject, as being an attack on their position in the state and in the nation, and which will also inspire distrust in those Catholics whose conception of their faith is somewhat more 'metaphysical', and somewhat less 'political'.

1. XXXIII, 562 ff.   2. XXXIII, 566.   3. XXXIII, 571.

THE CONSTITUTION: *UN HOMME EST TOUT*

Hanotaux is much more critical towards the constitution created by Bonaparte than towards the Concordat. The essence of this constitution is military; it is intended for war.[1] Therefore there must be unity. 'A whole generation must be poured into the same mould,' as the First Consul himself expressed it in the Council of State. Therefore there must be obedience.

My government [Napoleon said himself at St Helena] was the most solidly condensed, with the fastest circulation and the most immediate power for action which has ever existed. Nothing less was needed, in the face of the formidable difficulties by which we were surrounded. The prefects were little emperors on a small scale.

He, and he alone, was the representative of the people, of the sovereign people. The *Corps Législatif* ought really to have been called *Conseil Législatif*: it did not represent the nation. This constitutional explanation was given by himself in the *Moniteur* in 1808, when the whirlwind was already carrying him with it, according to Hanotaux's interpretation, and there was no more question of moderation.

This was by no means what had been expected of him in 1799 at the time of the *coup d'état*, nor even in 1804 when the Empire was established. The Consulate, as it had become, was a dictatorship. Hanotaux is prepared to applaud this, as contemporaries had done.

Anarchy is the weed which interferes with the production of a full harvest; every birth stands in need of authority, respected and obeyed, for its protection. Bonaparte was wise therefore to seize authority, and he exercised it, amid applause from his contemporaries, in such a way as to safeguard order by his administrative genius and the power of his administration. However, he made the mistake committed by the majority of dictators: he did not know how to give a reasonable limit in time to his necessary power. Instead of voluntarily terminating his dictatorial régime, he followed it wherever it lured him.[2]

In 1804, when the dictatorship of the triumphant general was replaced by a hereditary empire intended to last through the centuries, political circles imagined that the intention was to weaken the absolutism, that 'un-French warlike absolutism', as Hanotaux writes in another passage.

The public mind began to conceive a return to old French traditions, that is to say to the 'tempered' monarchy of Bodin and of Montesquieu. Without being in the least inclined to look to England for the example of parliamentary monarchy, the

1. XXIX, 262 ff.   2. XXIX, 838 ff.

THE ANTITHESIS AT THE END

men of sense and of experience would have been content with a constitution which allied to authoritarian forms serious guarantees of liberty.

And indeed the quotations from official declarations which at that moment the representatives of the State assemblies addressed to Bonaparte leave nothing to be desired on the score of explicitness.

Guarantees of public liberty; we beg for the solemn covenant desired and promised in 1789; a 'tempered monarchy' in accordance with what our greatest publicists have written.

Even Fontanes, the courtier *par excellence*, exclaimed: '*Non, citoyen premier consul, vous ne voulez commander qu'à un peuple libre*'.[1] Later, at St Helena, Napoleon declared that a better time and alleviation of the pressure would have come; but in reality he never wanted this.

It is for his failure to prepare for this slackening of the tension, for his unbridled surrender to his temperament, that Napoleon bears in the eyes of history so heavy a responsibility. We may be sure that he understood, for he understood everything; but he looked the other way, and to speak plainly, he was unwilling.

The Legislative Assembly was put definitely in the background in 1808. Napoleon's *sénatus consultes* and *décrets impériaux* were given force of law by the Court of Cassation; freedom of the Press had long since been abolished; all discussion, all debate, had been done away with; and in conclusion '*un homme est tout*' – a peevish remark which Napoleon let fall one day.

The Empire [says Hanotaux] is the Revolution without a constitution, although that Revolution had been accompanied by the cry: 'A constitution or death.'

This is indeed a very different conception of Napoleon and the Revolution than we have met with in Vandal or Masson. 'The Empire is not a system, it is a fact.' But Hanotaux understands how untenable was this state of affairs. 'A law,' he wrote, 'would have been needed for the very man who had deemed himself to be above the law.'

THE ADMINISTRATOR: *UN IMAGINATIF, UN ILLUSIONISTE*

Napoleon was the first and one might say the only administrator of the empire. One of his ministers, Mollien, who was the perfect Civil Servant, says: 'He wanted not only to govern France but to administer her from his army camp, and during military operations he did actually do this.'[2]

He wished to be informed in the most methodical and precise manner. His

1. XXIX, 279 ff.   2. XXIX, 597.

officials were always kept on the leash, and they had to give account of themselves to their suspicious and overworked master. Even when he was away at
the head of his army, and getting further and further from Paris, he insisted on
this. One realizes that in this way war meant that civil affairs were more or less
at a standstill; and under the Empire there was almost always war.

Napoleon works with never-failing accuracy on his data, his statistics, and
his reports; if this requires nights, he stays up.

But the mechanism of men and of things does not always respond. Wishing to
give them a single and straight impulse, the master sometimes pushes them off the
rails or makes them lose their balance. Nothing is more fascinating than the spectacle of this struggle between the strongest will the world has ever known and
the hardest task ever shouldered by a human being. Incomparable administrator
though Napoleon was, at times the impossible enterprise of fitting together two
contrasting periods and two opposing histories proves too strong for him. He was
too violent, too passionate . . . This is, to my mind, the characteristic trait. In spite
of his marvellous realistic activity, Napoleon remains *un imaginatif, un rêveur du
grand*. He overdoes his quickness of decision; he does not have himself in hand
completely. He is essentially a visionary and a talker about things . . . He who
wants to see in Napoleon the man of action alone, and blinds himself to the visionary
and the rhetorician, will find it hard to understand his reverses – and even his
successes.

Hanotaux here inserts a beautiful description of Bonaparte in the Council of
State, taken from the memoirs of Molé. Molé writes about 'the inexhaustible
verve, as the most characteristic trait of his mind', and shows him at the meeting,
lost in thought, taking pinches of snuff from his golden box, so much a man
meditating in solitude that those who were present kept a profound silence, but
then again, talking, talking, and his talk was nothing but thinking aloud.

Only compare this [says Hanotaux] with our other statesmen, with that expression-
less face of Louis XI, with the impassive Richelieu, with the frozen blood of
Talleyrand, and you will be able to gauge the abyss separating this great man from
the other great men of our own soil.

While talking, he forms projects, takes decisions, but only too often he neglects
or forgets his projects and his decisions almost as soon as they have dropped from
him. His correspondence contains, together with his grandiose and diverse
creations, an almost equally great number of 'false starts, impracticable schemes,
and failures'.

And this not only in administrative work but also in high politics.

Everyone knows how Napoleon fell under the charm of the colonial dream, how he abandoned it after San Domingo, ceding Louisiana to the United States; nor do I need to recall what a gigantic conception was the plan for the invasion of England, based on Villeneuve's naval operations which ended at Trafalgar; in the same way Napoleon successively put his faith in the Prussian alliance, the Russian alliance, the Austrian alliance, without finding a firm *point d'appui* anywhere, because he could not bring himself to make the necessary sacrifices. The man of the Concordat dragged the Pope to Fontainebleau, which was neither logical nor pleasing to the aesthetic sense.

In current administration, these whims multiply themselves, the gusts of wind swell ever more frequently to gales; his agents, never sure whether he will be satisfied or angry, tremble. Villeneuve had been disconcerted by the blasts of the imperial correspondence before Nelson's broadsides blew him to pieces. The plans are invariably impressive on paper. Some get carried into execution, but how many are abandoned for lack of means! For while Napoleon always demands of all his servants forcible and immediate execution, he generally places only moderate means at their disposal, and those in a niggardly fashion. Meanwhile he purposely mistakes their available resources, exaggerates them in words, grudges them in fact, to show surprise finally when results do not come in . . . This, the greatest defect of all that can mar a man of action, the maladjustment between the imagination and reality, is to ruin him . . . It might be said that Napoleon's correspondence is paved with illusions and disillusionments, and it is this changefulness, this scenic railway of heights and depths, of successes and failures, which explains the general fatigue, until in the end everything topples over into the abyss. . . .

In a word, the great man was great everywhere, but less in civil than in military matters. His civilian work too was of course brilliant, since (to quote the most forceful and aptest word he ever spoke) he cleaned up the Revolution, and since out of the malodorous mud of the Directorate he constructed a France of marble which for a moment filled the world with astonishment. But the great administrator, master illusionist, provided a plentiful crop of disappointments and ruins in the midst of all that brilliance. His appearance would be more harmonious, and his contribution to the history of France greater and even more beneficent than it actually was, if with a greater indulgence for men and a better judgement of obstacles he had tempered his Corsican impetuosity and his Florentine guile with a little French sense.[1]

I have not interrupted Hanotaux for quite a space. I must restrain myself from giving more quotations from the pages in which he elaborates this general appreciation of Napoleon as administrator, demonstrates the system in detail, and discusses the collaborators. I restrict myself to a single remark about what we have just read. It seems to me to be one of the happiest sketches of Napoleon at work which I have come across. Neither the mistakes he made nor their effects are minimized. Yet an impression is left of greatness and of unusualness. And how

1. XXIX, 602 ff.

much more convincing, how much more truthful does this appear than the over-idealized sketch we were given by Madelin. It is particularly the latter's unconditional praise for Napoleon the realist which sounds hollow by the side of this impressive study of the illusionist.

THE PIONEER OF THE BOURGEOIS CENTURY

The most original part of Hanotaux's study is that about *Social Transformation*.[1] I shall not try to follow the whole of his *exposé* of the rise of the bourgeois society in the nineteenth century. The important part is his attempt to examine how far there arose from the fragments of the *ancien régime* a new society, all in one piece, with a visage of its own – an order, a morality, and an attitude of mind – and what was the share of Napoleon in its creation.

The great thought of the reign, fusion, these words he had already quoted with approval.[2] Not only had the Revolution been adapted to the old order, civic liberties confirmed, and religion restored to a place of honour, but the social classes were shaken together into a new mixture. The *émigrés* had been enticed back and were being absorbed into the new leading class. Fashion had abolished the old elegance and colour, and had covered everything in sober black. Money alone established distinctions, and everybody worked equally hard to acquire it. Already in discussing the constitution Hanotaux had shown how the bourgeois society was being prepared. The revolutionary system of elections had made room for one of working with *notables* indicated by the government itself. The prime criterion for inclusion in the lists in each *département* was being among those who paid the highest taxes. After this the prefects had also to take into account birth, status of the family, etc. In doing this, says Hanotaux, the Emperor laid the foundations for 'Philippism'.[3]

Is it not surprising that Napoleon the hero of war, Napoleon the romantic genius, should have been the pioneer of this rigid solemn middle class, which esteemed property before all else and which was to reach its full glory under Louis Philippe, with his umbrella under his arm? Hanotaux is far from representing Napoleon as the only or even the main agent of the transformation. He sees it as the achievement of the whole nation, reacting against the confusion, loss of balance, and disruption of the crisis. No one of its component elements has led this development, not even the upper middle classes, among whom there continued to be much reserve and disapproval towards the Napoleonic régime. Napoleon himself was able to assist the process only where he moved with the current of his time; wherever he tried to row against it, for instance when he established his new military nobility, he failed. But in many respects he was in

1. XXXIII.   2. XXVI, 99.   3. XXIX, 298.

full sympathy with the tendencies that were gaining strength, and he was able to assist them by encouragement, by example, and by his actions.

Towards the financiers he was always distrustful. He completely lacked economic insight – we have seen how much Hanotaux emphasizes this in another connexion. And yet there was something which attracted him in the *entrepreneurs*, in the creators of goods and of employment; industry owed much to his régime, even if it was merely as the unintentional result of the Continental System, and he had a certain esteem for manufacturers. For this he was repaid with interest later by the followers of Saint-Simon; we have read earlier on (p. 286) the reflections of Leroux. But there are two points where Napoleon exercised personal influence to which Hanotaux specially draws our attention: 'his setting the example of hard work, and his preoccupation with respectability.'[1]

As to his industry, about this we have heard enough already to realize that it was impressive. Hanotaux contrasts Napoleon's mode of existence with that of the kings – how different it was to be once more, after his time, in the case of Louis XVIII and Charles X! This respect for labour, this steady conscientious consecration to the daily task, is an eminently bourgeois virtue which was to be glorified properly only in the new age.

As regards the other point:

Napoleon's personal morality was not on a very high level; manners he had none. His numerous *amours* smack of the garrison. He chucks women under the chin, and throws the most peculiar remarks at them. Such sentiments, habits, and tone are the rule at his court. There is an ugly side to all this magnificence.

This conceded, the master behaves himself, and it is his wish that others shall do the same. No acknowledged mistress, no display of scandals . . . Not much is improved in men's morals, on the whole; but by order from on high a mask of decency and propriety has been assumed.

The age of prudishness, of propriety, of hypocrisy, has been inaugurated. Here again one sees in Napoleon the union of conflicting tendencies, of bourgeoisie and romanticism.

And the war hero, the conqueror? One can – and this again makes him a real man of the nineteenth century – see in him the Emperor of officials. Who worked as hard at his desk? Who was such a devourer of regularly returned reports, drawn up on a fixed pattern? One might even call him the Emperor of professors, hater of free thought and of ideology though he was. For the *université*, with its rigid organization and hierarchy of the teaching personnel, has proved to be the most characteristic and the most durable of all his creations.

1. XXXIII, 95.

L'EMPIRE DE RECRUTEMENT

'The year 1807', thus Hanotaux opens his last article, 'is the year of fate in the reign of Napoleon.'[1] 1807 is the year of Eylau and of Friedland, followed by the unexpected denouement of Tilsit.

During his long absence from Paris, a change took place in the Emperor's person. He had suddenly become stout, heavier, slower in his movements, and also irritable. It was only in anger that he showed his old vivacity. There was the near defeat of Eylau, the hard work in Castle Finckenstein to avert the sudden threat of disaster. It is true that during this sojourn in the cold east Prussian winter he also knew love; it is the period of the little Polish countess Maria Walewska, the only one among his affairs which has the flavour of romance. It is true also that he kept his mind sufficiently free to steep himself in the affairs of peace, and that for instance he wrote a famous and really profound note about education, which was never put into practice. Yet it is to the heavy work, under the threat of danger and in the consciousness of impatience and disappointment stirring in France, that Hanotaux attributes the change.

Jena, the crushing of the still glorious army of Frederick the Great, had made him more proud than ever, and keen to venture on the most ambitious schemes. His aim now was 'to conquer the sea with the might of the land', as he wrote to Joseph. This means that he already saw Russia overthrown, behind her the East conquered, and Britain, which he declared from Berlin to be in a state of blockade (the Continental System), brought to her knees. Eylau, however, proved that he was facing heavier odds than ever before in his life.

It was, as Hanotaux expresses it, a warning from Providence. But could Napoleon harken to it? Was an interruption of the game, was a gradual retreat towards the Rhine not more dangerous even than a resumption of the struggle? Would the legend of his invincibility be proof against it? Would not the whole of his position in Germany – and worse, in Paris – be undermined? We catch a glimpse here of the theory of the fatality of Napoleon's continual further advances; but how much more acceptable is it in this limited form than in Sorel! Hanotaux says no more, and it seems perfectly justified, than that Napoleon, *having ventured too far, after Jena had obscured his judgement,* could not draw back. At Finckenstein he prepared a new battle, which was to be a victory. But what a problem! For his losses at Eylau had been extremely heavy. The *grande armée* had been used up; it hardly existed any more. How were new troops to be obtained? This became the compelling, torturing question. He was successful once more. Friedland caused Alexander to decide on peace, and Tilsit.

1. XXXIV, 824.

But what was Tilsit? Taking a very different view from that of Vandal, Hanotaux thinks the Tsar never had any other object than to gain time. And indeed, the same is true of Napoleon. Napoleon re-entered Paris triumphant, but he clung obstinately to his extravagant plans; and in spite of the anxieties through which he had passed, he continued to follow the line that was to lead him from difficulty to difficulty and at last to catastrophe.

It was a line (and this is what is brought out in Hanotaux's account) which weighed upon and upset the whole of his internal policy and his policy towards the territories which had been annexed, brought under his influence, or made dependent. More than ever France was 'in a state of siege'; and with France, the whole of Napoleonic Europe. Everything was subordinated to the first and principal requisite of this dizzy policy: men, soldiers. The Empire became *un empire de recrutement.*

A change of personnel at the centre accompanies the new course.

The Emperor has embarked upon a political enterprise which no longer agrees with the idea which men had at first formed of his usefulness to the national cause. Now that he is losing himself in the colossal struggle, and exceeds that moderation so dear to Frenchmen, the shrewd foresee his fall, while the docile, with hanging heads, follow their leader wherever he goes. The eagle takes his flight with out-stretched wings over the heads of the little band present at his start, and in a sense this group falls asunder of its own accord.[1]

The author now discusses Joséphine, Fouché, and Talleyrand. He recalls the latter's Strasbourg note of 1805, a document 'crammed with prophecies', and concludes that the separation was inevitable, since in the presence of this development into the impossible Talleyrand could no longer feel confidence in the master's star.

Napoleon, knowing what the inexorable intimate of the whole of his career means to him, dare not strike him down at one blow ... Talleyrand, freed for his part from all obligations towards a system that has never been anything but a period in *his* career, could already say what he was to write at a later stage, with perfect sincerity and unrivalled bad faith: 'I left the ministry in accordance with my wish.'

Let us note that Hanotaux, holding the judgement we know about Napoleon's policy, and full of admiration for the wisdom of the note of 1805, like most French historians fails to overcome his repugnance at Talleyrand's manoeuvres. And in fact, even now, he unites with his condemnation of Napoleon's far-reaching plans an admiration for the manner in which the Emperor, supported by second-rate ministers whose sole virtue was obedience and zeal, managed to communicate his energy to the whole body of his empire. 'A lesson of discipline, industry, and enthusiasm is spread to the farthest limits of greater France.'[2]

1. XXXIV, 835.   2. XXXIV, 841.

But the whole of his policy now turns on *recrutement*. Already at Finckenstein Napoleon had decided that henceforth the vassal states must produce their full quotà. It was after all a matter of making real this European unity which was at the same time benefiting from the immeasurable blessings of the French Revolution and from what Napoleon himself called *le beau idéal de la civilisation*.[1] Did the world agree with him on this point? All the kings, his own brothers, protest in the name of the national interests which they feel called upon to defend. It is that – and not, as Masson had tried to suggest, his personal dynastic feeling after the birth of the King of Rome – it is this reluctance and Napoleon's own obstinate persistence in his grandiose plans, and in demanding ever more fresh soldiers with whom to carry them out, that is the true reason why the federal Empire must become a unified Empire, why the Empire must for ever expand and absorb the whole continent.

When the King of Rome is born to Napoleon, according to Hanotaux,[2] he imagines that he will leave this son

a united, pacified world, which has been lifted to *l'idéal de la civilisation*. But this by no means implies, as has been asserted, a new Roman Empire. Napoleon has in mind something different from a repetition of the past. His original genius does not lend itself to imitation. It creates. He would certainly have looked upon it as an unforgivable insult if one had tried to draw a parallel between the dynasty he was creating and the very mixed lot of the successors of Augustus. He did not seek to model himself on Diocletian, not even on Marcus Aurelius.

To the last we see in Hanotaux's essays merciless criticism alternating with or even united to generous admiration. It is rather amusing to end on a passage in which Driault is called to order for having insulted the great man – Driault, whose convert fervour, as we have seen, had made him into the most enthusiastic of all admirers.

1. XXXIV, 832.
2. p. 858.

9 Georges Lefebvre

ANOTHER *UNIVERSITAIRE*

THE AUTHOR AND THE WORK

IN the well-known *Histoire Générale* of Halphen and Sagnac, *Peuples et civilisations*, the fourteenth volume, entitled *Napoléon*, was written by Georges Lefebvre, *maître de conférences à la Faculté des Lettres de Paris*. Its date is 1935. It is not a biography of Napoleon. It is a textbook for the history of the world during the period 1799–1815. The author knows that he must deal with many matters which were outside Napoleon's grasp or belonged to the opposite camp. The Anglo-Saxon countries preserved their liberal tradition, capitalism was developing, the middle class was preparing to take power, nationalities began to revolt. The uniformity which Napoleon imposed upon his part of the world was only outward appearance. Beneath is the diversity which will characterize the nineteenth century. But during this brief period everything seemed to be yielding to him, he was the leader of history. Therefore, concludes the preface, this volume appears under his name.

As a matter of fact, one finds in it a surprisingly complete picture of Napoleon. It is a textbook, detailed and condensed. But wherever one opens it, there is evidence of penetrating judgement, and the author has even found space for the inclusion from time to time of general reflections on events.

I have said before that I considered dealing with Lefebvre under the general heading of *Universitaires*. He is indeed a pure example of that class, and in a certain sense one can look upon him as being the very opposite of the typical but undistinguished *académicien* Madelin. Thinking of my division into *for* and *against*, I have no hesitation in placing him among the latter. And yet, just as we found in Hanotaux an *académicien* with a strong *universitaire* strain, we find in Lefebvre's vision something which transcends the merely professional quality as well as the party bias of the typical *universitaire*. If I introduce him to wind up the discussion, this does not mean that it is now terminated; there is no last word, there is no end. But it seems to me that Lefebvre has assimilated the discussion as it has proceeded so far, more harmoniously than Hanotaux, and not without a trace of the latter's influence.[1] Lefebvre is obviously aware of the problems as formulated in their

1. It was his reference to Hanotaux's various articles in the *Revue des Deux Mondes* in his bibliography which drew my attention to the latter's work.

many-coloured diversity by his predecessors. He solves them according to his own way of thinking: his book is far from being a series of samples from diverse conceptions, but in its unity it is richly varied. And although the true admirers of the Napoleonic tradition are bound to reject his interpretation, he is free from *parti pris*. He has an eye for the positive achievements, and above all he can appreciate the greatness of the figure. If I add to this that he writes vividly and to the point, and shows himself a man of imagination, I cannot resist a feeling of regret because the *universitaire* has allowed himself to be shut up in a textbook, and has left the great work in twelve volumes to the *académicien*.

ANOTHER PORTRAIT

After Taine, Hanotaux, and Madelin, although aware of the changes which made the young general almost unrecognizable in the megalomaniac Emperor, Georges Lefebvre has attempted to draw a portrait of Napoleon.[1] There are a number of traits which by now have become very familiar to us, but the portrait as a whole shows a remarkable tact and a fine balance.

His brain is among the most perfect that have ever been. His ever ready attention seizes indefatigably upon facts and ideas, which his memory registers and classifies. His imagination plays with them freely, and a state of incessant secret tension enables it tirelessly to produce those political and strategic theses which reveal themselves to him as sudden intuitions comparable to those of the mathematician and the poet. This happens especially at night when he wakes up suddenly. He himself speaks of 'the moral spark' and 'the after-midnight presence of mind'. This spiritual fire illumines through his glittering eyes the face, still 'sulphuric' at his rise, of the sleek-haired Corsican.[2]

This is what makes him unsociable; not, as Taine would have us believe, a certain brutality, as of a somewhat battered *condottiere* let loose upon the world in all his ferocity. He was only fair to himself when he said: 'I am not at bottom a bad sort.' He showed generosity and even kindness to his immediate environment; but between ordinary mortals and Napoleon Bonaparte, who was all effort and concentration, there could exist no common measure or true community. Out of this physical and intellectual disposition arose that irresistible impulse towards action and domination which is called his ambition. He saw clearly into himself: 'It is said that I am ambitious, but this is an error; or at least, my ambition is so intimately allied to my whole being that it cannot be separated from it.' It cannot be better expressed. Napoleon is before all else a temperament.

The author then remarks how well it suited Napoleon to be an officer. Giving orders agreed with his nature, and in Italy and in Egypt, and even in France, he introduced the military system into the government. He was able to consult, but

1. pp. 60–6.   2. See p. 32 above: Auguste Barbier's poem.

never to debate or to discuss. Hence his hatred for the ideologists, while for the confused and undisciplined yet formidable masses he had both hatred and contempt.

But there were in him several personalities besides that of the soldier, and it is this diversity which makes him so fascinating. There was the victim of early neglect who lived to enjoy a fortune. There was – a nobler trait – the man who wanted to know and understand everything. Entering active life after his studious youth, he remained *un cérébral*. Even though now he wants to be practical, he is still a typical man of the eighteenth century, a rationalist, a *philosophe*. He distrusts intuition, and believes in the power of reasoning.

In his conception of the unitary state, made of one piece according to a simple and symmetrical plan, he is entirely classical. At some moments his intellectualism reveals itself by his most marked characteristic, the dichotomy of the personality, the power to see himself live and to meditate wistfully on his own fate.

There follows, among other utterances, that noted by Roederer at the Tuileries (see p. 345).

Thus by a strikingly roundabout way this powerful and orderly mind slips from intellectualism into the romantic melancholia of Chateaubriand and de Vigny. But it is never more than a flash, and he pulls himself together at once.

A realist? In practice, in the knack of playing upon the passions and the interests of men, he is one, and to the highest degree. He has discerned very clearly what in the Revolution touched the heart of the nation and fitted in with his despotism. 'To win over the French, he announced himself both as the man of peace and as the god of war.'

A realist, however, only in execution.

A second personality lives within him, which has some of the features of the hero. It seems to have been born in him, as early as the days of the Military Academy, out of his longing to dominate the world, in which he felt himself despised, and especially to equal the semi-legendary figures of Plutarch and Corneille. What he coveted above all else was glory.

Alexander, the East; Caesar, Augustus, Charlemagne . . . He does not draw rules of conduct from these historical memories, they merely fructify his imagination and communicate an unutterable charm to action.

It is not so much his heroes' achievements which inflame his soul, as the sheer spiritual fire of which these are the tokens. He is an artist, a poet of action, for whom France and mankind were but instruments . . . This is why it is idle to look for the limit which Napoleon put to his policy, or for the goal at which he would have stopped . . . Thus we find in a psychological form that dynamism of temperament which struck us at the first glance. It is the romantic Napoleon, a force which seeks free play and for which the world is but an occasion for acting dangerously. The realist, on the contrary, can be recognized by his taking note of the possible when fixing his aim, and by his knowing where to stop.

But circumstances too are responsible for Napoleon's escape from reality. He had become French at a late date, and had never completely identified himself with the traditions and interests of the nation.

There has remained in him something of the uprooted person. Also of the man torn from his class: he is not entirely a nobleman nor entirely of the people. He has served the King and the Revolution without attaching himself to either. [This is why he was able, at the beginning, to place himself so successfully above parties, but also] neither in the old nor in the new order did he find principles which might have provided him with a norm or a limit. Unlike Richelieu, he was not curbed by dynastic fidelity, which would have subordinated his will to the interest of his master. Nor was he amenable to the civic virtue which could have made him a servant of the nation.

A successful soldier, a pupil of the *philosophes*, he detested feudalism, civil inequality, religious intolerance. In enlightened despotism he saw the way to reconcile authority and social and political reform. He became its last and most illustrious representative, and this is the sense in which he was the man of the Revolution. But his impetuous individuality never accepted democracy, so that he rejected the great expectation of the eighteenth century which inspired revolutionary idealism, the hope of a future when mankind would be civilized enough to be its own master.

Even care for his own safety could not restrain him. He dreamed only of stark and dangerous heroism. Was there a moral curb? No.

In his spiritual life he had nothing in common with the rest of mankind. Even though he knew their passions, which he applied with astonishing ability to his own ends, his attention was exclusively for those that can be used to reduce men to dependence. He belittled everything that raises them to altitudes of sacrifice, religious faith, patriotic enthusiasm, love of freedom, for in all these he feared obstacles for his own schemes. In his own youth he had been open to those sentiments which so easily conduce to heroic action. But circumstances gave him a different turn, and shut him up within himself. In the splendid and terrible isolation of the will to power, measure loses its sense.

With the aid of this sketch it is already possible to situate Georges Lefebvre fairly accurately. Though careful, with a typically modern bashfulness, to avoid moral terms, he shows traits that point to a spiritual descent from Mme de Staël.

When he points out that spiritual loneliness was the result of Napoleon's elevation of self, he even agrees with Taine, though guarding against the latter's exaggeration. He upholds the conception that Napoleon rejected the highest ideals which had animated the French Revolution, those of democracy and human dignity – thereby separating himself from conservatives like Vandal and Madelin, and even from Thiers. When he puts such emphasis upon the absence of a final goal in Napoleon's policy, upon his lack of measure, he places himself in opposition to both Sorel and Driault; and while in reducing everything to temperament he once more displays his affinities with the old *détracteurs*, from Mme de Staël to Lanfrey and Taine, his modern attitude reveals itself in the use he makes of the conception of romanticism. This we have already met in Guérard, Bainville, and Hanotaux. It helps Lefebvre, like Guérard and Bainville, to discern the greatness and beauty of the figure, to which the Barnis and the Lanfreys were blind. But like Hanotaux he attaches to the epithet an implication which as far as politics are concerned is very unfavourable, and in using it, and especially in the limits he sets to Napoleon's 'realism', he is clearly hitting at Madelin.

Yet when we come to look at the book more closely we shall be able to add a number of little traits to the figure – perhaps of Napoleon, certainly of the author.

THE DICTATORSHIP

Lefebvre's reserved attitude towards Napoleon had revealed itself at an even earlier stage of his book, when in a review of the war situation, and the possibilities of peace in 1799, he discusses the Directorate. His interpretation is intended to weaken the usual contrast which (having been indicated already by Armand Lefebvre and Thiers) had been so strikingly worked out by Vandal. He explains the evil reputation of the Directorate by the impossible financial situation which it had inherited from the Convention: worthless *assignats* withdrawn, a state bankruptcy, all credit gone, nothing but the receipts of taxation for financing the war. The régime struggled manfully with these difficulties, and introduced considerable improvements in the system of taxation. In the administrative sphere too there are good reforms to the credit of this much abused government; they were soon to benefit the First Consul. But inflation could not be avoided: the army suffered from it, hence its resentment against the 'lawyers'. The disintegration of the administration, of the policy, of public order, also resulted from it. The need for money explains why the Directorate came to practise its policy of exactions in the occupied territories and paid for the war out of its conquests. Lefebvre does not fail to add that the generals did not forget their own needs in applying this system.

By thus presenting matters, he links up with the previous volume in the series in which the Directorate had been dealt with by Guyot (see p. 241). At the same time he recognizes that the government failed to find really satisfactory solutions for urgent problems, and admits that in consequence, in leading political circles and among intellectuals in general, there was impatience and discontent and an inclination to try a stronger government, one in which power was concentrated, if not in the hands of a single man. Thus the 18th Brumaire is not an accident in his view, it is not in itself an event about which one might (as was Lanfrey, for instance) be seriously upset:

An inner necessity drove the Revolution to dictatorship, and not for the first time. [The author naturally thinks of Robespierre.] Nor was it an accident that it led to the dictatorship of a general. But it happened that this general was Napoleon Bonaparte, whose temperament even more than his genius could not easily acquiesce in peace and in moderation. Thus it was all the same something unpredictable that caused the scale to topple over towards the side of the *guerre éternelle*.[1]

But before passing to a review of Lefebvre's conception of the problem of war and peace – the main lines of which can already be predicted, with the help of this and previous quotations – let us say a word about the whole of the First Consul's constructive work.

A moment ago I established a connexion between this author and Mme de Staël, but it is necessary to observe that he takes a very critical attitude towards the practical policy of that great exponent of liberalism. He never fails to underline its bourgeois class character. The Jacobins, he said, in 1799 as in 1793, wanted a democratic dictatorship. Not so the ideologists of the salon of Mme de Staël. They did not even want a democracy. Mme de Staël summarized their programme, and it amounted to 'a representative system that would guarantee the power to the notables of money and of talent'. In the words of Lefebvre, this was nothing but 'a dictatorship of the bourgeoisie'; and as those who were aiming at this could only address themselves to the army (excluding, as they did, the people), they suddenly found themselves under an entirely different, a personal dictatorship. This supremely important change of régime, which introduced extreme centralization and placed the appointment of all officials – who had till then been elective – in the hands of the First Consul, was possible because the Revolution had swept away all group resistance, because the extreme decentralization on a democratic basis introduced by the *Constituante* obviously weakened the country against the danger from abroad, and because the ideologists – liberals, well-to-do and educated bourgeois, the notables in other words – though delivered from the democratic danger and in possession of all the jobs,

1. p. 58.

were still not satisfied and constantly allowed themselves to be tamed by Bonaparte's *'Voulez-vous que je vous livre aux Jacobins?'* Mme de Staël, 'who had hoped to govern France by means of Bonaparte or at any rate of Benjamin Constant', attempted opposition. On 5 January Constant delivered at the Tribunate the speech he had been discussing with her. 'At once the ruler became angry, and everyone took cover.'[1]

The methods of the dictator were those of a 'terrorist'.[2] Lefebvre says it without beating about the bush, and we have seen (pp. 326, 331) that this word 'terrorist' had become almost traditional among the *universitaires*. He writes this with reference to the pacification of the Vendée, but the proscription of the Jacobins after the attack with the infernal machine, and the establishment of special tribunals and of military commissions as an ordinary means of administration help him to complete the picture. *'Il faut du sang'*, declared Bonaparte in the Council of State when it dealt with the Jacobins (suspected after the attempt, but, as we know, innocent).[3]

When dealing with popular disturbances the First Consul was equally harsh. There were disturbances, and for a number of years to come, as the financial situation which had created so much trouble for the Directorate was not to be remedied overnight, and when the harvest failed it was difficult to obtain grain from abroad. Although Bonaparte, as we know, did his best to keep up the level of bread distribution in Paris by organizing the bakery trade, there were repeated periods of scarcity, with the usual accompaniment of unrest. If the agitation did not assume so serious a form as in 1789, when bread was also very expensive though not so expensive as in 1801 and 1802, this was due, says Lefebvre, not only to the absence of political and social troubles, but especially to the efficient organization of repression which had just been introduced.

Thus, popular excitement could only result in a still closer attachment of the propertied class to Bonaparte. He became the bulwark of society.

The crisis therefore helped him not a little in acquiring the Consulate for life in 1802.[4]

THE CONCORDAT

Towards the most famous constructive work of Bonaparte in his happiest years Lefebvre also adopts an attitude more critical than admiring. Let us devote a few words to the Concordat and the Code.

What the author points out in the first place is an observation we met for the

1. pp. 39, 80 ff.   2. p. 83.   3. p. 131.   4. p. 119.

first time in Driault (p.310). As he tersely expresses it,[1] the application made to the Pope to dismiss the French bishops amounted to the administration of a mortal blow to Gallicanism. But, he says, this old French tradition was totally alien to Bonaparte. How sharply an opinion like this differs from that of Masson, who gloried in the view that his hero had imbibed this doctrine with his extracts from Gerson (see p. 171). According to Lefebvre, Bonaparte saw nothing but the most immediate practical advantages. He considered it the only way of getting rid of a tiresome counter-revolutionary element. At the same time, imagining himself strong enough to keep the Roman Church under control, he wanted to use the religious renaissance for the sake of winning the counter-revolutionary aristocracy and middle class. Religion became once more *de bon ton* in good circles. 'Sensing the wind that blew', Chateaubriand 'proved the truth of Catholicism on its artistic qualities'. Fontanes, with more political acumen, took a wider view: 'The restoration of the cult had a social significance, and was to support the new class division.' This was the innermost intention of Bonaparte himself.[2]

The tone of a page like this differs sharply from that in which Madelin – or more especially the believing Catholic, Hanotaux – discussed the Concordat. It indicates a general attitude of mind on the part of the writer towards the great religious, political, and social problems which were involved in this measure. But a different appreciation and even a different interpretation of Bonaparte's action is the inevitable result.

THE CODE IN FRANCE

A general attitude of mind, anti-bourgeois, socialistic, also determines the judgement of the Code. No wonder that when one compares it with that of conservatives like Vandal and Madelin the accents are seen to fall very differently.

The famous saying of Bonaparte in the Council of State that the French had been made by the Revolution into so many grains of sand and that it was his endeavour 'to throw upon the soil of France a few blocks of granite, in order to give a direction to the public spirit' is unquestioningly accepted and admired by Madelin. 'Les masses de granite' is the title of a chapter of his larger work.[3] The measures with which Bonaparte wished to counteract the excessive individualism of post-revolutionary society were the institution of the Legion of Honour, the settlement of education, and the Code. The storm of opposition which rose

1. p. 120.
2. If the reader turns back to pp. 111 ff., 124, 322, 365, he will see how various were the interpretations of this aim and of Bonaparte's attitude to religion.
3. *Histoire du Consulat et de l'Empire*, IV, 166 ff.

against the Legion of Honour is described by Madelin as a curious sample of the continued effect of the Revolution's misconceptions. It was looked upon as a corporation, a grouping of privileged persons. As regards education, he first expatiates upon the deplorable neglect in which it was found by the First Consul and out of which he lifted it. He next cites from Napoleon's opinions on education his wish to enlist it in the service of national unity, his respect for the classics (we know – see p. 134 – that this means for *some* of the classics), his preference for the sciences: all this without analysis or criticism, and in a tone of the most cordial agreement. 'Meanwhile many other benefits were coming: work was proceeding on the Code.' In introducing the *Code civil* Madelin speaks of nothing but the high intentions for moral recovery which animated the First Consul, and for the work itself he has the phrase 'one of the finest portions of the building'.[1] He devotes to it a long and interesting discussion; he fairly summarizes the criticism to which it has been subjected, but only so as to lead up to the remark that every human work was bound to draw upon itself such criticism; and where he can he brings out the fact that the reactionary aspects one detects in it are due not to Bonaparte but to the lawyers. His conclusion is that this, the most impressive of the blocks of granite, also forms Napoleon's highest title to fame.

Hanotaux's view is very different.

The imperial policy [he writes] born of the policy of the Revolution, was not at its best where the protection of the weak, the poor, the isolated was concerned. Society is a pyramid which rests on its base, the people, makes them feel the whole of the weight. Let them accept and acquiesce; such is their lot. They have been guaranteed their political rights and their civil equality; this should suffice. As regards their economic rights, their claim to live, work, and enjoy prosperity, neither the State nor the nation cares. Property – that is all.[2]

Hanotaux does not blame Napoleon so much as public opinion for this; after the Revolution there was a holy terror of disorder, submission was called for, and yet the French nation still cherished a profound hatred for all social exception or privilege.

Faced with such sentiments, Napoleon, in spite of his great plans for reconstruction and consolidation, achieved nothing of permanent value for the masses. The age was stronger than he. The new society, by no means welded together by the vaunted blocks of granite, remained a dust cloud of human particles within the framework of a soulless administration rigidly subdivided into compartments. This dust could offer no resistance to imperial absolutism.

When later on he deals with the establishment of the imperial nobility, and has quoted the apology of St Helena that 'it is impossible to govern old and

1. op. cit. IV, 183.　　　2. *Revue des Deux Mondes*, XXXIX, 295.

corrupted nations without titles, decorations, harmless toys', he exclaims: 'How far we are here from the blocks of granite!...'[1]

Let us now see what Lefebvre makes of all this. He begins by remarking that the picturesque expression used in the Council of State conceals the intention 'to create bundles of interests, which are to be attached to the régime by advantage and honours and are expected to secure to it in exchange, through the influence they have upon wage earners, the obedience of the popular classes'. Intermediate bodies, corporate groupings, if you like; 'but he and only he was to create the social body'.

As conceived by Bonaparte the social hierarchy rested on wealth; nor was anything else possible, since he had seized power in conjunction with the middle class. The ideologists, indeed, by placing free education within the reach of all, had intended to raise talent to the level of property in the leadership of the State. But wealth once aquired has a natural tendency to reserve this privilege for itself, and Bonaparte shared the distrust of the rich for men of talent as long as they were poor: they formed a revolutionary ferment...

(Implied in this passage is a criticism of the educational settlement, and further on Lefebvre introduces his set treatment of the subject with a remark which places it at once in a different key from that which we observed in Madelin's work: 'Public education as designed by Bonaparte was in accordance with that social organization and with the authoritarian nature of the régime.') To continue my quotation from his analysis of the social hierarchy:

When Bonaparte proclaims himself to be the representative of the social revolution, he always reduces the great movement to the abolition of privileges, of which the consequence was the accession to power of the *bourgeoisie censitaire* [the well-to-do middle class which under the 'census' system after the Revolution was in exclusive possession of the suffrage]. At the decline of his despotism, the social régime of Year X will be seen to have laid the foundation for the July monarchy.[2]

'The *Code civil* was the bible of that régime.' As for Napoleon's personal share in it, Lefebvre remarks quite soberly that his direct interest was confined to the clause relating to the family.

He was intent on strengthening the authority of the father and the husband [this is expressly denied by Madelin], on robbing illegitimate children, if not recognized, of their heritage, and on minimizing that of those who have been recognized; also on retaining divorce, not without an eye to himself.

The Code, the author continues, possesses, like all Napoleon's work, a dual character. It confirms the disappearance of the feudal aristocracy and accepts the

1. ibid. p. 302; see p. 74 above.
2. *Napoléon*, p. 133 ff.; see the remarks of Hanotaux, p. 371 above.

social principles of 1789 . . . This is why Europe has seen in it the symbol of the Revolution, and why, wherever it was introduced, it ushered in the essential rules of modern society. Even though today this characteristic is out of date, not to restore its full freshness to the Code would be to misunderstand the history of the Napoleonic period and to preclude oneself from realizing the full implication of French domination. But the Code at the same time confirms the reaction against the democratic structure of the Republic. Drawn up with an eye to the interest of the bourgeoisie, it aims before all else at consecrating and sanctifying the rights of property. It looks upon this as a natural right, anterior to society, absolute, and belonging to the individual.

The State interest, as conceived by Napoleon and his lawyers, provides them with their second directive. It is on this ground, for instance, that expropriation is made possible. The authority of the head of the family is strengthened, but at the same time the right to make dispositions after death is limited.

But for those who possess nothing, the Code has nothing to say, except to protect their personal freedom by forbidding the lease or hire of services for an indefinite period. Proclaiming the freedom of labour, and the equality of citizens before the law, it in fact, as had been the wish of the Constituent Assembly, leaves the wage earners' labour to all the ups and downs of economic competition, looking upon it as a merchandise like any other. It repudiates the notion, which had emerged for a moment in 1793, of recognizing to the citizens the right to live. To the detriment of the wage earners, it even encroaches upon the principle of legal equality, since in wage disputes the employer only is believed upon his word. . . .

The Code then is the product of the development of French society, in so far as it has brought into being and into power the bourgeoisie. . . .

This, it will be noticed, is something very different from the paean of Madelin. Both Madelin and Vandal (see p. 329) recognize the bourgeois character of the famous law book and that it is, as Lefebvre proceeds to argue, a compromise between the old law and the new conceptions of the Revolution. But the first two are not in the least troubled by this. If one tries to express the difference between the views of the two conservatives and of the socialistically inclined Lefebvre not in political but in historical terms, one will have to point especially to the greater attention which the latter (following the example of authors like Aulard, Jaurès, and Mathiez) pays not only to the libertarian tendencies of the Revolution in its first phase (these had received full attention since Mme de Staël from an uninterrupted line of liberals and radicals) but also to the social tendencies of its second phase in 1793. It is only when these are ignored, or given no more than perfunctory attention, that the Code can be depicted as a natural and mature product of the great movement which Bonaparte took under his wing. When on the other hand one looks into these tendencies for an essential, important, and particularly hopeful part of the great movement, then one's regret at the destruction of the political and democratic aspirations is increased, and one sees still more in Bonaparte the man who deflected or arrested the course of the Revolution, the man of the reaction.

THE CODE OUTSIDE FRANCE

But like Mignet before him (see p. 37) Lefebvre makes a distinction between the Code in France and the Code in the part of Europe subjected to France. Here also, however, his views are far from the uncritical enthusiasm of Driault. He places the problem right in the centre of his account of the operation of the Napoleonic régime in the territories outside France, an account which is distinguished by its completeness and knowledge. A number of monographs, of which I have mentioned a few (p. 299 ff.), by French and foreign writers, have enabled the author to rise above the generalizations and superficialities of previous generations.[1] Here, if anywhere, one feels that the argument has yielded something.

Le grand empire, Lefebvre begins,[2] which Napoleon was trying more and more to make a political unit, must receive everywhere the same institutions and the same social structure as *l'Empire français*.

In the first place, Napoleon meant the introduction of his system of government to confirm his rule. He was anxious to raise his power and that of his vassals and allies beyond dispute: intermediate bodies, privileges, feudalism were to disappear, so that all might be the State's immediate subjects. It was desirable too that the law of succession should divide the large fortunes (see p. 295), that the aristocrats should become the sovereign's creatures and the priests their officials. At the same time all members of *le grand empire* lay under an obligation, which came before everything else: to supply money and men. [Hanotaux's phrase, *l'empire de recrutement*, will be remembered.] The *ancien régime* with its chaotic and slow administration could not mobilize the country's resources quickly enough; therefore there must be *tabula rasa* and introduction of Napoleonic bureaucracy in its place. From this point of view, the Emperor felt himself occasionally pressed to conquest by the desire to give free play to these methods, insufficiently appreciated, for instance, by Charles IV of Spain.

(We have here a rational and unromantic interpretation of the policy of 'regeneration', which a man like Prince Napoleon, to mention no others, thought a sufficient excuse for the dethronement of the Spanish Bourbons.)

Moreover, continues Lefebvre, Napoleon saw in the renovation of administration and society a means of winning the bourgeoisie and peasants, and he quotes the letter to Jérôme which I have already mentioned (p. 62). The essential

1. See his bibliographies, pp. 430, 440, 437, etc.   2. *Napoléon*, p. 427.

part of the social policy with which he meant to weld together the great empire was embodied in the Code. But

the jealous passion with which he tried to propagate this Code is not completely explained by realistic motives . . . The intellectual formation which he owed to the eighteenth century inspired him with a sincere aversion to feudalism, intolerance, and the muddled empiricism of the old administrations. He resumed the reforming work of the enlightened despots, but greatly as his task was facilitated by the tradition they had left behind, he surpassed them all in the boldness and rapidity of his action. His authoritarian mind, moreover, attributed to his work a character of perfection.

To illustrate this, Lefebvre quotes from yet another letter to Jérôme:

I think it ridiculous that you should make an argument of the opposition of the Westphalian people . . . If the people decline their own happiness, they only show their anarchical inclinations. They are guilty, and the ruler's first duty is to punish them.

'The expansion of French institutions', our author reflects, 'was one of the forms assumed by his lust for power.'

Nevertheless, he continues, the Emperor did frequently take circumstances into account, a fact which did not always help the operation of the system. The allied rulers had to be humoured; even in Italy, which generally speaking underwent his influence most profoundly, he allowed disruption to persist.

Enormous as was the work which he achieved, if one takes into account the brief space during which Napoleon's domination lasted, it remained fragmentary. And what was worse, in the sphere of social reforms, too, opportunist considerations come into conflict with the 'system'. As he needed money, and wanted to expand the extraordinary domain, the estates of princes who had been deposed, of émigrés, of the clergy came in very handy. Now tithes and feudal contributions constituted a considerable part of the importance of these estates. It would hardly have suited his book to let them go.

Outside France, too, it was impossible to fill all the posts in the new administrations with suitable men of non-noble birth.[1] The nobility was moreover indispensable for the courts of his kings.

1. I need hardly say that this does not apply to Holland. Indeed, as I have already pointed out (p. 302, note), the whole feudal question, the French annexation, and indeed the French influence in general from 1795 onwards, had much less profound significance in Holland than in many other countries. Lefebvre is perhaps not fully aware of this. When he writes that in Holland '*l'essentiel avait été fait par la République*' (p. 441), meaning the French Republic, he tends considerably to exaggerate the immediate French influence on internal development. In the first place much that was 'essential' was already present long before the French Revolution, and again, much that was done between 1795 and 1810 was partly the work of the Dutch. The most important exception

But as a consequence it became impossible to carry out the agrarian reforms in the radical way which would have been necessary to win the peasants and which had resulted in attaching the French peasantry to the Revolution. And indeed Napoleon everywhere discarded the 'Jacobins', who would have been fervently in favour of radical measures; he flattered the old nobility in France, and for himself sought a dynastic alliance. In the *empire* the Revolution was a fact for which he could deny responsibility; in the *grand empire* he had to carry that responsibility himself. Here was a contradiction which penetrated into the heart of the system. The peasants were sacrificed. Their contributions to the landowners, and even occasionally the tithes, were declared redeemable [instead of being confiscated]. This proved the great obstacle in the way of French influence as well as of Napoleonic reforms.

THE PROBLEM OF WAR AND PEACE

Lefebvre precedes his story of the rupture of the peace of Amiens with a short summary of the debate of which Napoleon's foreign policy has been the subject. Contemporaries, and Napoleon's first historians, he says, spoke of his ambition as being the source of all his wars; but afterwards this was found too simple, and a number of hypotheses have been constructed, agreeing or disagreeing with the Napoleonic legend. He indicates them all, without mentioning names; and then he continues (the names in square brackets have been added by me):

In each is to be found part of the truth, which yet as a whole transcends them all. It is true that those who helped Bonaparte into the saddle wanted to retain the natural frontiers, and that to defend these one could easily be tempted to go beyond them [Sorel]; but it is not true that this was the only means, or the safest, to protect them, and that in expanding his conquest his sole thought was of the interest of the nation. It is true that England was his constant and persevering enemy, and that by overthrowing him she triumphed definitely over France [Masson, Vandal, again Sorel]; but if in accordance with a maturely considered plan he was aiming at England alone, his continental policy would have been greatly different [same remark already made by Driault]. Even the blockade [the Continental System] of which so much is made [e.g. by Sorel] was suggested to him by the composition of *le Grand Empire*, rather than the other way about. Nothing would have pleased the new Alexander better than an adventurous expedition to Constantinople or to India [Bourgeois], but the larger part of his enterprise has only a cerebral connexion with that dream. It is a fact that he used to compare himself to Charlemagne and to Caesar and that he toyed with the idea of a political federation of the western world [Driault], but the intellectual desire to restore the past was not what drove him to action. In denouncing the hatred sworn by the allies to the soldier of the

was the unification of the laws by the French Code; and this was carried through under Louis Bonaparte.

Revolution, the legend gives evidence of a keen insight, and it is curious that so many historians should have overlooked the point. [We saw that Hanotaux emphasized this, and we shall see that Georges Lefebvre himself attaches great importance to the motif.] But he did not confine himself to the defensive.

There is no rational explanation by which Napoleon's foreign policy can be reduced to unity. He pursued simultaneously aims which at least for the moment were contradictory. In the last resort we must return to his 'ambition'. His contemporaries – who had before their eyes the theatrical apparatus of a luxury oppressive and loud in its novelty, accompanied by amorous adventures, quarrels of avaricious relatives, and thefts by servants – lowered it all, without denial of his genius, to the common level of humanity. Seen from a distance, the picture takes on a purer aspect, and his secret may be guessed: the heroic attraction of danger, the magic seduction of the dream, the irresistible impulse of the temperament.[1]

THE RUPTURE OF THE PEACE OF AMIENS

One sees how closely this interpretation is connected with the portrait. In the conception of Lefebvre, however immediately based upon a multiplicity of facts, there is a strong unity. It is not surprising to find that he will have none of the reasoning which lays the responsibility for the breach of the peace of Amiens on the British. Yet he by no means minimizes the Anglo-French antithesis as Napoleon found it, and his detailed explanation of economic and social conditions in the Britain of the industrial revolution, though less highly coloured than that of his namesake of almost a century ago (see p. 51), makes one realize most vividly what a dynamic spirit prevailed in Britain at that time and how it was transmuted into imperialism. An unwillingness to leave the Low Countries in the possession of France was, moreover, an ancient British tradition, which was felt there in all sincerity as being defensive. When in an earlier passage of his book[2] Lefebvre argues that it would have been possible for the First Consul upon his accession to consolidate the peace on the basis of the existing situation, that is to say with the preservation of the 'natural frontiers', it is from Prussia and Austria that he takes his starting point: it might have been possible to induce these two powers to acquiesce in the situation, the latter by giving up Italy. Without an ally on the continent, Britain would have had no chance. And sure enough, after Lunéville came Amiens.

There is no need to believe, says Lefebvre, ever conscious of the contrast between the old order and the new represented by the France of the Revolution, that Europe, so intensely hostile to the regicide Republic, would have given up for ever the idea of recapturing all or part of its amazing conquests. But this is not how the question should be put. For in 1799, as always, the problem for a statesman was

1. *Napoléon*, p. 144 ff.   2. p. 56 ff.

not to deflect the course of history [one cannot miss the thrust at Sorel here]; the question was merely whether France had a chance to secure peace for one or two decades, while keeping the natural frontiers, so as to recover her breath in order to defend them with even more strength than before. That the answer must be in the affirmative is not subject to doubt.

This amounts to saying – and immediately afterwards it is said in so many words – that it was Bonaparte's inadequate statesmanship, his 'temperament', by which France was dragged into new wars, and finally into disasters and the loss of the 'natural frontiers'. That it was Bonaparte, and not the bellicose spirit of the French nation, is strongly emphasized. Even the attempt by the Convention in 1794 and 1795 to fix the natural frontiers for ever by the constitution and by decree had elicited the condemnation of contemporaries; one of the ideologists, who in his blindness was to assist in preparing the 18th Brumaire, wrote in *La Décade philosophique* that this amounted to decreeing eternal war and the annihilation of all Frenchmen. In any case no one thought of transgressing the 'natural frontiers'. Italy was Bonaparte's personal playground, and to sum up, the responsibility was Bonaparte's.

How brilliant was the position of the First Consul after he had concluded the peace of Amiens!

The French nation longed for peace before all else; it had received it from Bonaparte's hands. It was attached to the social achievements of the revolution; Bonaparte had preserved them. Satisfied with its leader and proud of him, it did not yet realize that he intended to abuse his power and was pursuing objects which conflicted with its own. But the people did not want this leader to become king, and still less that he should create a nobility; while Bonaparte, in his heart, had broken with the Republic and with equality. Pleased with having reached the natural frontiers, the people did not in the least desire to go beyond them, while their master had already crossed them and was making war inevitable. They still saw in him the national hero, at the moment when he had ceased to answer this description.[1]

It is unnecessary after such an introduction to follow in detail Lefebvre's very precise narrative of the diplomatic relations which led to Amiens and to the rupture of Amiens. I merely note, in order to illustrate the difference from Madelin, that he says about the publication of Sebastiani's report: 'One is dumbfounded by so provocative an act.'[2] Nevertheless, he concludes:

There have been passionate debates about the responsibility for the rupture. Bonaparte's provocations are undeniable, but it is no less true that England broke the treaty and took the initiative for a preventive war, as soon as she could count on Russia. She tried to justify her conduct by pleading her concern for the European

1. *Napoléon*, p. 141.   2. *Napoléon*, p. 156; see p. 356 above.

balance. But she would not allow this system to extend over the ocean, which had been created by the God of the Bible to be English. As between Bonaparte and England there was not really anything but the clash between two imperialisms.[1]

THE EMPIRE: THE THIRD COALITION; 1813

The war, through the conspiracies encouraged by Britain, led to the murder of Enghien, which in turn led to the proclamation of the Empire and the consecration in Notre Dame.

The theatrical character of the consecration painted by David might fill Napoleon's heart with delight [Lefebvre writes in a characteristic passage] but it added nothing to his prestige. The people watched with a sceptical eye the strangely assorted procession and the festivities which succeeded each other throughout the month of December. No one believed his power to be strengthened. By restoring monarchy, and underlining the aristocratic character of the régime, he had even more emphatically separated his cause from that of the nation . . . Among the people, the spirit of the Revolution had not succumbed. Napoleon had seduced it by promising peace, he had made himself completely the master by resuscitating war. Now there was nothing to prevent him from giving way to his own nature. Imperial conquest, despotism, and aristocracy get free scope, while the nation can only watch in astonishment and disquiet. It has no choice but to follow for dear life the triumphal chariot of Caesar.[2]

One fact Lefebvre never allows us to forget; he gives it special emphasis in his careful narrative of the diplomatic negotiations. The wars are Napoleon's doing; France is dragged blindly into them and must willy-nilly follow in his wake. I shall not discuss Lefebvre's account of the origin of the Third Coalition and of the outbreak of the war on land in the autumn of 1805. But here is his conclusion, once more directed against Sorel, against the Sorel whom Bainville and Madelin had followed so slavishly:

The third coalition has been represented as a deliberate attempt to rob France of her natural frontiers. If the allies succeeded in defeating her, it goes without saying that they would take away her newly-won territories; but what really ought to be proved is whether England in 1803, Russia in 1805, took up arms solely with that purpose in mind; and for this proof we look in vain, even in the case of England. To begin with, the spirit of aggression, which cannot be denied, was fed by sentiments and interests which are left out of account entirely [here as elsewhere the author means by Sorel and his followers, who refer only to the 'natural frontiers']: the economic preoccupations and the maritime imperialism of the English, the megalomania and the personal jealousy of Alexander, the hostility of the European

1. op. cit. p. 158.   2. op. cit. p. 163.

aristocracy, so powerful in Vienna, and which was strengthened by causes of a social nature.

I remark in passing that economic and social factors have a prominence in Lefebvre's mind which gives a modern touch to his excellent and painstaking surveys of international affairs.

What is even more striking is the fact that Napoleon, as if on purpose, kept irritating this subdued ill will, caused uneasiness to all the powers, and exhausted the patience even of the feeble Austrian monarchy. Leaving aside the interests of the French nation, simply from the point of view of his own personal policy it was not in-dispensable to his authority to have the Duc d'Enghien kidnapped and to found the Empire, to incite England to action prematurely, to threaten the eastern ambitions of Russia, and above all to irritate Austria by changing the Italian Republic into a kingdom and annexing Genoa. Without sharing the revolutionary enthusiasm of the Girondins, he challenged the kings and the aristocracy in the same fashion for which it is usual to blame them, and he continued the noisy policy of intervention which has earned for the Directorate so much contemptuous criticism.

However this may be, the formation of the Third Coalition after the rupture of the peace of Amiens gave to his destiny its definitive direction. Not that from now on his failure was certain, as is often suggested [by Armand Lefebvre, Sorel, Bainville]: many more errors and unforeseeable accidents are required to bring about this ruin. But no way out was left, other than the conquest of the world.

The beauty of Lefebvre's book consists in the fact that he is able to present and continually to recall this general vision upon Napoleon and his régime, without neglecting the endless multiplicity of facts which determine and modify each particular instance. British imperialism, Austrian reaction, the personal policy of Alexander, none of these is blurred in order to make Napoleon's responsibility stand out with more sharpness. Lanfrey as well as Sorel becomes understandable in the interpretation of Lefebvre, without affecting the clarity of his own presentation.

As a single example I point to the attractive page in which he opposes Welling-ton and Napoleon. In the former he underlines 'the aristocratic *morgue*', he describes the high tone he adopts towards his officers, and his contemptuous description of his soldiers as 'the scum of the earth, a troop of rascals', and so forth.

At any rate [continues the author] pride of race tied him fast to his caste, and to the country of which it was in his eyes the lawful proprietor. He never had a thought but to save it, his dry soul, bare of imagination and affection, preserving him from the romantic individualism which ruined Napoleon, while lending to his genius an imperishable attraction.[1]

1. *Napoléon*, p. 424.

Equally characteristic is his treatment of the year 1813, which is as far from the over-simplified anti-Napoleon interpretation in Driault's article of 1906 as from the equally over-simplified pro-Napoleon interpretation in Driault's book of 1927 (see p. 267 ff.). Metternich is described as working at Napoleon's undoing. It is recognized that Napoleon could not accept Metternich's proposals without fighting; but above the circumstances of the moment, the author remains mindful of Napoleon's earlier mistakes which had led to his then inescapable difficulty.[1]

SPIRITUAL LIFE: INADEQUACY OF THE NAPOLEONIC IDEAL

It is impossible to summarize a textbook crammed with facts, in which the author usually indicates his conceptions, his judgement, with a mere word or an incidental clause. Before parting from Lefebvre, I wish to pick out a few passages which will give an idea of the richness of his material as well as of the spirit in which he deals with the phenomenon Napoleon. I choose for this purpose the two final sections of the first chapter (*La France impériale*) in his fifth book (*Le monde en 1812*). They are entitled *Le Gouvernement des esprits* and *L'évolution sociale et l'opinion*. Together they cover more than twenty pages, and we shall note only a few main points.[2]

'To lull men's minds by forbidding all criticism, while fostering their interests' was Napoleon's first method to obtain a docile public opinion, but it was not the only one. At times he had a clear insight into the positive power of the spirit, even above that of the sword, and at the very beginning conceived of the Concordat as a means towards the education of the faithful into a willing joyful obedience.

Here again the way in which Lefebvre discusses these matters strikes one by its complete lack of sympathy towards the Church. He goes into some detail about the advantages it saw in the relationship—advantages in money, in favours, and in influence – and also about the struggle which was being waged in the Emperor's environment for and against the interest of the Church, with Fontanes and the younger Portalis (who was to be snubbed so spectacularly in the full Council of State) as its pleaders, and Fouché as the anti-clerical who has preserved his revolutionary point of view. Finally he warns us that:

One must not measure the Church's influence upon the population by its material progress. In many regions indifference was considerable, and in the towns a public could always be found to applaud *Oedipe*[3] or *Tartuffe*. There is reason to believe, anyhow, that Napoleon had no wish to rechristianize France too profoundly; he

1. *Napoléon*, p. 532.   2. *Napoléon*, pp. 396–418.
3. Voltaire's first tragedy (1718), which was regarded as an attack on priestly arrogance.

had taken his measure to get a hold upon that section of his subjects who listened before all else to the priests; more than this did not interest him.

The success of this policy was, moreover, affected by the conflict with the Pope. Already in his discussion of the imperial consecration it was clear that Lefebvre did not succumb to the charm of the personality of Pius VII.[1] He now points out at once that the conflict between Emperor and Pope had no religious origin, a remark which Napoleon himself and afterwards his apologists have always been fond of making. No doubt

Pius VII resented the Emperor's Organic Articles and even more the conduct pursued with respect to the clergy of the Kingdom of Italy. But a rupture would never have ensued if the Pope had not been a secular ruler.

One consequence of the conflict undoubtedly was that

the clergy reverted to the royalism and counter revolution from which Napoleon had detached it by the Concordat. But the majority was reluctant to carry its opposition to extremes, for fear of losing the advantages obtained. As for the public, so long as worship was not interrupted and the *curé* not expelled, it took little notice. If the conflict revived the hopes of the royalists and favoured their intrigues, this was not in itself sufficient to shake the régime.

It is worth while to compare this estimate of the event with that of Hanotaux (see p. 366), to whom the rupture with the Pope, that is with God, meant the end of Napoleon.

In his description of the *Université*, Lefebvre places special emphasis upon the incomplete execution and results of the great plan. This was partly the result of lack of money, but there were other factors. The reformer overlooked the people; from the middle class he received through the schools what he wanted above all, able officials; but an idea that could have animated a whole generation and attached it to him was not his for the giving. This is shown not only by education, but by art and literature, which failed to reward his encouragement by a period of activity.

As worked out by Lefebvre, this idea amounts to a fairly thorough rejection of the Napoleonic episode. He admits that Napoleon lacked financial and technical means such as were at the disposal of later dictatorships for organizing their propaganda. (This remark, by the way, is a sign of the times: the parallel could not have been left out entirely in a book of 1935 – in a book by a leftish author, at any rate, for in Madelin's even later work one would look for it in vain.)

But [he continues], with his pretension to found a dynasty and a universal domination, he had nothing to teach which could convey anything to the French. They

1. *Napoléon*, p. 163.

who continued to serve him to the end faithfully and disinterestedly believed they were defending in his person the nation and the Revolution. The others could not take seriously the legitimacy of General Vendémiaire,[1] even though he had been anointed by the Pope. Thus he was able to drug or to oppress, not to master, the spirit of the people. Men's thoughts remained suspended between the two poles of tradition and the Revolution.[2]

SOCIAL LIFE: FAILURE OF THE FUSION

What I want to extract from the second of the sections to which I referred is mainly a remark which supports this last item. In his policy of social reconstruction Napoleon is shown by Lefebvre as leaning upon two incompatibles. Fusion – we saw how highly Vandal and after him Hanotaux thought of this slogan. Hanotaux certainly did not fail to discern, but Lefebvre is the first to state with full emphasis, that the fusion which the ruler had most at heart, that between the idea of the Revolution and the idea of Legitimacy, that between the newly emerging leading class and the *ralliés*, did not really materialize.

However far Napoleon might go in his denial of the ideas of 1789 ('nothing but weapons in the hands of malcontents, ambitious men, and ideologists', he called them at the end in speaking to Molé) – though he fill his court with the bearers of old names and flatter them by restoring ancient customs (since 1811 'the order of precedence marked by the *fauteuil*, the *tabouret*, the number of horses with the *carosse*, court dress, the curtsey . . .') – he had not really reconciled them. The two aristocracies continued to look at each other with distrust and contempt, in spite of the Emperor's attempt to unite them even by marriages – a means which he indeed liked to apply all along the line: the prefects in Dutch *départements*, for instance, were ordered to make out lists of girls with a good dowry, so that they might do their bit, by suitable marriages with young Frenchmen, towards bringing the leading class into the system. Himself he felt ill at ease in the midst of the *ci-devants*. They were on the lookout for the fall of 'Bonaparte'. And the fact is that he wished nothing less than their genuine restoration. If he had become the most powerful of enlightened despots, it was owing solely to the complete destruction of the French aristocracy at the moment of his appearance. In the provinces, where the old families had to see the new men occupying their former properties, relations were even worse.

The social revolution has created an unbridgeable chasm. The old aristocracy and

1. This nickname, which arose from Bonaparte's suppression of the Royalist rising against the newly formed Directorate in 1795, had a particular meaning when used by Royalists.
2. p. 407.

the new will long remain enemies and whatever Napoleon may say or do, in the course of the nineteenth century democracy will profit by their dissension and triumph once more.

It is entirely in the spirit of Hanotaux that Lefebvre goes on to argue that Napoleon's action has borne lasting fruit only where he worked in the direction of the social evolution itself. This was particularly so where he gave a chance to the bourgeoisie. Also in agreement with Hanotaux, Lefebvre pictures this bourgeoisie, while laying hold of the jobs after 18th Brumaire, as by no means won over in spirit. By way of reaction against despotism, British parliamentarianism once more becomes fashionable. It is in this connexion that Lefebvre, in speaking of the intellectual opposition of Mme de Staël and of Chateaubriand, makes a remark which would almost lead me to doubt whether I was right in counting him, even with the reservations I made, among the spiritual descendants of Mme de Staël. 'The significance of these cases', he says, 'lies only in their value as anecdotes', and he deems it of greater importance to establish by a number of less known indications, such as the audacious expression of war fatigue by the Chamber of Commerce of Lyons, that men were waiting for things to happen, that there was no feeling of confidence in the lasting character of the régime.

It will have been noticed before, not only that Lefebvre underlined the bourgeois character of Mme de Staël's policy, but also that he placed upon a low level the motives of Chateaubriand in writing *Le Génie du Christianisme*. This tendency to bring poets and intellectuals – and also, as we saw, the Pope – down a peg, and rather to listen to Chambers of Commerce, certainly does not fit very well in the line of liberal moralists which we can attach to Mme de Staël.

CONCLUSION: THE SIGNIFICANCE OF NAPOLEON

Insufficiency, failure – after all we have heard about misconceptions, mistakes, the habit of misleading, the question arises whether Lefebvre's judgement of Napoleon, though he finds something irresistibly great and fascinating in the figure, is not purely negative. Let me give, in answer and at the same time in conclusion, a brief summary of his findings.

After the failure of his gigantic undertaking – so he writes in effect – the Emperor has become, in the imagination of the poets, a second Prometheus, whose temerity was punished by divine power, the symbol of human genius struggling with fate. There are some, on the other hand, who have wanted to make him the plaything of historical determinism; wrongly so – the imperial dignity and the conquests beyond the 'natural frontiers' were his personal initiative. Even the thesis that this must fatally lead to his undoing, a thesis which would have its uses for the teaching of aspiring Caesars and for the good of mankind, cannot be upheld.

His personal ambition was not realized; but he has nevertheless left profound traces. In France he consolidated the new State by giving it, with a master hand, its administrative organization. The Revolution of 1789 had raised the middle class to power, a position which was subsequently contested by democracy [1793-4]. Under the Emperor's tutelage the notables regained their power, while their wealth and influence increased. Freed from the menace of the people, they set themselves to govern and to restore liberalism. In Europe the spread of French ideas, the influence of England, the progress of capitalism and consequently of the bourgeoisie, all tended to the same result. Napoleon contributed not a little to hasten this development by destroying the *ancien régime*, and by introducing the principle of the new order.

By his territorial rearrangements and his reforms he promoted, too, the awakening of the nationalities which had already begun. Rising capitalism was protected by his Continental System. Romanticism, already in a ferment, found in him the hero its poets needed. Wherever he went in the direction of the great currents of European civilization, his influence was considerable. 'If one wants to bring in historical determinism, this is the way in which it can be seen at work.'

Thus it also becomes intelligible that his legend has arisen so quickly.

Nevertheless, there is a contradiction between his personal endeavours and that which was lasting in his work and was preserved by the legend. He became more and more inimical to the Revolution, to such a degree even, that if he had had the time he would have ended by a partial denial of civil equality. He dreamed of a universal empire, yet for the French he remained the defender of the natural frontiers, while the liberals of Europe [in Italy, in Poland, in Belgium, even in western and southern Germany, even in Spain] put him up against the kings of the Holy Alliance as the defender of the nationalities. He established the sternest despotism, and it is in his name that the constitutional Bourbons were opposed. He was the idol of the Romantics, while the form of his thought as well as his literary and artistic taste were purely classical. . . .

The romantics alone were not altogether wrong, for what was classical in him was only his culture and the forms of his intellect. The spring of his actions, however, was the imagination, the irresistible impulse of the temperament. This is the secret of the charm which he will always exercise on men. If only in the passing fervour and confusion of youth, they will always be pursued by the romantic dream of power. There will always be those who, like the heroes of the novel of Barrès (see p. 146), will come to find exaltation at the Tomb.

This conclusion, however broad a vision it reveals, cannot be mine. I miss something in it. Let me, without trying to put my own conception in its place, which would go entirely beyond the purpose of this book, indicate what seems to me to be lacking.

In the first place I miss in it, far more than in his portrait, and in many other passages of the book, the spirit of Mme de Staël. I am far from wishing back the confinement of history within the limits of a moral trial, as we found it in Barni and Lanfrey. The modern abhorrence of big words and easy sentiments which characterizes Georges Lefebvre deserves appreciation, especially when, as in his case, it goes together with such a sharply practised eye for factual and material factors. These qualities not only guard him against excursions into ethics, they also make him aware of the temptations of chauvinism and of romanticism to which we have seen so many others succumb. Of romanticism indeed he not only displays striking understanding, but it is so close to his own heart that notwithstanding his entirely different political inclinations, he has not hesitated to quote, as his final word about Napoleon, Barrès and his young men by the tomb. But although romanticism conceived in the sense in which Lefebvre uses the word, is ever so profound a human characteristic, even though it is a merit of his work that he has been able to do justice to it in his presentation of the Napoleonic figure, I do believe that in the end it is given more than its fair share.

I would also like to draw more sharply the contradiction which the author himself notes between Napoleon's intentions and his achievements, and I should for instance like to see it stated more explicitly, in regard to the awakening of the nationalities, that it was only by oppressing them that the Emperor favoured them, that he did not in reality understand them, and that at most he tried intermittently to utilize them for his own purpose. Does not the word determinism, which Lefebvre smuggles in by a roundabout way, here too serve the purpose of masking personal responsibility in the historical process?

And so I come back once more to what I miss in his conclusion. I should like to see the eternal postulates of respect for the human personality, of the feeling for spiritual freedom, of lofty idealism, of truthfulness, taken into account when the final reckoning is made. It looks sometimes as though, for Lefebvre, to detect bourgeois class prejudice among Napoleon's contemporary opponents is a sufficient reason to rule them out of court. For him democracy is to be identified only with 'the people', the people who – silent, admiring even, without understanding – allowed everything to follow its course.

We know that the argument is going merrily on. Madelin will not be the last of his line. There will always be Frenchmen who subordinate social and spiritual needs to power and glory, to authority and order – or as Lefebvre would express it, to their own class interests – or who foster a respect for the Church either as an important means for social preservation or else from a sincere religious conviction. And bringing such inclinations to the study of Napoleon, they will till the end of time support another conception of some of his actions, and finally of the whole of his figure, than Lefebvre. But from the point of view which I indicated, too, even though one can accept his presentation most of the time, there will still be a good deal to say about his appreciation and his interpretation. The argument goes on.

Chronological Table

1769 August 15: birth of Napoleon Bonaparte.

1779 April: to the military Academy at Brienne in Champagne.

1784 October: to the military Academy in Paris.

1785 September: Lieutenant; to Valence.

1786 (September) till June 1788: on leave in Corsica.

1788 (June) till September 1789: with his regiment at Auxonne.

1789 (September) till February 1791: in Corsica. Takes part in party strife; soon in opposition to his former idol Paoli, who arrives on the island in July 1790. Leader of francophil and pro-Revolution party.

1791 (February) till June: again at Auxonne, with Louis.
June–Autumn: at Valence.
Autumn–May 1792: back in Corsica.

1792 June 20: witnesses crowd breaking into Tuileries.
August 10: also witnesses riot from which Louis XVI takes refuge with Legislative Assembly.
September 21: proclamation of Republic. Beginning of new calendar.

1793 March 3 till April: back in Corsica, whence escapes to Provence.
August: writes *Le Souper de Beaucaire.*
September 16: given command of artillery at siege of Toulon (Royalists and British).
December 17: fall of Toulon; stays on active service in Midi, in close co-operation with younger Robespierre.

1794 April: General of Artillery.
July 24 (*10 Thermidor an II*): fall of Robespierre. Arrest of Bonaparte.
August 20: liberated and restored in his function.
August–September: British prevent expedition to Corsica.

1795 May: appointed for expedition to Vendée, but lingers on in Paris.
August 22 (*30 Thermidor an III*): Convention ratifies new Constitution (of *an III*), which establishes five Directors supported by *Conseil des Cinq Cents* and *Conseil des Anciens.* Free elections of 5 Fructidor curtailed, however, from fear of reaction. Majority of 2/3 for *conventionnels* assured.
October 5 (*13 Vendémiaire an IV*): Bonaparte empowered by Convention to help Barras to subdue a Royalist rising in Paris.
October 30: the five Directors elected by the new Councils.

1796 February 23: Bonaparte given command of army destined for Italy.
March 9: Bonaparte marries Joséphine.

End April: Bonaparte compels King of Sardinia to conclude armistice by threatening Turin.

May 15: Bonaparte's triumphal entry into Milan (after Lodi). All Italian rulers in sphere of influence and subject to compulsory levies.

1797 February 2: Bonaparte takes Mantua after lengthy siege, having repelled all attempts to raise siege (Castiglione, Arcole, Rivoli).

Easter: anti-French riot at Verona; offers pretext to Bonaparte to overthrow the Venetian Republic.

April 18: Bonaparte signs preliminaries of Leoben with Austrians.

Summer: Bonaparte with Joséphine in castle Mombello near Milan. Cisalpine Republic founded.

September 3–4: *coup d'état* of Fructidor (Augereau deputy of Bonaparte).

October 17: Peace of Campo Formio, under strong influence of Bonaparte. Austria recognizes France's 'natural frontiers' and the Cisalpine and Ligurian Republics, and itself acquires Venetia. Congress of Rastadt for settling internal German affairs.

December 10: triumphal reception of Bonaparte by Directorate.

1798 April 12: the Directorate decides for expedition to Egypt, and gives command to Bonaparte.

May 19: sailing.

June 10: capture of Malta.

July 1: disembarkation at Alexandria.

July 21: victory of Pyramids.

August 1: Nelson destroys French fleet near Aboukir.

Autumn: increased tension between France and Austria (German affairs, Rastadt; Italian affairs) and France and Russia (Malta and Egypt).

December: Second Coalition formed by Paul of Russia, with Turkey, Britain, Austria, and Naples.

1799 Spring and Summer: French defeats; Archduke Charles ejects French from Germany, Suvorov from Italy. Royalist troubles in France.

February: Bonaparte enters Syria. Unsuccessful siege of Saint-Jean d'Acre.

July 25: Bonaparte back in Egypt, defeats Turks near Aboukir.

August 22: Bonaparte leaves Egypt.

September 25: Masséna defeats Russians near Zurich.

October: Brune defeats British and Russians, Bergen-Castricum.

October 9: Bonaparte lands near Fréjus.

November 9–10 (*18–19 Brumaire an VIII*): Bonaparte overthrows the Directorate and Legislative Assemblies; provisional triumvirate: Bonaparte, Sieyès, Roger-Ducros.

December 24: Promulgation of new constitution (of *an VIII*), drawn up by Bonaparte from concept with very different intentions by Sieyès. All power to First Consul. Senate; Tribunate (the only body with public debates); Corps Législatif; Council of State. Bonaparte First Consul, his colleagues Cambacérès and Lebrun.

1800 January: constitution approved by plebiscite.
  February 18 (*28 Pluviôse an VIII*): law about local administration.
  Summer: establishment of commission for *Code civil*.
  May–June: Moreau's successes against Austrians in Bavaria.
  May 15: Bonaparte crosses St Bernard.
  June 14: Marengo (in fact won by Desaix, who is killed) gives Bonaparte command of Northern Italy. Kléber assassinated in Egypt.
  September 25: British capture Malta.
  December 3: Moreau destroys Austrians near Hohenlinden.
  December 24: attempt on Bonaparte's life near Opéra (infernal machine).
  December 26: Paul I of Russia forms league of neutrals against Britain.

1801 January 8: Peace of Lunéville. Austria and the German Empire restore Peace of Campo Formio and recognize recently formed republics. Peace with Naples follows.
  February 8: Pitt replaced by Addington as Prime Minister of Britain.
  March 23: assassination of Tsar Paul I; accession of Alexander I.
  June 25, September 2: French capitulations in Egypt (Cairo, Alexandria).
  July 15: signature of Concordat.
  September 10: ratification of Concordat.
  October 1: peace preliminaries between Britain and France; beginning of negotiations at Amiens. Alexander of Russia soon makes peace.

1802 January–April: expedition to St Domingo. Overthrow of Toussaint l'Ouverture: his capture.
  January: at Lyons, Bonaparte invested with presidency of Cisalpine (henceforth Italian) Republic.
  March: notwithstanding constitution of Year VIII, Bonaparte causes Senate to expel opposition members from Tribunate and legislative body.
  March 25: Peace of Amiens.
  April: Concordat, together with Organic Articles, approved by Legislative body.
  May 15: Legion of Honour established.
  August 2: overwhelmingly favourable plebiscite about life Consulate. Constitution of Year X; Consul's powers still further increased, also those of Senate as against Tribunate and Legislative body.
  September 11: Piedmont annexed.

1803 January 30: Sebastiani's report about Egypt in *Moniteur*.
  March 13: Bonaparte's outburst against British Ambassador Lord Whitworth.
  March 24: powers granted to German Reichstag. French project for reorganization of German Empire: mediatizations (annexations) and secularizations (effect of peace treaties of Campo Formio and Lunéville).
  May 3: treaty for sale of Louisiana to U.S.A.
  May 11: Lord Whitworth leaves Paris.

December 2: army concentrated in camp of Boulogne, given name of armée d'Angleterre.

1804 February–March: discovery of conspiracy; arrest of Moreau, Pichegru, Cadoudal. Kidnapping of Enghien.

March 21: Enghien shot.

March 27: final text of *Code civil*.

May 18: Napoleon proclaimed Emperor by Senate. Constitution of Year XII, which imposes private sessions upon Tribunate as well, approved by plebiscite.

August 11: Francis II adopts title of Emperor of Austria.

December: Spain (Godoy) at war with Britain.

December 2: Emperor crowned at Notre Dame.

1805 March 30–August 18: Villeneuve ordered to open way to Britain; cruises between Cadiz and Antilles without meeting Nelson.

April 11: British-Russian alliance.

May 26: Napoleon crowns himself King of Italy at Milan.

June 4: Napoleon annexes Genoa.

August 9: Austria joins British-Russian alliance. Third Coalition.

August 18: Villeneuve, discouraged, runs into Cadiz.

August 24: Boulogne camp broken up. French army enters Germany.

October 20: capitulation of Ulm (Mack).

October 21: Villeneuve ordered to raise siege of Naples; utterly defeated at Trafalgar by Nelson.

November: Napoleon enters Vienna.

December 2: Austerlitz. Tsar Alexander continues war, while Emperor Francis sues for peace.

December 18: convention of Schoenbrunn, in which Napoleon buys off Prussia but also compromises it with Hanover.

December 26: Peace of Pressburg. Austria compelled to cede Venice to Napoleon's Kingdom of Italy and to recognize his influence over the whole peninsula. Bavaria acquires *inter alia* Tyrol, Württemburg, Austrian Swabia, Baden Breisgau. Dissolution of German empire.

1806 March 30: Joseph Bonaparte King of Naples and of Sicily; but in Sicily, Bourbons remain under protection of British navy. Murat Grand duke of Clèves and Berg; in Italy dukedoms established for ministers and marshals.

June 5: Louis Bonaparte King of Holland.

July 12: Rhine Confederation established, under Napoleon's protectorate.

July: peace discussions with Britain (Fox) and Russia; Napoleon hints at Hanover for Britain and Balearic isles for Russia.

August 6: Francis II resigns German Emperor's crown.

September 15: Prussia joins British-Russian coalition. Fourth Coalition.

October 14: Prussian armies destroyed at Jéna-Auerstaedt.

November 11: Decree of Berlin. Continental System established.

November 28: first French troops in Warsaw.

1807　February 8: Eylau; sanguinary and indecisive.

Spring: Napoleon at Finckenstein. Maria Walewska.

June 14: Friedland. Napoleon victorious.

June 24: Tilsit. Napoleon and Alexander meet on a raft in the Niemen.

July 9: peace. Establishment of Kingdom of Westphalia and Grand duchy of Warsaw. Alexander promises evacuation of Moldavia and Wallachia, and cedes Corfu to Napoleon. Vague eastern and anti-British agreements.

July–September: violation of Denmark by British navy.

September 18: Napoleon abolishes Tribunate.

October: Alexander declares war on Britain.

October 25: Napoleon concludes secret treaty with Spain for division of Portugal.

November 30: Junot occupies Lisbon.

December 17: Decree of Milan, directed against neutral trade and intended to make blockade of Britain watertight.

December–March 1808: Murat's gradual occupation of Northern Spain.

1808　February 2: Napoleon's letter to Alexander. Grandiose plans for conquest of India.

February: Miollis occupies Rome.

March 17: establishment of *Université impériale*. Fontanes Grand Master.

March 18: riots at Aranjuez; Charles IV compelled to abdicate in favour of his son Ferdinand.

End April: Spanish royal couple, Godoy, and Ferdinand arrive at Bayonne to submit their quarrel to Napoleon.

May 2: riots in Madrid; bloody repression by Murat (Dos Mayos).

May 10: Charles IV and Ferdinand, the latter under threats, cede their rights to Napoleon. Joseph appointed King of Spain. Murat becomes King of Naples.

July 20: Jospeh's solemn entry into Madrid.

July 23: Dupont capitulates at Baylen to Spanish *guerilleros*.

July 30: Joseph escapes from Madrid.

August: British gain strong foothold in Portugal.

September: Napoleon's demand, based upon intercepted letter, for dismissal of Stein in Prussia.

September 24–October 24: meeting of Napoleon and Alexander at Erfurt. Talleyrand warns Alexander and encourages Austria.

Beginning November: Napoleon enters Spain.

December 4: recapture of Madrid.

December 16: from Madrid, Napoleon outlaws Stein.

1809　Spring: agreement between Austria and Britain about new war. Fifth Coalition. Alexander remains neutral.

April 19–23: Napoleon fights battle against Archduke Charles in neighbourhood of Ratisbon.

April 28: Schill leaves Berlin, to foster rebellion in Westphalia.

May 13: Napoleon occupies Vienna.

May 21: French troops hard pressed near Aspern and Essling.

May 29: Andreas Hofer captures Innsbruck from Bavarians.

July 6: Napoleon restores his shaken prestige at Wagram.

July: from Schoenbrunn, Napoleon issues orders concerning Pope.

July 29: British descent upon Walcheren.

October 14: Austria concludes peace of Vienna, cedes Illyria to Napoleon.

December: threats of Napoleon against independence of Holland. In France, Louis receives demands for annexations.

December 15: Joséphine publicly announces acceptance of divorce. Two days earlier, Napoleon had ordered Caulaincourt urgently to demand from Tsar hand of his younger sister.

1810 January–February: French troops occupy Walcheren, then Bergen-op-Zoom, Breda, Dordrecht.

February 8: Napoleon organizes military administration of Spain, which has apparently been conquered after peace with Austria.

February 9: after evasive answer from Russia, Napoleon asks hand of Archduchess Marie Louise. He refuses to make promise to Alexander about future of Grand duchy of Warsaw.

February 21: Andreas Hofer shot at Mantua.

March 11: marriage of Napoleon and Marie Louise by proxy at Vienna.

March 16: Louis consents to a treaty ceding Brabant, Zeeland, and the land between Maas and Waal.

April 1: marriage of Napoleon and Marie Louise solemnized at Saint-Cloud.

July 9: whole of Holland annexed.

August 20: Bernadotte made Crown Prince of Sweden.

October 1: Masséna ordered to expel British from Portugal, occupies Coimbra; British entrenched behind Torres Vedras.

December 10: Oldenburg (belonging to Alexander's brother-in-law) and considerable part of Westphalia, Bremen, Hamburg, and Lübeck annexed.

December 31: Alexander's ukase favours British trade, already tolerated for a long time.

1811 Winter and Spring: Masséna driven back.

February: Napoleon, angered by Bernadotte's independent attitude, refuses to grant him Norway.

May 3: Masséna beaten near Fuentes de Onoro. Wellesley rewarded with title of Duke of Wellington.

June: Church Council of Paris.

August 5: majority of Council, under pressure, issues decree to limit papal right of institution.

August 15: at his birthday reception, Napoleon addresses ominous words to Russian ambassador (Oldenburg, Poland). He begins to draw up plan of campaign against Russia.

1812 Spring: military and diplomatic preparations.

January: Napoleon occupies Swedish Pomerania.

February 12: Prussia undertakes to grant Napoleon 20,000 auxiliary troops and free passage.

March 14: Austria promises 30,000 men for flank covering, against territorial advantages.

March: Cortes at Cadiz promulgates constitution for Spain.

March–April: Bernadotte receives from Alexander promise of Norway in exchange for Swedish help against Napoleon.

Beginning May: Napoleon at Dresden; 600,000 men against Russia.

May 28: instructions for de Pradt as ambassador at Warsaw excite Polish enthusiasm; but at the same time Napoleon wants to respect Austrian sensitiveness concerning Galicia.

July 22: Marmont defeated by Wellington near Salamanca. Soult compelled to give up siege of Cadiz in order to cover Madrid.

September 7: Napoleon defeats Russians near Borodino, where they try to hold up his advance.

September 14: entry into Moscow.

October 23: failure of attempted *putsch* by Malet in France.

October 25: beginning of retreat from Moscow.

November 26–27: crossing of Beresina, hotly contested by Russians.

December 5: 100 km east of Vilna, Napoleon leaves army, giving supreme command to Murat. Ney covers the retreat. Disaster of Vilna.

December 18: Napoleon reaches Paris.

December 31: Prussian general York concludes with Russia Convention of Tauroggen (neutralizing his troops).

1813 January 10: Senate promises Napoleon 350,000 new conscripts.

January 25: at Fontainebleau, Pius VII gives way to Napoleon's pressure and signs preliminaries for new Concordat.

February 22: Eugène evacuates Oder line and soon reaches Berlin.

February 28: Prussia concludes treaty of Kalisch with Russia. Appeal from Berlin by Russian general Wittgenstein addressed to German population.

March: Eugène evacuates Saxony too. French make a stand on the Elbe.

March 24: Pius VII withdraws his signature. Napoleon takes no notice.

April 7: Narbonne sent to Vienna, to offer Silesia in exchange for help against Russia and Prussia. Instead, Metternich offers armed mediation.

April 25: Napoleon takes over command of main army near Erfurt.

May 2: Luetzen. Saxony reconquered.

May 8: Napoleon enters Dresden.

May 21: Bautzen, a less decisive victory.

June 4: Armistice (offered by Tsar and King of Prussia) under mediation of Austria: till July 28. Prolonged till August 10.

June 14: Convention of Reichenbach. Britain undertakes to subsidize Russia and Prussia. Foundation of Sixth Coalition.

June 21: Joseph and Soult (Madrid being already evacuated) defeated by Wellington near Vittoria. Joseph flees to France.

June 27: Austria undertakes to cooperate with Russia and Prussia if Napoleon does not accept Austrian mediation conditions before end of armistice.

June 28: Napoleon receives Metternich at Dresden. After initial objections, accepts mediation and a Congress at Prague.

July 28: only now can Caulaincourt appear at Prague.

August 12: term having elapsed, Austria declares war on Napoleon. Napoleon's reply, containing concessions, arrives only next day.

October 18: after heavy engagements round Dresden, battle of Leipzig, in which Napoleon is defeated. Defection of S. German allies. Army has to fall back upon Mayence. Italy, N.W. Germany, and Holland lost.

November: Metternich now informs Napoleon from Frankfurt 'natural frontiers'. Napoleon replaces Maret-Bassano by Caulaincourt as Minister of Foreign Affairs.

December 1: the allies, made impatient, issue manifesto which throws responsibility for failure of negotiations upon Napoleon.

December 21: beginning of invasion of France.

1814 February 7: Congress of Chatillon. Metternich, uneasy about Prussia's plans, wants compromise. Alexander wants to continue. Napoleon, however, unable to agree to new demand of frontiers of 1792.

March 18: Congress disperses. Meanwhile Napoleon has achieved successes near Champaubert, Montmirail, Chateau-Thierry, Montereau, Craonne, Rheims.

March 20: Napoleon thrown across Seine. While he withdraws to Lorraine, Allies march on Paris.

March 31: fall of Paris. Napoleon at Fontainebleau.

April 3: Senate declares Napoleon has lost throne.

April 4: Marmont goes over to allies.

April 6: Napoleon abdicates.

April 11: Treaty of Fontainebleau, in which Napoleon accepts banishment to Elba.

April 23: Artois as *lieutenant-général du royaume* and Talleyrand as Minister of Foreign Affairs sign a convention which bring frontiers back in principle to line of 1 January 1792.

April 28: after humiliating treatment by populace, Napoleon embarks at Fréjus for Elba.

May 30: Peace of Paris, which confirms convention of April 23.

June 4: Louis XVIII 'grants' Charter. Throughout the year, increasing unrest in France owing to reactionary tendencies of restored régime.

November 1: official opening of Congress of Vienna. Talleyrand has already been acting as representative of Louis XVIII and of the principle of legitimacy.

1815 January 3: Britain, Austria, and France (Talleyrand) make alliance against Russia and Prussia, in Saxony-Poland affair.

March 1: Napoleon lands in neighbourhood of Antibes.

March 13: Allies at Vienna outlaw Napoleon.

March 18: Ney (who had promised Louis XVIII to bring usurper back in iron cage) throws himself into Napoleon's arms near Auxerre.

March 20: Napoleon occupies Tuileries.

April 22: new liberal constitution drawn up by Benjamin Constant. '*L'acte additionnel*.'

June 1: Champ de Mai.

June 7: new Chambers opened. Strong liberal opposition.

June 12: Napoleon leaves Paris to place himself at head of army. His plan is to strike before arrival of Russians and Austrians, and separate British from Prussians. Latter part fails at Quatre Bras.

June 18: Napoleon crushed near Waterloo.

June 21: Napoleon back in Paris. Chamber refuses to cooperate with him.

June 22: Napoleon abdicates. Fouché President of Executive Committee of Chamber, which opens *pourparlers* with allies.

June 25: Napoleon leaves Paris by order of Fouché, and withdraws to Malmaison.

June 29: upon approach of Prussian troops, and warned by Fouché, he goes to Rochefort to escape overseas. This proves impossible.

July 8: Louis XVIII back in Paris.

July 15: Napoleon surrenders to British. *Bellerophon* carries him to Plymouth.

August 7: transferred to *Northumberland*, which is to take him to St Helena, accompanied by Bertrand and Montholon (with their wives), Gourgaud and Las Cases.

October 17: steps ashore on St Helena.

December 9: after stay at the Briars, occupies Longwood.

1816 April 14: Sir Hudson Lowe, the new governor of the island, arrives.

December 31: Las Cases leaves St Helena.

1821 May 5: death of Napoleon.

1840 May 12: government declaration (Thiers) to French Chamber that Louis Philippe, having obtained consent of British Government, will order removal of body from St Helena.

December 15: burial at the Invalides. (Guizot now Prime Minister.)

Index of Authors

413

General Index